CRIMINAL PSYCHOLOGY and FORENSIC TECHNOLOGY

A Collaborative Approach to Effective Profiling

Edited by

Grover Maurice Godwin, Ph.D.

Research Assistant Professor
Justice Center
The University of Alaska–Anchorage

CRC Press
Boca Raton London New York Washington, D.C.

Front Cover: Helen M. Godwin

Library of Congress Cataloging-in-Publication Data

Criminal psychology and forensic technology : a collaborative approach to effective profiling / editor, Maurice Godwin.
    p. cm.
Includes bibliographical references and index.
ISBN 0-8493-2358-4
1. Criminal psychology. 2. Forensic sciences. I. Godwin, Maurice.

HV6080 .C734 2000
364.3—dc21

00-064150
CIP

Visit the CRC Press Web site at www.crcpress.com

Preface

Criminal psychology, forensic technology, and profiling. These three disciplines have received a wealth of media attention over the past decade. Consequently, due to public and professional interest, a plethora of books have been published. The technique of offender profiling, or classifying offenders according to their behaviors and characteristics, has been developing slowly as a possible investigative tool since 1841 and the publication of the *The Murders in the Rue Morgue* by Edgar Alan Poe, in which detective C. Auguste Dupin demonstrated the ability to follow the thought patterns of a companion while the pair strolled through Paris without speaking a word. Some years later, the art of using psychology to profile a criminal was used in 1888 in England, where Dr. Thomas Bond, a lecturer in forensic medicine, produced what could be recognized as a psychological profile of the perpetrator of the Whitechapel murders. Dr. Bond wrote to the head of the Criminal Investigation Division (Rumbelow, 1987:140):

> The murderer must have been a man of physical strength and great coolness and daring. There is no evidence that he had an accomplice. He must, in my opinion, be a man subject to periodic attacks of Homicidal and erotic mania. The character of the mutilations indicates that the man may be in a condition sexually, that may be called Satyriasis. It is of course possible that the Homicidal impulse may have developed from a revengeful or brooding condition of mind, or that religious mania may have been the original disease, but I do not think that either hypothesis is likely. The murderer in external appearance is quite likely to be a quite inoffensive looking man probably middle-age and neatly and respectable dressed. I think he might be in the habit of wearing a cloak or overcoat or he could hardly escape notice in the streets if the blood on his hands or clothes were visible.

> Assuming the murderer to be such a person as I have just described, he would be solitary and eccentric in his habits. Also, he is likely to be a man without regular occupation, but with some small income or pension. He is possibly living among respectable persons who have some knowledge of his character and habits who have grounds for suspicion that he is not quite right in his mind at times. Such person would probably be unwilling to communicate and would be suspicious of the police for fear of trouble or notoriety, whereas if there were prospects of a reward it might overcome his scruples.

Dr. Bond based his profile only on his professional experience, yet the claims he made would probably be accepted as thoughtful and intelligent by most police investigators today.

Since its emergence, offender profiling has been described by several different terms: psychological profiling, criminal profiling, criminal personality profiling, and criminal investigative analysis. Regardless of the descriptive label applied, profiling as an investigative tool today represents a less–than–educated attempt to provide law enforcement agencies with detailed information about the behavior of an unknown individual who has committed a crime. Most published accounts of profiling, which detail the methods employed by various individuals, have tended to take the form of semi-autobiographical books and journalistic articles rather than systematic academic work and, hence, are difficult to evaluate for accuracy or a scientific point of view. For example, most offender profiles emphasize the various psychological functions that murder has for the offender — not what varieties of action the murder actually consists of. Consequently, these profiles make little distinction between the overt crime scene behavior as it occurs in murders and the psychodynamic processes that produce that behavior. Hence, there is little attempt by profilers to differentiate aspects of the offender's motivations and life-style from aspects of his offending behavior.

Heuristics and Biases in Decision Making

Aside from a few studies (e.g., *Hunting Serial Predators*, Godwin, 2000), most published accounts that claim new findings in criminal profiling or serial offending are often a part of the cultural baggage passed down over the years, and are fraught with the frailties of human thinking. Conclusions are predominantly based on what has been written in the past. For example, some profilers claim that patterns associated with serial offending occur as a result of recognizable mental illness or mental disorder in the offender, and these disorders can be classified using a personality theory. However, psychological theory should never be treated as a vocabulary by so-called profilers or expert consultants to further their personal opinions, rather than a set of empirically derived hypotheses open to scientific analysis. For instance, in a newspaper article about Robert Yates, a serial murderer recently captured in Spokane, Washington, a former homicide investigator stated that the Yates case demonstrated that serial killers are individuals whose behavior cannot be predicted, yet a recently published journal article written by the investigator describes a theoretical typology by which sexual murderers' motivations are profiled. This is just one of the ways in which individuals attempt to blur the facts when it comes to taking responsibility for inaccurate profiles and the failure to link unsolved crimes.

Confirmation Bias

Numerous studies have demonstrated that people generally give excessive value to confirmatory information; that is, information which supports a particular position (Schwenk, 1988). Confirmation bias refers to a type of selective thinking whereby one tends to look for what confirms one's beliefs, and ignore or undervalue the relevance of contradictory information. This type of thinking results from deductive inferencing without supporting inductive research. For example, Wiseman, West, and Stemman (1996) found that in cases where psychics had contributed to police investigations, the psychics and the investigators they advised were only likely to remember those aspects of the case they were correct about and forget the incorrect assertions. Gilovich (1993) suggests that the most likely reason for excessive influence of confirmatory information is that it is easier to deal with cognitively. In other words, it is much easier to see how a piece of information supports a position than how it might count against it. This form of confirmatory thinking is prevalent in criminal investigations — especially serial crime investigations — and often results in misleading information and wasted man hours.

Selective Thinking

Selective thinking is the process whereby a person focuses on favorable evidence while ignoring unfavorable evidence. This kind of thinking is sometimes referred to as "tunnel vision." Selective thinking occurs when an investigator or profiler rejects alternative explanations in favor of simpler ones. This form of thinking is referred to as "Occam's Razor."

Post Hoc Fallacy

Post hoc fallacy, also called *post hoc ergo proper hoc* (after this therefore because of this) fallacy, is based upon the mistaken notion that simply because one event follows another, the first event is the cause of the second one. This form of reasoning in criminal investigations is the basis for many erroneous conclusions and failed investigations. For example, you have a "vision" that a body is going to be found in the water near a tree, and later a body is found in the water near a tree. To establish the probability of a causal connection between two events, controls must first be established to rule out other factors such as chance or some unknown causal factor (Riere, 1998). Anecdotes from law enforcement officers who use this approach and swear by it do not establish the probability of causal connection. Rather, a controlled study, comparing success rates with true detectors and fake ones, is the only way to establish the probability connection between two events.

From the previous discussion of the frailties of human thinking, we should be aware that offender profiles and many conclusions about what may have taken place during the commission of a crime can be distorted by easily recalled events, selective perception, and expectations that bias observations and conclusions. This process is called "illusory correlation," where unrelated variables, events, crime scene actions, etc. are believed to be correlated, when in fact no associations exist. Hence, the purpose of this book is to introduce alternative approaches that use systematic and scientific processes which aid in reducing illusory correlations and hindsight bias to improve the way crimes are investigated and offender profiles are generated, as well as to test their accuracy and applicability to criminal investigations.

Criminal Psychology and Forensic Technology is unique because it presents an array of topics fusing aspects of criminal psychology with forensic science methods in a collaborative effort to improve the way profiles are derived. Alternative approaches to crime solving and new research that contributes to the science of profiling are described. The format is simple and straightforward, and the information is designed for the generalist who may be just beginning a career as a law enforcement officer, or the student enrolling for the first time in a criminal justice or police–related degree program. *Criminal Psychology and Forensic Technology* is also geared to the professional with years of training and experience. The chapters are succinctly written and provide thorough examinations of their relevant fields. The book is perfect for students preparing essays or class reports on various crime detection procedures or criminal profiling techniques, and for professionals wishing to expand their knowledge of alternative investigative methods for application to real crime situations. Whatever the reasons for choosing this book, the reader will be enlightened and his knowledge about alternative investigative tools for solving crimes, scientific methods for reducing biases in investigative decision making, and ethical issues that surround the application of these investigative procedures will be greatly enhanced.

Grover Maurice Godwin, Ph.D.
Research Assistant Professor of Justice
University of Alaska–Anchorage
Anchorage, Alaska – 2000

Acknowledgments

I would like to take this opportunity to express my sincere thanks to Dr. Robert Langworthy, Director of the Justice Center at the University of Alaska-Anchorage, for his continued support and for providing me the opportunity to teach and pursue new directions in crime related research. I also would like to thank the entire staff at the Justice Center for helping me to complete this book. My appreciation also goes to the contributing authors, without whom I would never have been able to complete this publication. Finally, I would like to express my gratitude to all those at CRC Press who helped make my second book possible, and especially to my editor, Becky McEldowney. On a personal note, thanks to Clifford Curry and Bill Lyerly for keeping the East Coast sound alive.

About the Author

Dr. Grover Maurice Godwin is a research assistant professor of justice at the University of Alaska-Anchorage in the Justice Center, where he is a crime researcher, a grantsman, and teaches courses in criminal investigations, serial murder, and criminal profiling. He is also an adjunct professor at Vermont College of Norwich University in their distance-learning Master of Arts degree program, with a concentration in criminal investigative psychology. He earned his Ph.D. in investigative psychology from the University of Liverpool, England, and his Master of Science degree in criminology from Indiana State University. Dr. Godwin is the author of *Hunting Serial Predators: a Multivariate Approach to Profiling Violent Behavior* (CRC Press). He is also the author of several journal articles on psychological and geographical profiling. Dr. Godwin has worked as a consultant to police, developing psychological and geographical profiles. He has lectured in the United States and Europe on serial murder, cyber-stalking, and criminal investigative psychology. He is a former North Carolina police officer. Dr. Godwin's teaching and research includes concentration in areas of applied psychology, criminology, and criminal investigations. His current research interest includes developing a behavioral model of hackers and aspects of intrusion detection.

Web site: *http://www.investigativepsych.com*

Introduction

Criminal psychology encompasses a host of related disciplines such as personality theory, forensic psychology, environmental psychology, clinical psychology, and the relatively new field of criminal investigative psychology. While all these fields relate in some way to general psychology, certain segments within each field deal directly with criminality. Forensic psychologists testify in court as experts on the potential danger that is posed by a defendant. Environmental psychologists study how humans behave in the environment. Criminal investigative psychology is defined as the systematic examination of unsolved crime constituents and the application of scientific methods to supply investigative support to law enforcement. The main focus of this book is the field of criminal investigative psychology. This process utilizes an applied psychology/criminology perspective with the aid of multivariate statistical analysis in order to develop practical methods applicable to police investigations. Hence, the criminal investigative psychologist is interested in getting into the offender's "shoes" rather than his "mind." The field of criminal investigative psychology is comprised of a broad range of disciplines, with no one dominant field. Consequently, this book contributes in a variety of ways to the criminal investigative psychological process by bringing together alternative methods for solving crime.

When one thinks of forensic technology, several disciplines immediately come to mind such as medical and forensic detectives that have been made popular by television. A criminalist who collects and analyzes forensic clues such as blood and semen found at a crime scene is using just one type of forensic technology. However, forensic technology is juxtaposed to many disciplines, including criminal psychology, as this book will demonstrate. Forensic technology is defined in this book as any forensic tool or application that assists in solving crimes. For example, two alternative forensic tools used in criminal investigations that could complement each other are pollen analysis (palynology), which is the assessment of pollen grains and spores taken from a pollen sample found on a victim's clothing, and geographical profiling, which attempts to pinpoint the likely home base of an unknown offender based on relevant crime locations. For instance, using a geographical profile of the highest probable location for an offender's home base, pollen samples from the predicted suspect's home environmental surroundings could be compared to pollen samples taken from the victim's clothing or from some other evidential source for comparison. So, although articles detailing various forensic techniques and criminal psychology are found in separate chapters, many of the studies are uniquely interwoven, and if used together could form a powerful investigative tool.

Psychology theories are rarely forged with forensic techniques in an effort to solve crimes. One may ask, is this not what profilers do when they subjectively draw a mental picture of an unknown offender? Granted, it is the profiler's intent to use some aspect of psychology to paint a picture of a likely suspect in a crime. However, the process of drawing conclusions about an offender's personality and forensic clues left at a crime scene is based on deduction of past case experiences rather than systematic research. Not until this publication has there been a book devoted exclusively to combining aspects of psychology with forensic technology to solve crimes.

The book will be useful and interesting to social scientists, professionals, and students in the fields of criminology, criminal justice, police studies, psychology, sociology and behavioral studies. From a practical perspective, actual case studies are used to show how specific procedures relate to ongoing police investigations. The broad range of practical information will make *Criminal Psychology and Forensic Technology* a standard reference book for students of criminology, psychologists, detectives, police officers, and a variety of other types of investigators. A brief overview of each chapter is given below.

Section 1. Forensic Science and Criminal Investigations

In a crime where detectives are faced with few or no physical clues at the scene, they often turn their attention to forensic techniques to determine what occurred. The traditional forensic techniques that detectives routinely rely on are fingerprint analysis, plaster cast molding of a tire or shoe print, and analysis of hair and fiber evidence. More recently, the use of DNA analysis has improved the chances of solving crimes. While these approaches still remain an integral part of the investigator's crime-fighting arsenal, other lesser known forensic techniques are beginning to play a substantial role in bringing predators to justice.

When no obvious physical evidence has been left at the scene by a criminal, nature may play a role in bringing him or her to justice. Various environmental elements such as trees and leaves each have a unique DNA makeup, which can be transferred to a victim's clothing or, as in one murder case in Florida, to the suspect's truck bed. Three articles that deal specifically with alternative forensic techniques are the focus of Section 1. Each chapter is equally weighted with unique information that will assist investigators in understanding how the methods can be used in criminal investigations.

Section 2. Criminal Profiling: From Art to Science

This section introduces a series of writings providing insight into the highly controversial and often contradictory field of criminal profiling. Psychological profiling in its present form is flawed due to inferred deductive and clinical assumptions and "leap in the dark" conclusions about offender actions and characteristics based solely on gut feelings or derived from memories of past cases. This type of profiling can be empirically unsound and misleading for police investigations. As an alternative, Section 2 presents various forms of research which can lead to more productive profiles and better solutions to criminal investigations.

Section 3. Classifying Crime Scene Behavior: New Directions

A number of factors can interfere with adequate empirical evaluation into the variables that contribute to the success or failure of a profile or criminal investigation, and a more systematic and empirical approach to decision-making is needed. Contrary to the deductive process, where generalizations guide conclusions, the inductive process is an empirical approach, with conclusions derived from scientific analysis. For example, an inductive method derives general principles about the behaviors of serial murderers by empirically examining particular facts from a large number of solved cases in order to look for trends of behaviors over time. In contrast to the deductive process, which starts with assumptions about behavior, inductive profiling relies on data gathered from crime scenes, police reports, psychological evaluations, method examiners' reports, and victimology reports that is empirically analyzed to test a theory. The chapters in Section 3 describe the inductive process of determining how crime scene behavior relates to classification of the offender.

Section 4. Profiling and Linking Crimes

This section includes two important studies. Recognizing links between offender patterns is one of the most crucial skills of an investigator. Early recognition of similar patterns can lead to focusing resources, improving clearance rates, and ultimately saving lives. The first chapter describes how the non-metric multidimensional scaling procedure, Smallest Space Analysis, was used in linking the serial murder offenses of John William, Jr. in Raleigh, North Carolina. The results of this chapter support the notion that to correctly link unsolved crimes, behavior selection must be a valid indices of offender consistency, which can only be achieved through scientific research and replication using different data sets. The second chapter addresses the issue of linking murders committed by nurses or health care providers. The authors suggest that rapid epidemiological investigation could identify common exposure to one person and therefore prevent further harm to patients.

The third chapter provides a brief overview of the pitfalls associated with computerized linking databases such as VICAP, HITS, and HALT. These three chapters outline a number of ways in which linking offenses can be improved.

Section 5. Cyber-Crimes

With the rapid growth of information technology, a book on alternative methods for investigation crimes would not be complete without a section on computer crimes. While some law enforcement agencies are responding to cyber-crimes, most investigators are not fully aware of the problem and lack the expertise to pursue this type of criminal. The inherent problems with the definitions of hacker and cracker are addressed here. Gordon Meyer calls on his years of experience in computer technology to expose the myths about the computer underground world of hackers, phreakers, and pirates. Tim Jordan and Paul Taylor present a unique discussion on the sociology of hackers. They argue that at present there is no detailed sociological investigation of the hacking community, despite a growing number of racy accounts of hacker adventures. This excursion into the world of hacking and cracking can provide police investigators with alternative information about this emerging crime.

Section 6. Psycho-Geographical Profiling

It has been established that there is a relationship between solving crimes and having information about locations that criminals habitually travel to in the areas close to their homes. For example, the mental map we draw of an area changes over time, and often reflects how much time we spend in an area and the variability of our purposes for being there. Based on this premise, a field of crime analysis has emerged called geographical profiling. Geographical profiling is defined as the analysis of relevant crime locations in order to predict the likely home base area of the offender. Geographical profiling is quite different from the more traditional crime mapping technique that is often performed by crime analysts using a geographical information system (GIS). Rather than producing aggregate crime mapping results revealing hot spots, areas where a particular type of crime is clustering, geographical profiling is concerned with individual spatial behavior and predicting the offender's residence based on crime locations such as victims' body dump sites, abduction sites, and locations where physical evidence was found. Conversely, the term psycho-geographical profiling was coined by Dr. Maurice Godwin in 1995, while a doctorate student at the University of Liverpool in England. Psycho-geographical profiling differs from the traditional definition of geographical profiling in that it involves the use of theories from environmental psychology and other psychological literature in order to explain why criminals behave the way they do in the environment. Psycho-geographical profiling does not solve cases. Rather, this method provides an additional avenue of scientific investigation that, with the aid of other forensic specialities covered in this book, could re-focus an investigation. The actual search for the perpetrator remains completely in the hands of the police. Five chapters that specifically deal with the psycho-geographical behavior of criminals are featured in Section 6.

Section 7. Ethics in Profiling

Given the fact no formal requirements, educational or otherwise, must be met in order to qualify as a criminal profiler, it is most appropriate to conclude with a section that deals directly with the issue of ethics in profiling. In the first chapter, author Lynn Burnett brings to the surface several cases where profiles were rendered but later turned out to be totally wrong. The second chapter addresses the issue of ethics and forensic psychology, highlighting specific areas where conflicts of interest could arise. The authors provide several ways to deal with these types of situations. The final chapter explores the ethics of criminal profiling. The authors elegantly argue that due to various media portrayals of profiling, proliferation of the technique has gone virtually unchallenged without examination of its actual utility and accuracy. The chapter concludes with a discussion regarding the misuse of criminal profiling and the absolute absence of any guidelines for its application to criminal investigations.

A Final Thought

When all clues have been exhausted and the investigation is at a stalemate, *Criminal Psychology and Forensic Technology: A Collaboration Approach to Effective Profiling* is the alternative information source to turn to.

Contributors

Thomas W. Adair is a senior laboratory technician at Arapahoe County Sheriff's Office, Littleton, Colorado. He is also employed in the Department of Bioagricultural Sciences and Pest Management at Colorado State University, Fort Collins, Colorado.

Jonathan D. Alston holds an M.A. degree in criminology from Simon Fraser University in Canada. He is currently a Ph.D. candidate in criminology at The University of Alberta, Edmonton, Canada.

Michael D. Biderman is assistant professor in the Department of Psychology at the University of Tennessee at Chattanooga. He has special interests in computer analysis, mathematical models, and multivariate scaling techniques.

Carl E. Booth earned a B.S. degree in psychology from the University of Tennessee at Chattanooga and has been a detective with the Chattanooga Police Department since 1968. Detective Booth is also a consultant with Police Research Consultants.

Lynn Barkley Burnett is a health science professor, medical educator, and clinical ethicist. He has served as the medical advisor to the Fresno County Sheriff's Department for more than two decades, during which time he has informally advised other law enforcement agencies as well. Dr. Burnett has been a participant in numerous suspicious death investigations and hundreds of forensic autopsies, and has presented papers at the American Academy of Forensic Sciences examining homicide and sudden death. He has made contributions to the literature in the discipline of ethics, and has authored chapters for a textbook of emergency medicine addressing cocaine toxicity, sudden infant death syndrome, and domestic violence. Dr. Burnett's opinion is frequently sought in the resolution of ethical dilemmas involving patients hospitalized at Community Medical Center, where he is vice chairman of Medical Ethics.

David Canter is professor of psychology at the University of Liverpool, where he is director of the Investigative Psychology program. He has published 20 books and over 150 papers in professional journals, and lectured around the world on various aspects of scientific psychology.

Stephen Coleman is a fellow of the Center for Applied Philosophy and Public Ethics and a lecturer in ethics at Charles Stuart University's School of Police Studies, New South Wales.

Margaret Cox is a reader in archaeological sciences in the School of Conservation Sciences at Bournemouth University, England. She is the course leader in the master of science degree in Forensic Archaeology. She is a senior archaeologist at Gifford & Partners (consulting engineers). Her research interests include integrated management and monitoring of terrestrial wetlands; ecology and archaeology of Glasson Moss, Cumbria (English Nature); population of St. Augustine the Less, Bristol, AD 1000-1900; life and death in post-medieval towns and cities; Saxon cemetery populations in East Anglia; taphonomy; and forensic archaeology.

Andrew Day is a clinical and forensic psychologist currently working for the National Health Service in the U.K. He has previously worked in a number of forensic settings, including the prison service in both the U.K. and Australia, and in an offender treatment unit. His research interests include offender rehabilitation, service evaluation in criminal justice settings, and the role of anger in offenders.

Kriss A. Drass is a professor of criminal justice at the University of Nevada, Las Vegas. He has published extensively in the areas of racial differences in crime rates, criminal processing, and applications of QCA to describe various types of social behavior.

Charles Frost is professor emeritus of justice systems at Truman State University (Kirksville, Missouri) and visiting associate professor of criminal justice at Westfield (MA) State College. He holds a bachelor's degree from Tufts University and his masters and doctorate from the Fletcher School of Law and Diplomacy. Prior to his academic career he served with the Navy, the Central Intelligence Agency, the White House Drug Abuse Prevention Office, and the Drug Enforcement Administration. Dr. Frost's teaching interests include criminal intelligence collection and analysis, organized crime, comparative criminal justice systems, intelligence and national security, and international law. He has written extensively on report-writing techniques and the selection of intelligence personnel. He is a charter member of the International Association of Law Enforcement Intelligence Analysts and served as Secretary to the Board of Governors of the Society of Certified Criminal Analysts.

Edward J. Green is professor and head of the Department of Psychology at the University of Tennessee at Chattanooga. He is a consultant with Police Research Consultants and is the author of *Psychology for Law Enforcement*.

Andrew F. Hayes earned his Ph.D. in social psychology from Cornell University in 1996. He is currently a research statistician at the Amos Tuck School of Business Administration and an adjunct assistant professor in the Department of Psychological and Brain Sciences at Dartmouth College. His interests include computationally intensive statistical methodology, meta-analysis, multivariate statistics, and social psychology.

Tom Henderson is a senior registrar in psychiatry at Greater Glasgow Community and Mental Health Services, NHS Trust.

Terry Hutter is a geoscientist specializing in palynology, paleontology, and visual organic geochemistry. Dr. Hutter holds a Ph.D. in geology and palynology from Greenwich University. He is president of T.H. Geological Services, Inc., Sand Springs, Oklahoma.

Harvey Irwin is an associate professor of psychology at the University of New England, Australia, where he teaches a course in psychopathology. His principal research interests include the nature of dissociation and the dissociative disorders, the psychological consequences of childhood trauma, personality disorders, the origins and psychological functions of belief in the paranormal, and psychological bases of parapsychological experiences. He is the author of several books and over 100 articles.

Tim Jordan is a lecturer in sociology at Open University in England.

Brian Kidd is a consultant psychiatrist, Community Addiction Service, Bellsdyke Hospital, Central Scotland Health Care.

Richard N. Kocsis is a lecturer in violent crime investigation at the New South Wales Police Academy, Charles Stuart University. He is also unit chief of the Criminal Profiling Research Unit, an Australian national research center committed to the research and development of criminal profiling techniques for the assistance of all Australian law enforcement and fire investigation agencies.

Gordon Meyer began researching the computer underground in the mid 1980s. The paper reprinted here was seminal in what became the first ethnography of the hacker community. (The Social Organization of the Computer Underground, 1989.) Today, Gordon lives in the Silicon Valley where he works as a human interface designer for a well-known computer company.

Terance D. Miethe is a professor of criminal justice at the University of Nevada, Las Vegas. He is the author of three books and numerous articles in the areas of criminal processing, crime and victimization theory, and whistle-blowing as a method of exposing occupational deviance.

Ronald Nunn has been an officer in the New South Wales police service for the past 39 years. He is commander of the New England area command. He holds special interests in environmental disputes and the maintenance of public order.

Brodie Paterson is a lecturer at Forth Valley Campus, Stirling University, Scotland.

Cameron Stark is a consultant in public health medicine in Scotland.

Paul Taylor is a lecturer in sociology at the University of Salford in England.

Arvind Verma holds a Ph.D. in criminology. His dissertation involved development of new mathematical tools for criminal justice practitioners. Before joining the faculty at Indiana University, Professor Verma was a senior officer of the Indian Police Service. He served for 17 years in various capacities in law enforcement. His areas of interest are policing, research methods, criminal justice in India, fuzzy logic, geographical information systems, and mathematical applications.

Paul Whetham is a lecturer for the counseling program at the University of South Australia. He is a qualified clinical psychologist and has previously worked in social welfare settings and with young offenders in residential settings. He is interested in constructivist approaches to psychology, with a particular interest in the development of relationships in the clergy.

Dedication

This book is dedicated to my wife, Helen, and to Molly, my Weimaraner.

For the known and unknown victims and their families.

> One need not dwell on criminal motives to explain interpersonal crime —
> instead, one can take as given an offender predisposed to crime and proceed
> to analyze patterns of behaviors

A. Karemen
*Crime Victims: An Introduction to
Victimology* (1984)

Table of Contents

Forensic Science and Criminal Investigations

1

1.1 Forensic Archaeology: A United Kingdom Perspective

MARGARET COX

Forensic archaeology is defined in a United Kingdom context as the application of the principles and methods of the discipline of archaeology to locate and recover buried remains, and associated evidence, within the judicial framework. In the U.K., forensic anthropology is the analysis of skeletal material derived from forensic contexts. The two are distinctly different subjects. Most forensic archaeologists are not competent forensic anthropologists, and vice versa, although there are, as always, exceptions to this rule. In this chapter, I will elucidate the differences between U.K. and U.S. development and approaches, and discuss in some detail the key contributions currently made by forensic archaeologists within the U.K., and to the investigation of genocide on four continents.

1.1.1 Introduction to Forensic Archaeology and Anthropology

From a U.K. perspective, and perhaps wearing "rose-colored glasses," there appears to be an almost seamless continuum between anthropology and archaeology in the U.S., with forensic applications of both happily ensconced within. Not so in the U.K. Here, period-based archaeology encompasses a wide range of traditionally defined specialties including biological anthropology, environmental archaeology (e.g., palynology and entomology), and geophysical prospection. Despite the best efforts of U.K. practitioners and exponents, forensic applications of archaeology and anthropology are largely shunned by the majority of mainstream archaeologists and anthropologists, where they are seen as somewhat ghoulish and irrelevant to the intellectual goals of both disciplines. This situation is unfortunate, and it is hoped that with time this barrier will be removed. The use of forensic data as archaeological analogues will assist in this process.[1]

In a forensic context, anthropology would seem to be the lead discipline in the U.S., with archaeology providing invaluable contextual information for recovered human remains but little more. This is despite the pioneering works of Morse et al.[2] and Sigler-Eisenberg,[3] and the later contributions of

Killam[4] and France et al.[5] In the U.K. that relationship is reversed, and for the most part, anthropological skills are not involved at all.[1]

To place forensic archaeology and anthropology in its developmental framework, we have to look to the U.S., where forensic anthropology developed from the 19th century. While the first documented case is arguably the investigation of the fate of Jezebel in the Old Testament,[6] a more factual basis for its origin lies with the work of Thomas Dwight in the 1870s.[7] Dwight's contribution was followed by such notables as Dorsey at the close of the century,[8] and by the 1960s the concept and practice of forensic anthropology was well integrated into the U.S. legal system.[9] Works by Snow and Işcan[10] describe the development and evolution of the subject in detail. It is not surprising that the forensic applications of biological anthropology were first developed in the U.S. Consider the favorable context and stimulus of the diverse range of variables responsible:

- War-dead repatriation and the consequent need for identification has been fundamentally important in the development of both biological and forensic anthropology.
- Relatively low population density and vast expanses of uninhabited land have all encouraged murderers to dump victims' bodies in such areas, confident that the remains will be skeletonized before recovery.
- The bodies will also probably be scavenged and scattered by the range of insect, avian, and faunal scavengers that the U.S. is home to.

The situation in the U.K. is very different. Here, the application of biological anthropology is almost totally confined to archaeological specimens, and in the rare cases where skeletons are recovered in a forensic context, the forensic pathologist usually undertakes the examination, despite his or her relatively limited experience of examining skeletal material.[11] The reasons for this are equally as diverse:

- We do not repatriate our war-dead.
- We do not have large areas of uninhabited land.
- We have a relatively low murder rate (approximately 800 in 1998), few of which are either dumped or buried.
- The U.K. has a temperate climate and wet (often clay) soils which retard decomposition.
- Most victims of murder whose bodies are recovered are found before skeletonization takes place, and where such victims are buried and recovery delayed, they are usually wrapped in synthetic materials, retarding decomposition.

- Where a corpse is exposed, scavengers are limited to insects, with little current evidence to suggest avian activity as a serious consideration.[12] Foxes and badgers are the principle faunal species likely to be involved in scavenging.

The U.K. situation is exemplified by the results of a recent survey of all U.K. police forces, which shows that 99% have never used the services of a forensic anthropologist.[11] Nevertheless, despite a dearth of interest by our medicolegal services in the potential of anthropology to judicial enquiries, the 1990s saw the rise of forensic archaeology as an investigative tool. Clearly, our understanding of the terminology is somewhat different from our U.S. counterparts, so exactly what do we mean by the term?

While archaeological techniques were occasionally employed earlier, forensic archaeologists were first employed in the U.K. in the Stephen Jennings case in 1988.[7] Since that time, largely reflecting the diligence and perseverance of Professor John Hunter (University of Birmingham), its use has slowly spread until today most police forces have employed archaeology for certain cases. As developed and defined in the U.K., forensic archaeology encompasses a broad range of aspects and expertise which are presented in the order of magnitude in which each is currently employed:

1. Search and location
2. Recovery and excavation of human remains and other materials
3. Recording the burial context
4. Facilitating the work of other forensic experts by appropriate sampling and recording of the burial environment, e.g., toxicology, entomology, ballistics, palynology, and soil analysis
5. Interpreting and reporting findings, and presenting evidence in court
6. Forensic anthropology
7. Conservation of recovered materials using passive conservation methods to meet new legislative requirements (Criminal Proceedings and Investigations Act, 1996).[4,7]

Consequently, whereas in the U.S. archaeological skills are largely confined to the excavation of remains already located, in the U.K. the remit is much wider and includes a breadth of archaeological skills which are not generally applied in the U.S. The function and rationale of each will now be discussed briefly. More attention is given to issues not previously considered in standard texts on this subject.

1.1.2 Search and Location

The methods utilized in the search for a buried victim or other materials (e.g., buried stolen goods, weapons) are the most significant and frequent input of archaeological techniques to the U.K. justice system. The Forensic Search Advisory Group, established in 1995, is most often called upon by the police to assist in the location of missing remains (FSAG, 1999) and to participate in devising an appropriate multidisciplinary search strategy for any particular case.

Forensic archaeologists frequently work alongside other experts. These can include cadaver dog handlers, ground penetrating radar specialists (GPR), and aerial multispectral and thermal imagery operators. Where appropriate, they employ a sequenced approach designed to narrow down the search area using a range of skills before more closely examining a specific area using a further suite of expertise. Such methods include:

- Cartography (including geological)
- Aerial photography
- Field skills, i.e., vegetation change, topography
- Geophysical prospection
- Evaluation of "hot-spots" by excavating sondages or small evaluation trenches across them, ruling out natural or irrelevant features and identifying areas of criminal activity.

1.1.2.1 *Cartography*

When the investigating authorities have identified a search area in relation to a specific crime involving concealment, possibly by burial, the first step has to be the examination of a range of appropriate maps. These must include a geological map, as in some parts of the U.K., outcropping and near surface solid geology of such materials as granite or limestone will, in the former case preclude, and in the second deter, any attempts at digging. Even chalk is immensely difficult to dig into deeply, and the presence of it in an area will almost certainly infer that any burial will be relatively shallow. Similarly, deposits of drift geology such as clay, which tends to be waterlogged, can impede the use of certain investigative methods, such as GPR.

Conventional maps will show areas of woodland, settlement, degree of slope, rivers and other bodies of water such as lakes, and roads, tracks, and footpaths which might have been used as access routes. Such knowledge will inform any search strategy, and will document changes over time.

Other types of mapping can be useful. Land that is subject to protection as nature reserves or agricultural conservation schemes will almost certainly have been subject to vegetation and land-use mapping, and subsequent vegetation change will be monitored by regular aerial photography. Such data is held in England and Wales by organizations such as English Nature and the Royal Society for the Protection of Birds, as well as by relevant government departments. It can provide a baseline from which to assess any recent change that could indicate criminal activity.

1.1.2.2 Aerial Photography

Surface change such as vegetation acceleration or retardation as a consequence of ground disturbance can be seen from the air using conventional aerial photography; even single graves can be identified in some circumstances. Photographs are preferably taken at an oblique angle during clear weather when the sun is low in the sky (i.e., winter months, or summer mornings or evenings). Vegetation stress due to the proximity of decaying cadaver(s) can be seen using infrared photography, and heat emitted as a consequence of either insect infestation or putrefaction and autolysis can be detected using aerial thermal imagery, as can heat differentials between disturbed and undisturbed soils.[13] Baseline data from which to observe more recent change can also be obtained by comparing pre-existing aerial photographs in any of the forms mentioned above (vertical or oblique, traditional, infra-red, or multispectral imagery), with those recently taken. In the U.K., complete coverage of air-photographs have a fine enough degree of detail to indicate archaeological features. Taking photographs of an area subsequent to its becoming an area of search and comparing such information with pre-existing but preferably recent (i.e., no more than five years) coverage can be immensely useful in highlighting areas of change or disturbance.

Equally as important as aerial photographs is prior knowledge of previous land use and the location of services. The position and date of installation of water and gas mains, electricity and television cables, septic tanks, and soak-aways are essential. In areas of settlement it is important to know the date of the construction of such garden features as ponds, patios, extensions to buildings, and outbuildings. Patios are, in my own experience, a favored medium under which to dispose of victims, as are soak-aways.

1.1.2.3 Landscape and Vegetation Appraisal

The use of line-searches by police officers causes the forensic archaeologist considerable consternation, as such an approach can be potentially catastrophic, damaging surface indicators of disturbance. The typical police response of digging what appear to be randomly sited holes in a search area can be even more damaging, and unless they are exceptionally lucky will have no greater chance of success than of finding a needle in haystack. However, a minimalist but carefully considered and informed search by experienced archaeologists can be invaluable in detecting evidence of soil disturbance or vegetation change indicative of the numerous impacts of a burial on plant regimes.

When examining a particular search area for topographical and vegetation anomalies it is imperative to have a basic understanding of geology, the soil sciences, and the affects of such processes as colluvium and alluviation on the landscape. The experienced eye can differentiate between natural soil change and changes that are anthropogenic in origin. Similarly, an under-standing of the impact of soil types and different hydrological regimes on taphonomic processes is crucial to be able to predict the condition of any surviving human remains[14] and associated materials, such as clothing.[15]

It is also essential to have some knowledge of the local flora and the effects of disturbance, changes in pH, nutrient enrichment, increased mois-ture retention, and changed water-levels. The burial of a decaying body will effect all of these processes at different times and to a different extent in the decomposition process, hence an understanding of taphonomic change is crucial.[16] Such change will be moderated or enhanced by such variables as pre-deposition insect infestation, depth of burial, cause of death, previous health and weight of the victim, toxicology, and presence and nature of clothing or body coverings. The burial of a victim can cause overlying vegeta-tion to be stressed, to die, to be accelerated, or simply to be anomalous in terms of normal plant succession in the area. It can also disturb a dormant seed bank and result in the colonization of plant species not presently visible locally. A recently excavated experimental grave (containing a Soay sheep) on the chalk down-land in Dorset provides a useful example. The grave was clearly demarked by the almost exclusive colonization of a member of the Compositae (daisy) family, which though common in the area before inten-sive farming took over, is now only rarely seen but known to like disturbed ground. Similar species exist for most soil types, and it behooves the archae-ologist to either have an awareness of them or to involve a botanist. A burial in an area of acid grassland has the potential to encourage the success of plant species tolerant of alkaline conditions after a period of months follow-ing burial, reflecting proteolysis.[14] This might be a useful indicator and assist in locating a grave. A further consideration is that awareness of vegetation regimes local to a grave is essential for the involvement of any subsequent palynological or botanical analysis.

Field searches can involve a trained cadaver dog, and in the U.K. such animals are used in conjunction with ground probes which are believed to release gases associated with decomposition. In the U.S., most dogs are air-scent only. In both cases, the success of this method is very much dependant on the temperature and humidity being moderate, not extreme, and on wind strength and direction. Dogs can form a useful part of a multi-pronged approach to cadaver detection.[4]

1.1.2.4 Geophysical Techniques

This aspect of forensic archaeology is long overdue for a full appraisal in the literature. A useful, if dated, summary can be found in Hunter et al.[7] The two principle methods employed directly by archaeologists in the U.K. are resistivity and magnetometry surveys. The benefit of both methods is that they are not intrusive and can be carried out quickly, and the results processed in the field.

Resistivity survey measures the electrical resistance of the buried soil. An electric current is passed between two probes pushed a few centimeters into the ground surface. This is undertaken within a measured grid and the results plotted within the defined area. Resistance is affected by the moisture content of the soil, which is altered in areas of below-ground disturbance. Variation of the probe separation allows an estimation of size and depth of anomalies.[7] Resistivity is less effective on waterlogged soils than free-draining ones, and is unlikely to give useful results in heavily disturbed soils.

Soil disturbance not only alters moisture retention levels locally, but will also cause local anomalies in the magnetic field. Magnetometry can be used to detect such change. This method involves no probing and is also carried out within a grid. Magnetometry will also pick up evidence of buried ferrous metals which might be associated with a burial. It is less effective than resistivity in urban contexts where building materials include fired clay products, fragments of which may be in the garden soils. It is adversely affected by steel pipes, metal fences, and other ferrous debris, and is not effective in heavily disturbed sites.

A further method that is employed in the U.K. is GPR. Although now becoming more frequently used, GPR is not a standard procedure employed by archaeologists, and in forensic cases outside specialists are involved if the circumstances suggest GPR might be an appropriate method to employ. GPR transmits a short pulse of electromagnetic energy into the ground and measures the reflection of the context. Producing almost instant results, it detects anomalies that represent a discontinuity in substrate. This method is best employed by operators experienced in forensic work, as its most challenging aspect is interpretation of the data. A considerable amount of experimental work is being undertaken by the FSAG using GPR as well as resistivity and magnetometry on experimental burial sites. GPR cannot be used on waterlogged sites or if the ground is uneven or heavily vegetated. However, unlike resistivity and magnetometry, it can be used through concrete and paving slabs, and within buildings, thus saving considerable time and resources.

Ideally, as many appropriate methods as possible are used and the results from each are compared and contrasted, compiling a series of "hot-spots" for further evaluation. What such methods detect are below-surface anomalies which may reflect a burial but can also reflect natural and other anthropogenic activities.

1.1.2.5 *Other Search Methods*

Perhaps uniquely in this volume, this chapter does not attempt to understand the criminal psyche. What experience has shown, however, is that perpetrators will conceal victims in extraordinary places and on occasion go to considerable lengths to conceal the presence of the grave. The more experience gained, the more it becomes apparent that rules of thumb for dump site situations are only that. Regardless of patterns of behavior discussed in the literature,[4] bodies may be found almost anywhere, including such counterintuitive sites as the middle of a field, such as near Fareham, Hampshire in 1996 (Rai case). While being aware of known patterns of criminal behavior, it is crucial to retain an open mind.

Alternative approaches can be adopted where more traditional search and location methods cannot be applied. Augers, or ground probes, that remove samples of the buried soil can be useful in criminal investigations. Different types of augers are used for different soil types. When the author was asked some 15 years previously by the police to assess, as discretely as possible, whether a victim was buried in one of a series of legitimate graves in a group of cemeteries, the above methods could not be employed. As the depth of the legitimate burials was known by the cemetery authorities and made available to us, augering was used to assess the grave fill down to the depth of the original burial. This method was successful in locating a body. It took only minutes to examine each grave, and was inexpensive and unobtrusive in a sensitive setting. Augers can also be used as a survey tool and auger transects undertaken as a search method. Clearly, augers are not affective in stony soils and gravels, but in experienced hands can be very effective tools.

When, for various reasons, none of the above methods can be used on a site where there is every reason to believe a grave may be concealed, a last resort is to strip off the vegetation and top soil using plant machinery equipped with a wide toothless bucket. On smaller areas, such stripping could be done by hand. A colleague and I have used machine stripping successfully in a mass grave location in the Balkans where the perpetrators dumped spoil to a depth of up to one meter over the entire search area and littered it with waste metal. This method can be fast and effective, a good machine operator being the principle requirement. Once the overburden of topsoil and vegetation is removed, the archaeologist can examine the exposed surface for evidence of grave cuts through the natural undisturbed substrate. Anomalous features can then be quickly examined to see if they are of interest to the inquiry. In some substrates grave-cuts are likely to become ill-defined due to hydrological conductivity (e.g., alluvial deposits in flood planes or sands), excessive root or rodent disturbance, or because the substrate is already very disturbed. While the former two criteria are unlikely to happen within a forensic framework (in the U.K. 70 to 75 years), in such cases narrow evaluation trenches can also be cut systematically and strategically across the site to ensure that nothing is missed. Evaluation trenches are not advisable when seeking individual graves but can be useful when attempting to locate mass burials. An adaption of this technique is to remove material known to have been deposited on a site (for whatever reasons) after a burial has taken place, by machine, and then apply geophysical methods upon the original ground surface. The use of archaeological techniques for locating and excavating mass graves is discussed in further detail by Skinner.[17] In view of the amount of work in this field over the last five years or so, this paper is rather dated, but nevertheless useful until a more up-to-date review is presented.

1.1.3 Excavation and Recovery

The fundamental principle underlying archaeological excavation and recording is that the digging of a grave will cause discontinuity in the medium into which it is cut and that it will itself conform to the laws of stratigraphy. Consequently, the approach to excavation is a destructive process and must be sequential and thoroughly recorded to allow the evidence to be reconstructed and interpreted for the courts. In order to accurately record the stratigraphy of a grave and the location of any materials within that stratigraphic context, archaeologists excavate the fill of a grave in spits, or layers of five or ten centimeters, depending on the circumstances of each case. Each layer is retained in a sealed sterile container for further analysis and individually numbered. It is imperative to be able to say which layer any materials found within a grave came from, as this could be crucial in successfully linking a perpetrator to the site. Generally, a forensic grave will be excavated in two halves so that a section of the fill showing clearly any layers or differences can be accurately recorded. The fill will be removed this way until the top of the cadaver or skeleton is exposed.

A major difference between archaeological and forensic graves is that in forensic cases, unless the grave, is very shallow, a trench will be dug around one or two sides of the grave, allowing the grave walls to be removed. This enables the victim to be more easily recovered than from above. This method does preclude close scrutiny of the removed grave walls in deep graves, and evidence of tool marks and possibly flakes of paint from tools may be lost as a consequence. Unlike in archaeological graves, in forensic cases, whether cadavers or skeletons, the remains are not scrupulously cleaned in situ, as this may remove crucial forensic evidence. Enough of the body will be revealed to record its position and its relationship to any other objects or materials recovered. The body or skeleton will then be removed by methods appropriate to the particular circumstances.[7,18] Thereafter, in the U.K. the analysis of the remains will almost certainly to be undertaken by the forensic pathologist, at the direction of HM Coroner.

Once the body has been removed, the archaeologist will complete the excavation of the grave and fully record it. Particular attention must be paid to recording evidence of tool marks in the grave walls and base, and evidence of shoe prints in the base. Survival of such features is heavily dependent on soil type (i.e., shoe prints may survive in clays but not on chalk) and on wetness/dryness. The degree of organic content in the soil is a further factor here, as the activity of earthworms can be such that the degree of disturbance they cause can remove footprints from an organic soil context. This proved to be the case in experimental graves dug by the author on chalk, where several centimeters of organic mulch were placed at the bottom of a grave for the sole purpose of leaving deep footprints for students to recover in training excavations a year later. No trace of the footprints survived, the worms having clearly been very active in the organic matrix.

Careful excavation and recording of the grave itself is a crucial component of the archaeologist's remit and should not be considered secondary to recovering the remains. The type of question the archaeologist may be asked in court is whether or not he or she considers that the grave was dug with care and consideration, or in haste and with little care. In the U.K., the consequences of an archaeologist's interpretation of the evidence may be crucial in deciding whether a perpetrator is charged and convicted of murder or manslaughter. This is an onerous responsibility, as is so much that is associated with this type of work.[19,20] Photography will be used for recording, as well as drawn plans and records showing levels. Digital photography is presently not an acceptable format in the U.K. courts. Full written records will be made of the whole process, including the reasons certain approaches were adopted as well as details of those methods, and the results. An illustrated report will then be prepared for the courts.

1.1.4   Passive Conservation of Materials

The adoption of the Criminal Procedure and Investigations Act (1996) into English law in 1998 has placed an important new obligation on the investigating authorities. Under s.23(1), authorities are obliged to conserve evidence from a case until after the trial process is complete — where no-one is convicted, or, in the case of a conviction, until after a perpetrator is released from prison. In serious cases, this can mean retention of evidence for twenty years or more. At present the U.K. authorities have neither the space nor expertise to undertake this responsibility satisfactorily — that is, in order that material can be re-examined in its original form, in the case of an appeal or retrial some years later. Biological samples present particular problems in this respect.

Archaeological conservators, however, often working within museum environments, have a wealth of expertise in material science and have the knowledge base and expertise in order that a wide range of organic and inorganic materials can be conserved. Present archaeological theory and new scientific developments require that such conservation is passive and that it does not, if possible, alter the original state of the object or material in order to conserve it. The reason for this is the wealth of biomolecular methods available to archaeologists in the new millennium. Archaeological conservation involves a wide range of considerations, including appropriate packaging, environmentally controlled storage facilities, and consideration of the impact of light on materials. The ramifications of this legislation require further clarification in the courts but are potentially onerous for the police as the storage space, expertise, and cost are potentially enormous. Nevertheless, this highlights another area of potential archaeological contribution to the process of justice.

1.1.5 Forensic Anthropology

As stated above, the use of biological anthropology in a judicial context in the U.K. is unusual. For example, in the high profile serial murder case of Fred and Rosemary West, where the skeletonized remains of twelve young females were recovered, no anthropologist was involved. Recently, in a mass disaster in the U.K. where it was believed that victims had been incinerated, offers of expertise from archaeologists and anthropologists specializing in cremated bone recovery and analysis were declined. Recovery was undertaken by police officers, with the help of forensic pathologists and the analysis by the pathologists. That the U.K. judicial system facilitates and tolerates a system where such work is undertaken by individuals with neither the expertise nor experience to undertake either recovery or analysis to the best possible level, and where offers of help from those with both are ignored, is astonishing. It would appear to reflect a system within which the pre-eminence of the pathologist is unthinkingly assumed by the police authorities and the courts.

Occasionally though, the anthropologist might be involved. It is not the place of this chapter to summarize the role of the forensic anthropologist, and the reader is referred to such works as Reich[21] and Ramey Burns.[22] Suffice to say that their role is to uncover as much information as possible that will contribute to identifying the remains through individuating characteristics such as ancestry, sex, age at death, stature, parity status, evidence of trauma and disease in life, and handedness. The forensic anthropologist may also contribute towards the determination of cause of death, e.g., gunshot wounds, strangulation, blade or blunt weapon trauma, and manner of death.

While forensic anthropology per se is only infrequently practiced in the U.K., it must be noted that anyone undertaking forensic archaeology must have a basic understanding of anthropology. In order to be able to excavate human skeletal remains from any context, archaeological or forensic, it is imperative to have a good understanding of human skeletal morphology. In the U.K., many traditional archaeologists do not currently have this level of understanding and, as McKinley and Roberts[23] note, "The fact that all excavators have a skeleton does not ensure their knowledge of what one looks like." The forensic archaeologist must know what bony elements should be present in fetal remains, in those of an infant, and at every stage of development and maturation, including degenerative changes. It is imperative that the individual recovering remains understands sequences of ossification centers and epiphyseal fusion. There must be an understanding of where in the body "stones" of various types might be recovered, where sesamoid bones might occur, where ossified cartilage might be found, and what each looks like.

As with use of archaeology within the judicial framework, employment of anthropological techniques should not be a simple unquestioning transference of skills from an archaeological context to a forensic one. A key consideration is that most of the methods anthropologists use to determine the key characteristics of ancestry, sex, and age are all subject to margins of error and degrees of probability that may be problematic for the courts. While the use of 95 percent confidence is acceptable when analyzing archaeological material, it is less satisfactory in court, as it implies a one in twenty chance of being wrong.[20] Equally, the use of statistics such as discriminant functions, derived from material of specific genetic and socio-economic backgrounds, is inappropriate when a victim's background is different from the group on which the function was derived. Since little is known about most victims at this stage in the proceedings, this will almost always be the case. An area of anthropological analysis that requires further research is the assessment of disease processes prevalent in modern western society (e.g., AIDS, multiple sclerosis, cystic fibrosis) upon the skeleton, and how such disease processes are influenced by treatments and consequential sequelae. While the study of paleopathology is well developed and has forensic relevance in third world contexts, many of the infectious diseases are not relevant in westernized societies, while many more remain virtually unexplored.[24]

1.1.6 Attitude and Application

1.1.6.1 Adaptation

Archaeologists in the U.K. working on archaeological sites and materials are guided by theory, rules and regulations, codes of conduct, and protocols adapted over many decades of practice and set out by our professional body, the Institute of Field Archaeologists. While adaptation and even innovation is acceptable in unusual contexts, for example, wetlands or underwater, generally there is little divergence from accepted procedures. However, the key to successful integration of archaeology into the forensic context is to retain knowledge of everything you would normally practice in an archaeological context as a tool-kit of options, and to bring to bear whichever of these is appropriate to any particular forensic context. If none are directly appropriate, then modify an existing approach or devise a new one. A key constraint is recognition of the objectives of the investigators and applying archaeological principles and methods as appropriate. Similarly, such factors as cultural dictates, terrain, time constraints, health and safety, the presence of military rule with its oppressive machinery of arms and personnel, fear, insecurity, dislocation, and emotionally charged environments all will generally influence procedures and practice.

The ability and willingness to act expediently and employ lateral thought are essential skills of the forensic archaeologist. Hoshower sensibly advocates the abandonment of a rigid adherence to textbook archaeology which has evolved to maximize the potential of archaeological sites.[25] She advocates the adoption of flexible, common-sense, streamlined approaches in forensic cases. The challenge for the archaeologist is to devise the most appropriate method meeting the legal and humanitarian requirements of individual cases, methods which do not sacrifice the integrity of data or the ability to offer confident interpretation. The archaeologist almost always has to devise such a strategy very quickly, often under the scrutiny of other experts, with little or no time for reflection. It is without doubt a challenging role.

1.1.7 Conclusion

Ultimately, the credibility of the archaeologist will be tested in court, and it should always be remembered that no matter who invites you to participate in an investigation, your duty is to the courts. Credibility in court relies very much upon experience and qualifications as well as having the essential professional and interpersonal skills to give evidence in court with confidence and credibility. It is not enough to be a proficient archaeologist; forensic archaeology demands a much wider range of skills to ensure that your contribution fits inside current legal constraints. An understanding of basic criminal law and of courtroom and crime scene procedures and obligations is essential. With the increasing deployment of forensic archaeology to the investigation of genocide, recently known to have taken place within four continents, the range of associated expertise increases. Some understanding of international legislation and protocols is a fundamental requirement of the forensic archaeologist in this arena. At the start of a new millennium, it is with some satisfaction that U.K. trained forensic archaeologists are contributing to the investigation of serious crime in North and South America, Europe and Australia.

1.2 Palynology: A New Tool for the Forensic Investigator

TERRY HUTTER

In its inception, "pollen analysis" (palynology) was principally the assessment of pollen grains and spores. Pollen grains are best understood as the containers which embody the male gametophyte promulgatory portion of the seed plants (angiosperms and gymnosperms). Spores, on the other hand, are the resting and dispersal stages of a cryptogam/fruiting body (pteridophytes, bryophytes, algae, and fungi). The science of palynology has evolved to include, in addition to spores and pollen, a variety of plant and animal microfossils and micro-organics.

In 1944 Hyde and Williams,[26] acknowledging the expanding science of pollen and spore analysis, originated the term palynology to embrace this expanding science. For the duration of the 1940s, palynology, though still concerned largely with the science of modern spores and pollen, also included forms recovered from sediments and coals. Hence, the expression "the study of acid resistant microfossils" is sometimes substituted for the term palynology. Eventually, other resistant micro-forms/organics that survived the acid preparation process of hydrochloric acid (HCl), hydrofluoric acid (HF), and other inorganic caustic chemicals, were loosely referred to as palynomorphs. Indeed, as the science of palynology is now defined, a palynomorph can refer to spores, pollen, chitinozoa, polychaete worm jaws, acritarchs, algal cysts, and animal and vegetable tissues.

Though used in investigations as far–ranging as climatic change studies to allergy studies, the fledgling science of palynology found its first broad support with petroleum exploration companies in the 1950s, where its usefulness was described as near magical.[27] This predominance of the use of palynologists by petroleum exploration companies continues today. Presently, and in conjunction with technological expansion, we are on the eve of a new revelation in palynology — forensic palynology.

It has long been recognized that the toughness of the organic structure of palynomorphs, specifically spores and pollen, enhances their survivability and resistance to decay in comparison to other biological materials. Secondly, variations in the form, sculpture, and stylings of many palynomorphs provide an invaluable means of identifying and differentiating them, increasing their usefulness in taxonomic studies. In addition to recognizable characteristics and preservability, the abundance of palynomorphs in the environment is of foremost value to the forensic investigator. Soil, leaf litter, even dust contains palynomorphs which may provide clues to the geographical locale or habitat from which a sample comes. Matter from tires, packaging material, soil from shoes, dust from clothing, material from beneath fingernails, even samples from the digestive tract may yield sufficient palynomorph recovery for analysis and the reconstruction of recent movements.

1.2.1 Historical Perspective

Erdtman described possibly the first use of forensic palynology in Austria in 1959 while on a journey down the Danube near Vienna, solving a murder case in which a man disappeared and his body was never recovered.[28] The investigation did yield a probable suspect for the murder, and a pair of muddy shoes was taken into evidence. Palynomorphs were recovered from the mud on the shoes and indicated a presence of the modern pollen spruce (pine), willow, and alder, in addition to fossil hickory pollen estimated to be approximately 20 million years old, from the Tertiary geologic period. From this retrieved palynomorph data, Wilhelm Klaus, of the University of Vienna, determined that only a small area 20 kilometers north of Vienna could contain this same palynomorph assemblage. The suspect, when confronted with this locale as the scene for the murder, confessed and showed authorities where he had buried the body, in the area predicted by Wilhelm Klaus.[27]

Probably the most noted mention of forensic palynology in the United States occurred on a television show popular in the 1970s, Hawaii Five-O. The particular show contained a plot where a group of thieves in Hawaii were tracked to their hideout by examination of the pollen trapped in their abandoned car's air filter. The pollen was deemed by the palynologist to be representative of plants found only in a particular area of the island, the hideout. In truth, this may be one application of forensic palynology.

Though few cases utilizing forensic palynology are in evidence in the United States, a murder case involving corn/maize pollen (Zea mays) is significant. In the late 1970s in rural Illinois an individual was kidnaped, assaulted, and murdered with an ax. Subsequent to the murder, the victim's car was stolen. Thereafter, transients were arrested for breaking and entering in a town near where the murder victim's car was abandoned. Suspicious of the transients' story, but with no real evidence to link them with the abandoned car and the scene of the crime, the Illinois Bureau of Investigation turned to forensic palynology and Dr. James King of the Carnegie Museum for assistance (personal communication). Pollen analysis of a transient's shirt revealed it was covered with fresh pollen, especially in the area of the shoulders. This information indicated that the transients had recently run through a field of maize in bloom. The only such field in the area was located between where the murder victim's car was abandoned and the town where the transients were arrested. However, the transients stated that they had never been near the location in question. Subsequent to the palynology report, investigators questioned people living and working near the maize field. Several positive identifications from this follow-up investigation, as well as the corn pollen identification, led to a confession of the murder by the transients. (Case #77CF65, Illinois vs. Bobby Cole and Arthur Wilson, Macoupin County, Illinois.)

In another brutal murder case in the United States, the victim's hands and feet had been removed by the assailant in an effort to prevent fingerprint identification. A search of the area where the body was recovered revealed no clues to the victim's place of origin or the geographic location where the murder took place. However, recovered clothing from the body was tested using forensic palynology, which revealed palynoflora indicating an area nearly 100 miles north of the area where the body was found. That information narrowed the search locale and aided investigators in pinpointing the area where the victim lived, and eventually the scene of the crime. Civil, misdemeanor, and other such cases of less tragic consequences are also amenable to forensic palynology.

In one such case in New Zealand, a suspect fled the scene of a crime on a motorcycle.[29] The motorcycle became stalled on a muddy hillside, where the suspect abandoned it and fled on foot. Later, the suspect arrived at the local precinct and tried to reclaim the motorcycle, saying that it had been stolen from his home the previous evening. Denying that he had ever been in the area where the motorcycle had been abandoned, the suspect allowed the police to search his home, where they recovered a pair of muddy boots. The mud on the boots contained an identical grouping of palynomorphs to that collected from the muddy hillside.

As in the United States, many countries monitor the trading of agricultural commodities. In a case in England, a product advertised as "Yorkshire Clover Honey" was suspected of being adulterated. A palynological investigation revealed that in addition to palynomorphs typical of the Yorkshire area of England, the honey contained significant portions of four other pollen types indigenous to Eastern Europe. It was determined that the majority of the honey originated in Eastern Europe, and the party was charged and found guilty under the British Trades Description Act.[30]

Another case, though not brought to a legal conclusion, was when a large shipment of honey purchased by the United States Department of Agriculture (USDA) for the Farm Subsidy Program was analyzed for its palynomorph content. As USDA agents suspected, it was not entirely of domestic origin. A forensic palynological evaluation of the honey indicated that approximately six to ten percent of the honey mixture was indeed produced outside the United States.

Forensic palynology has even been used in zoning disputes of local jurisdictions. A large medical manufacturing company in the midwest had located its facilities in a rural setting to reduce problems with airborne contaminants and reduce cost-prohibitive air filtration during the manufacturing of its product. Years later, a local quarry operator sought to open a new facility a few miles from the medical manufacturing company, with access to and from the quarry being a new two-lane gravel road passing less than a quarter mile from the medical manufacturing company. The quarry operator's argument was that their travel on the gravel road would not produce additional particulates in the air than what would be produced seasonally by the cornfields surrounding the medical manufacturing company. Corn pollen, generally spherical, and large in comparison with other pollen types, does not travel a significant distance in any great numbers. Instead, it falls from the corn flowers at the top of the plant to pollinate the ears of corn directly below. Conversely, the dust and particulate matter placed into the air by the passing trucks would stay suspended and travel great distances. Resultant knowledge of the pollination style of corn crops and the travel of micellular particles on air currents led the local jurisdiction to deny the application of the quarry operator, thus saving substantial expense by the medical manufacturing company on new filtration equipment.

Until recently, the New York City Police Department Crime Lab maintained a palynologist on staff — Dr. Stanley, who was instrumental in solving several criminal cases. One case involved a shipment of cocaine hydrochloride that was seized in a New York City drug raid. Though the suspects were not caught, the raid and subsequent cocaine seizure yielded important trafficking information. Palynological analysis of the cocaine hydrochloride revealed a number of different pollen suites that indicated the cocaine was processed in South America (probably Bolivia or Columbia), then sent to a locale in northeastern North America where it was cut and packaged and finally sent on to New York, where it was cut again and was being prepared for distribution when seized.[31]

Overall, documented forensic palynology cases are few and far between in the United States. Currently, the only country that seems to have fully tapped the enormous potential of forensic palynology and the acceptance of palynomorph evidence in civil and criminal court cases is New Zealand, though Australia and Malaysia are initiating programs. In an effort to learn why forensic palynology was not more widely used, Drs. Vaughn Bryant, John Jones, and Dallas Mildenhall sent questionnaires to leading law enforcement agencies and forensic labs in the United States, Canada, and the United Kingdom (personal communication). They discovered that forensic palynology is rarely used, not because the science lacks validity, but because it is not widely known or understood how palynomorph data can be used to resolve questions related to legal or criminal matters.

1.2.2   Palynomorph Production and Environments

Pollen and spore production within a given area and environment is of great significance to the forensic palynologist. If one has knowledge of the production and dispersal patterns of pollen and spores of indigenous plants in a given geographical area, then one knows what palynomorph assemblages would be expected for samples collected from a specific locale. For example, samples examined from a given area not exhibiting the expected palynomorph assemblage, as well as the presence of other palynomorph assemblages in atypical numbers, could suggest an anomaly. This anomalous pattern gives the forensic palynologist clues, and indicates the need for scrutiny.

As a corollary to known production and dispersal patterns of the indigenous plants of a given geographical area, a perimeter/location customarily bears a palynological marker endemic to its floral occupants. Just as individuals decorate and bring familiar objects into their dwelling, they tend to bring into their living environment palynomorph-producing objects specific to their wants and desires. To verify this human propensity, one only has to drive through any suburb and notice the shrubs, flowers, grasses, and other such plants to establish that each dwelling has a specific owner as well as additional occupants. This is also true of the outside palynomorphs brought into the dwelling, and may even indicate a particular place of employment. As an example, consider the rapist or burglar concealed in the shrubs and flower beds outside his intended victim's residence. The forensic investigator may have a crude indication of foot prints in the soil, indicating the suspect's place of concealment, but little other evidence to tie the offender to the scene of the crime. However, recovered palynomorphs from the clothes and shoes of an offender may indicate a palynomorph assemblage specific to the scene of the transgression or concealment. Such forensic palynological investigations may also provide clues to a supposed fight between victimizer and victims in a garden area, or articles of clothing dropped in one area and transported to another area where they are recovered by investigators. The potential for the use of palynology incorporated into forensic investigations is endless. However, as in all scientific procedures, certain protocols and collection procedures must be maintained and adhered to.[32]

1.2.3   Forensic Palynomorph Collection

One of the most important aspects of forensic palynology is the collection of palynomorph samples. Ideally, these forensic samples should be collected by either a competent palynologist or an investigator trained in such forensic collecting techniques. Collected samples need to be maintained contamination-free throughout the duration of the case. Accurate records of the collecting procedures as well as the provenance of each sample during each stage of the investigation, in addition to their later utilization throughout the case, should also be preserved.

When forensic palynology is deemed advantageous for particular samples or a specific case, one must first consider what kind of material is available for analysis. This consideration indicates how the material should be collected as well as what palynological processing procedures are to be utilized after collection. Of the sample types applicable to forensic palynological investigation, the best results are from the dirt, mud/soil, and dust associated with a crime scene, victim, or suspect. Sources for this type of sample may be clothing, shoes, vehicles, skin, or even appliances bearing an electromagnetic source. In conditions where dirt and mud have been dried on objects, one should use a soft, clean, fine brush to first clean the surface before collecting the material. This removes the possibility of surface contamination of palynomorphs that may have adhered to the mud or dirt after it had dried. Collection of each forensic sample should consist of picking up the samples or gently scraping them from the surface with a clean instrument. Once collected, each sample should be placed in a sterile plastic container, sealed and marked for provenance.

In certain environmental conditions it may be necessary to use new paper envelopes to maintain sample integrity and stability. In the case of minimal sample availability, one may use transparent cellophane tape for collection purposes. This is especially useful in the collection of dust samples. The tape used in sampling should be folded and stuck back onto itself to maintain the integrity of the sample and reduce the possibility of outside contamination and each tape piece placed in a labeled sterile plastic container. Once in the laboratory, the forensic palynologist can use solvents to free the collected material from the tape. Cloth and other such woven items are also useful in the trapping and ultimate collection of palynomorphs. Micellular particles such as dust, spores, and pollen are constantly settling on exposed surfaces. If one doubts this premise, view the light source in any movie theater to see this micellular material floating in the subtle air drafts around the theater. Woven articles left exposed to these subtle air drafts of the atmosphere will ultimately become coated with this micellular material. Comprising this micellular material the forensic investigator will find, in addition to the palynomorphs, micro fibers and biological elements such as shed skin cells which become trapped in the fibers of such material. Woven articles exposed to the "palynomorph rain" of an area may be excellent indicators of place of origin or usage. For example, rugs become indicators of the micro-niche in which they were placed, and baskets often contain palynomorphs in the spaces between their weave.

If an item is to be recovered for palynomorph investigation, the entire article should be collected for examination if possible. Once back in the lab, the forensic palynologist can remove the pollen by thoroughly rinsing the item or item fragment in a solution of hot, soapy, distilled water. Distilled water should always be used, since many municipal water systems, though free of microbes, are rarely free of spores and pollen. When a suspect item cannot be maintained for later examination, the cellophane tape method of palynomorph collection may be used, even though it may be a less effective technique. An excellent and often overlooked vehicle for palynomorph entrapment is hair. Wind blows through hair and palynomorphs in the air become trapped in the spaces between the hair strands. Natural oils produced by the individual aid in the palynomorphs' adherence to the hair strands.

The collection of palynomorphs need not be restricted to humans. Often companion animals will carry a similar palynomorph assemblage as their owners. Stock animals might be traceable to their original owners. Hair on fur coats, hats, and other such personal items are excellent palynomorph traps from which evidence may be extracted. Such evidence can indicate the owner's association with a crime scene as well as his or her association with narcotics such as marijuana, heroin, and cocaine. Additionally, humans often use cosmetic applications, sprays, and other cosmetics that apply a sticky coating to the hair shaft, which aids in the entrapment of airborne palyno-morphs. A simple washing of the hair with warm distilled water and mild detergents will loosen the trapped palynomorphs. The resulting effluent can be collected and stored in sterile plastic containers for later examination.

1.2.4 Forensic Palynology and Illegal Drugs

Currently, a primary application of forensic palynology is the tracing and identification of illegal drugs. Forensic palynology can tie specific locales and individuals to specific consignments of illegal drugs, or it can indicate whether drugs recovered from seemingly unconnected locales can be tied to a common shipment.[31] Additionally, it may be useful to connect a seizure of illegal drugs to a specific processing laboratory, the precise location of a distribution facility, or the shipment's geographic origin.

For example, consider marijuana, one of the plant kingdom's most pro-lific producers of pollen. When marijuana cultivation, harvesting, and pack-aging occurs in the open, large amounts of marijuana pollen, in addition to indigenous pollen, incorporate to become a part of the processed marijuana.

Thus, analysis of pollen samples from seized shipments are susceptible to being traced to their place of origination. Conversely, in a situation where marijuana is grown and processed in the confines of an artificial growing facility, little of the outside indigenous pollen flora will be incorporated into the processed and shipped marijuana. This may increase the difficulty of locating the precise geographic source for the marijuana's production and packaging.

Nonetheless, as all marijuana plants produce copious amounts of pollen, personnel, clothing, furniture, appliances, dust, dirt, as well as everything coming into and out of such a closed environment will bear the pollen of the marijuana being produced inside. This would also be true of the air-exchange system, its filters, as well as effluents coming from the facility. It is therefore an easy task to connect individuals and materials with a known or suspected marijuana-producing facility, as everything their pollen grains come into contact with will be contaminated. In rare instances is any portion of the production of heroin or cocaine confined to an enclosed facility. The initial methodology in the production of heroin is the collection of flowing sap induced by incising the outer surface of the immature seed pod of specific species of the poppy plant, whereas the beginning of cocaine production is the collection of substantial measures of the leaves of the coca plant. The sticky sap of the poppy plant is generally allowed to dehydrate in the open, as are the leaves of the coca. Both the dehydrated poppy sap and dried coca leaves are usually further processed in the open. Because most of these processes generally occur in a single locale, pollen from other indigenous plants in the area is incorporated into both the heroin and cocaine samples. This representation of indigenous palynomorphs will be reflected in every part of the refined heroin and cocaine from the point of origination to the point of consumption.

Just as heroin and cocaine contain pollen indicative of their respective points of origin and processing, so will their packaging materials, vehicles, and personnel. All will contain traces of a similar palynoflora. Fibrous as well as woven packaging materials have many of the palynomorph trapping propensities, as does hair. It is also not uncommon for the paper money associated with such illegal drug transactions to be a source for the collection of said palynofloras and aid in the tracing of drug transactions.

1.2.5 Additional Forensic Palynology Applications

Forensic researchers in New Zealand have even advocated the collection of palynomorph samples in association with investigations of human remains.[33] Dallas Mildenhall recommends the collection of samples from the stomach, small intestine, and colon areas during autopsy, as well as the scraping of nasal/sinus passages for later palynomorph analysis. An examination of these recovered palynomorphs may produce clues to where a victim had been just prior to death as well as where he or she ate her last meal. In the case of a struggle, palynomorphs may indicate the locale of the assault and ensuing encounter. Samples collected from the clothes and remains of a victim may be tied to locale, as well as to the clothes of the suspect who was also involved in the assault.

In instances where skeletal or severely decomposed remains are recovered, forensic palynomorph samples should still be collected. Samples beneath and protected by the position of the victim may yield indications as to the season when the victim's remains were concealed. Palynomorphs recovered from the victim's hair or clothing may yield indications of the time of year the offense occurred, as well.

1.2.6 Palynomorph Processing

It should be understood by the investigator that laboratory extraction of palynomorphs is a destructive process — that is, in an effort to remove, refine, and concentrate palynomorphs it is typically necessary to alter, dissolve, or destroy all of the non-palynomorph waste. As such, the study of palynomorphs is often referred to as the study of acid resistance microfossils/forms. What this means to the case investigator is that material from which palynomorph recovery is attempted will generally not be available later for other types of forensic testing. For this reason, forensic palynology should be performed last. Equally as important is the maintenance of forensic protocol for testing and transferring evidence. Utilization of these standard forensic practices significantly reduce and substantially negate the possibility of contemporaneous palynomorph contamination.

Extraction procedures of palynomorphs may vary due to the type of material being processed, however, of key importance is the sample size available for processing. When ample material is available, standard palynomorph extraction vessels, procedures, and chemicals such as Hcl, HF, and potassium hydroxide usually suffice. Often, though, there is little material to process, and therefore, qualified acid-resistant vessels are needed as well as modifications in standard palynomorph processing techniques. It should also be understood that the techniques used in the extraction process are predominantly targeted at the disintegration, dissolution, or otherwise removal of the non-palynomorph portion of the sample, which often results in a concentration of the recovered palynomorphs. These palynomorphs are then collected and mounted on glass microscope slides for later analysis and storage.

1.2.7 Hydrochloric Acid (Hcl)

The use of Hcl is necessary to remove any calcium carbonate in the sample. If any portion of the sample is suspected to contain carbonates, it is preferable to begin with this technique. When the use of HF is also deemed necessary in the preparation of a sample, Hcl digestion should precede that of the HF treatment. Treatment of the sample in this manner consists of adding a cooled 10% solution of Hcl to the palynomorph residue until all visible reaction ceases. The use of hot Hcl is discouraged due the possibility of corrosion of the walls of the palynomorph. After digestion, the sample should be neutralized with distilled water.

1.2.8　Hydrofluoric Acid (HF)

The use of HF is indicated if there is presence of silica in the sample which may obscure mounted palynomorphs. Due to the abundance of clays and quartzose sands in the environment, the use of HF is generally standard in palynologic processing. HF is an extremely corrosive reagent, and all prescribed precautions should be taken during its use. It is recommended that protective garments and eye protection suitable for use with HF be used at all times. Glass vessels are not to be utilized for HF.

Treatment of a sample should be initiated with the introduction of a small quantity of a 30 to 40% solution of HF to the palynomorph residue. As the reaction is exothermic, care should be taken to add the solution slowly, since any expanding clays in the sample may cause the residue to rapidly boil and spill out of the containment vessel. Ultimately, the HF solution should be added to the sample in excess of the reaction. When an excessive amount of silica is present, it may be necessary to place the containment vessel holding the palynomorph residue and HF solution in a hot water bath to speed the dissolution of the silica portion of the residue. After dissolution of the silica, allow the remaining residue to settle and decant the HF solution. Repeatedly add distilled water to allow to settle, then decant and add distilled water sample to neutralize.

1.2.9　Potassium Hydroxide (KOH)

The treatment with KOH should be done with caution. If this procedure is done improperly, the caliber and quality of the resulting palynomorphs may be diminished. Where there is an abundance of organic debris, as in peats and organic-rich soils, KOH may be indicated to rid the sample of the humic materials. When the sample size is sufficient, treatment with KOH should be accompanied by acetolysis.

A portion of the palynomorph residue should be placed in a vessel, and a 10% solution of KOH added. Place the vessel containing the solution and palynomorph residue in a hot water bath for up to fifteen minutes, stirring the residue occasionally to desegregate the organics in the sample. The addition of water to the solution may be necessary to ensure that the liquid does not exceed a 10% solution of KOH. After a maximum time of ten to fifteen minutes, the solution should be passed through a fine sieve. Palynomorphs will pass through, with the sieve retaining large plant material and mineral grains for potential macro-forensic study. The fine sieved portion of the residue should be quickly neutralized with distilled water and removed from the remaining solution with a ten millimicron sieve. The discarded liquid may vary from a dark brown to straw yellow color due to organic colloids.

1.2.10 Acetolysis

The treatment of the sample utilizing acetolysis is deemed necessary when the sample contains oils, protoplasm, and intine remains from pollen and spores as well as large amounts of cellulose. If the sample contains humic materials with only trace amounts of silicates, then acetolysis should follow treatment of the sample with KOH. If there is a noticeable silicate or mineral content to the sample, then acetolysis should follow the treatments of the sample with Hcl and HF and their neutralization with distilled water.

The reagent mixture used in acetolysis is one part sulfuric acid [H_2SO_4] to nine parts acetic anhydride [$(CH_3CO)_2O$] by volume, which may give a nearly explosive reaction with any water remaining in the palynomorph residue. For this reason, it is best if the palynomorph residue is first dehydrated before proceeding with acetolysis. To dehydrate the sample, suspend it in a solution of glacial acetic acid [CH_3COOH]. Allow the palynomorphs to settle, then decant the remaining solution of glacial acetic acid. Add a small portion of the acetolysis mixture to the palynomorph residue and gently suspend the two with a stirring rod. Place the vessel containing the suspended palynomorph/acetolysis mixture in a hot water bath for one to two minutes, depending on the nature of the cellulose present in the sample. Centrifuge the mixture and decant the acetolysis solution into cold running water, being careful to maintain the concentrated palynomorph mixture in the base of the centrifuge tube. Resuspend the palynomorph mixture in glacial acetic acid and decant. At this point, the remaining palynomorph mixture can be rehydrated and neutralized in distilled water.

1.2.11 Staining

Unstained palynomorph material can be studied by the forensic palynologist.[32] Additionally, acetolysis generally leaves modern palynomorphs with a slight yellow color. Nevertheless, other researchers may prefer an enhancement of the palynomorph's features through the technique of staining. For this purpose, the organic stains aqueous safranine and fuchsin may be employed. However, to ensure that the stain will be effective and consistent throughout the sample, a 10% solution of KOH should be added to the final neutralization wash before decanting.

To stain the organics, add to the resultant palynomorph residue a mixture of 5% aqueous safranine or fuchsin solution at the admixture ration of one drop stain solution per milliliter of distilled water/palynomorph residue combination. Stir this palynomorph mixture thoroughly, add distilled water, let the palynomorphs settle, and decant or siphon off the staining mixture. Wash, stir, settle, and decant the palynomorph mixture until the supernatant remains clear. If the palynomorphs are darkened in excess by the stain, it can be removed with a wash of diluted 10% Hcl.

1.2.12   Mounting Preparation

Whether a single or a series of digestion treatments were necessary to prepare the sample for palynological evaluation, the sample should be neutralized before mounting of the palynomorph residues. As bright-field microscopy is the commonly preferred method for examination of palynomorphs, these residues will need to be mounted on glass coverslips and affixed to glass microscope slides. However, in an effort to facilitate examination of the processed sample, it may be necessary to separate possible unwanted organic debris from the palynomorphs.

A technique common to many forms of palynological preparation is heavy liquid separation with zinc bromide [$ZnBr_2$], zinc chloride [$ZnCl_2$] or a bromoform/alcohol mixture utilizing a specific gravity solution ranging from 2.0 to 1.65 (depending on preservation and carbonization of the palynomorphs). Due to the possibility of accidentally discarding data and the resulting challenges in court, this author advocates eliminating all use of heavy liquids in forensic palynology sample preparation. Nevertheless, it may be necessary to separate unwanted organic debris. For example, filtration using nylon sieves has been successfully used.

Selective size fractions ranging from 250 millimicrons to 5 millimicrons have proven to be most useful for the separation of unwanted organic debris and the concentration of similar palynomorph types and sizes. To facilitate filtration of the palynomorph-bearing effluent, it may be necessary to use a nylon millimicron sieve or a series of such sieves with an ultrasonic probe. The author has found that a commercially available bull sperm separator is appropriate. As with all forensic preparations, it is necessary to maintain cleanliness in the laboratory, including all utensils.

Disposable condoms should be stretched over the probe before each use. Non-destructive separation methodology is preferred over the use of heavy liquids, as it allows the researcher control over the subdivision of the sample, thereby aiding in organic and taxonomic documentation of the palynomorph sample.

1.2.13 Bright-Field Mounting

In preparation for bright-field mounting on a glass slide, the palynomorph residues will need to be affixed to thin glass coverslips ranging in average thickness from 0.13 to 0.17 mm. As with all aspects of forensic palynology preparation, the coverslips should be cleaned with ethyl alcohol to remove manufacturer's lubricants, dust, and any such contaminants. Depending on whether the palynomorph preparation is maintained in distilled water or alcohol, a small amount of either cellosize solution or polyvinyl alcohol solution should be added to the sample.

These solutions not only disperse and prevent clumping of the organics but also attach the organics to the coverslip. Transfer a portion of the sample, containing the proper mounting solution, to a coverslip with a micropipette and allow the sample to dry. This will permanently secure the specimens to the coverslip, keeping all of the specimens in a single focal plane, aiding in examination and documentation of each sample. After drying, the cover slip should be inverted and permanently mounted on an ethyl alcohol precleaned glass slide, using a mounting medium. This places the organics below the surface of the coverslip, secured to the glass slide.

Palynologists have for years utilized various mounting mediums to affix the organic strew-mount coverslips to glass slides. For the purpose of forensic palynology, there is a need for permanent maintenance of the slides and their contained palynomorphs. In this vein, Elvacite, a commercially available plastic polymer, is recommended. Elvacite is durable, and even though its refractive index is slightly inferior to other mounting media, its use presents no problem for the forensic palynologist or for subsequent microphotography. Elvacite can be purchased in a fine granular form and is best dissolved in a solution of toluene/xylene. The Elvacite/toluene/xylene mixture is sparingly applied to a cover slip-sized portion of the cleaned microscope slide. The cover slip is inverted and placed on the Elvacite and left to cure on a warming tray. The palynomorphs are now secure from outside contamination and ready for analysis.

1.2.14 Summary

Although the science of palynology is a mature discipline, forensic palynology is rarely utilized in criminal investigations. In the early 1990s, finding little in the literature concerning forensic palynology, palynologists Dallas Mildenhall and Vaughn Bryant conducted a survey of many U.S. law enforcement agencies (personal communication). Their findings indicated that very little was known about forensic palynology. Mildenhall, in various reports, pointed out that "most forensic palynomorph evidence is regarded as circumstantial and that its usefulness is based on an ability to associate a suspect, or object, with the scene of a crime." He goes on to state that this perceived impression is one of the reasons pollen data have not been utilized more widely as evidence in court. Given this, technology, sampling methodology and processing procedures, and facilities have evolved to the stage where micro-evidence is a reality in the forensic sciences, and forensic palynology has a great potential as a tool for the criminal investigator.

Though it remains frequently unused throughout much of the world, forensic palynology is well known among the countries of the southern Pacific Rim, especially New Zealand, where it is often used in civil and criminal matters. Perhaps as we enter the new millennium, forensic palynology will become a standard in the arsenal of applications utilized by legal analysts as well as a majority of law enforcement agencies in the United States.

1.3 Forensic Entomology: A Valuable Resource for Death Investigations

THOMAS W. ADAIR

Insects are the life blood of our world. They are the largest group of animals on the planet, and many taxonomists estimate that at least three quarters of a million species have been described, with as many as three million species yet to be identified. As Holden pointed out, "bugs are not going to inherit the earth...they own it now." With this in mind, it should come as no surprise that some insects are important to man. Their importance may be economical, agricultural, medical, and even forensic in nature.

The use of insects in medico-criminal investigations enjoys a long practice. The oldest reported case dates to 1235 A.D. in China when a local "Death Investigator" determined that the presence of adult flies on the washed sickle confirmed the guilt of a murder suspect, who subsequently confessed to the crime.[34] Other authors, such as Smith[35] and Catts and Haskell[36] give excellent accounts of historical case work. In spite of this history, however, the current number of practicing forensic entomologists remains disturbingly low. As a result, many law enforcement investigators remain unaware of the valuable role insects can play in a criminal investigation.

Generally, among law enforcement practitioners, maggots and other insects have traditionally been regarded as unpalatable byproducts of the decomposition process. The sights and smells of a heavily infested corpse can be very disturbing, and these invaders are often looked upon as pests. These pests are often washed down the autopsy table with little regard to their evidentiary value. The challenge to investigators is to realize that insects can be our partners in solving crime. Their presence on a corpse can provide valuable information not attainable from any other source.[37]

While forensic entomologists may offer a variety of analyses in both criminal and civil matters, they are most often called upon to examine insects recovered from deceased individuals. Following death, a corpse can be quickly colonized by a variety of necrophagous and saprophagous arthropods, especially insects. This faunal succession of invertebrates also includes parasitic and

29

predacious species of the necrophagous insects, omnivorous species which feed on the corpse and invading insects, and adventive species which may utilize the corpse as a temporary habitat. This faunal succession is a valuable phenomenon to entomologists, as it often assists them in understanding the history of the corpse. As each species of insect arrives and feeds on the body, they invariably change the corpse, thereby making it attractive to the next group of insects. The lines separating these successional waves are far from distinct, as environmental and biological systems vary from location to location.

During warm months, flies (Diptera) are the main decomposers, and are the major invertebrate fauna on carrion. Adult flies of the families Calliphoridae (blow flies) and Sarcophagidae (flesh flies) may arrive within a few minutes after death. After locating on a corpse, gravid females will then lay their eggs (Calliphoridae) or larvae (Sarcophagidae). Usually these species favor the natural orifices but may also be preferentially attracted to sites of trauma such as gunshot injuries, sharp force, and blunt force trauma.

These flies undergo what is known as holometabolous, or complete, metamorphosis. There are three larval growth stages called instars which are each separated by a molting. This is followed by a wandering phase and then the pre-pupal and pupal stage. The pupal stage is easily recognized as the outer skin darkens to a reddish brown to black color with the developing pupa inside. These pupae can be found in the soil, adjacent leaf litter, or clothing of the victim. The pupae are immobile and assume a barrel shape, similar in appearance to rodent droppings. After development, the adult fly will emerge, leaving the durable puparium behind.

The stage of development of the larvae (maggots) of these flies is the most reliable indicator for estimating what has traditionally been referred to as the time since death, or post mortem interval. Entomologists have been studying these rates of development for different species and have established reliable data on how quickly each stage develops under varying temperatures. For example, once the adult female fly deposits her clutch, a kind of biological stop watch is started. Once the species and the stage of development is established, the entomologist can then review the temperature data from the crime scene and determine how long it would have taken the maggots to reach the observed stage of development.

There is agreement among entomologists that the longer a corpse has been exposed, the less precise the estimate will be, although this is not always the case. This time frame is commonly referred to as the post mortem interval, or time since death. This is a familiar term in death investigations, and caution is warranted in its use in entomology, as "time estimate" is not actually measuring the time since the victim died. Rather, entomologists are measuring the time since the corpse was first colonized by the insects analyzed. While this difference may seem trivial, there is sound reasoning for the distinction.

While flies may locate on a corpse immediately following death — often within minutes — and begin oviposition or larviposition, there are a variety of biological, situational, and environmental factors which could hinder the arrival of adult flies. Temperature and humidity are by far the most influential environmental factors. Generally, adult flies will not be active in flight when ambient air temperatures fall below 10°C. It follows that a corpse dumped in a field during a period of cold temperatures will not immediately be colonized by these species — even though death has occurred. Likewise, concealment (temporary or prolonged) of the corpse by means of burial or placement in a location inaccessible to adult insects (e.g., metal drum, car trunk, water) will also retard or prevent this "clock" from starting. Additionally, once the corpse is physically accessible by adult flies, it may have advanced to a stage of decomposition that is unattractive to adult flies and unsuitable for maggot development. The degree to which these factors influence a particular analysis must be determined on a case by case basis. Failure to consider these factors could lead to a serious error in the estimate of time since colonization. Furthermore, use of the term "time since death" can cause a misunderstanding by law enforcement personnel unless clarification is made by the entomologist as to whether he actually believes that colonization occurred immediately following death.

1.3.1 Other Types of Investigation

1.3.1.1 Entomotoxicology

Entomotoxicology has become a powerful tool to the criminal investigator. Studies by Nolte et. al,[38] Goff and Lord,[39] Wilson et. al,[40] and Sadler et. al[41] have greatly expanded our understanding and appreciation of insects as reservoirs of toxins and drugs. As the maggots feed on the soft tissue of the corpse, they also ingest associated substances which may be revealed through toxicology. The metabolites of several prevalent illegal drugs such as cocaine can be detected even though the tissue from the corpse may be unsuitable. Because maggots do not suffer from the destructive processes of decomposition, these drug constituents may be recovered long after death has occurred.

1.3.1.2 Cases of Abuse and Neglect

Forensic entomologists are sometimes asked to examine maggots recovered from living subjects who are victims of abuse or neglect. These victims are often among the elderly and infancy populations. Some individuals in these populations are physically unable to adequately care for themselves and depend on others to properly manage their hygiene. When this care is neglectful or absent, adult flies may oviposit in areas such as bed sores or dirty diapers. Using the same principles as in death investigations, an analysis of

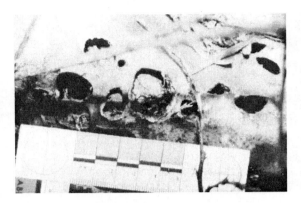

Figure 1.3.1 A clothed human male corpse in advanced stages of decomposition discovered along a rural dirt road in El Paso County, Colorado.

the age of the maggots in these areas may reveal the extent (in time) of the neglect or abuse. This may be crucial information when deciding how to charge the offender and prosecute the crime.

1.3.1.3   Geographical Isolation or Origin

Although uncommon, entomologists are sometimes requested to determine whether a particular species has a restricted origin that may aid investigators. This type of analysis was portrayed in the movie *Silence of the Lambs*, when entomologists determined the origin of an exotic moth which was placed in a murder victim's throat. The information then led customs agents to the individual who had imported the moth to the United States. While many forensic species have a wide distribution (some Holarctic), others may be somewhat isolated to a particular region or location. This may be due to environmental requirements of the species, loss of habitat, or both. Recent studies in DNA population affinity among insect species groups have suggested that populations of the same species may be differentiated by location, although future studies need to be conducted.

1.3.2   Case Studies

1.3.2.1   A Murdered Army Private

In late December of 1997, a clothed unidentified human male corpse in an advanced stage of decomposition was discovered along a rural dirt road in El Paso County, Colorado. The victim had over 20 sharp force injuries observed in the clothing, desiccated tissue, and skeletal elements of the trunk (Figure 1.3.1). An examination of the victim revealed numerous pharate adults of the hairy maggot fly *Chrysomya rufifacies*. These adults were fully formed but still encased within the puparia. This was the first reported collection of *C. rufifacies* from a human corpse in Colorado. The remains were autopsied by both the El Paso County Coroner's Office and the Armed Forces Institute of Pathology. The victim was later identified as a member of the United States Army stationed at Fort Carson in Colorado Springs, Colorado.

Collections of *C. rufifacies* in Colorado can be described as extremely rare. DeJong reports only two state records [Denver County (1996) and Otero County (1994)] for this species.[42] These previous collections were from fox and badger carcasses, respectively.

The ecological role and medical importance of the "hairy maggot fly", *C. rufifacies* (Macquart), is well known. Baumgartner reported that *C. rufifacies*, after its introduction, spread rapidly through the southern United States and often ran dominant in the regional blow fly fauna.[43] Richard and Ahrens reported the first collection of *C. rufifacies* in 1982 from the continental United States in Texas.[44] Greenberg reported that this species, a native of the Australasian region, has been collected from human corpses in southern California as early as 1987.[45] While this fly is common throughout the southern United States, reported temperature tolerances of this species indicates that it may only seasonally invade temperate regions like Colorado. Byrd and Butler report that ambient air temperatures below 15°C will typically cease pupal development.[46] The potential ability of this fly to permanently displace other native dipterian species along the front range of Colorado seems unlikely, given its lower temperature thresholds. However, *C. rufifacies'* distinct advantage is its ability to become piedacious under conditions of decreasing food supply. As such, the competitive nature of this fly cannot be ignored by the forensic investigator, as native Diptera can be temporarily displaced or cannibalized following initial colonization.[47]

Air temperature records available from Peterson Air Force Base, 3.0 km from the crime scene, indicated that after September 20, 1997, ambient air temperatures would have been too low to allow *C. rufifacies* to reach the observed stage collected from the corpse. Using the temperature data, a minimum time of infestation for *C. rufifacies* was determined to be between September 1 and 4, 1997. Subsequent identification of the victim revealed that he was reported absent without leave (AWOL) on August 30, 1997. Two suspects were developed during the investigation, and one confessed. Without the analysis of the entomological evidence in this case, there would have been little hope in establishing a nexus between the time of disappearance and the victim's death. Both suspects were tried and convicted by the United States Army for murder.

While the collection data of *C. rufifacies* in Colorado is limited, information to date suggests that *C. rufifacies* invades the lower elevations along the front range of Colorado primarily between mid-July and mid-September. During this same period, *Phormia regina* (Meigen) and *Lucilia sericata* (Meigen) are the dominant blow flies collected from human corpses (personal observation by senior author). The seasonal invasion of *C. rufifacies* is unlikely to permanently displace either of these important blow flies in Colorado, but its presence on a corpse may significantly aid in the determining the time of colonization. In the above murder case, the presence of large numbers of pharate *C. rufifacies* indicated a narrow window of infestation due to its apparent intolerance to low temperatures.[46] Because of the significant time between the death and discovery of the victim in this case, an analysis of other more temperature tolerant species of Calliphoridae would have yielded a much wider window surrounding the time of adult oviposition, and may not have aided in securing a confession.

1.3.2.2   The Missing Man Who Wasn't

In mid-July of 1998, the skeletonized remains of an adult male subject were found scattered across an open area in the foothills of the Denver metro area in Jefferson County. There was evidence of animal scavenging activity, which accounted for the dispersed nature of the remains. This area is on a south–facing slope with medium-sized scrub oak scattered across the location where the victim was found. Drug paraphernalia was recovered with the remains but no identification could be found. The victim's clothing consisted of a T-shirt and blue jeans. The skeleton was sent to a forensic anthropologist and odontologist to establish the physical characteristics of the victim so the data could be searched against missing person reports.

Recovered with the victim's remains were large numbers of eclosed puparia of the black blow fly *P. regina* (Meigen). This cosmopolitan fly can be found year round in Colorado along the front range, and is one of the most commonly collected species from human corpses. The presence of large numbers of eclosed puparia indicated that the population was killed during a significant drop in ambient air temperature.

Using temperature data from a weather station approximately 10 km from the crime scene, it was determined that the pupae were killed, at a minimum, during the last two weeks of March or early April 1997. Armed with this information, investigators began searching missing person records for that time period with negative results. The description of the victim was printed in the media, and through a series of acquaintances the victim's family was contacted in California and informed of the victim's description. The family had never reported the victim missing but confirmed that they lost contact with the man the last week of March in 1997. The family forwarded medical and dental records to the Jefferson County Coroner's Office, where a positive identification of the victim was made.

Figure 1.3.2 Clothed body of an adult white male found laying in a drainage washout covered by a mattress, Eastern Arapahoe County, Colorado.

1.3.2.3 Where Have You Been?

In November 1996, a deceased adult white male was found along a rural dirt road in eastern Arapahoe County, Colorado. No vehicle was found at the scene. The victim was fully clothed and laying in a drainage wash-out which was covered by a mattress. The victim was in a supine position with his legs bent at the knees (Figure 1.3.2). Numerous second and third install larvae of the black blow fly *P. regina* (Meigen) and *Calliphora terraenovae* (Macquart) were recovered from the victim at autopsy. Autopsy finding revealed that the victim died of natural causes associated with severe alcohol abuse. These findings were supported by subsequent investigation and reports from family and friends of the victim, who confirmed his heavy drinking. Weather records were obtained from the Buckley Air National Guard Base approximately 1.5 km from the crime scene. After weather data was examined, it was determined that the victim had been dumped in the location and colonized 9 to 10 days prior to discovery.

Law enforcement investigators had located a witness who claimed to have seen the victim in the same position two weeks prior to the discovery date. The witness had been in the area target shooting and was adamant about the sighting. The author was contacted about this discrepancy and responded that the witness must be mistaken, as the victim could not have been in the location 14 days prior to discovery. It was suggested that investigators put a day planner in front of the witness and make him account for every day of the two week period. After this meeting, the witness confirmed that he was in fact mistaken and that he had been in the area 10 days prior to the discovery of the victim.

Once the victim was identified, it was determined through the investigation that his vehicle, wallet, and credit cards were missing from his Denver residence. A review of the victim's credit card charges and an examination of the signatures by a questioned document examiner revealed that the victim had driven to Texas about three weeks prior to his discovery. Shortly after his arrival in Texas, the victim's signature changed on his receipts. Several days later the victim's vehicle was stopped by Texas authorities and another man was found to be driving and using the victim's identity. The victim was not in the vehicle at the time of the stop. The unidentified suspect was not arrested or identified by Texas authorities, but was later identified by Colorado investigators as an acquaintance of the victim's.

After being contacted by Colorado investigators, the subject gave the following account: the subject admitted that the victim had died after a period of extremely heavy drinking. The two had reportedly been drinking all weekend, and employees of several local motels verified that the individuals had been ejected from their establishments because of their drunken behavior. The victim was then reportedly left in his vehicle with the windows rolled up for approximately 8 to 10 hours on a hot day while the subject continued drinking in a local bar.

On returning to the vehicle the subject found the victim dead. He panicked and drove the victim back to Colorado. After returning the victim to Colorado, the subject immediately returned to Texas (apparently to finalize a drug deal) and it was then that he was stopped by the Texas authorities. The subject would not elaborate as to where the victim was placed for the few days he was absent, however, investigators believe that the victim was placed inside an outbuilding belonging to an acquaintance of the subject.

The subject returned from Texas for the second time and stated that he dumped the victim at the scene nine days prior to the discovery of the victim. A credit card receipt from the victim's card (signed by the subject) confirmed that it was used to purchase gasoline at a station approximately 3 km from the scene on the same day. Investigators have yet to determine the location of the victim prior to his dumping, as all parties continue to be uncooperative.

References

1. Cox, M. and Bell, L., Recovery of human skeletal elements from a recent U.K. murder enquiry: preservational signatures, *J. Forensic Sci.*, 44, 945-950, 1999.

2. Morse, D., Duncan, J., and Stoutamire, J., *Handbook of Forensic Archaeology and Anthropology*, Rose Printing, Springfield, Illinois. 1983.

3. Sigler-Eisenberg, B. B., Forensic research: Expanding the concept of applied archaeology, *Am. Antiquity*, 50, 650-655, 1985.

4. Killam, E. W., *The Detection of Human Remains*, Charles C. Thomas, Springfield, Illinois, 1990.

5. France, D. L., Griffin, T. J., Swanburg, J. G., Lindemann, J. W., Deavenport, G. C., Trammel, V., Armbrust, C. T., Kondratieff, B., Nelson, A., Castellano, K., and Hopkins, D., A multidisciplinary approach to the detection of clandestine graves, *J. Forensic Sci.*, 37, 1435-1750, 1992.

6. Martin, A. L., The application of archaeological methods and techniques to the location, recovery and analysis of buried human remains from forensic contexts, unpublished M.A. dissertation, University of Bradford, 1991.

7. Hunter, J. R., Martin, A. L., and Roberts, C. A., Eds., *Studies in Crime: an Introduction to Forensic Archaeology*, Seaby/Batsford, London, 1996.

8. Stewart, T. D. and George, A., Dorsey's role in the Luetgert case: a significant episode in the history of forensic anthropology, *J. Forensic Sci.*, 23, 786-791, 1978.

9. Snow, C. C., Forensic anthropology, *Ann. Rev. Anthrop.*, 11, 97-131, 1982.

10. Isçan, M. Y., Rise of forensic anthropology, *Yearb. Am. J. Phys. Anthrop.*, 31, 203-230, 1988.

11. Black, S., Forensic osteology in the United Kingdom, *Human Osteology in Archaeology and Forensic Science*, Cox, M. J. and Mays, S., Eds., Greenwich Medical Media Ltd., London, 2000, chap. 29.

12. Yeates, R. R., A case study to determine the effects of bird scavenging upon decomposing human remains using a pig carcasss (*Sus scrofa*) in mimicry, unpublished M.Sc. dissertation, University of Bournemouth. 1999.

13. Scollar, I., Tabbagh, A., Hesse, A., and Herzog, I., *Archaeological Geophysics and Remote Sensing*, Cambridge University Press, Cambridge.

14. Gill-King, H., Chemical and ultrastructural aspects of decomposition, in *Forensic Taphonomy: the Postmortem Fate of Human Remains*, Haglund, W. D. and Sorg, M. H., Eds., CRC Press, New York, 1997, chap. 6.

15. Janaway, R. C., The decay of buried human remains and their associated materials, in Hunter, J. R., Martin, A. L., and Roberts, C. A., Eds., *Studies in crime: an Introduction to Forensic Archaeology*, Seaby/Batsford, London, 1996, chap. 4.

16. Haglund, W. D. and Sorg, M. H., *Forensic Taphonomy: The Postmortem Fate of Human Remains*, CRC Press, New York, 1997.

17. Skinner, M., Planning the archaeological recovery of evidence from recent mass graves, *Forensic Sci. Int.*, 34, 267-287, 1987.

18. Haglund, W. D. and Reay, D. R., Problems of recovering partial human remains at different times and different locations, *J. Forensic Sci.*, 38, 69-80, 1993.

19. Cox, M. J., Crime scene archaeology is one of the most frightening areas of archaeology in which to practice, *The Field Archaeologist*, 23, 14-16, 1995.

20. Cox, M. J., Aging human skeletal material, human osteology, in *Archaeology and Forensic Science*, Cox, M. J. and Mays, S., Eds., Greenwich Medical Media Ltd., London, 2000, chap. 4.

21. Reich, K. J., Ed., *Forensic Osteology II: a Decade of Growth*, Springfield, Illinois, 1997.

22. Ramey Burns, K., *Forensic Anthropology Training Manual*, Prentice-Hall, New Jersey, 1999.

23. McKinley, J. and Roberts, C. A., Excavation and post-excavation treatment of cremated and inhumed human remains, *Inst. Field Archaeologists*, technical paper No. 13, 1, Birmingham, 1993.

24. Aufderheide, A. C. and Rodriguez-Martin, C., *The Cambridge Encyclopedia of Human Palaeopathology*, Cambridge University Press, Cambridge, 1998.

25. Hoshower, L. M., Forensic archaeology and the need for flexible excavation strategies: a case study, *J. Forensic Sci.*, 43, 53-56, 1998.

26. Hyde, H. A. and Williams, D. A., The right word, *Pollen Anal. Circ.*, 8:6, 1944.

27. Woods, R. D., Spores and pollen: a new stratigraphic tool for the oil industry, *Micropaleontology*, 1:368-375, 1955.

28. Erdtman, G., *Handbook of Palynology*, Hafner Publishing, New York, 1969.

29. Mildenhall, D. C., Deer velvet and palynology: an example of the use of forensic palynology in New Zealand, *Tuatara*, 30: 1-11, 1988.

30. Moore, P. D., Webb, J. A., and Collinson, M. E., *Pollen Analysis*, Blackwell Scientific, London, 1991.

31. Stanley, E. A., Application of palynology to establish the provenance and travel history of illicit drugs, *Microscope*, 40:149-152, 1984.

32. Mildenhall, D. C., Jones, J. G., and Bryant, V. M., Forensic palynology in the United States of America, *Palynology*, 14: 193-208, 1990.

33. Mildenhall, D. C., Forensic palynology, *Geol. Soc. N. Z.*, newsletter, 58:25, 1982.

34. McKnight, B., *The Washing Away of Wrongs: Forensic Medicine in Thirteenth-Century China*, University of Michigan Press, Ann Arbor, 1981.

35. Smith, K. G., *A Manual of Forensic Entomology*, British Museum of Natural History, London, 1986.

36. Catts, E. P. and Haskell, N. H., *Entomology and Death: a Procedural Guide*, Joyce's Print Shop, Clemson, S.C., 1990.

37. Adair, T. W., *A Field Manual for the Collection and Preservation of Entomological Evidence*, Arapahoe County Sheriff's Office Crime Laboratory, Littleton, Colorado, 1999.

38. Nolte, K. B., Pinder, R. D., and Lord, W. D., Insect larvae used to detect cocaine poisoning in a decomposed body, *J. Forensic Sci.*, 37(4):1179-1185, 1992.

39. Goff, M. L. and Lord, W. D., Entomotoxicology: a new area for forensic investigation, *Am. J. Forensic Med. Pathol.*, 15(1):51-57, 1994.

40. Wilson, Z., Hubbard, S., and Pounder, D. J., Drug analysis in fly larvae, *Am. J. Forensic Med. Pathol.*, 14(2):118-120, 1993.

41. Sadler, D. W., Richardson, J., Haigh, S., Bruce, G., and Pounder, D. J., Amitriptyline accumulation and elimination in calliphora vicina larvae, *Am. J. Forensic Med. Pathol.*, 18(4):397-403,1997.

42. De Jong, G. D. and Chadwick, J. W., Additional county records and a correction to the checklist of the calliphoridae (diptera) of Colorado: a new state record for chrysomya rufifacies, *J. Kansas Entomol. Soc.*, 70:47-51,1997.

43. Baumgartner, D. L., Review of chrysomya rufifacies (Diptera: calliphoridae), *J. Med. Entomol.*, 30:338-352,1993.

44. Richard, R. D. and Ahrens, E. H., New distribution record for the recently introduced blow fly chrysomya rufifacies (Macquart) in North America, *Southwest. Entomol.*, 8:216-218,1983.

45. Greenberg, B. H., Chrysomya megacephala (f.) (Diptera: calliphoridae) collected in North America and notes on chrysomya species present in the new world, *J. Med. Entomol.*, 25:199-200,1988.

46. Byrd, J. H. and Butler, J. F., Effects of temperature on chrysomya rufifacies (Diptera: calliphoridae) development, *J. Med. Entomol.*, 34:353-358,1997.

47. Holden, C., Entomologists wane as insects wax, *Science*, 246:754-766,1989.

Criminal Profiling: From Art to Science

2

2.1 Criminal Intelligence – The Vital Resource: an Overview

CHARLES FROST

A criminal intelligence system is a vital resource for crime control. Such a system not only enhances the effectiveness of an agency's component law enforcement arms but also, as a central repository of criminal intelligence information, contributes to a more productive exchange of information among law enforcement organizations. Operational intelligence collection and analysis support both routine case investigations and complex investigative research projects. Strategic intelligence analysis serves a broad spectrum of crime control needs both within and without the agency; internally in the areas of planning, the allocation of resources, and the development of sound law-enforcement strategies; and externally in responding to requests for crime trend analysis.

2.1.1 The Need For an Intelligence System

A vital criminal intelligence system involves more than compiling data that is used primarily to react to immediate investigative needs. Lack of a fully developed strategic and tactical intelligence capability seriously hinders the ability of a law enforcement agency to accurately measure and prevent organized, serious crime within its jurisdiction, or to anticipate crime threats that can significantly affect the jurisdiction from without. This, in turn, has been a stumbling block in the development of scientific crime control strategy that would have a measurable impact on the effects of crime.

2.1.2 Information

Information is unprocessed data of various kinds that may be used in the production of intelligence. A sizable volume of such information may be retrieved from computer databases.

2.1.3   Intelligence

As a functional activity, intelligence is the end product of information that has been subjected to the intelligence process: planning/direction, collection/evaluation, collation, analysis, and dissemination or reporting. By its very nature, intelligence is a form of knowledge that is usually more than information but less than firmly established fact.[1] In its broadest terms, intelligence is knowledge and foreknowledge that can be used to advance or defend the interests of organized society.[2] Ideally, intelligence provides meaningful, useable knowledge that is accurate and timely. Such intelligence gives the consumer a factual description of a state of affairs, an interpretation of current events, or the forecasting of future events or trends.[3]

2.1.4   The Intelligence Process

The intelligence process encompasses a series of interrelated functions:

1. Planning the intelligence effort, often as a formal or joint exercise, involving the setting of priorities and specific requirements for collection of information
2. Directing the intelligence effort, usually by management, in accordance with agreed plans or guidelines
3. Collecting pieces of information from various sources
4. Evaluating that information as to its accuracy and usefulness
5. Collating or systematically organizing the information for storage and retrieval
6. Analyzing the information to determine its meaning in reference to a criminal investigation or assessment
7. Disseminating or reporting the findings of the analysis.[4]

The intelligence process may be conveniently represented as a cycle, and is often called the intelligence cycle. Some schematic diagrams give the erroneous impression that the intelligence process must be followed in rigid sequence. In actual practice, the functions are not necessarily sequential: management may query the analysis section on matters that were not foreseen in the planning process; a competent analysis that falls short of expectations because of insufficient information may spur better targeted collection; a productive source or acquisition of information may induce the analysis section to recommend broadening the scope of their research; and so on. Figure 2.1.1 more accurately represents the interrelated nature of the functions of the intelligence process than would a simple cycle diagram.

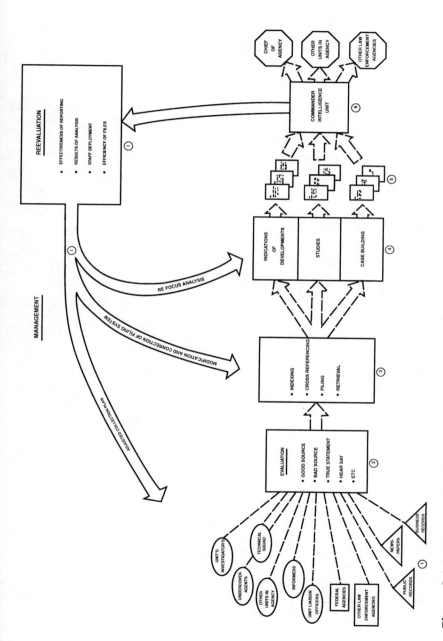

Figure 2.1.1 The intelligence process.

2.1.5   Criminal Intelligence

Criminal intelligence refers to the holdings of information on known or suspected persons involved in criminal activity or the conclusions resulting from the analysis of criminal data and information collected on persons known or suspected of being involved in criminal activity.[4]

2.1.6   Tactical Intelligence

Tactical intelligence affords direct and immediate support to investigative activity. This immediately usable information has been quickly retrieved from manual files or computer databases and has not been subjected to comprehensive analysis. Name checks, identifiers, criminal histories, criminal associations, and street prices for drugs are typical items of tactical intelligence. Such information is usually needed on a short-term basis, or for relatively uncomplicated cases.[2,4] Formal reports would not be a likely form of dissemination for intelligence of this nature.

2.1.7   Operational Intelligence

Operational intelligence details patterns, modus operandi, and vulnerabilities of criminal organizations.[2] Rather than focusing on the offenses committed by individual violators, operational intelligence affords a broader understanding of the workings of the criminal enterprise: superior-subordinate relationships, formal versus informal leadership, the rules of the organization, its management practices, its degree of dominance in particular criminal industries, and the factors that contribute to its success. Intelligence activity of this type results in the production of formal reports that may include recommendations for future action.[2,3] The direct application of this enforcement–oriented analysis to an active operation leads to better prioritization of cases for maximum enforcement effectiveness against criminal activities as well as the most efficient utilization of investigative resources.[5]

2.1.8   Strategic Intelligence

Strategic intelligence provides an overview of the scope and character of criminal activity, contributing to the development of effective strategies (e.g., prevention, containment, attrition, or displacement) to reduce the harmful economic and social effects associated with one or more categories of criminal activity. Strategic intelligence analysis serves the needs not only of the originating enforcement organization but also of legislative and executive consumers that depend upon its insights in developing broad policy and programs. Thus, for example, an analysis of the supply of illegal drugs would deal with the sources of drugs, the number of people involved in drug abuse and drug distribution, the volume of drugs consumed, the corresponding money drain from economy, the health consequences, and other societal costs associated with drug abuse.

2.1.9   Crime Data Analysis

Crime data analysis involves a systematic study of daily crime activities in order to determine the types of crimes being committed, where and when these crimes are being committed, and the types of persons being victimized. This activity typically produces statistical outputs detailing the incidence of crime by city subdivision and neighborhood by day of the week and time of day. State-of-the-art crime mapping software programs can generate a variety of crime incidence map overlays. The primary purpose of crime data analysis is to identify high-incidence crime neighborhoods for higher-order crime pattern analysis.

2.1.10   Crime Pattern Analysis

Law enforcement agencies should not be content with knowing the statistical probability of crimes happening based on where and when these crimes have previously occurred. Statistics only allow management to set goals for crime prevention in general localities without specific targets. "Revictimization" (repeat crime) studies illuminate the "hot spots" in the crime map but do not explain why people, places, and things are being revictimized. True crime pattern analysis starts from the assumption that law enforcement must target specific perpetrators if it is to break the cycle of revictimization. Through analysis of reports, the crime intelligence analyst creates a profile of each known offender, the offender's MOs (style of entry, day of the week, time of day, choice of goods to be burglarized, fencing outlets), his or her associates, and the associates' MOs. For example, combining the mapping of burglary incidents with a knowledge of suspects' activities builds up a more meaningful analysis of burglars' crime patterns, with the result that law enforcement can concentrate its attack in a particular area and achieve noticeable proactive effect.[6]

2.1.11   Management Orientation of Intelligence

2.1.11.1   Strategy Is Key to Proactive Enforcement

Central to effective law enforcement is strategy. The essential component of an effective criminal law enforcement strategy is an intelligence system. The capacity to understand the criminal environment provides law enforcement with a factual basis for strategic planning and resulting enforcement action. The ultimate function of the intelligence system is to develop criminal data through an ordered process, thereby affording an informed approach to strategic law enforcement planning, and giving direction to investigative and

enforcement operations. Information that is fully processed through the
intelligence system and not merely random dissemination of raw data provides law enforcement with intelligence relating to the capabilities, vulnerabilities, and intentions of criminal organizations or individual criminals. This
essential knowledge enhances law enforcement's ability to accurately assess
and effectively investigate, prosecute, and disrupt criminal activity.[7]

2.1.12   Intelligence Analysis Serves Management

Intelligence analysis enables the law enforcement administrator to allocate
the agency's resources to deal more effectively with serious crime. The investment of precious investigative resources toward crimes which are marginally
injurious to the community must be made within the context of fiscal reality.
This mandates an intelligence capacity able to assess whether the commitment of these resources is rational or whether important societal benefits
would be realized. The integration of intelligence with operations is clearly
the answer to efficiently managing investigative resources, particularly given
today's fiscal climate. As Dintino[8] pointed out:

> Intelligence is a management tool. It is meant to facilitate planning, decision-
> making and policy development. One of the best reasons for intelligence is
> that it serves to systematically look ahead to develop a set of alternatives
> with which to meet unforeseen or dimly lit future eventualities.

Operational intelligence analysis is indispensable in documenting the nature
and extent of organized crime for the purpose of obtaining grand jury indict-
ments. Intelligence is used most productively in selecting targets for special
investigative attention. One of the most powerful weapons against organized
crime is the investigative grand jury. In most cases, however, a grand jury
can be impaneled only with a strong showing that organized crime is a
problem in that jurisdiction. Intelligence, as a process, offers law enforcement
a coherent, rational, and above all consistent methodology in addressing this
enduring social problem — organized crime.[9]

   In arriving at criminal target selection decisions, enforcement, intelligence, planning, evaluation — and, indispensably, top management — are
key players in a mutually reinforcing interaction. Top management plays its
traditional role of planning, goal setting, and policy making, while day-to-day
tactical decision making remains with field enforcement managers. The aim
of top management should be to orchestrate the enforcement effort in accordance with overall crime control strategy without becoming deeply enmeshed
in operational matters. Improving responsibility for immobilization of designated targets is the touchstone of success. With assigned targets, the interface
between intelligence and enforcement should take on new vitality. Intelligence

analysts, instead of having to sell self-initiated products to reluctant investigators, will find that field enforcement groups are seeking all the help they can get from intelligence to help them in attacking their assigned targets.[10]

2.1.13 A Model Intelligence System: Unified, Prioritized, Collectively Managed

2.1.13.1 The Goal to Be Adopted

To assure that operational components of law enforcement agencies have an effective intelligence function, a single and centrally directed criminal intelligence system should be established. The system should prioritize data collection and analysis in accordance with a criminal intelligence steering committee, with member agencies represented. Intelligence activity should be mutually supportive at the center and in the field. Personnel should be designated among member agencies for special duty assignments to receive and distribute intelligence advisories by querying the intelligence center for support and report information indicative of emerging crime patterns.

2.1.14 The Need for Unified Direction

Fragmentation and isolation of criminal intelligence activity reduces the effectiveness of field enforcement efforts. It also weakens the ability of central management to conduct strategic planning and to efficiently allocate limited resources. As we move into the 21st century we must develop a sophisticated collection, analytical, and reporting capability to serve the needs of both central planning and field enforcement.

2.1.15 Proactive Purpose

A vital criminal intelligence system involves more than compiling a repository of data used primarily to react to immediate investigative needs. Instead, it should be formal, prioritized, and directed by the collective planning of program managers, resulting in solid support for policy development and enhanced enforcement programs.

2.1.16 Action-Oriented

Intelligence should not be produced for its own sake, nor should intelligence analysts indulge in mere intellectual abstractions. Intelligence assessments are prepared for the purpose of advising managers and/or operational law enforcement officers. Analysts need a structured environment in order to make their most useful contribution to the intelligence system. The analytical effort needs to be carefully programmed to ensure that analysts are addressing the most important tasks, bearing in mind the need for reasonable flexibility.

The planning, prioritization, and direction that flows from the criminal intelligence steering committee will enable the intelligence analyst to clearly understand the dynamics of the institutional situation and its implications for his/her role.

2.2 Construction of Offender Profiles Using Fuzzy Logic[*]

ARVIND VERMA

Although fuzzy logic is being used extensively in electronics and mathematical sciences, it has found little or no application in the social sciences, especially criminology. As a mathematical system, fuzzy logic generalizes the Boolean logic and can be a very useful tool for the social sciences, where concepts and terms involve shades of meanings. This paper outlines the essential mathematics behind this approach and develops a technique that could be useful in building offender profiles from fuzzy descriptions provided by witnesses. The paper also suggests several other possible areas of applications of this mathematical system.

Descriptions of suspects that police officers receive are often fuzzy in nature. Offenders are described as "tall", "dark", "young," or even "rude", terms that are imprecise and admit a range of possibilities. In fact, policing itself involves many issues that are fuzzy and difficult to measure exactly. For example, officer's services are often evaluated as being "good" or "average," while gang activity related areas are described as "dangerous" or "rowdy". All these characteristics are essentially fuzzy, and therefore difficult to use with common statistical techniques.

The concept of fuzzy variables will be introduced here to criminal justice practitioners, and a fuzzy logic-based mathematical procedure will be described that is capable of handling such variables. Although fuzzy logic has become a much talked about technique in mathematical and engineering literature, it has not yet found application in social science fields, though some researchers such as McDowell[11] and recently Wu and Desai[12] have mentioned the possible use of this mathematical system in criminological research work. This chapter will present the mathematics behind fuzzy logic and outline a mathematical technique that uses fuzzy logic in the construction of offender profiles. Several areas of application will be suggested for

[*] Originally published in *Policing: An International Journal of Police Strategies and Management*, 20:408-418, 1997.

police and practitioners within the criminal justice field, where this mathematical field can be useful.

2.2.1 Nature of Fuzzy Variables

In everyday conversation we use imprecise and implied terms like "it's a hot day", "it's an early morning meeting", and "there is only a short time allotted to each speaker." Ordinarily, we understand intuitively the implied meanings of these terms even though each is individual-specific. Thus, for some people, early morning implies a time period before 9:30 a.m., while for others it may be 6.00 a.m. Yet we can communicate easily in such fuzzy terms that the best computer is unable to replicate. There are several reasons for this difference, but a significant characteristic is the capability of human beings to communicate in fuzzy terms. "The difference between human brain and the computers lies in the ability of the former to think and reason in imprecise, nonquantitative terms."[13]

It is this proficiency that makes it possible for humans to decipher different scripts and handwriting, comprehend a variety of sounds, interpret multiple meaning responses, and focus on information that is relevant in order to make decisions. Unlike the computer, human brain has the power of reasoning and thinking logically, but also of understanding things globally, peripherally, and holistically. Cognition is possible even though a term may be imprecise or have several shades of meanings. Unlike the computer that deals with dichotomous categorizations, human beings communicate in nuances that may have multiple interpretations. Thus, a human being can perceive a piece of information that is fuzzy in nature and respond to it in an unambiguous, clear manner by using a range of possible interpretations.

At present, our analytical procedures generally follow the Boolean logic system, in which the law of the excluded middle is deeply entrenched. For this reason, we can deal with data that can have only two possible interpretations — it is either true or false, means yes or no, and so on. This system precludes any possibility of a situation falling in between, not true, but not false either. The Boolean logician would place this into an "impossible" category and thus reject its validity. Yet, from experience we know that there are situations in which it is not possible to take either of the extreme possibilities. For example, a police detective may narrow down the suspects by deciding that "he is not innocent but not guilty either" at some early stage of investigation.

Realizing the need to deal with such unfixed cases, Zadeh[14] developed a new form of logic system that he called fuzzy logic, in which he stipulated that an element can be a member of a given set in an uncertain manner. Unlike the classical mathematical set theory in which an element can be only in two situations, a member of the set or not its member, fuzzy logic generalizes the possibilities and introduces the concept of shades of membership patterns. It therefore incorporates the condition that an element is either a member or not a member of some set but also extends the condition by introducing the possibility of membership falling in mixed modes.

Apart from the natural generalization to the concept of belongingness, another clear advantage of using such a theory of logic is that it allows the structuring of all that is separated by imprecise terminology. Uncertain situations, language, thoughts, expressions, feelings, and even perceptions can now be modeled by mathematical techniques based upon this system of logic. The system is essentially based upon the axiom that there exist "fuzzy sets or classes with unsharp boundaries in which the transition from membership to non-membership is gradual rather than abrupt."[15]

2.2.2 Fuzzy Set Theory

A set S is said to be fuzzy when an element can belong partially to it, rather than having to belong completely or not at all. Fuzzy set theory therefore begins with an assignment of grade of membership values which are not restricted to 0 (non-membership) or 1 (full membership). In classical set theory, membership is binary, since there are only two possible states, membership and non-membership. Conventionally, these are assigned the values 1 and 0, respectively. These two values comprise what can be called the valuation set, which is the set of possible membership values. However, a set is said to be fuzzy if the valuation set contains values between 0 and 1. In most versions of fuzzy set theory, the valuation set is the interval [0,1]. The higher the membership value, the more an element belongs to the concerned set S.[14,16]

The valuation set need not contain numerical values. Verbal membership values have also been utilized by Kempton[17] in his anthropological studies of fuzzy linguist categories such as "absolutely not a"; "in some ways a"; "sort of a"; "primarily a", "best example of a" etc. These membership values are merely an ordered set of verbal hedges, but they successfully elicit fuzzy judgments from respondents, as Nowakowska[18] points out. Given the concept of degree of membership in the set S, the corresponding degree of membership in "not-S" ($\neg$ S) called the negation of S is denoted as $mS(x) = 1 - mS(x)$ where $mS(x)$ is membership value in S (Smithson, 1982).

2.2.3 Modeling Offender Profiles

The unreliability of witnesses in identifying criminal suspects is well known to most police officers.[19–21] Therefore, the focus on modeling the ways offenders perceive their likely targets appears a promising procedure to locate likely offenders.[22–25] In a recent article, Brantingham and Brantingham outlined what they describe as the pattern theory of crime, in which they suggest that offenders develop a kind of mental template when searching for suitable targets.[26]

However, in these cases, there is no established technique to profile such a template, since it is so individualistic and involves a large number of factors.

We know, and the pattern theory asserts, that despite such individual differences there are set patterns that can be seen. Police detective work is indeed dependent on deciphering patterns determined by habitual actions of offenders. In the commission of almost any kind of crime, every offender adopts a fixed mode of behavior in terms of chosen time period, target preference, region of operation, and even the manner of committing the crime. In police terminology, this behavior is described as the "modus operandi" of the offender, and a good detective attempts to establish this by looking for recognizable patterns in the commission of a crime. Thus, in burglary cases, the pattern sought is the time, place, mode of entry into the premises, and items stolen or left behind. In serial killings, apart from the place, time and mode of killing, characteristics of the victim, nodes of the residence, workplace and acquaintances of the offender may form the set pattern, or modus operandi, as demonstrated by Alston's study of serial rapists found in Section 6 and Rossmo's geographical profiling technique.[27]

Since the variables and factors that assist the police in establishing the modus operandi are imprecise in nature, it is difficult to develop any of the standard mathematical techniques to profile the offender. However, as described above, the new kind of mathematics based upon fuzzy logic appears to be useful in creating templates of offenders. We will develop a mathematical routine that models the modus operandi procedure followed by the police investigators. This fuzzy logic-based mathematical technique can assist in making sense of the evidence provided by the witnesses. As a practical example, we will use the case of motor vehicle theft in which multiple offenses by a single individual are more probable, but the technique could be applied to any type of a offense.

2.2.4   Technique

Let Ω be the set of auto suspects. An auto thief (suspect) $p = \Omega$, can be categorized by assigning to it the values of a finite set of fuzzy parameters relevant to him or her. Examples of such parameters may include places or times of operation, preferred vehicle type, busy or isolated road conditions of theft sites, value of the vehicle or the goods inside, mode of getting into the car, purpose of theft, and so on, where the highlighted parameters are fuzzy in concept.[14] Each parameter is specific to some feature of the offender p in question.

Thus, p can be associated with a mathematical object $F_k = [m_1(p), m_2(p), m_3(p), \ldots m_r(p)]$ where $m_i(p)$ is the measurement procedure of parameter i and $m_i(p)$ is that particular value. For example, we may have $m_j(p)$ = time period, i.e. day or night; or $m_k(p)$ = place, which refers to the boundary limits of some particular neighborhood; $m_l(p)$ = value in terms of costly or low-priced car, and so on.

Here F_k will be called the pattern class, and many such pattern classes $F_k \in I$ of mathematical objects could be associated with p. This will depend upon the various combinatorial values of $m_i(p)$ where I = 1 ... r. The set F of all such mathematical objects will be called the pattern space. The objective is then to assign a given object to a class of objects similar to it, having the same structure. According to Zadeh, such a class is often a fuzzy set F_y.[14] A recognition algorithm when applied to it yields the grade of membership $M_F(p)$ of p in the class F. In case the parameter is exactly known, such as the time of theft (someone may have noticed the car being driven away), then the grade of membership in time parameter will be 1, in accordance with the definition of fuzzy set.

We will first define a fuzzy pattern class F based upon the parameters in question. The easiest way of doing this is to assign this class a "deformable" prototype constructed through the information available from convicted and old suspects.[28] The assignment can be done by giving an interval of measures to each of the selected variables. Thus, young may mean 15 to 19 years of age, costly may imply a dollar value of around $5,000, etc. Other features such as ethnicity, casually dressed, tall, or local could also be added, based upon the information made available from victims' statements or detectives' knowledge about the active suspects. The measurement of these variables could be carried out through some form of smaller or larger scale developed for this purpose.

A prototype may then be something like: {young, Asian, smart looking, Robson/Granville street areas, evening, (prefers) Japanese cars, medium valued, lighted locations, (uses) duplicate keys... and so on}. All these are fuzzy variables with a range of membership values. However, with larger data sets of suspects, and over the years, more and more information gets built into the system which would help in reducing some of the fuzzy measurements or in building more representative prototypes.

Finally, a new auto theft offense will be analyzed about its attributes and for its membership values in each parameter. Some definite information will always be available, such as the make of the car and place of theft. Based upon these values and the information provided by the complainant or witness, the investigating officer can then assign the values of 1 or 0 or decide upon the grade of membership into other parameters.

Mathematically, let $F_k \in I$ be a fuzzy prototype pattern class defined by the fuzzy features $f_1 ... f_r$, where f_i is the fuzzy values of feature i. Symbolically, $F_k = \{f_1 ... f_r\}$ where f_1 is (tall), f_2 is (Chinese looking), f_3 is (...around Robson street) f_4 is (busy street...), f_5 is (shabby clothes) and so on. Each f_i will be having an interval of values. For example, busy may imply a situation when

15 to 25 cars pass a street crossing per minute, information about some suspect hanging around Robson street could mean the area is within four blocks on either side of Robson street, and so on.

F_k will have a minimum value n obtained by aggregating all the minimum values of f_i, and similarly a maximum value m. An object p, who is a suspect of this theft, will be characterized with respect to the class F_k by the r membership values– –f_k $m_i(p)$, i = 1 ... r. The value of p, denoted by $M_{F_k}(p)$ will be constructed by aggregating the $m_i(p)$s in some manner. This $M_{F_k}(p)$ can then be compared to the maximum and minimum values of different prototype pattern classes $F_k \in I$ which provides a numerical measure of the likelihood of a suspect belonging to a specific pattern class F_k (a group of suspects or a particular gang).

2.2.5   Aggregation Techniques

Several aggregating schemes have been developed by Zadeh et al.[29] and Smithson,[30] however, a literature review suggests that the choice of aggregation is very context-dependent.[28] Rather, two simple aggregation techniques were suggested in Zadeh's original paper and could be profitably utilized.[14]

Given an object *p* with membership values $F_k \in I$ $m_i(p)$ where i = 1 ... r and each F_k is a feature class, we can extend the classical union and intersection of ordinary set theory concepts to these fuzzy sets also by the following procedure:

$\cap$ (mA, mB) = min (mA, mB) and

$\cup$ (mA, mB) = max(mA, mB) where

$\cap$ is the logical 'and' and $\cup$ is the 'or' operator on the fuzzy sets A, B.

These operators have all the properties of any set theoretic operation like idempotency, commutativity, associativity and distributivity. Moreover, these also satisfy the following relationships:

1. min(0, A) = 0 for any A ≠ 0.

2. max(1, A) = 1 for any A ≠ 1.

Therefore, the min-max operation can be used for aggregation of the various profiles.

Another useful technique is the product operators:

$\cap$ (mA, mB) = m A*m B and

$\cup$ (mA, mB) = m A + m B – mA*mB.

The product operators have all the properties listed above except idempotency and distributivity. However, we can replace idempotency by an inequality since we know that for any positive numbers x and y, such that $x < 1$ and $y < 1$,

$$x*y \ \ min \ (x, y).$$

Finally, after selecting some assigning procedure (say the min-max one) the value $M_{F_k}(p)$ can be calculated by aggregating all the values $m_i(p)$ for $i = 1 \ldots r$.

Usually there are several fuzzy pattern classes $F_1 \ldots F_s$ and the problem could be to assign a given object to a definite class. When the membership values $M_{F_i}(p)$ are available, p can be assigned to the class F_k such that

$$M_{F_k}(p) = \max j \ M_{F_j}(p), j = 1 \ldots s,$$

otherwise, a new pattern class F_{s+1} may be created for p.

2.2.6 Hypothetical Example

Consider the situation in which an investigator obtains some fuzzy information about the suspect from the descriptions provided by few eyewitnesses. In such a hypothetical situation, the fuzzy terms could be analyzed following the technique as mentioned above. For instance, suppose the witnesses mentioned that the offender was tall, with brown color hair, wearing dirty clothes and was a young person. As indicated, these are fuzzy terms that mean different characteristics to different witnesses. To determine the overlapping range of these characteristics, the investigator could hold an in-depth examination of their perceptions to fix a range within which they could be describing these characteristics.

Consider the fuzzy characteristic tallness. It is fuzzy because for one witness 166 cms. and above is the height that makes a person tall. For a second witness, only a height of 172 cms. and above is tall, while for the third witness, a person is tall if he/she is over 170 cms. How about 168 cms. or 166 cms.? Is this height "tall" for the first witness? A detailed examination of this witness' perception may suggest that for him/her, any person of height 165 cms. or below is definitely not tall (membership value is 0), while 166 to 167 is tall, perhaps with 0.15 membership value. It is possibly 0.7 for 169 to 170 and 1 for over 173 cms. Thus for each witness, there is a minimum range of height of membership value <0.1 and a maximum range of value >0.9 for describing the fuzzy characteristics of tallness. As suggested above, the police investigator could obtain this information and possible ranges with membership values by a detailed examination of perceptions of each of the witnesses. This may be done by displaying a measuring scale and letting the witness point out the range over which he/she considers someone as "tall."

Such membership values could then be obtained for the other characteristics by developing a suitable scale of references. Thus, shades of brown on a scale of ten could be shown to the witnesses to determine the minimum and maximum placement of membership values for the fuzzy description of 'brownness' of hair. Thus, for witness 1 the brownness may begin with the shade marked 4 with membership value of 0.1 and may end with value 0.9 for the shade marked 8 on this scale. For each witness, a range of shades could similarly be determined for what they perceive as brown. Finally, each of the fuzzy characteristics that the witnesses provided about the suspected offender could thus be reduced to a range of numbers on a suitable scale. From these given values, the minimum and maximum values provided by the subjective judgment of each of the witnesses could then be determined. Finally, the investigator could use the average of the min-max values or other combinations, like min-min and max-max to experiment with different kinds of profiles. This may be determined by judging how well the information matches with other evidence available to him/her.

2.2.7 Implications

The realization that certain concepts and descriptions may be fuzzy in nature is important to assist the investigators in narrowing down the list of suspects. Instead of treating every piece of information given by the witnesses as having a definite meaning, the detective would do well to understand that some of the information is fuzzy in nature and therefore will admit a range of possibilities. Thus, as the first step, the detective may find it useful to ask the witness at the time of recording the statement to provide some indication of upper and lower inclusions for the particular fuzzy descriptor. For example, if the witness says that the offender was a tall person, the detective could ask him/her to characterize people at the scene as tall and short. This will provide some indication of the range the witness is implying and would be more useful to the detective than simply recording the suspect description as "tall."

Undoubtedly, it is impractical to expect investigators to use the mathematical technique described above in all circumstances. However, exposure to the concept of fuzzy variables and some training about the different ways of measuring them would be useful for police detectives. The technique outlined above may be initially reserved for the big cases, in which every clue needs to be finely probed. Cases such bank robberies and car-jackings are executed within a matter of minutes, giving victims and witnesses only a fleeting glimpse of the offender(s). These cases therefore generally involve fuzzy descriptions, which could be aggregated by a technique similar to one described above to provide a range for investigators to focus upon. Serial offenses, too, provide an example in which descriptions from several witnesses have to be closely reconciled. Based upon the information provided by different witnesses, the detectives could use fuzzy logic based methods to determine how "well-built" the offender(s) may be and thus be able to reconstruct a sharper profile.

Fuzzy logic techniques can also be useful to police managers for analyzing other kinds of data that is non-dichotomous and fuzzy in nature. For instance, fuzzy logic can be a promising tool for improving decision making in the police department. Job evaluations that involve ratings such as "good", "poor", "average" are difficult to interpret since different supervisors have different perceptions of these ratings. However, each of these ratings could be assigned a range of values and then reconciled through fuzzy logic methods to judge what constitutes "good" for all the supervisors.

Similarly, rather than classifying neighborhoods as "dangerous", "tough", or "troublesome" for extra deployment and special attention, the patrol officers may be trained to provide a range of gradation for these areas in order to make deployments more appropriate and cost effective. Thus, areas victimized by gang activity have boundaries that are fuzzy in nature.

Instead of designating the whole region as the "turf" of some particular gang, the patrol officers could be trained to see that the region could be divided into a range of dominance. Using some measurement scale, portions of the region could be identified as being partially a turf (say, 0.2 inclusion value) or overwhelmingly (0.9 inclusion value) under the dominance of that particular gang. This may be useful in planning cost-effective resources for surveillance or patrolling purposes.

Above all, the understanding that certain variables are fuzzy in nature will enhance police capabilities and can also improve our understanding of police behavior, action, and organizational culture. The discretion used by officers in making arrests, in stopping and questioning people is commonly based upon fuzzy factors. Thus, variables like "race", "age", "socioeconomic status", "appearance", that influence discretion exercised by the police, such as Dunham and Alpert,[31] Black and Reiss,[32] Davis,[33] Smith and Visher,[34] and Klinger[35] are essentially fuzzy in concept. The application of fuzzy logic-based techniques could be useful in examining the range that begins to affect officer's perceptions.

The reasons police officers stopped and questioned a particular "dark", "lower class" person may perhaps be explained by realizing that these are fuzzy parameters. The police officers may be using a graded scale to make their decisions in which not every dark, lower class person is a suspect but some particular ones are, for whom these parameters have a high inclusion value in the fuzzy perception of the officers. What constitutes these high values and how to identify and measure them remain important questions that require an empirical examination of officer's perceptions. In this examination, the measurement procedure as outlined above could similarly be applied. Undoubtedly, fuzzy logic has immense and rich possibilities for police related subjects.

Fuzzy logic can also provide a powerful method for applications in other criminal justice fields. A large category of data such as citizen responses, attitudes, and opinions are generally fuzzy in nature where possibilities for the utilization of this form of mathematics are extensive. A possible application could be in the field of comparative studies in law. It is generally acknowledged that international comparative legal studies are difficult since the meaning of offenses differs considerably.[36-40] For instance, "law" in Chinese language may mean "fa: a set of rules" or "shizhaifa: a living law". Similarly, "legality" could mean "fazhi: rule of the law or rule by law" in translation. It is interesting to note that Chinese scholars define another kind of legality, "socialist legality" a fuzzy concept in itself!

Legal terms like "good faith" of section 52 Indian Penal Code (IPC) or "lurking" house trespass of section 443 of IPC (Government of India, 1966),[41] "goondaism (Government of India, 1975),[42] "hooliganism" (liu-mang: in Chinese law) have different shades of meaning and interpretations. Further, legal terminology that is commonly used in almost all the written codes, like "human rights", "official responsibilities", "social morality", "duties of the citizen", "due process", "fundamental rights", "autonomy", "reasonable person", and "due diligence" are commonly used but have different meanings to different people. These are undoubtedly fuzzy in nature and could admit a large number of different interpretations.[43]

One possible way to estimate the commonality between two definitions from different legal systems could be to describe them in different situations that vary in stages. For example, a set of circumstances could be construed that define activities ranging from "goondaism" to being "lawful" in the Indian Law. The Chinese scholars could then be asked to identify the range where the situation could be labeled as "hooliganism" according to the Chinese law. The proportion of situations that match could provide an estimate of the comparative elements between the two legal terms, "goondaism and hooliganism". The use of fuzzy logic technique in similarly determining the common range of meanings of other such legal terms is therefore likely to assist in the comparison of the two legal systems. This obviously calls for a new form of research, but the possibility is immense and exciting.

Fuzzy logic techniques are likely to be useful for qualitative analyses too. Qualitative researchers collect data through various ethnographical techniques, like hermeneutics, that attempt to interpret the subjectivity of some phenomenon. They always face the problem of matching their records with one another and even with their own subsequent research work. Reliability of their technique is generally considered doubtful due to the natural differences that arise in replicating their data collecting procedures. Validity also becomes a problem, since in attempting to give meaning to their observations, the language is left open to interpretation.

Data collection through observational methods that involves more than one observer is always problematic when attempting to reconcile the records of all the researchers, since there are bound to be differences in the significance of the observed events. The same action may be interpreted differently by several researchers. For one researcher, a police officer may appear only to be "insensitive", while for another he/she may actually be "hostile". These are the possibilities that qualitative practitioners acknowledge openly, since for them such observations do depend upon the researchers' insight, and they may look at people and events from different angles. It is here that fuzzy logic could assist by quantifying these differences and thus reducing the range of their possible interpretations. By realizing that "sensitivity" (or its apparent absence) is a fuzzy concept and admits a range from "definitely insensitive" to "possibly hostile" the two researchers could reconcile their difference by agreeing that the police officer may be placed in a particular range. Since fuzzy logic can deal with such shades of meanings, it is reasonable to expect that it could begin to reconcile these individual differences.

Clearly, fuzzy logic-based techniques have the capability of providing a vast range of applications in the criminal justice field. A strong mathematical technique that can handle imprecise and fuzzy data is undoubtedly going to strengthen the analytical capabilities of social researchers. Above all, by exposing the readers to the concept of fuzzy variables and the mathematical base of fuzzy logic and by suggesting various ways in which it can be applied in criminal justice fields, this information may initiate a new research process. However, a great amount of research is required before fuzzy logic-based techniques emerge as powerful tools of analysis for police and criminal justice fields.

2.3 Reliability, Validity, and Utility of Extant Serial Murderer Classifications[*]

MAURICE GODWIN

Serial murderers have received attention from both the academic community and the entertainment world since the FBI first published accounts of its profiling principles. The topic was made popular by the Oscar-wining film *Silence of the Lambs*, and follow-ups such as *Seven*, *Copycat*, and *X-Files* making the headlines. However, beyond the victims' pin pictures that help create the sensationalism in these movies and books, there have been few, if any, reliable examinations of serial murder classification schemes. The following article examines some current typologies used to classify serial murderers, including the first systematic review of the FBI's organized and disorganized serial murder typology.

2.3.1 The Origins of the FBI Serial Murder Project

The FBI's initial project on serial murder began in 1978.[44,45] The impetus for the project was to conduct personal interviews with serial murderers about their crimes in order to find out how they were successful at avoiding capture.[44] The FBI serial murder project was given added attention in Washington, D.C. in the early 1980s due to public outcry of the murder of a six year old boy in Florida by a serial murderer.[45] Therefore, due to public pressure, the FBI serial murder project was brought to the forefront and given the necessary U.S. Government funding, which eventually lead to a unit being established in Quantico, Virginia called the Behavioral Science Unit (BSU). In 1995 a restructuring phase combined the BSU, Violent Criminal Apprehension Program (VICAP), and the National Center for the Analysis of Violent Crime into one unit, calling it the Critical Incident Response Group (CIRG).[46]

The primary purpose of the serial murder project was to use interviews with convicted killers as a basis for constructing future classifications, which then could be used to aid police investigations. A series of interviews with 36 incarcerated offenders, of whom 25 were defined as serial murderers

[*] Originally published in *The Criminologist* (U.K.), 22:194-210, 1998.

(i.e., the killing of three or more individuals over time) took place between 1979 and 1983 in the U.S.A. The interviews were guided by an unstructured checklist of questions. Prior to the interviews, data sources on each offender and his crimes were obtained by reviewing crime scene photos, physical evidence, court transcripts, victim reports, autopsy reports, prison records, and psychiatric reports. However, no detailed analysis of this material has ever been presented. Instead, a simple dichotomy was claimed to emerge from the project by which offenders were classified either as organized or disorganized. The assignment of the offenders to either the organized or disorganized category was based on the appearance of the victims' attire or nudity, exposure of victims' sexual parts, insertion of foreign objects in body cavities, or evidence of sexual intercourse.

The FBI posits in the literature that the organized and disorganized scheme was developed to classify a sub-group of serial murderers, that is, sex-related murders, where motive was often lacking.[45] This also can be interpreted that where the murderer is emotional and no organization can be deciphered from his actions at the crime scene, there is no motive. Because of the apparent lack of motive, FBI profilers decided to look for evidence of planning, irrationality, or some form of discord at the crime scene to determine whether the offender was organized or disorganized. The organized and disorganized typology is then used to classify the murderer's personality, depending on the category of the crime scene.

There are weaknesses in the organized and disorganized dichotomy. For example, there is no explanation in the literature of the differences between the organized and disorganized serial murderer. Rather the organized and disorganized dichotomy seems to describe the different levels of aggression in serial murderers, although no literature source acknowledges this. The differences in organized and disorganized crime scenes are usually explained in the form of a psycho-dynamic drive; the dynamic drives are: 1) revenge, and 2) sadistic.[45,47] The focus of these drives is seen in terms of lasting urges, formed through early life experiences. These experiences are organized especially around conflict.

The differences between the two types appear to originate from several traditional theories of aggression and personality disorders. For example, it is alleged that the organized offender has the ability to maintain some control over his aggressive behavior, while the disorganized offender is unable to maintain control. There is, however, a third type, the mixed offender, which is rarely discussed in the literature. The mixed type was added to accommodate offenders who did not fit into either the organized or disorganized category.[48]

2.3.2   The Organized Serial Murderer

According to the FBI classification, the organized (nonsocial) serial murderers are generally assumed to be cunning, and spend vast amounts of time planning murders, whether consciously or not, and this behavior is reflected at their crime scenes.[45] Another assumption is that the serial murderer's planning is expressed in his preoccupation with, and constant need for control.[49] FBI profilers claim that crime scenes tend to echo this aspect through the condition of the body, the body's state of dress, selection of restraints and weapons, body disposal sites, and method of approach.[50,51]

The organized serial murderer is described as one who is positively antisocial but often more gregarious, quite normal on the outside, maintaining normal relationships. He will be more forensically aware, mobile, creative, adaptive; he often has a certain preferred type of victim. Although victims' bodies are normally concealed, he will tease the police by leaving some bodies open to view. The FBI posit that the organized type serial murderer is out to shock and offend the community and taunt the police because he feels so much more powerful than them.[50] The offender will likely be a police buff and usually collects items relating to law enforcement.[50]

In the FBI study, imprisoned serial murderers classified as organized were assumed to have had an angry frame of mind at the time of the murder, but their behavior was calm and relaxed during the commission of the crime. The organized crime scene is described as having a "semblance of order existing prior to, during, and after the murder."[45] It is suggested that the murder is planned, and the offender is likely to used a con or ploy to lure his victims to their deaths. For example, the individual may strike up a conversation or pseudo-relationship with his victims. For organized killers, who consciously plan their murders, selection of the victim is believed to be a first step in acting out their fantasy; victims are thought to be chosen because of their symbolic similarity to someone in the killer's life or because of meanings the offender assigned to particular actions, such as hitch hiking. However, the FBI provides no empirical research supporting its theory that serial murderers target specific victims for psychological reasons.

The organized offender is seen as one who usually remembers his thoughts prior to each murder and improves on his planning with each subsequent killing. The offenders' planning and control over their victims are noted by the use of restraints, for example, ropes, chains, handcuffs, belts, or clothing. The offender is most likely to bring a weapon to the crime scene and take it with him when he leaves. The organized serial murderer is also forensically aware, and rarely leaves incriminating evidence behind. The FBI suggests that the organized serial murderer is more likely to rape and torture victims prior to death, while the disorganized types are more likely to mutilate and perform post-mortem sexual acts. However, these assumptions have been challenged by several researchers.[52,53]

The organized typology has several shortcomings. The FBI suggests that organized serial murderers kill to act out their "control and dominance,"[55] while at the same time they maintain that prior to the murder, the offender is feeling frustration, hostility, anger, agitation, and excitement, all of which indicate that the crime is emotional, and revenge seems to be the primary drive.[45] In other words, the FBI claims that serial murderers who kill in an emotional rage have control of their behavior at the crime scene.

The revenge (nonsocial) drive explanation for repetitive murder is that it is the offender's unconscious effort to discharge aggressive drives toward another person who represents a significant other from past life experience. The act supposedly originates from the Oedipal trauma of a seductive or rejecting mother and a punitive or absent father. The ego's defenses cannot prevent the action, but can direct it towards an alternative object, the victim. The rationale of the revenge formulation is that the relationship between a child's parents sets the pattern not only for sexual and aggressive behavior, but for general standards of expressing and prohibiting all sorts of behavior.

The drawback to the aggressive revenge drive theory is it assumes that conflicts invariably express themselves in Oedipal language. This may be true for some serial murderers, for example, David Berkowitz, Son of Sam, who shot couples in their cars apparently as stand-ins for the biological parents who had abandoned him. The revenge focus for serial murder may have some validity, however, the Oedipal theory neither explains why some serial murderers need to seek revenge repeatedly, nor why convicted killers do not necessarily demonstrate weakened defenses in other aspects of their lives. It seems reasonable to conclude that an individual who is so tortured by Oedipal thoughts that he acts them out is going to reveal similar behavior in other areas of his life. Clearly, the revenge focus seems too broad an explanation for describing individual differences in serial murderers.

2.3.3   The Disorganized Serial Murderer

Freud concluded in his *Theory of Sexuality* that with such perversions as sexual murder and necrophilia, "It is impossible to deny that in their case a piece of mental work has been performed which, in spite of its horrifying result, is the equivalent of an idealization of the instinct."[55] Freud's statement seems to set the direction for the classification of the serial murderer's aggression as a sexual perversion, and many theorists have argued that the disorganized murderer kills primarily for sexual gratification.[45]

The asocial (disorganized) serial murderer is described as a loner, withdrawn, and more cowardly in his crimes.[56] His crimes are often committed without a plan, and the victims are usually attacked in a blitz style. Some researchers suggest that the disorganized crime scene reflects a serial murderer whose motivation consists of uncontrolled sexual drives, reflected by the murderer's inability to control impulsive behavior or change his action in consideration of others.[49]

Other researchers suggest that the psychological gain for the disorganized serial murder is sexual exploitation of the victim in the form of torture.[45] However, the term "torture" was not defined by the researchers. The literature asserts that a sadistic sexual drive is the impetus for the disorganized serial murderer.[45,50,53] What is derived from this perspective are biases gleaned from offenders' self-reports. Consequently, no exploration of the different emphases murder has for different offenders is considered.

Traditionally, the sadistic aggressive explanation suggests that the offender derives sexual gratification by the infliction of pain and degradation on living victims. It is argued in the serial murder literature that the etiology for serial murder is sexual gratification.[57] The sexual attack is posited to be a way to degrade, subjugate, and ultimately destroy the victim. In the sadistic drive formulation, it is postulated that the offender kills out of sexual frustration because of a specific need for an object he can humiliate and torture. Some researchers also claim that sadism reassures the individual of his power by easing his worries about, for example, castration.[58] However, Storr discounts the sadistic sexual gratification theory.[59] Rather, he suggests that the murder has less to do with sex and more to do with pseudo-sexual activity, power, and control. Fox and Levin[60] concur with Storr's view, and point out that domination is a crucial element in serial crimes with a sexual theme. Another problem is the traditional definition of sadism. For example, no consideration has been given to the offender's perspective — that during the course of a violent attack, determining when sadistic gratification begins or ends is problematic. It may be more logical to consider violent behavior as a continuum of actions.

The disorganized offender is also described as one who shows no forensic awareness, often leaving fingerprints, bloody footprints, semen, and evidence of little or no preparation for the murder by selecting weapons of opportunity. Ressler and his colleagues point out that the disorganized serial murderer is not likely to use restraints because the victim is killed immediately.[45] In the disorganized type murder, the victim is depersonalized by cuts and stab wounds to specific areas of the body. Other examples of depersonalization and sadistic acts on victims occur in the form of inserted objects, which the FBI suggests is a form of regressive necrophilia and sexual substitution rather than an act of mutilation or control.[45,51] Additional sexual exploits may include features such as mutilation, disembowelment, amputation, and vampirism.

The literature suggests that victims of the disorganized killer typically show signs of overkill and excessive blunt trauma to the facial area, which is thought to indicate that the victim knew her attacker.[45] Also, the lack of organization is often noted by the offender making no attempt to conceal the victim's body, leaving her in the same location in which she was killed.[51]

2.3.4   Discrepancies in the Organized and Disorganized Dichotomy

If we look closely at the FBI's description of organized and disorganized types, there appear to be some discrepancies in their "narrative descriptions" when compared to the respective "crime scene checklist". The narrative version of the disorganized type actually seems to contain a number of organized types of behaviors that require extensive planning and forethought. For example, behavior such as post-mortem sexual activity, revisiting the crime scene, and the use of gloves would appear to indicate cognitive planning and an instrumental focus. However, the checklist, which is the list of descriptive words that are assigned to each crime scene type (cf. Ressler[45]), seems to reflect more a mixture of revenge and expressive aggression. The actions of blunt trauma to the face and blitz attack are embedded with a primary focus, sexual gratification. The combination of these modes of behavior is commonly cited as indicative of the organized serial murderer, however, actually they appear to represent disorganization rather than organization. The hypothesis that serial murderers who perform mutilations, post-mortem sex, and cannibalism are also disorganized is certainly open to question.

In addition to these discrepancies, there are two further shortcomings in the organized and disorganized offender typology. First, the behaviors that describe each type are not mutually exclusive; a variety of combinations could occur in any given murder scene. This is, of course, a weakness in all the murder classification schemes discussed in this chapter. Second, there is no discussion of why serial murderers have the need to repeatedly murder. Both the revenge and sadistic drives seem too vague. The organized and disorganized scheme also provides no reason why serial murders select some victims and pass up others. The organized and disorganized labels appear to be clinical assessments, similar to those found in the DSM-III-R. Hare argues that the antisocial personality disorder criteria in DSM-III-R is primarily a measurement of antisocial and criminal behavior and does not measure the affective and interpersonal characteristics of the personality disorder commonly associated with individuals displaying psychopathological behavior.[61]

2.3.5   Reliability of the FBI Serial Murderer Sample

In the FBI project, 36 killers were interviewed, 25 of whom were classified as serial murderers and 11 single or double killers.[45,47,55] A sub-sample of the 36 offenders were classified as disorganized and organized (Ressler et al., 1988). Thirty-three of the offenders who participated in the interviews were white. The offenders who agreed to participate in the final project were reportedly motivated by various reasons, such as making restitution to victims, to obtain attention, or to gain some legal advantage. For example, some of the offenders interviewed "had not completely exhausted their legal appeals prior to the interviews."[44] Furthermore, the offenders who refused to be interviewed were predominately white, intellectual, and motivated not to participate on advice from their attorneys, and were most likely to have organized behavior, which could account for the higher ratio of disorganized to organized murderers. Rather than interviewing a representative sample of killers, the FBI examined a small, select set of incarcerated offenders who were interested in volunteering. Thus, the FBI sample must be viewed as biased, although exactly how much is difficult to tell without a description of the population the subjects were drawn from to compare with the sample.

2.3.6   Inferring Behavior from Fantasy in the FBI Model

One theme that dominates serial murder classifications is the role that fantasy has in facilitating the murders. Ressler and his colleagues argue that "sexual murder is based on fantasy."[45] Several methodological constraints become relevant when inferring motivation through fantasy, for example the distortion most likely found in self-report studies. The FBI's serial murder classification relies on self-reports of personal history background and elements of how the crime was committed. However, research by Lewis et al., in a study that required independent confirmation of reports of trauma (e.g., those found in hospital or on police reports at the time of the incidents), found that convicted killers tend to under-report histories of trauma and deny symptoms of psychiatric disorders.[62] For example, during the interviews with serial murderers, the FBI researchers ultimately found the disorganized murderers' unanimous assertions of heterosexuality to be unreliable, but the researcher's suspicions were not aroused about whether retrospective accounts of the offenders' fantasy states prior to the murders were accurate.

In a later study, Prentky and his colleagues examined the role of fantasy in serial sexual murder by comparing 25 serial sexual murderers taken from the FBI sample with 17 single-victim sexual killers.[63] The study found that the serial group differed significantly from the single homicide group on measures of intrusive fantasy. However, the Prentky study has several weaknesses. First, part of the data sample was borrowed from the FBI serial murder project, which, as discussed earlier, has inherent biases. Similar to the FBI's studies, the Prentky study is so embedded with a mixture of clinical and motivational assumptions that no clear differences are made between fantasy and planning. Shapiro cautioned that historical explanations of pathology are simply too narrow a base from which to derive the complicated forms of sadism.[64] Second, the Prentky study used a control group, single sexual murderers, but the study methods were not matched to those used with the serial murderer group. This is rather vexing because there were no interviews of the offenders in the single-victim group. Instead, data were taken from police archives. DeHart and

Mahoney point out that researchers who choose to distinguish between one-victim murderers and serial murderers run into ambiguities in scientific and legal classification of serial murderers, which may diminish the validity of the data.[65] Third, the Prentky study compared a distinct sub-group of serial sex murderers with single-victim murderers who, over time, may not be likely to have the opportunity to exhibit bizarre sexual behaviors as the serials. Finally, the study used fantasy to distinguish between the types of offenders, which is highly susceptible to subjective interpretation.

Further complications come to light when using inferred motives and fantasies to develop a classification model of serial murder. Serial murderers often alter or exaggerate their claims for egocentric or status reasons. The FBI classification model of serial murder is constructed under the assumption that normal people do not have sadistic fantasies, or if they do, the fantasies are different from those experienced by serial murderers. One assumption is that childhood fantasy is usually positive, and thus serial murderers' childhood fantasies are oddly violent. Another assumption is that serial murderers show an unusually early onset of fetishistic behavior, when in fact the literature suggests that fetishism begins to develop in children somewhere around the age of five.[66]

Fantasy is described in the FBI motivational model as a linear relationship between a dominant mother, abusive personality, and arousal levels.[67] However, Terr found that abused children could become either aggressive or withdrawn, and children with non-abusive backgrounds demonstrated a range of responses from psychosis through neurosis.[68] This suggests that subtle yet crucial distinctions may be overlooked when an interviewer inquires only whether or not the offender's mother was dominant in his childhood. Lion further suggests that inferring fantasy from violent crimes such as rape and serial murder is problematic.[69] Gresswell and Hollin pointed out that little research has been published on how pervasive sadistic fantasy is within the general population or on the precise relationship between fantasy offending and real offending.[82]

2.3.7 Validity of the FBI Serial Murder Model

Using a five-stage development criteria, Busch and Cavanaugh[70] examined two classification models of serial murder proposed by the FBI.[71,72] They determined that the FBI classification model fits two stages: 1) unfounded statements not supported by data collection, and 2) unevaluated case reports without rigorous evaluation of other contributory factors. The remaining stages of the criteria were: 3) scientific case reports of individuals or small groups, 4) select population studies of particular sub-groups, and 5) epidemiological studies of larger random samples or a significant proportion of a small population.

Busch and Cavanaugh concluded that serial murder classifications were weak because they were descriptive and were not generalizable to the full population of serial murderers at large.[70] They also found that the two studies depended on ad hoc data, which tended to confirm the assumptions of the researchers.[70] Busch and Cavanaugh further argued that the motivational model for serial murder proposed by the FBI lacked statistical support, and warn that conclusions drawn from the crime scene variables inevitably produced a bias favoring confirmation of the assumptions.[70] Canter also questions the motivational based murder classifications by pointing out that the offender's actions are known to police, but not his motivation.[73]

2.3.8   Lack of Empirical Operational Definitions

A continual source of conflict in the FBI's serial murder model is the lack of defined concepts in the organized and disorganized dichotomy. An example of lack of defined concept is, in the FBI project, fantasy which was positively coded if the daydreaming content included intentional infliction of harm in a sadistic or sexually violent way.[63] The problems with this form of deductive reasoning are demonstrated in one serial murder case where, on one hand, the FBI profilers interpreted the bizarre positioning of a victim's body to represent a Hebrew letter as evidence of planning rather than fantasy, and on the other hand, they interpreted the refinement in techniques used to immobilize victims as evidence of fantasy rather than planning.[45] Katz points out that any model of serial murder which accepts blanket statements about motivation and does not carefully examine victim/offender interaction and the interaction of behavioral sequences in the actual murder may be misleading.[74]

2.3.9   False Dichotomization of Variables

A typical example of false dichotomization of variables and the lack of mutually exclusive concepts in the FBI typology is demonstrated in the following scenario: how would a police investigator classify an organized serial murderer with good intelligence, sexual competence, and who is geographically mobile (car) who commits a spontaneous, depersonalizing murder in which the victim's body is left at the crime scene, which are characteristics of a disorganized killer? In this example the profilers assume that the motivational factor that caused the violent criminal behavior will be indicated by study of the patterns in the external characteristics of violent offenders. Their assumption is that the antecedent factor for a series of murders is due to both an emotional outburst and some intrinsically abnormal personality in the offender, and that the offender's personality will be reflected in the way he carries out his crimes. This perspective sees motivation and personality as the same process, and neglects the emphasis that each explanation may have for different individuals.

2.3.10   Utility of the FBI Serial Murder Model

The theories on which the FBI serial murder classification is built are rather perplexing. First, there is the clinical classification which sees differences in offenders rather than crimes. These classification typologies seem to paint a picture of the offenders' mental illnesses, rather than trying to distinguish between their crimes.[67] Here, motive is thought to be some form of anger or rage towards society or a targeted group of individuals, and the offender harbors his emotional reactions to the point where they explode. These trends may be explained in terms of displacement of anger from other targets, or the feeling of lack of power. Stephenson has reviewed such displacement theories as general explanations of criminal behavior and found little evidence for them.[75] Second, there is the motivational classification that suggests that the internal forces or predispositions that drive a sadistic killer to murder repeatedly are mental representations of vicarious gratifications.[45,76] In other words, the murderer, who has no conscious emotion, is driven by thoughts and fantasies. This perspective is usually derived by relying on self-reports of serial murderers to classify the offender's mental state, and in turn to classify crime scenes. However, the FBI profilers suggest that the sadistic serial killer is influenced by a continual fantasy. The problem with this form of deductive reasoning is that motives are inferred and are assumed to be related to intrinsic thoughts and mental illness, and the exploration of behavior is totally neglected. Not surprisingly, in a recent study of different profiling approaches, Wilson and his colleagues [77] examined the validity and utility of diagnostic evaluations [76] and profiles developed from crime scene analysis.[45] They concluded that the "majority of profiles are mildly to severely flawed." [77] Other approaches to profiling serial murderers appear to be not much better. Given this, it might be more productive to adopt an approach that focuses more on behavior.

2.3.11   The Personality to Behavior Confusion

The actions of serial murderers from a behavioral approach looks at behaviors that can be observed rather than the individual's internal workings. As John B. Watson argued many years ago, "only individuals can observe their perceptions and feelings, but someone else can observe your actions." [78] Consequently, it seems more reasonable to consider crime scene actions as experiences of behavior rather than particular manifestations of intrinsic psychopathology.

The behavioral approach to classifying serial murderers' actions suggests that an individual's actions are the result of interaction between personality characteristics and the social and physical conditions of the situation. An inductive behavioral approach to modeling serial murderers sees behavior as mostly being consistent across a number of situations rather than specific to a particular environmental context. By employing the inductive behavioral approach, trends in how serial murderers behave from one crime to the next can be explored. Researchers often assume that personality traits are consistent, so that an offender can be characterized according to enduring personality characteristics. However, individuals are not uniformly rewarded across different crimes. The offender may learn to discriminate between contexts in which certain behavior is appropriate and those in which it is not. Rather, aggressive actions are differentially rewarded, and learned discriminations determine the situations in which the individual will display a particular behavior. This suggests that diverse behaviors do not necessarily reflect variations of the same underlying motive but often are discrete responses to different situations. Therefore, a behavioral classification model of serial murder may be more representative of serial murderers at large than a model developed from personality traits.

2.3.12   Other Perspectives on Classifying Serial Murderers

2.3.12.1   Sewell's Approach

Using Megargee aggression theories, Sewell analyzed the serial murderer Ted Bundy from literature dealing with Bundy and from Sewell's own involvement as an investigator on the Chi Omega sorority house murders at Florida State University.[79] Sewell applied Megargee's algebra of aggression to Bundy's crime scene behavior for this one crime event. Briefly, Megargee's theory of criminal behavior posits that "an individual automatically weighs alternatives and chooses a response to a situation which maximizes his or her benefit and minimizes potential pain distress."[79] Sewell's analysis found that Ted Bundy's behavioral characteristics provide a clear application of Megargee's algebra aggression:

> Bundy's overall violent response exemplified an instigation to aggression which was grounded in his rage against women and magnified by his need for excitement, attention, and ego gratification. His habit strength drew on his repeated successful acts of violence...to obtain control of the victims and the unsuccessful attempts by a number of states to charge him with these crimes. A number of situational factors added to his predisposition towards violence as an acceptable response.

Sewell's study concluded that Ted Bundy's motive for murder was that he chose a violent response as an acceptable reaction to many situations.[79] However, a review of Sewell's study found that he omitted some critical behavioral information concerning Ted Bundy's killing career. Although it could be argued that the Chi Omega murders were opportunistic and relatively unplanned, Bundy's other murders were very much thought out with deliberation and intent. To use Bundy's behavior in murders towards the end of his killing career is misleading, because in those murders Bundy was more emotional due to the pressure of trying to elude the police. Therefore, his instrumental need of post-mortem sexual activity had dissipated. Sewell failed to acknowledge this difference in his study. In other words, Sewell's study used one murder incident in which Bundy was clearly frustrated, and extrapolated it to Bundy's entire criminal career.

2.3.13   The Holmes' Approach

Serial murderers have been classified by other researchers.[50,56,80,81] Holmes and Holmes (1996) classified serial murderers into four types:

1. Visionary serial murderers, whose impetus to kill is propelled by voices they hear or visions they see
2   Mission serial murderers, whose impetus to kill is a need on a conscious level to eradicate a certain group of people
3. Hedonistic serial murderers, who are labeled lust or thrill murderers, and whose crimes have sexual overtones to them
4   Power/control serial murderers, whose impetus to kill is driven by a need for sexual gratification and the complete domination of their victims.

The Holmes' classification scheme appears to be a type of story line, offering reasons serial murderers murder rather than an empirical model distinguishing between offenders and offenses. Gresswell and Hollin point out three weaknesses in the Holmes' serial murder typology: 1) the classifications are not mutually exclusive, 2) the classifications are not exhaustive, and 3) the classifications fail to pick up interactions between the murderer, the victims, and the environment, and do not appear to be flexible enough to accommodate a serial murderer who may have different motives for different victims or changing motives over time.[82] Another weakness in the Holmes' classification model is that the data is not provided on which the conclusions are based.[47]

2.3.14   Hickey's Approach

Hickey's study on serial murderers and their victims is based on data collected on 203 serial murderers of 34 females and 169 males.[50,53] The dates of the crimes range from 1795 to 1988. Hickey's research focused mainly on victims of serial murderers rather than the offenders' crime scene behaviors. Hickey's study on serial murder is considered to be one of the most thorough in the literature. Hickey developed a taxonomy of motives from his data, and he states that serial murderers' motives appear to focus on "financial security, revenge, enjoyment, and sexual stimulation."[53] However, there are several problems with Hickey's motive types. It is likely that most researchers would exclude many of the female serial murderers that Hickey included in his study. Hickey included females who could be labeled as "black widows," meaning that they usually killed for profit. Of the 34 female murderers in his study, 53% killed for profit sometimes, while in 41% the motive for murder was entirely financial profit. It is interesting to note that Hickey did not rely on self-reports but rather data obtained from case files.

The data on male serial murders was less than forthcoming in Hickey's study. He did not discuss many behavioral characteristics, and when they were highlighted, they were used descriptively. Consequently, no attempt was made to empirically explore the relationship between serial murderers who murdered out of revenge and the distances they traveled to commit their crimes, and although he did discuss differences in spatial behavior, it was not in relation to crime scene actions.

Despite the shortcomings in Hickey's study, he does provide a useful descriptive model on predisposition factors and facilitators that could influence the serial murderer. He refers to his model as the "trauma-control model for serial murder."[53] Hickey suggests that the triggering mechanism in the serial murderer may be some form of trauma in which the individual is unable to cope with the stress of traumatic events. Hickey points out that individuals deal with traumatic events differently, and some deal with past trauma in a more destructive framework.

One interesting finding in Hickey's study was, although no exact percentage figure is given, he found that serial murderers who were serial rapists were also abused. In a similar vein, Hazelwood and Warren reported in their study on 41 serial rapists that 76% had been sexually abused as children.[83] This finding is interesting because it could give an indication that a common feature in serial murderers' backgrounds could be some form of a traumatic experience.

2.3.15 The Dietz Approach

Dietz and his colleagues made a descriptive study of 30 sexually sadistic serial murderers.[80] The purpose of their study was to gather information on personal characteristics and crime scene details common among such murderers. Seventeen of the subjects were classified as serial murderers, five of whom were originally in the FBI's sample population. The remaining subjects were drawn from a pool of cases maintained in the FBI's National Center for the Analysis of Violent Crime. The data used were archival documents (i.e., self-reports and police records) describing the offenders' crimes.[80] The study found that 93% of the sexual sadists were organized, and suggested that fantasy was the motivational factor behind the murders.

The ratio of organized to disorganized offenders in the Dietz study was considerably higher than in the FBI's project. The high proportion of organized offenders was probably due to biases in the sample; that is, a distinct sub-group of offenders, sexual sadistic murderers who were most likely to have organized behavior. Another form of bias in the Dietz study was the combination of a small sample size with a priori diagnosis suppositions made about the offenders, which appear to confirm the assumptions of the researchers.

2.3.16   Keppel and Walter Approach

Keppel and Walter proposed a theoretical classification by which sexual murderers' motivations could be profiled.[81] They described four types of sexual murderers: 1) power-assertive rape-murderer, 2) power-reassurance rape-murderer, 3) anger-retaliatory rape-murderer, and 4) anger-excitation rape-murderer. The power-assertive rape-murder is described as a series of acts which the rape is planned and the murder is an unplanned response of increasing aggression to ensure control of the victim.[81] The actions are characterized by forceful aggression and intimidation.[81] In the power-assertive rape-murder, Keppel and Walter suggests that the homicide becomes one of maintaining control over a vulnerable victim, and the killer demonstrates mastery of the situation by taking charge by the use of an assertive image and dominating violence.[81] The power-reassurance rape-murderer is described as rape that is planned followed by an unplanned overkill of the victim.[81] In this type of sexual murder, the authors suggest that the killer is motivated by an "idealized seduction and conquest fantasy."[81] Keppel and Walter point out that this type of killer expresses his sexual competence through seduction and when that fails, the murder allows the offender to reintroduce the fantasy system. The anger-retaliatory rape-murder is where the rape is planned and the initial murder involves overkill.[81] This type of offender murders for purposes of retaliation, getting revenge on women due to poor past relationships with women. The final type of sexual murder is the anger-excitation rape-murder, where both the sexual assault and murder are planned for the purpose of inflicting pain and terror on the victim for personal gratification.[81] This type of murder involves sadistic acts precipitated by highly specialized fantasies.[81]

Keppel and Walter appear to have borrowed their typology from a previous theoretical rape classification scheme first proposed by Cohen[84] in 1971, which was revised later by Groth et al.[85] in 1977, and again modified by Hazelwood and Burgess[86] in 1987. Some of the weaknesses in the original rape classification scheme are still prevalent in the Keppel and Walter model. The caveat of overlapping behaviors is problematic in the Keppel and Walter sexual murder model, and there is no discussion of any systematic analysis from which the described offender types may be validated. As a result, the perspective derived from the Keppel and Walter typology emphasizes the various psychological functions that sexual murder has for the offender, not the actual varieties of action the murder consists of. Consequently, the classification scheme makes little distinction between the overt crime scene behavior as it occurs in murder and the psycho-dynamic processes that produce that behavior. There is little attempt to differentiate aspects of the offender's motivations and life-style from aspects of his offending behavior. Any attempt to understand the actions that occur in murder offenses requires the classification of offense behavior as distinct from classification of the offender in either psychological or sociological terms.

There are also several unique weaknesses to the Keppel and Walter sexual murder typology originally not found in the rape classification scheme. The typology gives no consideration for an offender who commits a completely random crime. In each of the sexual murder types, either the rape or murder is planned. In an attempt to validate their sexual murder typology, Keppel and Walter surveyed a group of incarcerated murderers at the Michigan State Penitentiary who were given the four classification types and asked to describe which type fit them best. This process could hardly be considered scientific. In sum, Keppel and Walter's sexual murder types are described and then illustrated by case studies, and the differences between them are briefly discussed. The lack of data does not allow for exploration of the general applicability of the proposed classifications, because no background information on samples or population has been published. Hence, these are generalized classifications in need of empirical refinement.

2.3.17 Investigative Process Management

Given the problems with these approaches, how should we proceed? One way might be through the Investigative Process Management (IPM) approach.

2.3.18 Induction as Systematization

The view I have adopted is that induction is not a method of inference to the best explanation, but to the best "systematization." Induction, in this way, is used as an instrument of inquiry; it affords a mechanism for arriving at the best available estimate of the correct answer to factual questions. For example, during a criminal investigation, questions arise most pressingly where the information in hand does not suffice; i.e., when questions cannot be answered in terms of what has already been established. Here arises what Peirce calls the ampliative methodology of inquiry — the sense of going beyond the evidence in hand. Investigators need to do their best to resolve questions that transcend accreted experience and outrun the reach of the information already at their disposal.[87] In this regard, it becomes necessary to have a device for obtaining the best available, rationally optimal answers to the information in hand. Arriving at answers inductively should not be a matter of mere guesswork, but of responsible estimation. It is not just an estimate of the true answer that we want, but an estimate that is sensible and defensible. Induction thus represents a cognitive effort at closing all information gaps in such a way that we can regard it as epistemically well advised to accept the indicated results. In this sense, the inductively derived answers are arrived at by systematization with "real world" experience.

2.3.19   Deriving Inductive Profiles from Deductive Experiences

Providing answers to a criminal inquiry requires systematization of information at hand. Using this information we want to arrive at rational conclusions rather than depending on suppositions. But, why should Investigative Process Management be a matter of the systematization of question-resolving conjecture with experience? The answer lies in the consideration that system-building is not an end in itself, it is a process subject to objectives and the systematization of data in its original form.

The starting point in any police inquiry is set by factual questions about the case, to which we need to have the best available answers. At this juncture a "this-or-nothing" argument comes into operation. The investigator's only access to information about cases is through his interaction with past criminal cases. The same applies to those individuals who have studied criminal behavior in a clinical environment. Such interaction is what experience is all about. Here, of course, "experience" must be broadly construed to encompass the entire gamut of interaction with nature-generated clues that serve as grist to the mill of inquiry. The investigator, researcher, or clinician must have knowledge of nature, and experience is the only source of that knowledge that is available. The empiricist insight holds good: we have no alternative but to fall back on experience as factual information about the world.

To be sure, experience alone cannot do the whole job. For one thing, it only relates to particular cases. Questions about the world usually involve some element of generality, and empiricists have always had to confront the vexing problem of rationalizing the cognitively crucial step from particular experiences. There is no alternative to relying on experience for the reference points of the theoretical triangulation through which our knowledge of the world is generated. If information about criminal matters of objective fact is obtained, this must be on the basis of experience supplemented by principles of inductive systematization to make rational exploitation possible. Past observations are our only avenue of contact with what happens in the world. If anything can validate claims to generalized factual knowledge, then experience, while limited and imperfect, can do so.

As John Henry Newman wrote: "We are in a world of facts, and we use them, for there is nothing else to use."[88] If we do not call on experience to validate our cognitive claims in the factual sphere, then nothing can do so: if anything can, then experience can. In this sense, the inductive approach used within IPM, the view adopted in this research, is a matter of not only systematization with experience, but systematization of experience as well.

On the whole, extant classifications reviewed in this chapter are inherently flawed due to weak operational definitions and inferred deductive assumptions made about offender actions and characteristics. In its present form, this leads to empirically unsound and misleading profiling of serial murderers for police investigations. For example, as mentioned earlier, Prentky and Ressler suggest that fantasy is the motive for serial murder, however, they provide no literature to support their theory. Their claims appear to be deductive conclusions based on offenders' self-reports, which are highly susceptible to misleading and false information.

The serial murder typologies reviewed in this paper, outside of Hickey's study, seem rather vexing. No explanations are given regarding how the offender's criminal personality is formed. Some researchers argue that the offender is affected by some manifestation of mental illness, while others argue that pre-dispositions and sometimes fantasy is the motive for murder. The problem is that neither mental illnesses nor fantasies are motives, therefore, it is not possible to specify exactly what is responsible for the serial murderer's actions. An offender who is mentally ill may have different reasons for murder than an offender who appears normal, yet may be driven by fantasies.

The IPM approach is genuinely ampliative rather than inferential; it does not unravel the inner ramifications of the pre-existing state of informational affairs, but relies on bringing new information to our disposal. Accordingly, inductive profiling in this vein is the operative method of a goal-oriented method of classifying serial murders; it is at bottom a matter of praxis, a process of ultimately practical rather than strictly theoretical character. This fact is critically important from the standpoint of justification or validation research. Experience plays a substantial role in filling in the gaps. Thus, while recognizing that humans sometimes see illusory associations between variables when actually there are none, it is important to recognize that associations between variables may go unnoticed due to lack of experience. Such an approach, however, requires an appropriate methodology, and perhaps the most appropriate is Facet Theory.

2.3.20   A Move towards a Facet Classification of Serial Murderers

An alternative to classifying serial murderers into rigid types, organized and disorganized, for example, is the inductive thematic Facet Model that sees the criminal's behavior as shaped by daily life experiences and interpersonal relationships with others. In other words, the way the individual treats others when he is not offending may affect the way he carries out his crimes.[90]

Facet Theory offers a new approach to classifying serial murderers that may be practical for police investigations. There are two immediate advantages. First, serial murder investigations are faced with a great deal of information of investigative value that may be derived from simple overt aspects of an offense. Facet Theory can be helpful in that serial murders often involve subtle behavioral information which has value, but detailed analysis of the overt actions of the murder usually overshadow these actions. One example of how the inductive faceted profiling process could assist police in a serial murder investigation is a study carried out by this author on the spatial behavior of 54 U.S. serial murderers.[90] The study found that the locations at which victims were abducted were centrally located close to the offenders' home bases rather than at any number of the body dump locations.[90] Second, Facet Theory can use offense and offender variables that have been inductively related and empirically replicated for linking crimes to a common offender.

2.4 Criminal Psychological Profiling in Violent Crime Investigations: a Comparative Assessment of Accuracy *

RICHARD N. KOCSIS
HARVEY IRWIN
ANDREW F. HAYES
RONALD NUNN

There has been little empirical study of the abilities that contribute to proficient performance in psychological profiling. The authors sought to address this issue by comparing the accuracy of psychological profiles for a closed murder case generated by groups differing primarily in characteristics posited to underlie the profiling process. In addition to a sample of professional profilers, the study recruited groups of police officers (representing the role of investigative experience), psychologists (with insight into human behavior), university students (with skills in objective and logical analysis), and self-declared psychics (who rely on an intuitive approach). Another group of participants compiled a generic profile of murderers without knowledge of the specific case given to other groups. Despite the small size of the sample of profilers, there were indications that this group had a set of profiling skills superior to the individual skills represented by the other expertise groups. Additionally, the performance of psychologists was better in some respects than that of police and psychics, suggesting that an educated insight into human behavior might be relatively pertinent to psychological profiling. It would seem that psychics relied on nothing more than the social stereotype of a murderer in their production of the offender's profile.

The objective of this study was to investigate the skills underlying the effective performance of criminal psychological profiling. The fundamental role of a psychological profiler is to use information gathered at the scene of a crime and from victims and witnesses in order to construct a biographical sketch that is as specific as possible to the type of person who perpetrated the crime.[91-93,56] The offender profile typically includes identifying personality

* Reprinted with the permission of Sage Publications from an earlier manuscript appearing in the *Journal of Interpersonal Violence*, Vol. 15, April, 2000.

traits, behavioral tendencies, and demographic characteristics. Notwithstanding some highly fanciful depictions of psychological profiling in the mass media, these techniques have assisted police services in a number of criminal investigations. Although it is only in occasional instances that an offender profile is sufficiently specific to have led directly to the apprehension of the offender,[94,95] the profile evidently can assist the investigators' thinking on a case and help to narrow the range of potential suspects; in conjunction with other investigative procedures, psychological profiling thereby can make some contribution to the eventual identification of the offender.[56,96] Although the efforts of a psychological profiler may be of practical value, there has been little empirical study of the abilities that mark a proficient profiler. In the present study, this issue was addressed by comparing the performance of professional profilers with that of other groups believed to have some type of expertise potentially pertinent to the task of profiling.

While acknowledging that the approach of the American FBI to psychological profiling has been subject to some criticism,[56,73] it remains fair to say that the most internationally renowned program for training psychological profilers is that conducted at the FBI Academy in Quantico, Virginia by members of the FBI's Behavioral Science Unit (BSU). In this light, it is appropriate to consider the views of some principals of the BSU concerning the skills of profiling. According to Hazelwood, Ressler, Depue, and Douglas, the key attributes of successful profilers include an appreciation of the psychology of the criminal, investigative experience, the ability to think objectively and logically, and intuition.[97] Each of these characteristics will be addressed in turn.

2.4.1 Appreciation of the Criminal Mind

Hazelwood and colleagues argue that an understanding of the type of person who committed a given crime requires an appreciation of how a criminal mind might function.[97] Although the authors believe that this skill is not learned in a classroom, they do acknowledge that a background in the behavioral sciences may be helpful. In part, therefore, this factor constitutes an understanding of human, especially criminal, psychology. To sharpen the distinction between this factor and that of investigative experience, it might be best to operationalize the former in terms of demonstrable psychological skills. In the present study, the significance of psychological skills to profiling was assessed through the use of psychologists as one of the experimental groups asked to perform a profiling task.

2.4.2 Investigative Experience

In the professional opinion of Hazelwood and his colleagues, "no amount of education can replace the experience of having investigated crimes."[97] Indeed, despite the claim of the BSU to take due account of research findings, the FBI's handbook for profiling practice, *The Crime Classification Manual*,[98] was constructed almost entirely on the basis of the criminal investigative experience of FBI agents. The value of such experience evidently goes beyond an emerging awareness of patterns in criminal behavior; rather, it is said to relate to an appreciation that nothing should be taken at face value: the experienced investigator is more inclined to consider possibilities beyond the obvious.[97] Thus, in their intense focus on individual details of physical evidence it seems that experienced police personnel approach the task of criminal profiling in a very different way than do behavioral scientists.[99,100] By inviting a group of experienced police officers to perform a profiling task, the present study sought to gauge the relative importance of investigative experience. This is certainly not to claim that police have no relevant skills other than experience, but by comparison with other groups in the project, experience is their most distinguishing characteristic.

2.4.3 Objective and Logical Analysis

Hazelwood also depicts the effective profiler as one who can think logically without being diverted by personal feelings about the crime, the perpetrator, and the victim.[97] Thus, in constructing a profile all subjective impressions about the offender being, for example, "an evil thug" or "a sick pervert" must be set aside in favor of a description of the offender as might be given by this person's friends and neighbors. The capacity for objective and logical analysis was tapped in the study by recruiting a group of university science and economics students who had had no training in behavioral science but had been trained to set aside personal impressions in the rational analysis of factual information.

2.4.4 Intuition

A capacity for objective logical analysis might be an essential characteristic of the successful profiler, but in the popular image the psychological profiler is not quite so analytical. The media often depict the profiler as able to evoke apparently mystical visions of the way in which the crime was committed. Thus, many lay people see profilers as "fitting somewhere between a clairvoyant and a witchdoctor,"[101] and even some police reportedly look askance at offender profiling as "one step removed from witchcraft."[46] Forensic psychologists generally have been at pains to discount such depictions of the processes of psychological profiling.[102,103] It may be surprising, therefore, to find that Hazelwood nominates the psychic-like faculty of "intuition" as an important facet of psychological profiling.[97] Holmes and Holmes also refer to the intuitive element of psychological profiling, describing it as "the art dimension of profiling," as distinct from the elements of skill.[56] Indeed, during the investigation of many crimes police services evidently have invited psychics to use their intuitive faculties to assist in solving the case. Rigorous scientific investigation has yet to validate psychics' utility in criminal investigations,[104,105] and instances of spectacular failures of psychics in this context have been reported by Randi,[106] but there also are numerous anecdotal accounts of psychics' accurate identification of an offender.[107] The value of intuitive processes to psychological profiling therefore remains an open question. Be this as it may, in deference to the view by Hazelwood and his colleagues that some intuition is involved in successful profiling, the study reported here included the recruitment of a group of self-described, predominantly professional, psychics.

There may well be additional abilities that serve to enhance the practice of psychological profiling. Hazelwood and colleagues, for example, also propose the value of "common sense."[97] Under the comparative group design used in the study, however, it is difficult to nominate a naturally occurring group of adults that distinguishes itself in terms of this characteristic. More fundamentally, the operational distinction of common sense from the factors of objective, logical analysis and investigative experience is highly problematic. We therefore decided to focus on a comparison of the four above types of expertise to that of the professional profiler.

At least two broadly similar studies have been reported in the literature. Pinizzotto and Finkel gave details of two closed criminal cases (a rape and a homicide) to groups of profilers, detectives, psychologists, and students.[108] Profilers were found to write richer, more detailed offender profiles than did the other groups and at least for the rape case, the profilers' descriptions contained a greater number of correct items of information. Only 15 items of offender information were processed by Pinizzotto and Finkel, and there was no scrutiny of the types of information on which profilers were more accurate.[108,109] Another study by Reiser and Klyver made use of a sample of psychics.[110] In this investigation, however, psychics' and students' offender profiles were compared to those by detectives, not professional profilers. The total number of accurate statements in the profiles did not differ significantly across groups.

A valid argument can be raised about the representation of the utilized cases in these studies (and that within the present manuscript) as being particularly amenable or unamenable to profiling. However, given logistical restraints that arise in such research, a case study approach is typically the most viable. Consequently, it is essential to increase the number of such studies in order to eventually generate an extensive database.

The present study endeavored to advance the current literature in two principal respects. First, it sought to compare the performance of professional profilers to that of four other groups marked by expertise independently proposed by Hazelwood to bear on the skills underlying offender profiling. Second, it was planned that an attempt be made to identify the specific types of offender information about which the profilers were more accurate.

The relative profiling accuracy of these five groups may help to clarify the nature of the skills involved in psychological profiling, but it might be argued that such group comparisons would do nothing to demonstrate the extent to which profiling requires any expertise whatsoever. The relative accuracy of the groups' performance would not necessarily attest to the absolute accuracy; all groups' profiling efforts could still be poor. One way to index the accuracy of a group's profiling performance would be to see how many characteristics of the offender were correctly predicted by members of the group. This index, however, is potentially misleading in that it is confounded by the number of offender characteristics canvassed in the investigation and by the number of characteristics that are actually known about the offender. An alternative way to index the efficacy of a group's profiling performance would be to show that the number of offender characteristics correctly identified is better than that achieved by a group that is not given any details about the specific case other than its type (viz., murder). Inclusion of such a group in the design allows a test of the hypothesis that group profiling performance is more than a simple restatement of commonly held social stereotypes about offenders. A trend by any of the profiling groups to correctly conclude that the offender in the given case was primarily motivated by an "uncontrollable impulse," for example, would hardly evidence an incisive profiling performance if people unfamiliar with the case also often attribute this motive to murderers in general. The possible role of this factor in the construction of psychological profiles is indicated by Campbell's claim that profilers are no better than bartenders in the depiction of the offender of a crime.[111] To take account of the possible influence of popular criminal stereotypes on profiling performance in the study, a secondary analysis was planned whereby the performance of the expert groups was compared to that of a sample unfamiliar with the specific case. This type of analysis does not appear to have been incorporated in the designs of previous studies.

2.4.5 Method

2.4.5.1 Participants

Five groups of adults participated in the primary part of the study. The groups were selected with regard to the relevance of their expertise to psychological profiling, and thus for convenience the groups are termed profilers, police, psychologists, students, and psychics.

The group of profilers comprised 5 people (4 men and 1 woman) ranging in age from 27 to 48 years ($\bar{x} = 41.4$). Selection of participants for this group was based on a demonstration that the person had been consulted by a law enforcement agency for the purpose of constructing a psychological profile in the course of a criminal investigation. Invitations to participate in the study were sent to over 40 active profilers in several countries. The participation rate of profilers therefore was low.

The police group comprised 35 people (28 men, 5 women, and 2 of unknown gender) ranging in age from 26 to 45 years ($\overline{x}$ = 32.1). All members of this group were current police officers involved in active duties and had a minimum of 5 years experience in an Australian state police service with a component in criminal investigations. The sample of psychologists comprised 30 Australians (9 men, 20 women, and 1 of unknown gender) ranging in age from 21 to 68 years ($\overline{x}$ = 38.8). All had completed at least three years of accredited training in psychology but had not formally studied forensic or criminal psychology. To index the role of objective and logical analysis, a sample of Australian university science and economics sophomores was recruited. This group comprised 31 participants (11 men and 20 women) ranging in age from 20 to 52 years ($\overline{x}$ = 32.5). The students did not qualify for any of the other groups in the study, that is, they were not profilers, police officers, or psychologists, and they did not profess to be psychic. The remaining group comprised 20 (4 men and 16 women) Australian self-declared psychics, ranging in age from 25 to 60 years ($\overline{x}$ = 41.3). The participants in this group believed they possessed some form of paranormal ability that could assist them in identifying a criminal offender and indeed, if consulted by police, the psychics would be willing to use this ability to construct an offender profile for an ongoing criminal investigation.

In addition to the groups used in the comparative assessment of areas of expertise in psychological profiling, one other group was used to survey the stereotypical profile of a homicide offender. This sample, designated the stereotype group, comprised 23 Australian university economics students (14 men and 9 women) ranging in age from 17 to 30 years ($\overline{x}$ = 19.7).

2.4.6 Materials

The study entailed the completion of a specially constructed survey inventory in five collated parts. The first part of the inventory was a detailed report of a previously solved homicide investigation. The case description was based on information in files of an Australian state police service and comprised a scene of crime report, a forensic biologist's report, a forensic entomologist's report, a ballistics report, a report of a preliminary post mortem examination, a pathologist's post mortem report, basic details of the identity and background of the victim, a schematic plan of the crime site, and nine captioned photographs of the scene of crime and the body of the deceased, the latter showing the extent of injuries suffered by the victim. The case report thus contained a summary of all relevant information available to investigators prior to their determination of the primary suspect (the person ultimately convicted of the homicide).

In the second part of the inventory, participants were asked to sign a declaration that they were not previously familiar with the facts of this case. Details of the participant's age and gender also were requested here.

The participant's construction of a profile of the offender in the given case was sought in three stages in the remaining sections of the inventory. Participants initially were asked to write a detailed description of the person they envisioned as the offender in the case. No guidance was given on writing this account other than to suggest that it include "any and every personal and physical characteristic that could assist police officers in their endeavors to apprehend the offender."

After they had written the open-ended description, participants were presented with a 45-item multiple-choice questionnaire surveying physical characteristics of the offender, cognitions related to the offense, behaviors associated with the offense, and personal history. Some of the items in this questionnaire were modeled on those devised by Pinizzotto.[109] While the questionnaire contained 45 items, only 33 are relevant to the analyses reported here. These 33 questions and the instructions given to the participants prior to completing the questionnaire can be found in the Appendix.

The final section of the profiling task addressed the personality characteristics of the offender, and these were surveyed by means of the Adjective Check List (ACL).[112] The ACL comprises 300 adjectives descriptive of personality, temperament, and character. Respondents are asked to check those that are applicable and to leave unchecked those that are not applicable. For the purpose of this study, participants were asked to complete the ACL so as to depict the personality characteristics of the offender.

2.4.7 Procedure

The survey inventory was completed by mail by the profiler group. In part for reasons of security, the inventory was administered in person to the members of all other groups; in a few instances, people were tested individually, but most were tested in groups. Group sessions typically were convened in large rooms such as lecture theaters and classrooms.

In administering the survey inventory, the researcher explained the objective of the project and the procedure for completing each of the forms. The researcher also responded to any request for clarification of procedural matters, but no clarification of information in the case report was given; indeed, at this stage the administrator of the inventory knew almost nothing about the personal characteristics of the offender in the test case. Participants were not permitted to discuss collaboratively the case information. No time limit was imposed in completing the profiling task.

At the request of a small number of individual participants, the test conditions were slightly tailored so as to facilitate the best possible profiling performance, provided that these modifications did not compromise the security of the test. Thus, in one instance the inventory was individually administered in a "shrine" in which the psychic participant believed her "energy would be maximized."

Participants in each of the five "expert" groups completed the survey inventory under this procedure. Additionally, the stereotype group was given the three sections of the profiling task and asked to use these to depict "a typical murderer" without having seen the case report. These data were solicited for the purpose of a secondary analysis to assess the extent to which the expert groups were able to identify offender characteristics beyond what might be widely assumed as stereotypical of the perpetrator of a homicide.

After the completion of all testing, the survey inventory was given to the principal police officer who originally had conducted the official investigation of the test case. This officer completed the inventory in order to provide the correct answers to the profiling task. Before completing the forms, the police officer consulted original case notes to refresh memories of the case, but it seems these memories still were highly vivid in any event.

2.4.8   Results

The written offender profile solicited in the first stage of the profiling task has not yet been subjected to statistical analysis. Data from this form were gathered for another purpose and may be reported in the future.

2.4.8.1   Measures of Accuracy

Our primary purpose was to assess the degree to which participants differing in the skills, abilities, knowledge, or experience potentially pertinent to the construction of an accurate profile actually differed in successfully identifying the characteristics of the person who committed the offense described to them in the survey inventory. To accomplish this, we constructed two omnibus measures of accuracy and four sub-measures of accuracy sensitive to different dimensions or features of the offense or offender. Each measure was defined as the number of questions about the crime and/or offender relevant to that dimension that the participant answered "correctly." A question was answered "correctly" if the respondent gave the same response as the police officer who conducted the original investigation. The police officer's response was of course based on information known after the perpetrator was identified and convicted. In Appendix I, we provide the questions pertinent to each dimension. The dimensions are described below.

2.4.8.2   Physical Characteristics

Six questions asked the participant about the physical characteristics of the offender that would yield a rough visual description of the offender (e.g., sex, age, height).

2.4.8.3   Cognitive Processes

Seven questions related to the offender's contemplation of the offense (e.g, degree of planning, previous violent fantasies, subsequent reflections).

2.4.8.4   Offense Behaviors

Seven questions asked the participant about the behavior exhibited by the offender just before, during, or just after the offense (e.g., protecting his/her identity from the victim, modifying the crime scene after the offense).

2.4.8.5   Social History and Habits

Ten questions concerned features of the offender pertinent to his or her social status and behavior (e.g., marital status, relationships and friendships, make and model of car). Two omnibus measures of profiling accuracy were used.

2.4.8.6   Total Accuracy

This omnibus measure of accuracy was defined simply as the total number of questions from the four sub-measures described above that were correctly answered.

2.4.8.7   P&F Accuracy

The other omnibus measure of accuracy was constructed using questions similar to the ones used by Pinizzotto and Finkel.[108] This accuracy measure contained twelve questions, nine of which were on one of the four sub-measures described above and identified in the Appendix with an asterisk. The additional three questions can be found in the Appendix. The sole purpose of this measure of accuracy was to provide a means of comparing our results to the results described by Pinizzoto and Finkel.[108]

2.4.9   Differences between Expertise Groups

To compare the performance of the five groups, six individual analysis of variances were conducted on each measure of accuracy. We first describe the results of the two omnibus measures of accuracy and then proceed to the four sub-measures of accuracy.

Table 2.4.1   Profile Accuracy (Mean Number of Questions Correct)

| | Group | | | | | |
	Psychics	Students	Psychologists	Police	Profilers	$F(4,116)$
Omnibus Measures						
Total	11.30	12.03	12.57	11.60	13.80	2.02+
P&F	4.05	4.45	4.13	3.91	5.00	1.00
Submeasures						
Cognitive Processes	2.60	2.03	2.27	2.49	3.20	1.44
Physical Characteristics	2.80	3.42	3.63	3.43	3.60	3.47*
Offense Behaviors	3.65	3.64	4.03	3.09	4.00	3.20*
Social History and Habits	2.25	2.94	2.63	2.60	3.00	0.73
Personality						
Total Correct	27.70	26.84	34.03	22.03	24.60	3.58**
Total Checked	54.45	47.26	60.27	39.89	42.60	2.87*

$+p < .10$ $*p < .05$ $**p < .01$

Reprinted with the permission of Sage Publications from an earlier manuscript appearing in the *Journal of Interpersonal Violence.*

2.4.9.1   *Overall Accuracy*

As can be seen in Table 2.4.1, the five groups did differ in their total accuracy, but only marginally so, $F(4,116) = 2.018$, $p < .10$. Follow-up comparisons using Tukey's HSD failed to uncover any reliable differences between the groups, however. No differences were observed on the omnibus measure of accuracy based on the research of Pinizzotto and Finkell, $F < 1$.[108]

2.4.10   Components of Accuracy

Individual ANOVAs on the four subscales revealed that the groups did differ statistically in the identification of the physical characteristics of the offender, $F(4,116) = 3.468$, $p < .02$, and the identification of the offense behaviors, $F(4,116) = 3.196$, $p < .02$). Follow-up comparisons using Tukey's HSD procedure showed that psychologists correctly identified more of the physical characteristics of the offender and more of the offense behaviors than did the police officers. Psychologists also correctly identified more of the physical characteristics of the offender than did the psychics. No other comparisons were statistically significant.

2.4.11   On the Accuracy of Profilers

The analysis above would seem to cast serious doubt on the claimed abilities of profilers and their usefulness in criminal investigations. In spite of their training, knowledge, and experience, profilers did no better than anyone else

Table 2.4.2   Profile Accuracy: Profilers vs. Nonprofilers

	Profilers	Nonprofilers	$\underline{t}(118)$
Omnibus Measures			
Total	13.80	11.92	1.81*
P&F	5.00	4.14	1.29+
Submeasures			
Cognitive Processes	3.20	2.33	4.54+
Physical Characteristics	3.60	3.37	0.60
Offense Behaviors	4.00	3.58	0.80
Social History and Habits	3.00	2.64	0.54
Personality			
Total Correct	24.60	27.40	−0.45
Total Checked	42.60	49.64	−0.58

+$\underline{p}$ < .10   *$\underline{p}$ < .05

Reprinted with the permission of Sage Publications from an earlier manuscript appearing in the *Journal of Interpersonal Violence.*

in the correct identification of features of the offender or offense. But a visual examination of the means in Table 2.4.1 tells a somewhat different story that seems to contradict this analysis. Notice that the profilers did <u>descriptively</u> outperform all other groups on the two omnibus measures of accuracy and two of the sub-measures (cognitive processes and social status and behavior). On the other two sub-measures, the profilers were second most accurate, with the difference between them and the most accurate group (psychologists) negligible and easily attributable to sampling error. The analysis described above tests whether the five groups differ from each other, not whether a certain group or groups tend to outperform certain other groups. But one of our goals was to examine the performance of profilers relative to other groups that may possess relevant skills or knowledge. To examine the question as to whether profilers tend to be more accurate in their profiles than the other groups, a more sensitive analysis was undertaken.

To conduct this analysis, the psychics, psychologists, students, and police officers were collapsed into one group, which we will refer to as the "nonprofilers." The mean number of questions answered correctly for this new larger group was then compared to the same mean derived only from the five profilers. These means are displayed in Table 2.4.2. As can be seen, a consistent pattern is clearly present. On every measure of accuracy, the profilers answered more questions correctly than the nonprofilers. Furthermore, this difference was statistically significant on the total accuracy measure, $\underline{t}(118) = 1.81$, $\underline{p} < .04$ one tailed, and marginally so using the omnibus measure based on Pinizzotto and Finkel, $\underline{t}(118) = 1.29$, $\underline{p} = .10$ one tailed.[108]

On the individual analyses of the sub-measures of accuracy, the profilers were only marginally more accurate than the nonprofilers in the identification of the cognitive processes of the offender, t (118) = 1.54, p < .07, although again, as can be seen, the effect was in the same direction for all subscales. When the four tests on the subscales are meta-analytically combined using Stouffer's procedure, modified for nonindependence between the measures (Strube, 1985), Z = 1.77, p < .04. This leads us to the vague conclusion that the profilers are more accurate than the nonprofilers on at least one of the subscales, but we cannot specify precisely which one or ones.[113,114]

2.4.12   Insights into the Personality of the Offender

Up to this point we have focused exclusively on the "objective" features of the offender and the ability of different groups to correctly identify those features. Might they differ in their ability to describe the psychological characteristics of the offender (i.e., whether he or she can be described as aggressive, neurotic, extroverted, etc.)? Our approach to this question is only exploratory, and impeded partially by ambiguities as to how to measure whether or not a respondent is "correct" in his or her psychological description. We resolved this ambiguity here by continuing to use the impressions of the investigating officer as the authority, and comparing the respondent's psychological profile derived from responses to the adjective checklist with the investigating officer's profile. A measure of accuracy was derived by computing the number of adjectives that the respondent checked as descriptive of the offender that the investigating officer also checked. We also noted the absolute number of adjectives that were checked by the respondent and used this as a measure of the respondent's tendency to ascribe any characteristic to the offender.

Interestingly, the five groups did differ in the accurate identification of the psychological characteristics of the offender, $F(4,116)$ = 3.58, p < .01. Using Tukey's HSD procedure, the psychologists were more accurate than the police officers. All other comparisons were not significant. However, this same pattern was found when we examined the total number of adjectives checked. The groups did differ from each other in how many characteristics were ascribed to the offender, $F(4,116)$ = 2.87, p < .05, with the only significant difference being the tendency for psychologists to check more adjectives than the police officers. After controlling for the number of adjective's checked in analysis of covariance, the groups were equally accurate in their descriptions of the psychological characteristics of the offender, $F(4,115)$ = 1.94, p > .10.

2.4.13   Better than Bartenders?

The preceding analyses showed few differences between the groups in their ability to accurately identify features of the offender in this case, although

Table 2.4.3 Performance of the Social Stereotype Group

	Mean Correct	Significantly Different From
Omnibus Measures		
Total	9.78	Psychologists, Students, Police, Profilers
P&F	3.04	Students, Profilers
Submeasures		
Cognitive Processes	2.35	None
Physical Characteristics	2.09	Psychologists, Students, Police, Profilers
Offense Behaviors	3.61	None
Social History and Habits	1.74	Students
Personality		
Total Correct	28.48	None
Total Checked	50.17	None

Reprinted with the permission of Sage Publications from an earlier manuscript appearing in the *Journal of Interpersonal Violence.*

there was some evidence upon closer examination that profilers excel compared to nonprofilers in at least some sense. One potential explanation for the similarity in their performance is that when they answered the questionnaires, all participants may have relied on a common social stereotype of the likely features of people who commit such crimes. That is, perhaps the information specific to the case was in effect not used at all and instead the respondents answered the questionnaire by relying on stereotype-based knowledge (e.g., murderers tend to be male, mid 20s, poorly educated, asocial). We addressed this question by comparing the performance of each group to the performance of a group who were given no specific information about the case itself and who were merely asked to respond to the questionnaire. We refer to this group as the "stereotype" group. The responses of this group give us a means of determining how accurate a profile based on a social stereotype would tend to be. These comparisons were done on the two omnibus measures of accuracy as well as the submeasures and those based on responses to the adjective checklist. Within each accuracy measure, a Bonferonni correction of 5 was applied to compensate for multiple tests. In other words, a comparison was deemed statistically significant only if p was equal to or less than .01.

The results of these analyses are displayed in Table 2.4.3. As can be seen, on two measures (total correct and physical characteristics) all but the psychics produced a profile that was more accurate than one based only on the social stereotype. On the measure based on Pinizzotto and Finkel,[108] only the profilers and students produced a more accurate profile compared to the stereotype group. Finally, only the students outperformed the social stereotype on the social history and habits measure. All other comparisons between the expert groups and the stereotype group were not significant.

2.4.14   Discussion

One incidental but nonetheless noteworthy finding of the study was the low participation rate by profilers, despite all assurances of confidentiality given in the invitations to take part in the study. This may have been due in part to some reluctance by profilers to have their skills subjected to empirical evaluation. British profiler Paul Britton, for example, remarks that psychological profilers tend to exhibit exceptionally strong professional rivalry and jealousy, and thus they may be hesitant to expose any shortcomings in their profiling expertise when there is no personal gain in their doing so.[101] Any such tendency among the relatively small population of professional profilers is clearly a major impediment to the conduct of scientific investigation of the skills involved in psychological profiling. If it achieves little else, we hope this paper will encourage profilers to be more sympathetic to researchers' requests for their participation in scientific investigations. The small size of the sample of profilers compromised the capacity of the study to establish statistically significant differences between the performances of the expertise groups, but some interesting trends nevertheless were evident. At least in some sense the profilers were more accurate on the task than were the other expertise groups (see Table 2.4.2), so it would seem that the collective skills of profilers are superior to the individual skills represented by each of the comparison groups.

This is not to say, of course, that these individual skills are equally important to the practice of profiling. In comparison to the police and perhaps the psychics, the group of psychologists showed superior performance in several components of the task. The study's findings therefore might be taken to suggest that specifically psychological knowledge is more pertinent to successful profiling than investigative experience and intuition. Admittedly, the data on the offender's psychological characteristics are to some degree ambiguous in this respect, because the psychologists were inclined to check a greater number of identifying characteristics; but this finding could also be interpreted to indicate that psychologists are able to depict the offender's personality in a relatively multifaceted fashion, whereas the other groups tend more to a one-dimensional characterization. In any event, the study does encourage the view that an educated insight into human behavior could play an important role in the process of psychological profiling. At the same time, it must be stressed that the psychologists' performance did not differ significantly from that of the student group, so it remains uncertain whether the psychologists' advantage over some other groups was predominantly in regard to specific knowledge of behavioral science or in some respect also to a broader capacity for objective and logical analysis.

The performance of the group of police officers, on the other hand, was not strong. This finding is somewhat at odds with the claim by Hazelwood that investigative experience is the most essential factor in successful profiling.[97] The commonly voiced view that psychological profiling cannot be taught in the classroom[46,97] might deserve reconsideration. That is, police training academies might usefully give greater attention to formal instruction in this area. More explicit empirical scrutiny of this issue is called for.

The performance of the self-declared psychics also warrants comment. The accuracy of the psychics was not high, and indeed, unlike all other groups used in the project, these participants showed no insight into the nature of the offender beyond what reasonably could be gleaned from the prevailing social stereotype of a murderer. Notwithstanding anecdotal reports of the successful use of psychics in a police investigation, the present study certainly does not serve to encourage reliance on psychics by police services. In this respect, the findings confirm those of previous controlled research,[104,105,110] and extend the latter by implying that many "forensic psychics" might rely on nothing more than social stereotypic images as the basis for their predictions. At the same time, the occasional report of a psychic's advice being helpful to a criminal investigation will presumably serve to keep this issue open.

An anonymous referee has raised the possibility that the data simply reflect differences in intelligence across groups. This point clearly needs further exploration in future studies with covariance of I.Q. with group assignment and profile accuracy scores. However, as a rudimentary insight into the possible influence of I.Q. in the present study, consideration will be made between the educational standards of the groups. On this point, it is interesting to note that the educational level of detectives (undertaken by all police participants) in the present sample is equivalent to a postgraduate qualification in criminal law. Yet police demonstrated a lower trend in profile accuracy than most other groups. In contrast, three of the five profilers' highest tertiary qualification was only a bachelor degree. Consequently, the present samples seem to demonstrate an inverse trend in their educational achievements in comparison to the outcomes of their profiling accuracy.

Finally, an extensive amount of literature documents the inability of psychologists' professional assessments to be any more reliable than those offered by lay persons.[115] Clearly, consideration of this point must be examined in future research which identifies psychological skills for a crime profiling task. However, it must be clarified that previous literature deals with issues related to psychological assessments for such purposes as personality assessments, prediction of recidivism, dangerousness, etc. Although colloquially referred to as Psychological Profiling, the requisite task of the present study predominantly deals with the inference of offender demographic features from crime scene evidence and represents a different task from that which has been previously examined and typically undertaken by psychologists. Indeed, the process of profiling is described as an inverse process to a clinical diagnosis where the evidence of behaviors are present and are used to describe features of an unknown individual.[46,57,67,116] Thus, the present study does make a tentative original contribution to understanding the abilities of psychologists in this distinct task.

In conclusion, it must be emphasized that there remains a need for further research into the skills involved in successful psychological profiling. The present study has generated some suggestive trends, but it also has some methodological limitations of which one should be mindful. The small size of the profilers' group not only impedes the chances of statistical significance, but also raises substantial doubts about this group's representativeness of profilers as a whole. Additionally, the profiling task entailed just a single murder case. Thus, the study's findings could have been biased by the extent to which that case is typical of all murders, the extent to which its solution is transparent, and the extent to which murder is a crime conducive to the application of psychological profiling techniques. Finally, the study relied on the observations by Hazelwood et al.[97] as a guide to the underlying skills of psychological profiling. There may, of course, be other relevant skills that warrant scrutiny in future studies.

References

1. Harris, D. R., Maxfield, M., and Hollady, G., Basic elements of intelligence, *U.S. Department of Justice, Law Enforcement Assistance Administration*, Washington, D.C., 1976.

2. Frost, C. C. and Morris, J., *Police Intelligence Reports*, Loomis, CA: Palmer Enterprises, 1983.

3. Kedzior, R., *A Modern Management Tool for Police Administrators: Strategic Intelligence Analysis*, Toronto: Criminal Intelligence Service, Canada, 1995.

4. Peterson, M. B., *Applications in Criminal Analysis: a Source Book*, Westport, CT: Greenwood Press, 1994.

5. Royal Canadian Mounted Police, *Criminal Intelligence Program: Implementation Guide*, Ottawa: June, 1991.

6. Eldridge, L., *Applying Criminal Intelligence to Community Policing: the Sheffield (U.K.) Case*, unpublished paper, 1998.

7. Royal Canadian Mounted Police, *Criminal Intelligence Program: Roles and Functions*, Headquarters Criminal Intelligence Management Steering Committee, Ottawa: August, 1991.

8. Dintino, J. J. and Clinton, L. P., The investigative function: Reassessing the quality of management, *The Police Chief*, June, 55-88, 1984.

9. Coe, C. C., Domestic police intelligence: capturing its history and reflecting on its future, *Intelligence: the Ultimate Managerial Tool, Law Enforcement Intelligence Unit*, 1983.

10. Frost, C. C., The catalyst role of intelligence in drug law enforcement, *The Police Chief*, June, 69-70, 1976.

11. McDowell, C. P., False alligators and fuzzy data: a new look at crime analysis, *The Police Chief*, 57 (3):44-45, 1990.

12. Wu, Jian Kang and Desai, N., Identifying faces using multiple retrievals, *Ieee Multimedia*, 1(2):27-38, 1994.

13. Zadeh, L. A., Fu, K. S., Tanaka, K., and Shimura, M., Eds., *Fuzzy Sets and Their Applications to Cognitive and Decision Process*, New York: Academic Press, 1975.

14. Zadeh, L. A., *Fuzzy Sets, Inf. Control*, 8:338-353, 1965.

15. Kaufmann, A., *Introduction to the Theory of Fuzzy Subsets*, Vol. I, New York: Academic Press, 1975.

16. Zimmerman, H. J., *Fuzzy Set Theory and its Applications*, Leiden: Klerwer, 1985.

17. Kempton, W., Category grading and taxonomic relations: a mug is a sort of cup, in Smithson, M., *Fuzzy Set Analysis for Behavioral and Social Sciences*, New York: Springer-Verlag, 16-17, 1987.

18. Nowakowska, M., Methodological problems of measurement of fuzzy concepts in the social sciences, *Behav. Sci.*, 22:107-115, 1977.

19. Clifford, B. R. and Bull, R., *The Psychology of Person Identification*, London: Routledge and Kegan Paul, 1978.

20. Home office report of the departmental committee on evidence of identification in criminal cases, *Devlin Report*, London: HMSO, 1976.

21. Mayhew, P., Crime in public view: surveillance and crime prevention, in P. J. Brantingham and P. L. Brantingham, Eds., *Environmental Criminology*, Prospect Heights, IL: Waveland Press, 1991.

22. Bennett, T., Burglars choice of targets, in D. J. Evans and D. T. Herbert, Eds., *The Geography of Crime*, London: Routledge: 176-192, 1989.

23. Cornish, D. B. and Clarke, R. V., *The Reasoning Criminal: Rational Choice Perspectives on Offending*, New York: Springler-Verlag, 1986.

24. Cromwell, P. F., Olson, J. N., and Avary, D. W., Breaking and Entering: an Ethnographic Analysis of Burglary, Newbury Park, CA: Sage, 1991.

25. Rengert, G. F. and Wasilchick, T., *Suburban Burglary*, Springfield, IL: Charles C Thomas, 1985.

26. Brantingham, P. J. and Brantingham, P. L., Environment, routine and situation: toward a pattern theory of crime, in R. V. Clarke and M. Felson, Eds., *Routine Activity and Rational Choice: Advances in Criminological Theory*, Vol. 5, New Brunswick, NJ: Transaction Publishers, 1993.

27. Rossmo, K., *Geographical Profiling: Target Patterns of Serial Murderers*, unpublished doctorate thesis, School of Criminology, Burnaby: Simon Fraser University, 1995.

28. Dubois, D. and Prade, H., *Fuzzy Sets and Systems: Theory and Applications*, New York: Academic Press, 1980.

29. Zadeh, L. A., Fu, K. S., Tanaka, K., and Shimura, M., Eds., *Fuzzy Sets and Their Applications to Cognitive and Decision Process*, New York: Academic Press, 1975.

30. Smithson, M., *Fuzzy set analysis for behavioral and social sciences*, London: Springer-Verlag, 1987.

31. Dunham, R. G. and Alpert, G. P., *Critical Issues in Policing: Contemporary Readings*, Prospect Heights, IL: Waveland Press,135-136, 1989.

32. Black, D. and Reiss, A. J., Police control of juveniles, *Am. Soc. Rev.*, 35: 63-77, 1970.

33. Davis, K. C., *Police discretion*, St. Paul: West Publishing, 1975.

34. Smith, D. A. and Visher, C., Street level justice: situational determinants of police arrest decisions, *Soc. Probl.*, 29: 167-178, 1981.

35. Klinger, D. A., Demeanor or crime? An inquiry into why 'hostile' citizens are more likely to be arrested, *Criminology*, 32: 475-493, 1994.

36. Kuner, C. B., The interpretation of multilingual treaties: comparison of texts versus the presumption of similar meaning, *Int. Comp. Law Q.*, 40(4):953-964, 1991.

37. Booysen, H., The wide meaning, the narrow meaning and an international law meaning of Article viii(2)(b) of the International Monetary Fund Agreement. *Comp. Int. Law J.*, 26(3):352-363, 1993.

38. Peletz, Michael G., Sacred texts and dangerous words: the politics of law and cultural rationalization in Malaysia, *Comp. Stud. Soc. Hist.*, 35(1):66-109, 1993.

39. Brugger, W., Legal interpretation, schools of jurisprudence, and anthropology: some remarks from a German point of view, *Am. J. Comp. Law*, 42(2):395-422, 1994.

40. Yang, C., Public security offences and their impact on crime rates in china, *Br. J. Criminology*, 34(1):54-68, 1994.

41. Government of India, Indian Penal Code, Nasik: *Government of India Press*, 1996.

42. Government of India, Maintenance of Internal Security Act-1975, Faridabad: *Government of India Press*, 1975.

43. Tamanaha, B. Z., Post-1997 Hong Kong: a comparative study of the meaning of high degree of autonomy, *Calif. West. Int. Law J.*, 20(1):41-66, 1989.

44. Ault, R. L., Jr. and Reese, J. T., Psychological assessment of criminal profiling. In Committee on the Judiciary (1984), in *Hearing Before the Subcommittee on Juvenile Justice of the Committee on the Judiciary United States Senate Ninety-eighth Congress. First Session on Patterns of Murders Committed by One Person in Large Numbers with no Apparent Rhyme, Reason, or Motivation*, July 12, 1983, Serial No. j-98-52, Washington, D.C.: U.S. Government Printing Office. Reprinted from FBI Law Enforcement Bulletin, 1980. September 1-4, 1980.

45. Ressler, R., Burgess, A. W., and Douglas, J., *Sexual Homicide: Patterns and Motives*, Lexington, MA: Lexington Books, 1988.

46. Douglas. J. and Olshaker, M., *Mindhunter*, New York: Scribner, 1995.

47. Lester, D., *Serial Killers: the Insatiable Passion*, Philadelphia, PA: The Charles Press, 1995.

48. Ressler, R., Douglas, J., Burgess, A. W., and Burgess, A. G., *Crime Classification Manual*, London: Simon and Schuster, 1992.

49. Brown, J. S.,The psychopathology of serial sexual homicide, *Am. J. Forensic Psych.*, 12, 11-24, 1991

50. Hickey, E., *Serial murderers and their victims*, 2nd ed., Belmont, CA: Wadsworth, 1997.

51. Douglas, J. and Burgess, A., Criminal profiling: a viable investigative tool against violent crime, *FBI Law Enforcement Bull.*, 55, 9-13, 1986.

52. Meloy, J. R., *Violent Attachments*, New Jersey: Aronson, 1997.

53. Hickey, E., *Serial Murderers and Their Victims*, Pacific Grove, CA: Brooks and Cole, 1991.

54. Freud, S., Beyond the pleasure principle, in J. Strachey, Ed., *The Complete Psychological Works of Sigmund Freud*, Vol. 18, London: Hogarth Press, 1962.

55. FBI Law Enforcement Bulletin (1985), Classifying sexual homicide crime scenes: Inter-rater reliability, reprinted in *NCAVC criminal investigative analysis: sexual homicide*, Quantico, VA, 1990.

56. Holmes, R. M. and Holmes, S., *Profiling Violent Crimes: an Investigative Tool*, 2nd ed., Sage: CA, 1996.

57. Dietz, P. E., Sex offender profiling by the FBI: a preliminary conceptual model, in M. H. Ben-Aron, S. J. Hucker, and C. D. Webster, Eds., *Criminal Criminology: the Assessment and Treatment of Criminal Behavior*, Pittsburgh, PA: American Academy of Psychiatry and Law, 1985.

58. Revitch, E. and Schlesinger, L. B., Murder, evaluation, classification, and prediction, in S. B. Kutash, L. B. Schlesinger and Associates, Eds., *Violent Perspectives on Murder and Aggression*, San Francisco: Jasey, 1978, 138-164.

59. Storr, A., *Human destructiveness*, New York: Basic Books, 1972.

60. Fox, J. and Levin, J., *Overkill: Mass Murder and Serial Killing Exposed*, New York: Plenum Press, 1994.

61. Hare, R. D., *Without Conscience*, New York: Pocket Books, 1991.

62. Lewis, D. O., Pincus, J. H., Bard, B., Richardson, E., Prichep, L. S., Feldman, M., and Yeager, C., Neuropsychiatric, psycho-educational, and family characteristics of 14 juveniles condemned to death in the United States, *Am. J. Psych.*, 145, 584-589,1988.

63. Prentky, R. A., Burgess, A. W., Rokous, F., Lee, A., Hartman, C., Ressler, R., and Douglas, J., The presumptive role of fantasy in serial sexual homicide, *Am. J. Psych.*, 146, 887-891, 1989.

64. Shapiro, D., *Autonomy and Rigid Character*, New York: Basic Books, 1981.

65. DeHart, D. D. and Mahoney, J. M., The serial murderer's motivations: an interdisciplinary review, *Omega*, 29, 29-45, 1994.

66. Caputi, J., *The Age of Sex Crime*, London: The Women's Press Ltd., 1987.

67. Burgess, A. W., Hartman, C. R., Ressler, R. K., Douglas, J. E., and McCormack, A., Sexual homicide: a motivational model, *J. Interpersonal Violence*, 1, 251-272, 1986.

68. Terr, L., Childhood traumas: an outline and overview, *Am. J. Psych.*, 148, 10-20, 1991.

69. Lion, J., Pitfalls in the assessment and measurement of violence, *J. Neuropsychiatr. Clin. Neurosciences*, 3, 540-543, 1991.

70. Busch, K. A. and Cavanaugh, J. L., The study of multiple murder: preliminary examination of the interface between epistemology and methodology, *J. Interpersonal Violence*, 1 5-23, 1986.

71. Ressler, R., Burgess, A., and Douglas, J., Rape and rape-murder: one offender and twelve victims, *Am. J. Psychiatr.*, 140, 36-40, 1983.

72. Ressler, R., Burgess, A., D'Agostino, R., and Douglas, J., Serial murder: a new phenomenon of homicide, paper presented at the tenth triennial meeting of the International Association of Forensic Sciences, Oxford, England, 1984.

73. Canter, D., *Criminal Shadows: Inside the Mind of the Serial Killer*, London: Harper-Collins, 1994.

74. Katz, J., *Seductions of Crime*, New York: Basic Books, 1988.

75. Stephenson, G. M., *The Psychology of Criminal Justice*, Oxford: Blackwell, 1992.

76. Liebert, J., Contributions of psychiatric consultation in the investigation of serial murder, *Int. J. Offender Ther. Comp. Criminology*, 29, 187-200, 1985.

77. Wilson, P., Lincoln, R., and Kocsis, R., Validity, utility and ethics of profiling for serial violent and sexual offenders, *J. Psychiatr., Psychol. Law*, 4, 1-12, 1997.

78. Hilgard, E. R., *Divided Consciousness: Multiple Controls in Human Thought and Action*, New York: Wiley, 1977.

79. Sewell, J. D., An application of Megargee's algebra of aggression to the case of Theodore Bundy, *J. Police Criminal Psychol.*, 1, 14-24, 1985.

80. Dietz, P. E., Hazelwood, R, and Warren, J., The sexually sadistic criminal and his offenses, *Bull. Am. Acad. Psychiatr. Law*, 18 163-178, 1990.

81. Keppel, R. and Walter, R., Profiling killers: a revised classification model for understanding sexual murder, *Int. J. Offender Ther. Comp. Criminology*, 43:417-437, 1999.

82. Gresswell, D. M. and Hollin, C. R., Multiple murder: a review, *Br. J. Criminology*, 34, (1), 1-13, 1994.

83. Hazelwood, R. R. and Warren, J., Serial rapists, *FBI Law Enforcement Bull.*, 18-25, January, 1989.

84. Cohen, M. L., The psychology of rapists, *Semin. Psychiatr.*, 3, 307-325, 1971.

85. Groth, A., Burgess. A., and Holmstrom, L., Rape, power, anger, and sexuality, *Am. J. Psychiatr.*, 134, 1239-1243, 1997.

86. Hazelwood, R. R. and Burgess, A. W., An introduction to the serial rapist, *FBI Law Enforcement Bull.*, 16-24, September, 1987.

87. Peirce, C. S., Ampliative reasoning, in N. Rescher, *Induction: An essay on the Justification of Inductive Reasoning*, Oxford: Blackwell, 1980.

88. Newman, J. H., *Apologia Pro Vita Sua: Being a History of His Religious Opinions*, London: Oxford University Press, 1870.

89. Godwin, M., *Hunting Serial Predators: a Multivariate Classification Approach to Profiling Violent Behavior*, Boca Raton, FL: CRC Press.

90. Godwin, M. and Canter, D., Encounter and death: the spatial behaviour of U.S. serial killers, *Policing Int. J. Police Management Strategies*, 20, 24-38, 1997.

91. Bartol, C. R. and Bartol, A. M., *Psychology and Law*, Pacific Grove, CA: Brooks/Cole, 1994.

92. Jackson, J. L. and Bekerian, D. A., Does offender profiling have a role to play? In J. L. Jackson and D. A. Bekerian, Eds., *Offender Profiling: Theory, Research and Practice*, Chichester, U.K.: Wiley, 1997, 1-7.

93. Turco, R. N., Psychological profiling, *Int. J. Offender Ther. Comp. Criminology*, 34, 147-154, 1990.

94. Teten, H. D., Offender profiling, in W. G. Bailey, Ed., *The Encyclopedia of Police Science*, New York: Garland, 1989, 365-367.

95. Oleson, J. C., Psychological profiling: does it actually work? *Forensic Update*, 46, 11-14, 1996.

96. Gudjonsson, G. H. and Copson, G., The role of the expert in criminal investigation, in J. L. Jackson and D. A. Bekerian, Eds., *Offender Profiling: Theory, Research, and Practice*, Chichester, U.K.: Wiley, 1997, 61-76.

97. Hazelwood, R. R., Ressler, R. K., Depue, R. L., and Douglas, J. C., Criminal investigative analysis: an overview, in R. R. Hazelwood and A. W. Burgess, Eds., *Practical Aspects of Rape Investigation: a Multidisciplinary Approach*, 2nd ed., Boca Raton, FL: CRC Press, 1995, 115-126.

98. Douglas, J. E., Burgess, A. W., Burgess, A. G., and Ressler, R. K., *Crime Classification Manual*, London: Simon and Schuster, 1993.

99. Jackson, J. L., Herbrink, J. C. M., and van Koppen, P., An empirical approach to offender profiling, in S. Redondo, V. Garrido, J. Pérez, and R. Barberet, Eds., *Advances in Psychology and Law*, Berlin: de Gruyter, 1997, 333-345.

100. Jackson, J. L., van den Eshof, P., and de Kleuver, E. E., A research approach to offender profiling, in J. L. Jackson and D. A. Bekerian, Eds., *Offender Profiling: Theory, Research and Practice*, Chichester, U.K.: Wiley, 1997, 107-132.

101. Britton, P., *The Jigsaw Man*, London: Bantam Press, 1997.

102. Canter, D., *Profiling as poison*, on-line article, available: http://www.liv.ac.uk/ InvestigativePsychology/invpub.htm, August, 1998.

103. Harrower, J., *Applying Psychology to Crime*, London: Hodder and Stoughton, 1998.

104. Reiser, M., Ludwig, L., Saxe, S., and Wagner, C., An evaluation of the use of psychics in the investigation of major crimes, *J. Police Sci. Admin.*, 7, 18-25, 1979.

105. Wiseman, R., West. D., and Stemman, R., An experimental test of psychic detection, *J. Soc. Psychical Res.*, 61, 34-40, 1996.

106. Randi, J., Atlanta child murderer: psychics' failed visions, *Skeptical Inquirer*, 7(1), 12-13, 1982.

107. Lyons, A. and Truzzi, M., *The Blue Sense: Psychic Detectives and Crime*, New York: Warner, 1991.

108. Pinizzotto, A. J. and Finkel, N. J., Criminal personality profiling: an outcome and process study, *Law Hum. Behav.*, 14, 215-233, 1990.

109. Pinizzotto, A. J., Criminal personality profiling: an outcome and process study, unpublished doctoral dissertation, graduate school, Georgetown University, 1988.

110. Reiser, M. and Klyver, N., A comparison of psychics, detectives, and students in the investigation of major crimes, in M. Reiser, Ed., *Police Psychology: Collected Papers*, Los Angeles, CA: LEHI, 1982, 260-267.

111. Campbell, C., Portrait of a mass killer, *Psychol. Today*, 9: 110-119, May, 1976.

112. Gough, H. G. and Heilbrun, A. B., *The Adjective Check List: Manual*, Palo Alto, CA: Consulting Psychologists Press, 1983.

113. Becker, B. J., Applying tests of combined significance in meta-analysis, *Psychological Bulletin*, 102:164-171, 1997.

114. Darlington, R. B. and Hayes, A. F., *Vulnerability, Specificity, and the File Drawer Problem in Meta-Analytic Probability Poolers*, submitted for publication, 1998.

115. Monhan, J. and Steadman, H. J., Eds., *Violence and Mental Disorder*, Chicago: University of Chicago Press, 1994.

116. Douglas, J. E. and Olshaker, M., *Journey into Darkness*, London: Heinemann, 1997.

Offender Characteristics Questionnaire

Instructions: This questionnaire systematically surveys the principal charac-teristics of the offender who committed this crime. For each item, indicate your prediction of the offender's characteristics by circling the appropriate number in the response column. If you think you know the correct answer but your answer is not among the options, choose the option that is closest to your answer. If you are unsure of the correct answer, simply <u>guess</u> at it. Make sure you complete each item.

Questionnaire Items

Physical Characteristics

*1. The offender is (1) male; (2) female.
*2. The offender is aged (1) 1-12 years; (2) 13-17; (3) 18-25; (4) 26-35; (5) 36-45; (6) 46-55; (7) over 56 years.
*3. The offender's ethnic background is (1) Anglo-Saxon; (2) Mediterranean; (3) Eastern European; (4) Middle Eastern; (5) Asian; (6) Aboriginal; (7) Afro-American; (8) Other.
4. Offender's general build: (1) thin; (2) average; (3) solid; (4) fat.
5. Offender's height: (1) very short; (2) short; (3) average; (4) tall; (5) very tall.
6. Offender's hair color: (1) brown; (2) red; (3) blonde; (4) black; (5) gray; (6) none/bald.

Cognitive Processes

7. Prior to the offense, was the offender familiar with the location where the offense took place? (1) yes, highly familiar; (2) yes, vaguely famil-iar; (3) no.
8. Did the offender feel comfortable in the area where the offense took place? (1) yes; (2) no.

*9. Previous relationship between the offender and the victim: (1) blood relatives; (2) mutual acquaintances, but not related by blood; (3) offender knew victim, but victim did not know offender; (4) complete strangers.

10. What was the primary motive for the offense? (1) revenge; (2) uncontrollable impulse; (3) show of power; (4) feelings of inadequacy; (5) frustration; (6) jealousy; (7) other.

11. The offense was (1) totally unplanned, spontaneous; (2) thought of previously but never actually planned; (3) some planning; (4) carefully planned.

12. Prior to the offense did the offender have fantasies about killing someone? (1) no; (2) yes, sometimes; (3) yes, often; (4) yes, constantly.

13. Did the offender experience any remorse about the offense? (1) yes, a great deal; (2) yes, some; (3) no.

Offense Behaviors

*14. At the time of the offense, did the offender live within a five kilometer radius of the location where the offense took place? (1) yes; (2) no.

15. Did the offender take any precautions to protect his/her identity from the victim? (1) yes; (2) no.

16. How did the offender initially approach the victim? (1) slowly/casually; (2) with a con or ploy to detain the victim; (3) belligerently; (4) by surprise (e.g., from behind or during sleep).

17. Did the offender use force before committing the actual offense? (1) no; (2) yes, primarily to gain control over the victim; (3) yes, primarily to intimidate the victim; (4) yes, primarily to see the victim suffer; (5) yes, primarily in a drive for revenge; (6) yes, primarily in anger.

18. After the offense, did the offender alter the victim's body in any way (e.g., rearrange clothing, reposition body?) (1) yes; (2) no.

19. After the offense, did the offender do anything to alter the crime scene? (e.g. remove evidence, cleaning up?) (1) yes; (2) no.

20. Did the offender take away from the crime scene any possessions of the victim? (1) yes; (2) no.

History and Habits

21. The offender's marital status: (1) single; (2) married; (3) living in a defacto relationship; (4) divorced.

22. The offender's highest level of education: (1) nil; (2) did not complete primary school; (3) completed primary school; (4) dropped out of high school; (5) completed high school; (6) completed technical college course; (7) completed university degree.

*23. The offender's general employment history: (1) student, not yet employed; (2) mostly unemployed; (3) irregular, part time employment; (4) regular work as a laborer; (5) regular semi- skilled work; (6) regular skilled work; (7) professional.

24. The offender's current religious belief: (1) Protestant; (2) Catholic; (3) Greek Orthodox; (4) Jewish, (5) Muslim; (6) Buddhist; (7) Taoist; (8) nil (atheist, agnostic); (9) other.

25. Offender's history of romantic relationships: (1) no prior relationships; (2) very few brief casual relationships; (3) a few relatively long casual relationships; (4) many short casual relationships; (5) many long casual relationships; (6) a few relatively short serious relationships, (7) a few relatively long serious relationships; (8) many short serious relationships; (9) many long, serious relationships.

26. Offender's history of (nonromantic) friendships: (1) no friendships; (2) very few brief casual friendships; (3) a few relatively long casual friendships; (4) many short casual friendships; (5) many long casual friendships; (6) a few relatively short deep friendships; (7) a few relatively long deep friendships; (8) many short deep friendships; (9) many long deep friendships.

27. Did the offender ever serve in the armed forces? (1) yes; (2) no, but thought of it; (3) no.

*28. The offender's alcohol consumption: (1) nil; (2) low; (3) medium; (4) in binges; (5) high.

*29. How old is the offender's vehicle? (1) none owned; (2) 1-2 years old; (3) 3-5 years old; (4) 6-10 years old; (5) over 10 years old.

*30. Condition and model of offender's car: (1) does not apply; (2) "flashy" model in excellent condition; (3) conservative model in excellent condition; (4) "flashy" model in good condition; (5) conservative model in good condition; (6) "flashy" model in poor condition; (7) conservative model in poor condition.

Pinizzotto and Finkel
All questions starred above, plus:

31. The offender's work habits: (1) steady, dependable, hard worker; (2) misses work frequently, but works well when present; (3) attends work frequently, but works poorly when present; (4) misses work frequently, and works poorly when present.

32. Does the offender have a juvenile record of assaults? (1) yes, several; (2) yes, one or two; (3) no.

33. Does the offender have adult convictions for assault? (1) yes, several; (2) yes, one or two; (3) no.

Classifying Crime Scene Behavior: New Directions

3

3.1 Exploring the Social Context of Instrumental and Expressive Homicides: An Application of Qualitative Comparative Analysis*

TERANCE D. MIETHE

KRISS A. DRASS

Using data from the FBI's Uniform Crime Reporting Program's (UCR) Supplementary Homicide Reports, the method of Qualitative Comparative Analysis (QCA) is used to examine whether instrumental and expressive homicides are similar or unique in their social context (i.e., combinations of offender, victim, and situational characteristics). Instrumental and expressive homicides are found to have both common and unique social contexts, but the vast majority of homicide incidents involve combinations of individual and situational factors that are common in both general types of homicides. Among subtypes of instrumental (i.e., rape, prostitution, and robbery murders) and expressive homicides (i.e., lovers triangles, brawls, and arguments), there is wide variability in their prevalence of unique and common components. After a discussion of these results, illustrations of how QCA may be used in other areas within criminology are presented.

3.1.1 Introduction

There are various ways to classify types of criminal homicide. State statutes distinguish between criminal and non-criminal homicides, degrees of murders, and types of manslaughters. Law enforcement agencies often categorize homicides according to the characteristics of the offender (e.g., gang versus non-gang), the victim (e.g., child murders, teen violence, elderly victims), or situational context or attributes (e.g., domestic violence, stranger assaults, drive-by shootings, robbery-murders, road rage, or workplace homicides). Lawyers, social scientists, and law enforcers also classify homicides in terms of motive. Common motives for homicides include trivial altercations, jealousy, revenge, romantic triangles, robbery, sexual assault, burglary, and disputes in drug transactions.

* Originally published in *Journal of Quantitative Criminology*, 15(1), pp. 1–21, 1999. With permission.

These motives are often subclassified to differentiate between two general types of homicides: "instrumental" and "expressive" homicides.

Using data from the FBI's Uniform Crime Reporting Program's (UCR) Supplementary Homicide Reports and the method of Qualitative Comparative Analysis (QCA), the present study examines whether instrumental and expressive homicides are qualitatively different in their social context (i.e., combinations of offender, victim, and situational characteristics). We do this empirically by identifying the most prevalent combinations of individual and situational elements unique to each type of homicide, as well as those common to both, through a systematic process of holistic comparison.

3.1.2   Instrumental and Expressive Crimes

The distinction between instrumental and expressive crimes has been widely used in criminological research. Instrumental crimes are those conducted for explicit, future goals (such as to acquire money or improve one's social position), whereas expressive offenses are often unplanned acts of anger, rage, or frustration.[1-7] The instrumental–expressive distinction often parallels the differences between planned (premeditated) and spontaneous ("heat of passion") offenses.

Across a variety of different crimes, it has been a common practice of criminologists to consider instrumental acts as qualitatively different from expressive acts. Taxonomic systems for rapists, for example, employ the instrumental–expressive distinction as a fundamental dimension.[8,9] The instrumental–expressive distinction is also a critical dimension in typologies of motor vehicle theft, vandalism, political terrorism, workplace violence, and intrafamily assaults.[10-14] Violent crimes are often distinguished from other offenses (like corporate crime) based on their relative frequency of instrumental and expressive motives. The presumed difference in the relative frequency of expressive and instrumental motivations for violence in the North and South has been used as an explanation for regional variation in homicide rates among African Americans.[15] Furthermore, studies of criminal careers have employed this distinction, asserting that early criminal careers begin with the commission of expressive crimes, and serious criminal careers are often continued for instrumental reasons.[16]

From the perspective of crime control, the relative prevalence and nature of instrumental and expressive crimes has important policy implications. Under the deterrence doctrine, the threat of legal sanction is considered most effective for instrumental crimes by persons with low commitment to a criminal lifestyle.[17-19] Expressive crimes, in contrast, are often viewed as undeterrable by legal sanctions. Other crime prevention and intervention strategies are also tied directly to the instrumental–expressive distinction. Treatment programs for impulsivity and anger management, for example, are directed at the control of expressive acts, whereas an assortment of social betterment measures (like job training, family counseling, and educational enhancement) are often advocated as corrective actions to abate the conditions that motivate instrumental crimes. Crime control efforts through environmental design and situational crime prevention techniques may be equally effective for both instrumental and expressive crimes, by increasing the costs for the reasoning instrumental offender and decreasing the opportunities for spontaneous or expressive criminality.[20,21] Regardless of the particular crime control strategy, however, it is widely assumed that instrumental and expressive crimes are unique in the characteristics of their offenders, victims, and situational elements.

When applied to the study of homicide, particular circumstances and motivations are often categorized as either instrumental or expressive crimes. Arguments, brawls, romantic triangles, youth gang killings, and other interpersonal disputes are typically classified as expressive acts because their dominant motivation is the violence itself.[2,6,22] Killings that occur in the commission of another felony are the most commonly classified instrumental homicides. While many homicides in these felony-type circumstances are often a side effect of another criminal act,[23] these killings are usually classified as instrumental crimes because the death of the victim is a potentially expected outcome in the pursuit of the primary goal.

Previous research provides empirical support for this subclassification of homicide circumstances as instrumental and expressive crimes. Interviews with convicted robbers, for example, indicate that a majority of these offenders were motivated by instrumental reasons such as getting money and purchasing drugs.[24–26] Most muggers do not intend to kill their victims,[23] but the precipitating actions that result in the robbery are clearly motivated by instrumental pursuits. Youth crime, especially when it occurs in a group context, is often described as impulsive, situational and opportunistic, spontaneous, and non-utilitarian. Street fights are the major triggering event in gang-related homicides,[2] providing additional support for the classification of youth gang homicides as expressive offenses. However, for other homicide situations (e.g, revenge or "payback" killings), it is difficult to classify motive unequivocally on an instrumental-expressive dichotomy.[22]

While most criminological research treats instrumental and expressive acts as distinct entities, several alternative conceptualizations have been employed in past studies. Block and Block, for example, consider expressive and instrumental motives as different points along a continuum.[1] These authors also note that both types of motives may be present among the same types of crimes. For instance, street gang violence may result from instrumental, entrepreneurial activities, such as drug trafficking, whereas other violent gang situations involve impulsive, emotional, expressive outbursts (Block and Block, 1993). In contrast, Felson interprets all aggressive behavior as goal-oriented or instrumental because "it is an attempt to achieve what people value."[27] From this perspective, even expressive acts of violence done in anger reflect an instrumental reaction to perceived wrongdoing.

3.1.3   The Current Study

While the instrumental-expressive distinction is widely used in criminological research and policy, there is still debate about its usefulness and validity as a basis for differentiating types of crime. Research in this area often assumes that instrumental and expressive motives are conceptually distinct, producing qualitatively different types of crime. However, some researchers argue that instrumental and expressive acts are best viewed as polar ends of a continuum, thus allowing for the possibility that a crime contains elements of both. Under Felson's conceptualization, this distinction by motive is not very useful because all violent acts ultimately have instrumental motivations.[27]

The purpose of the current study is to address these issues by examining empirically whether instrumental and expressive homicides are qualitatively different in their social contexts (i.e., particular combinations of offender, victim, and situational factors). Three basic questions underlie this research. First, do instrumental and expressive homicides have similar or different structures in terms of their particular offender, victim, and situational attributes? Second, what are the common and unique characteristics of these homicide types? Third, is the relative prevalence of these unique and common characteristics the same among subsets of instrumental homicides (like rape– and robbery–murders) and expressive homicides (like love triangles, brawls, and arguments)?

Previous research provides mixed predictions about whether different individual and situational attributes underlie different homicide motives. Under Felson's assertion that all aggressive actions derive from the same basic instrumental values, both expressive and instrumental homicide should occur in the same contexts and share common explanatory factors because uniquely expressive motives do not exist.[27] A finding of different contexts for instrumental and expressive homicides would question the characterization of a singular motivational structure for all homicides. In contrast, other researchers, such as Decker[6] and Maxfield[23] observe that expressive violence is more concentrated among persons in primary or intimate relations, whereas instrumental violence is more common among strangers. Decker also contends that persons excluded from mainstream urban life (e.g., young black males) are more prone to deviate from this pattern of primary-expressive and stranger-instrumental homicides.[6] These latter observations suggest that unique combinations of individual and situational factors may underlie different homicide motives. We employ the method of QCA to examine more systematically these rival claims about the prevalence of unique and common characteristics of instrumental and expressive homicides.

3.1.4 Data Description and Methods

Data from the Supplementary Homicide Reports (SHR) are used in this study to examine the common and unique features of instrumental and expressive homicides. Characteristics of the sample and the measures of key variables are described below.

3.1.5 Supplementary Homicide Reports (SHR)

The SHR program involves supplementary information on murders and non-negligent manslaughters that are provided by law enforcement agencies as part of the FBI's Uniform Crime Reporting Program. SHR data include information on the characteristics of the offender and victim, and the situational elements and circumstances surrounding each homicide.[27] The data for this study include all single-victim, single-offender homicides for the years 1990 to 1994 that had non-missing data on the relevant variables. Over three-fourths of the homicides in which victim and offender characteristics were known involved one-on-one events. Similar to other researchers,[28] our analysis is restricted to this most common type of homicide situation because of the ambiguity surrounding classification of individual attributes in multiple victim-offender homicides.

As a source of information on homicide, the SHR files are the single most comprehensive data source on individual cases. Similar to other UCR data, a limitation of this source is that reporting of crime data by law enforcement agencies is done on a voluntary basis. Other particular problems with the SHR files, such as missing data and ambiguity in the classification of circumstances, are widely known.[23,29–32] For the time frame utilized for this study, missing data on offender characteristics (like gender, age, and race), the victim-offender relationship, and the specific circumstances or motive were found in about one third of the cases. While non-random undercounting of homicide situations, missing data, and problems with initial police classification of motives are major problems with this data source,[23,29] the SHR files are nonetheless utilized here because they still represent the most comprehensive national data on homicide situations.

3.1.6 Measures of Variables

The major variables include type of homicide, offender characteristics, victim characteristics, and situational elements. Offender, victim, and situational elements are used to examine the common and unique configurations that underlie instrumental and expressive homicides.

Instrumental homicides involve all felony-type circumstances in the SHR data, including robbery, rape, burglary, drug offenses, motor vehicle theft, and other felony-type situations.[33] Robbery-homicides are the most common type of offense in this classification. Expressive homicides include arguments, brawls, romantic triangles, and youth gang killings. Arguments are by far the most common triggering event for all homicides and for this presumed group of expressive homicides. Previous research has used a similar classification scheme for differentiating instrumental and expressive motives.[6,22,23] When missing data and homicides with unclear motivations, such as sniper attacks or baby sitter killings, are excluded from the analysis, about one fifth of the homicides are classified as instrumental crimes, and the remaining four fifths are considered expressive crimes (see Table 3.1.1).

The specific offender characteristics used to differentiate types of homicide include gender, race, and age. Similar variables are included as victim characteristics. Situational elements involve the victim-offender relationship, gun use, and location of the homicide. The race of the offender and victim is coded as either White, African-American, or Hispanic. The age of the offender and victim includes the categories "less than 20," "20 to 39 years old," and "40 and over." Our selection of these particular categories is based on the growing public interest in youth homicide and the underlying age distributions in the sample. These age categories are also similar to those used in past homicide studies.[6] Following the Maxfield and Decker approach, the victim-offender relationship is coded into the categories "strangers," "acquaintances," and "family members/intimates." Weapon is coded to compare deaths involving firearms with those involving direct personal contact (e.g., knives, sharp objects, blunt objects, fists). The location of the offense contrasts large urban areas (population over 100,000) with smaller cities and towns. Combined, we consider this particular set of offender, victim, and situational elements to capture major components of the social context of crime events that have been examined in past research.[34,35]

Looking at the modal categories for the variables (see Table 3.1.1), homicides in the total sample most often involve offenders who are male, African Americans, and between the ages of 20 and 39 years old. The typical victim in this sample also possesses the same characteristics. Concerning situational elements, victims and offenders are acquaintances in the majority of homicides, and over half of these killings involve a firearm and happen in an urban setting. Most of these patterns hold for both instrumental and expressive homicides. However, a notable difference is that stranger assaults are far more common among instrumental crimes, whereas slayings of family members or intimate parties (like boyfriends) are more common among expressive homicides.

3.1.7 Analytic Procedures

Comparing modal categories allows us to describe similarities and differences in the general features of instrumental and expressive homicides. However,

Table 3.1.1   Frequencies, Codings, and Value Labels for All Variables (N = 34329)

Variables	Value Labels[a]	N	% Total	% Instrumental	% Expressive
Type of Homicide					
Instrumental		7005	20.4		
Expressive		27324	79.6		
Offender Characteristics					
White[b]	OWHITE	11621	33.9	30.0	34.8
African American	OAA	18751	54.6	62.2	52.7
Hispanic	OHISP	3957	11.5	7.7	12.5
Under 20 Years of Age	O < 20	6517	19.0	25.5	17.3
20 to 39 Years of Age	O20-39	21184	61.7	64.5	61.0
40 Years of Age or Older[b]	O40+	6628	19.3	10.0	21.7
Male	OMALE	30048	87.5	94.4	85.8
Female[b]	OFEMALE	4281	12.5	5.6	14.2
Victim Characteristics					
White[b]	VWHITE	13047	38.8	42.6	36.8
African American	VAA	17364	50.6	49.7	50.8
Hispanic	VHISP	3918	11.4	7.7	12.4
Under 20 Years of Age	V < 20	4642	13.5	15.1	13.1
20 to 39 Years of Age	V20-39	21062	61.4	54.4	63.1
40 Years of Age or Older[b]	V40+	8625	25.1	30.5	23.7
Male	VMALE	26319	76.7	77.6	76.4
Female[b]	VFEMALE	8010	23.3	22.4	23.6
Situational Characteristics					
Victim and Offender Acquaintances[b]	ACQUAINT	18843	54.9	51.4	55.8
Victim and Offender Family or other Intimates	FAM/INT	9706	28.3	9.1	33.2
Victim and Offender Strangers	STRANGER	5780	16.8	39.5	11.0
Gun Used	GUN	22564	65.7	65.0	65.9
No Gun Used[b]		11765	34.3	35.0	34.1
Urban Setting	URBAN	18408	53.6	57.1	52.7
Non-urban Setting[b]	RURAL	15921	46.4	42.9	47.3

[a] Descriptive labels used to represent categories in the QCA results.
[b] Excluded category. For all variables, 1 = Yes and 0 = No.

these comparisons do not tell us whether there are similarities or differences in the way offender, victim, and situational attributes *combine* to form actual criminal events. To answer this question, we need an analytic approach that makes holistic comparisons, identifying similarities and differences in the combinations of offender, victim, and situational characteristics that define the contexts within which instrumental and expressive homicides occur.

The method of Qualitative Comparative Analysis[37–39] is used in this study to identify the common and unique features of instrumental and expressive homicides. An analysis using QCA begins with the construction of a truth table. A truth table lists all unique configurations of the offender, victim, and situational variables appearing in the data, along with the corresponding type(s) of homicide observed for each configuration. The truth table provides information about which configurations are unique to a category of the classification variable and which are found in more than one category. By comparing the numbers of configurations in these groups, we obtain an estimate of the extent to which homicide types are similar or unique.

QCA then compares the configurations within a group, looking for commonalities that allow configurations to be combined into simpler, yet more abstract, representations. Briefly, this is done by identifying and eliminating unnecessary variables from configurations. QCA considers a variable unnecessary if its presence or absence within a configuration has no impact on the outcome associated with the configuration. For example, suppose configurations ABC and ABc (where upper case indicates presence or 1, and lower case indicates absence or 0) both produce the same type of crime. Since both configurations produce the same outcome, they would be assigned to the same category of the classification variable. QCA would consider variable C to be irrelevant when combined with A and B (i.e., within the context of A and B) since Y occurs regardless of the value of C. Thus, QCA would replace these two configurations (ABC, ABc) with the single, simpler configuration AB. However, variable C is removed only from these two configurations; it may be necessary to produce Y when combined with other variables. It is in this manner that QCA produces case-based rather than variable-based results.

QCA repeats these comparisons until no further reductions are possible. Redundancies among the remaining reduced configurations are eliminated, producing the final solution: a statement of the unique features of each category of the typology. When applied to criminal event data like the SHR, the results can be interpreted as profiles of the basic types of situations in which homicides occur.

Compared to standard statistical procedures like regression and ANOVA, QCA is a case-oriented approach that considers each case holistically as a configuration of attributes. For example, QCA assumes that the effect of a variable may be different from one case to another, depending upon the values of the other attributes of the case. Through systematic and logical case comparisons based on the rules of Boolean algebra, QCA identifies commonalities among these configurations, thus reducing the complexity of the typology. The end result of QCA is a typology that allows for heterogeneity within groups and defines categories in terms of configurations of attributes.

When applied to the study of instrumental and expressive homicides, QCA provides answers to several questions about their structural characteristics. First, how many different configurations of offender, victim, and situational characteristics are observed for instrumental and expressive homicides in the SHR data? Second, how many of these configurations are common to both instrumental and expressive homicides? Third, how many of these configurations are unique to instrumental homicides and to expressive homicides? Fourth, what is the nature and relative prevalence of each unique configuration of instrumental and expressive homicides? By addressing these questions, QCA provides a systematic method for examining the nature and magnitude of the similarities and differences between instrumental and expressive homicides.

3.1.8 Results

We begin our analysis by looking at the distribution of configurations of individual and situational elements by type of homicide. This information, obtained from the truth table, allows us to identify how much heterogeneity exists within each category and how well the instrumental-expressive dichotomy differentiates homicide events. The following two steps are used to assign outcome values to configurations in the truth table.

First, we identified each combination of independent variables present in the data and recorded the number of times that the combination was observed with an instrumental homicide and with an expressive homicide. This resulted in a simple contingency table in which the combinations of independent variables were the rows, and type of homicide the columns. Second, we used the cell frequencies for each type of homicide to recode or eliminate combinations that were observed relatively infrequently. A combination of independent variables was coded instrumental in the truth table if it was observed with at least five instrumental homicides and expressive if it was observed with at least twenty expressive homicides. A minimum cell frequency of five for instrumental homicides was used because this is a general rule of thumb for identifying minimum cell frequencies in the analysis of contingency tables, and a minimum cell frequency of twenty for expressive homicides was utilized to make our coding rule proportional to the marginal distribution of the homicide variable (approximately 80% of the homicides in our data are expressive). Combinations with cell frequencies below both of these minimums were not included in the truth table.

Table 3.1.2   Truth Table Summaries of Unique and Shared Homicide Situations for Instrumental and Expressive Homicides

	Instrumental				Expressive			
	Configurations		Cases		Configurations		Cases	
	N	%	N	%	N	%	N	%
Classified as Unique	144	51.4	1574	27.4	121	47.1	6174	27.8
Common to Both (Unclassified)	136	48.6	4181	72.6	136	52.9	16019	72.2
Total Observed	280	100.0	5755	100.0	257	100.0	22193	100.0

We constructed our truth table using this minimum cell frequency rule for two reasons. First, QCA gives each configuration in the truth table equal weight in terms of its impact upon the final solution. While it is important to include and model as much of the diversity in the data as possible, the coding rule helps to ensure that our results are not overly sensitive to relatively idiosyncratic situations. Second, a minimum cell frequency rule helps minimize the impact of coding error on the classification of configurations as common to both instrumental and expressive homicides. Using this rule, a reasonable minimum of both instrumental and expressive homicides, rather than a single one, must be observed before a combination is considered common to both rather than unique to one. Thus, in the final truth table analyzed using QCA, a combination of individual and situational factors was considered common to both instrumental and expressive homicides if it was observed leading to at least five instrumental homicides and at least twenty expressive homicides. Summary information about the distribution of configurations by type of homicide in the truth table are presented in Table 3.1.2.

3.1.9   The Prevalence of Unique and Common Configurations

As shown in Table 3.1.2, our coding rule produces a truth table containing 280 different configurations of offender, victim, and situational attributes associated with instrumental homicides. These 280 configurations describe the types of situations leading to instrumental homicides for 5,755 observed cases. A total of 144 of these configurations (51.4%) were classified as unique to instrumental homicide (i.e., they never, or rarely ever, resulted in an expressive homicide). These 144 unique configurations account for a little over a quarter (27.4%) of the total number of instrumental homicides in our analysis.

Table 3.1.2 also reveals that expressive homicides outnumber instrumental homicides by almost 4 to 1 (22,193 cases versus 5,755 cases). However, although many more expressive homicides occurred during this period, there is less diversity in the types of situations producing expressive homicides. Our truth table identifies only 257 different configurations of individual and situational elements among these 22,193 cases of expressive homicide. Of these, 121 (47.1%) are classified as unique to expressive homicide. These unique configurations account for 27.8% of the total number of expressive homicides in our analysis.

As we have previously stated, a QCA analysis begins with the construction of a truth table. A truth table summarizes data holistically, in terms of combinations of attributes associated with an outcome. Summary information describing the truth table for instrumental and expressive homicides reveals a great deal about the unique and common features of the social context of homicide for the period under study (see Table 3.1.2). Specifically, when we look just at the different configurations of offender, victim, and situational attributes that define the social context of homicide, we find evidence that both instrumental and expressive homicides are, to some extent, qualitatively distinct types of crimes. A little more than half (51.4%) of the instrumental homicide configurations are unique and a little less than half (47.1%) of the expressive configurations are unique. In total, there are 401 different combinations of individual and situational factors producing homicides: 144 unique to instrumental homicide, 121 unique to expressive homicide, and 136 common to both. These combinations represent different social contexts that are more or less conducive to instrumental and/or expressive homicides.

However, these results also show that these unique social contexts are not very prevalent. For both instrumental and expressive homicide, the unique configurations account for about a quarter (27.4 and 27.8%, respectively) of the observed cases. This indicates that most homicides occur in situations that cannot be clearly differentiated on the basis of the presumed motive of the offender. Nonetheless, as illustrated shortly, these common configurations do vary somewhat in terms of their relative prevalence among instrumental and expressive homicides, suggesting the existence of a continuum along which situations can be classified as more or less prevalent among instrumental and expressive homicides.

3.1.10 The Specific Profiles in Instrumental and Expressive Homicides

The next step of our analysis involves using QCA's minimization algorithms to identify common patterns within this diversity. The results can be interpreted as profiles of the basic types of situations in which homicides occur. These results are presented as dot plots[40] in Figures 3.1.1, 3.1.2, and 3.1.3. The y-axis labels describe the types of homicide situations, while the graphs depict the percentage of cases associated with each type. A tilde symbol ($\sim$) indicates a zero value for a variable (i.e., logical not). We use more descriptive value labels in these figures where possible to make the configurations easier to interpret. For ease of presentation, we report only those core combinations that account for at least 1% of the observed cases.

Figure 3.1.1 provides a dot plot representation of the core combinations of offender, victim, and situational characteristics unique to homicides classified as instrumental. One configuration is clearly dominant in terms of its relative frequency. This configuration involves a situation in which the offender is male, the victim is a non-Hispanic female, and the offender and victim are strangers. A total of 361 (22.9%) of the unique instrumental homicides involved this combination of attributes. Further, given the way QCA produces a solution, this particular combination of attributes is not found among the situations unique to expressive homicides or those situations common to both. That is, the combinations in Figure 3.1.1 identify features that differentiate unique instrumental homicides from all other homicides in our analysis. Many of the other unique configurations underlying instrumental homicides include situations involving specific combinations of male offenders who victimize non-Hispanic strangers with guns. Only three of the most prevalent profiles defined as uniquely instrumental homicides involved teenage offenders, and in each of these cases the offender was also non-Hispanic and male.

The core combinations of individual and situational attributes describing the social context of homicides classified as expressive are presented in Figure 3.1.2. Once again, one reduced configuration is dominant in terms of its relative frequency. This configuration refers to homicides between family members or other intimates, involving guns, and occurring in urban settings. A total of 1770 (28.7%) of the unique expressive homicides contain this combination of attributes, and this particular combination (like the others in Figure 3.1.2) is not found among situations unique to instrumental homicides or situations common to both. Looking at the other configurations in Figure 3.1.2, we see that the involvement of family members or other intimates, and offenders and victims with the same racial/ethnic background are features important for differentiating expressive homicide situations from instrumental homicide situations.

Core combinations of individual and situational attributes that describe situations common to both instrumental and expressive homicide are graphically illustrated in Figure 3.1.3. These configurations are those that were observed with at least five instrumental homicides and at least twenty expressive homicides. Thus, in the truth table, these configurations cannot be classified as either uniquely instrumental or uniquely expressive. However, they can be treated as a special "unclassified" or remainder group and analyzed in terms of the features that differentiate them from both uniquely instrumental homicides and uniquely expressive homicides. Aside from the nature of the specific combinations, the percentage of unclassified instrumental and expressive homicides accounted for by each configuration are also presented in Figure 3.1.3.

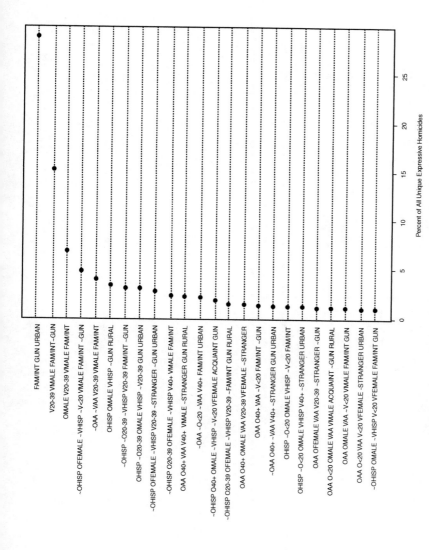

Figure 3.1.1 OCA plot representation of the core combinations of offender, victim, and situational characteristics unique to homicides classified as instrumental.

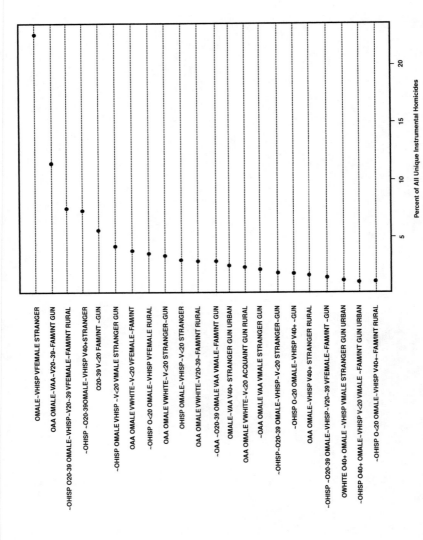

Figure 3.1.2 QCA model of the most prevalent types of unique expressive homicides.

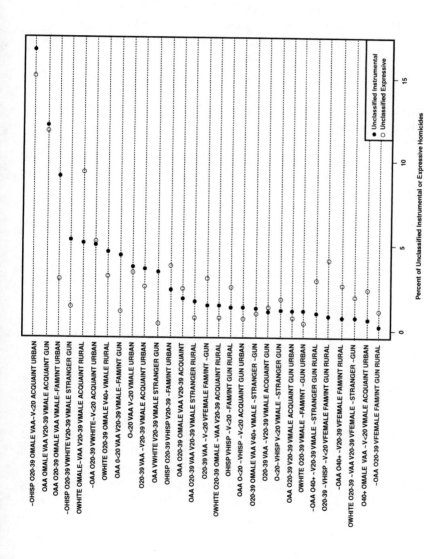

Figure 3.1.3 QCA model of the most prevalent types of situations common to both instrumental and expressive homicides.

Comparison of the relative placement of plot symbols for each configuration reveals that some combinations are relatively more prevalent among instrumental homicides, some relatively more prevalent among expressive homicides, and some about equally prevalent across both types of homicide. For example, the first configuration in Figure 3.1.3 accounts for 16.6% of the unclassified instrumental homicides and 15.0% of the unclassified expressive homicides. Thus, situations involving a non-Hispanic male offender, 20 to 39 years of age, an African-American victim over 20 years of age who is an acquaintance, and an urban setting are a little more likely among instrumental than expressive homicides. The second configuration in Figure 3.1.3 identifies a situation equally common to both unclassified instrumental and expressive homicides, while the third configuration identifies a situation that is relatively more prevalent among the unclassified instrumental homicides than it is among the unclassified expressive homicides. Thus, while all of the situations described in Figure 3.1.3 can lead to either an instrumental or expressive homicide, they can be seen as defining a continuum of social contexts that are relatively more or less prevalent within each category.

3.1.11   Unique and Common Configurations Underlying Subsets of Homicide Situations

Thus far, we have shown that instrumental and expressive homicides do have unique social contexts, although most homicides occur in situations that are common to both. However, a final question is whether some kinds of instrumental homicides and some kinds of expressive homicides are more likely to occur in unique situations. Tables 3.1.3 and 3.1.4 answer this question by presenting a summary of the proportion of unique and common configurations of individual and situational factors that underlie major subtypes of instrumental and expressive homicides.

As shown in Table 3.1.3, subsets of homicide situations that are often classified as instrumental crimes vary dramatically in the relative proportions of their uniquely instrumental profiles. About two thirds of slayings involving rape or prostitution have a social context that is unique to instrumental homicides, and slightly over half of the homicides in burglary situations are also unique to instrumental homicides. While murders that occur during robberies are often portrayed as the ultimate instrumental homicide,[23] they share a similar social context to instrumental homicides in only about one third of these crimes. Fewer than 10% of homicides involving narcotic law violations or gambling have social contexts that are unique to instrumental homicides, with the vast majority of these homicides involving combinations of individual and situational factors that are common to both instrumental and expressive homicides. Under these conditions, the common practice of classifying different felony-type homicides as exclusively instrumental crimes

Table 3.1.3   Distributions of Unique and Shared Homicide Situations by Subtypes of Instrumental Homicide

Subtype	Unique to Instrumental		Common to Instrumental and Expressive		Total	
	N	%	N	%	N	%
Rape	145	67.4	70	32.6	215	100.0
Robbery	841	33.9	1643	66.1	2484	100.0
Burglary	147	51.6	138	48.4	285	100.0
Larceny	11	20.4	43	79.6	54	100.0
Auto Theft	27	33.8	53	66.2	80	100.0
Arson	29	32.6	60	67.4	89	100.0
Prostitution	19	67.9	9	32.1	28	100.0
Other Sex Offense	21	30.0	49	70.0	70	100.0
Narcotics Law	168	9.0	1694	91.0	1862	100.0
Gambling	0	0.0	47	100.0	47	100.0
Other Felony	166	30.7	374	69.3	540	100.0

Table 3.1.4   Distributions of Unique and Shared Homicide Situations by Subtypes of Expressive Homicide

Subtype	Unique to Expressive		Common to Instrumental and Expressive		Total	
	N	%	N	%	N	%
Lovers Triangle	248	21.4	910	78.6	1158	100.0
Brawl under Alcohol	302	23.2	997	76.8	1299	100.0
Brawl under Drugs	46	10.4	397	89.6	443	100.0
Argument over Money	289	19.5	1196	80.5	1485	100.0
Other Arguments	5098	30.1	11817	69.9	16915	100.0
Youth Gang	191	21.4	702	78.6	893	100.0

would grossly distort any substantive conclusions about the social context of instrumental homicides.

Contrary to the pattern for subtypes of instrumental homicides, none of the subtypes of homicide situations that are often classified as expressive crimes display unique profiles (see Table 3.1.4). For each subtype, the vast majority of offenses involve combinations of individual and situational factors that are common to both instrumental and expressive homicides. Homicide situations involving brawls, lovers triangles, youth gangs, and arguments exhibit greater internal consistency than subtypes of instrumental homicides, but none of these "expressive" acts have social contexts that are exclusively found among expressive homicides. In other words, subsets of expressive homicides are best treated as having individual and situational elements similar to both instrumental and expressive homicides.

3.1.12 Conclusions and Implications

Criminologists have employed the fundamental distinction between instrumental and expressive motivations across a variety of crime types. The current research examines whether these two general motivations for homicide are associated with either common or unique combinations of offender, victim, and situational elements. QCA models indicate that the social contexts of instrumental and expressive homicides are both unique and common. Of the 401 total configurations of individual and situational factors, slightly more than one third (36%) are unique to instrumental homicides, nearly one third (30%) are unique to expressive homicides, and the remaining one third of the configurations are common to both general types of homicide. Among those homicides that had social contexts common to both general types of homicide, some of the particular profiles were more commonly found among instrumental homicides, while others were more typical of the configurations involving expressive homicides. Comparisons within subtypes of instrumental and expressive homicides revealed wide variability within and across these general categories.

The current research was motivated by an ongoing debate about the nature and usefulness of the instrumental-expressive distinction. Most researchers have assumed that instrumental and expressive crimes are qualitatively distinct, while others characterize these general types as polar ends of a continuum. The work by Felson, in particular, suggests that this distinction is of little practical value because all offenses ultimately are thought to involve a pursuit of instrumental goals.[27]

Our results provide support for some of these arguments in the following ways. First, the fact that only one third of the combinations of individual and situational factors are common to both crime types supports the claim that instrumental and expressive homicides are qualitatively unique in their social contexts. However, this claim of uniqueness is tempered by the finding that only about one fourth of all homicides are accounted for by these unique configurations of attributes. Second, the finding of both unique and shared social contexts, as well as differentiation within those particular configurations common to both instrumental and expressive homicides, supports the treatment of the instrumental-expressive distinction as an underlying continuum. Third, the fact that the majority of homicides have social contexts common to both, and that some particular types of homicide situations (like rape and prostitution) often involve social contexts that are unique to instrumental homicides, may be interpreted as somewhat consistent with the argument that all crimes derive from instrumental goals. However, the findings of unique configurations for expressive homicides are clearly contrary to expectations based on this perspective.

The most important conclusion that derives from our analysis, however, is that characterization of homicides as either instrumental, expressive, or a combination of the two is a complex issue.[22] Both within and across these general crime categories, there is enormous variation in the nature and prevalence of particular combinations of offender, victim, and situational factors. Under these conditions, the treatment of instrumental-expressive crimes as a simple dichotomy results in a gross misrepresentation of both their common and unique signatures.

As illustrated in the current study, we think the QCA approach has enormous potential for studying crime across a variety of contexts. Whenever researchers are interested in comparative analyses (e.g., are there differences between recidivists and non-recidivists, murders and non-murders, organizational and occupational offenders, or novices and career criminals?), QCA provides a methodological framework for evaluating the similarity and uniqueness across these categories. Compared to statistical approaches that are variable-driven and typically assume that a variable's impact is linear and constant across levels of other variables, QCA begins with the assumption of maximum complexity and uses logical rules to uncover simpler patterns within the data.

In the current research context, QCA yielded results that are theoretically and substantively meaningful. Contrary to the prevailing assumptions that instrumental and expressive homicides are distinct forms (and that specific subtypes of killings are unique manifestations of these two general types), our analysis indicates that these homicides typically share the same particular combinations of offender, victim, and situational characteristics. The task for further research is to explain why these particular individual and situational combinations are associated with homicides across a variety of motives and circumstances.

3.1.13   Acknowledgments

The authors would like to thank Richard McCorkle and the anonymous reviewers for their instructive comments.

3.1.14   Notes

While Block and Block (1993) emphasize the instrumental-expressive continuum, this theoretical conceptualization often reduces to a simple dichotomy in statistical models of crime types and empirically-based taxonomies. For example, Block and Christakos (1995) acknowledge the instrumental-expressive continuum, but then proceed to identify homicide syndromes that derive from dichotomizing instrumental and expressive motives as one of their classification criteria. As discussed briefly, our analysis permits an empirical evaluation of the proper conceptualization of these two general types of homicide by determining whether instrumental and expressive crimes are fundamentally unique or share the same combinations of offender, victim, and situational factors.

It is important to note that many city-wide studies of homicide have lower proportions of missing data because it is easier in a particular local jurisdiction to perform a more in-depth search of alternative records (e.g., police, court, newspaper) to fill out missing information (Block, 1976; Decker, 1996; Polk, 1994; Wilbanks, 1984). However, with the exception of the Chicago homicide files, most city-wide studies lack a sufficient number of observations for analyses that require complex, multiple classification of attributes. SHR data do not have this problem.

It is not unusual to use some type of frequency-based rule when assigning configurations to construct truth tables in a QCA analysis, especially with large samples. For examples of other studies using some kind of frequency-based rule, see Amenta, Carruthers, and Zylan (1992) and Ragin, Mayer, and Drass (1984).

QCA is distributed by the Center for Urban Affairs and Policy Research at Northwestern University. To obtain QCA, and working papers about QCA, contact: Audrey Chambers, Director of Publications, Center for Urban Affairs and Policy Research, 2040 Sheridan Road, Evanston, IL 60208-4100.

By focusing on the more prevalent patterns in the data, we do not mean to imply that the other findings are theoretically uninteresting or unimportant. In fact, one of the strengths of QCA is its ability to identify uncommon or "deviant" patterns that can lead to a more complete understanding of the data. However, we feel that a focus on more prevalent combinations is appropriate given our interest in evaluating the general usefulness of the instrumental-expressive distinction for identifying and differentiating types of homicide situations.

While a series of increasingly complex interaction terms may be included in regression models and modifications of the general linear model, multicolinearity and other estimation problems often occur in these statistical applications. In contrast, QCA begins with the most complex configuration of the data and works to find less complex patterns. It is within this context that we think that QCA is superior to standard statistical approaches for the analysis of crime events.

3.2 Death by Detail: A Multivariate Model of U.S. Serial Murderers' Crime Scene Actions

MAURICE GODWIN

While some aspects of police work have been studied in depth — for example, police decision making in connection with an arrest — very little is known about the way in which detectives work toward identifying suspects in serial murder investigations. In order for the classification of serial murderers to be more than educated guess work, conclusions must be based on empirical research of consistencies in criminal behavior, and the relationship of those actions to aspects of an offender that are available to the police in an investigation. The crime scene actions of 96 U.S. serial murderers, who had each killed three or more victims on different dates and in different geographical locations, were examined in relation to their first, middle, and last offense in order to test three hypotheses: that serial murderers will have some structure in their actions within the series that are common to those offenses; that there will be certain thematic behaviors in any murder committed by a sample of serial murderers that are more typical than behaviors in similar murders; and there will be consistency across the three offense series for the offender samples. The non-metric multivariate statistical analysis procedure, Smallest Space Analysis (SSA), was used to analyze a total of 288 victims. The SSA results supported a four-theme classification model, reflecting offenders' modes of interaction with their victims. The present study has a number of practical consequences for police investigations, and if replicated with other data sets could form the basis of a powerful investigative support tool for building a computerized linking system.

3.2.1 The Challenge of Classifying Serial Murderers

Since its emergence, several terms have been used to describe the technique of offender profiling — for example, psychological profiling, criminal profiling, criminal personality profiling, and criminal investigative analysis.[41–43] However, despite the descriptive label applied, profiling as an investigative tool today represents a less than educated attempt to provide law enforcement agencies with detailed information about the behavior of an unknown individual who has committed a crime. Most published accounts of profiling, especially those

125

of serial murderers, have tended to take the form of semi-autobiographical books and journalistic articles rather than systematic academic work and, therefore, are difficult to evaluate from a scientific point of view.[44]

In the past decade, social scientists have turned their attention to profiling serial murderers by grouping their crime scene actions into theoretical categories.[45-47] Yet despite the significant loss of life and the cost of extended police investigations, an empirical examination of the crime scene behavior of serial murderers has never been carried out. A few anecdotal illustrations have been recorded by retired agents from the FBI Behavioral Science Unit in their memoirs,[48,49] acknowledging that the interaction between offender and victim is an important factor in serial murder investigations; however, these have not been related to any empirical studies testing hypotheses. As a consequence, a fuller understanding of serial murderers' behavior has academic merit and will facilitate more effective law enforcement.

Profiling serial murderers should proceed on the assumption that to understand crimes of this nature, we need to consider psychological issues relevant to behavior in general — for example, the offender's perception and interpretation of his actions and their likely consequences, and the emotional framework within which the person operates. Crime scene behavior, like any other behavior, is a function of the whole personality of the individual. Human behavior does not take place in a vacuum, but occurs in a concrete social situation. Hence, the specific circumstances of a set of actions between offender and victim need to be understood in order to give a useful account of any related behavior.

The crime scene presents a large amount of information about the perpetrator's actions. In order for the classification and linking of serial murderers' offenses to be more than educated guesswork, conclusions must be based on empirical research of consistencies in criminal behavior and the relationship of those actions to aspects of an offender that are available to the police in an investigation. Therefore, a model of any violent crime, especially that of serial murder, should be built on the central hypothesis that offenders differ in their actions when committing crimes and that these differences reflect different interactions between the offender and victim. However, most published literature on variations in serial murderers' behaviors have neglected victim/offender interpersonal actions that occur during a crime. Rather, research has tended to combine accounts of crime scene actions with explanations of motivations, intentions, personality attributes, and other inferred offender characteristics.[50-54]

A serial murder, whether committed for sexual sadistic purposes or revenge, is just a label for what is, in fact, quite complex behavior. However, this label tells us little about the individual who carries out that behavior. For example, current models of serial murderers are embedded with demographic statistics, offender self-reports, and offense descriptions mixed in an intuitive manner to create groups that conform to the researchers' preconceptions. Another drawback to such serial murder typologies is that they tend to put the sexual serial murderer in the same classification as killers who act on emotional impulses by suggesting that sadistic sex is the dominant focus in all serial murders. In reality, though, is it not clear how to decide which type a particular serial murderer is.

The serial murder literature points to a number of aspects of the offender's actions occurring in a crime. The most obvious of these is the dichotomous model of organization and disorganization proposed by the FBI.[47] This theoretical model divides serial murderers into two types according to the interplay of aggression and sex.[47] The first serial murderer type is one who struggles against his impulses. Ressler and his colleagues suggest that his crimes are disorganized, and he often leaves his crime scenes in disarray.[47] His driving motive is sexual gratification. The disorganized serial murderer has an aggressive aim — a displaced anger murderer. In this type, sexual and aggressive impulses are not well differentiated and feed off each other.[47] The second serial murderer type is labeled a sociopath.[47] Ressler and his colleagues point out that this type of killer is driven by sadistic sexual urges, seeking to humiliate his victims.[47] The offender's actions are organized; that is, the crimes have been planned to a degree, and the offender rarely leaves forensic clues at the crime scene.[47] These offenders are often referred to as lust murderers.[54] Other research also points out that sex is an integral part of the serial murderer's attack.[53]

Conversely, some researchers argue that it is not aggression and sex that drive the serial murderer, but rather power and control. Groth and his colleagues suggest that sex in the crime of serial murder is pseudo-sexual, not a true sexual act.[56] Originally developed as a clinical model for rape, the Groth model has been theoretically related to serial murderers by Keppel and Walter.[57] Keppel and Walter point out that the serial murderer has inherent doubts about his general adequacy, including sexual adequacy, and seeks to control victims through intimidation. To alleviate these feelings of sexual inadequacy the offender seeks revenge on women for wrongs believed to have been done to him in the past.

Other studies, also from a clinical perspective, attempt to classify serial murderers based on the degree of sadism in the crime.[50,58] However, clinical approaches make little distinction between overt crime scene behavior as it occurs in an offense and the psycho-dynamic processes that produce that behavior. Hence, there is little attempt to differentiate aspects of the offender's motivations and life-style from aspects of his offending behavior. However, any attempt to understand the actions that occur in a serial murder requires the classification of offense behavior as distinct from classification of the offender in either psychological or sociological terms. The perspective derived from clinically-based serial murder typologies emphasizes the various psychological functions of murder for the offender, not the actual varieties of action of the crime.

Although each serial murder typology previously discussed is logical, contradictions are inherent between them. At the very least, questions are raised about how a quest for intimacy and desire for power are combined in actual behavior in murders — if at all. A further weakness was highlighted by Meloy, who emphasized that murder is based upon psychological contact with a person, whether for aggression or intimacy reasons.[59] Meloy's opinion raises the issue of whether serial murderers have an internalized perception of a potential victim prior to the murder.

3.2.2   The Role of the Victim in Serial Murder

It could also be argued that rather than sexuality, aggression, or sadism, the desire for attachment (intimacy) is dominant in serial murderers. By drawing attention to the subjective aspects of the interpersonal contact of serial murderers with their victims, a theoretical framework for classifying crime scene behavior can be proposed. Such a perspective draws attention to behavior that goes beyond physical contact to an attempt at some sort of personal relationship with the victim. This theory is similar to that of "personification" proposed by Sullivan in 1953, which refers to a complex, organized cognitive pattern — a mental image — of a particular person, although not necessarily a real one.[60] Here, the individual's mental image is constructed out of experiences, deriving from interaction with other persons. Similar literature on the view of others can be found in child trauma studies.[61] Analyzing child trauma produced modifications in both technique and theory to accommodate the reality that people do not only belong to themselves but are created by relationships with others. Klein points out that an individual's experience of his behavior is not influenced only by the reality of traumatic relationships but by the imagined meaning the person assigns to them.[62]

In a similar vein, Swann discusses a self-verification process through which people induce others to verify their self-images.[63] This process has been demonstrated in the maintenance of both positive and negative relationships; thus people tend to adopt interaction strategies that elicit self-confirmatory feedback from others. It might be expected, then, that individual differences in the interpersonal styles of serial murderers would be highlighted in their interactions with their victims. For instance, Meloy suggests that in social situations attachment can be observed in normal or pathological patterns of proximity-seeking towards a victim.[59] Meloy further argues that in a psychological context, the mental representation of the individual is imbued with certain affects and maintains an enduring and relational quality in the mind of the perpetrator, although not necessarily based on reality. As such, it would be anticipated that differing degrees of aggression would play a role in the serial murderer's interpersonal contact with his victims.

As the above discussion suggests, killers have different cognitive perceptions of their victims before and during a crime which reflect the personal narratives of these men in their everyday life. One possibly is that serial murderers, who see their victims as "vehicles" on which to vent their anger and rage, could kill repeatedly to re-enact impersonal, fearful attachment conflicts.[64] Fearful attachment occurs in individuals who exhibit an impersonal thematic style. This type of person is seen as introverted, aloof, and socially avoidant.[65] Kagan points out that the fearful attachment type of individual is prone to anxiety due to feeling rejected.[66] For example, Miller states that killers who treat their victims in an impersonal way see themselves as powerful people with strong feelings of self-confidence during the murder but otherwise live lives of unbearable shame.[67] Consequently, it could be expected that serial murderers who score low on intimacy with their victims and demonstrate low mastery of the situation are more likely to reveal themes of behaviors during their crimes which have an affective (emotional) aspect. For example, offenders who fit this type are more likely to leave forensic clues and less likely to plan their crimes.

Conversely, there is also the possibility that serial murderers see their victims as objects, a kind of prop for acting out their sadistic torture and sexual fantasies. These types of serial murderers express dismissing attachment. Dismissing attachment is a term applied to individuals who are self-assured; for example, they exhibit controlling and calculating behavior.[65] Bartholomew points out that individuals with dismissing behavior appear to be able to isolate their affective reactions from their cognitive representations of early events and develop a view of themselves as impervious to future rejection. In other words, these types of killers have mastered the style of maintaining superficial relationships with others and are able to lure victims using cons and ploys.

Birtchnell suggests that this form of depersonalization is a way of denying the emotionality of the victim by treating her as an object.[68] Laing also refers to this form of depersonalization as reification, the ability to look at a person as an object of interest.[69] Gacono and Meloy point out that it is possible that most criminals are detached from their victims and appear to have little capacity to form affectional bonds with others.[70] So, although in terms of everyday behavior the serial murderer who sees his victims as objects is dismissive of others when he is not offending, he could actually display a high degree of personal attachment in the way in which he deals with his victims. It could be expected that serial murderers who score high on intimacy with their victims and demonstrate a high mastery of the situation are more likely to reveal themes of behaviors during their crimes that suggest they have cognitive control, such as pre-planning the crime and being forensically aware.

3.2.3   Research Objectives

The classification model of serial murder proposed in this study does not carry direct implications for the internal dynamics of the offenders. Rather, the study attempts to derive inferences about the crime scene behavior of serial murderers from the details of the way their crimes were committed. The study proposes that more objective accounts of what really happens in the course of a serial murder will relate in part to the link between the offender and the victim. This objective was important from a practical point of view, because it allowed the study of the material available in police records.[71]

The basis for developing a classification system of serial murder was the fact that variables derived from a crime scene will not have random interrelationships, but rather would reveal grouping of offenses with consistently related actions. Deriving groups of consistently related crime scene actions is important from the perspective of building a crime linking system. Empirically determining the salient behaviors of serial murderers can assist police investigators in prioritizing suspects and linking crimes.

There are a number of ways in which associations between crime scene behaviors of serial murderers can be established. The framework adopted in this study is characterized as a psycho-social behavioral approach, in which the offenders' interactions with their victims will tell us how they carry out their crimes, and subsequently how consistent they are from one offense to another. Crime scene actions that show associations between offenses will help classify behavior into common themes. Implicit is the need to identify those behavioral traces at a crime scene which can be used as variables for this research. Such traces of behavior may be seen as discrete acts, which constitute one element within a series of actions which combine to form an underlying structure to a crime scene.

The central task of the study is to establish whether there were any interpretable themes within the co-occurrence of the actions across all the serial murder cases. In order to represent the relationship of every variable to every other variable, the data will be subjected to Smallest Space Analysis (SSA-I), one of a series of non-metric multidimensional scaling procedures.[72] Smallest space analysis (SSA) is a multidimensional scaling technique that finds the best fit within a specified dimensionality between a matrix of association and a geometric representation of those associations as distances in a Cartesian space (i.e., the axes have no external reference). The advantage of SSA over other algorithms lies in its robustness and rational step-size.[73] This is mainly because the algorithm only attempts to find the best fit between the ranks of association coefficients and the ranks of distances in the geo-metric space. Such a matching of ranks can give a mathematically more efficient solution and are less sensitive to extreme values, which is why the procedure is called "smallest space analysis." It also leads to the procedure being recognized as non-metric.

SSA is also appropriate to many psychological studies, such as the present one, as psychological hypotheses are usually about the relative associations between entities rather than their absolute differences. The resulting SSA geometric representation is thus often more amenable to direct interpretation in relation to a set of hypotheses than procedures using metric algorithms or specific, externally defined axes. Another advantage that SSA has over other procedures is that SSA only takes into account the positive co-occurrence between variables. For example, if two variables are both absent from the records, this will not increase the association. As such, SSA is deemed to be the appropriate statistical procedure to measure the association for data drawn from police records, because it is not known whether absent infor-mation was recorded.

3.2.4   General Hypotheses

The general hypotheses central to this research are:

1. Serial murderers will display certain crime scene behaviors that they share in common
2. There will be groups of serial murderers who will consistently display signature behaviors that are more typical than any other group, and;
3. The analysis of the data will reveal four thematic, mutually exclusive regions that make up the offender's modes of interaction with his victims. The four themes of behavior are:

    *   Affective-Vehicle
    *   Affective-Object
    *   Cognitive-Vehicle
    *   Cognitive-Object

It is possible that the four thematic modes occur in any combination across a range of murders. This would suggest that none of the explanations provides a basis for distinguishing among serial murder offenses. A com-pletely random combination of any behavior with any other would suggest that there is no consistently coherent distinction among the four crime scene themes above. Hence, a null hypothesis would suggest that no inter-pretable relationships will be found between the actions that occur in serial murder offenses.

A second possibility is that a subset of conceptually related actions — for example, sadistic acts where the offender has a personal attachment to his victim — will consistently occur together. Such a grouping would support the hypothesis of the specific theme of victim as an object related to that behavior. However, in the event that different methods of killing the victim (e.g., bludgeon and ligature) co-occur but the style of sexual assaults (e.g., post-mortem sex, attempted sexual assault) were independent of each other, there would be support for the impersonal attachment towards the victim as a vehicle as a coherent salient aspect of the offender's focus. A grouping such as this would support the theme related to that behavior.

Finally, a third possibility is that all of these aspects of offense behavior might be identified in details of an actual event and they therefore would combine to provide a composite model of serial murderers' offense behavior. Such an empirical model would be expected to have an interpretable structure to it. For example, those types of behaviors that are likely to be associated with a cognitive thought process, such as planning the crime, disfiguring the victim's body, and postmortem sexual activity would be expected to have some empirical relationship distinctive from the affective elements where more impulsive behaviors, such as blitz attack and non-completed sex acts, are likely to be found. Scientific evidence for the second or third possibility discussed above would contribute to an empirical model of serial murder practical for police investigations and for building a linking database to identify murders committed by one offender.

3.2.5 Data Acquisition and Content Analysis

Details about serial murderers and their offenses are generally found in written form in state and local police files and court records; during the last few years, most police records have been maintained and stored in computerized databases. Because serial murder cases often remain unsolved for months and even years, the process of maintaining accurate information in police files becomes problematic. This dilemma is further compounded by the fact that most data collected by police are not intended for research purposes, and therefore the information is not organized in an orderly fashion. In recent years, though, the management of case data for all crimes has greatly improved due to the development of computerized police databases.[71]

Data representing the first, middle, and last murder offenses of 96 U.S. serial murderers who murdered 288 victims were drawn from various police sources. Three-fourths of the data (75%) were collected by this author by making an on-site visit to the Homicide Investigation and Tracking System (HITS) unit in Seattle, Washington.[71] Twenty percent of the research data were collected from other homicide reports — for example, the FBI's Violent Criminal Apprehension Program (VICAP) and New York State Homicide

Investigation and Lead System (HALT) files, which were originally located within the case files at the HITS unit. The remaining five percent of the data were obtained from court transcripts by accessing LEXUS and WESTLAW, American on-line law databases. To facilitate the data collection, a crime analyst from the HITS unit initially guided the author through the use of the HITS murder data base for extracting relevant information on solved serial murder cases. Definitions of the crime scene behaviors can be found in Appendix I. The data for this study do not represent a skewed set of solved serial murders found only in one particular geographical area or data base. Rather, the solved cases were selected randomly from a broad range of sources comprising 42 states.

In 90% of the cases, neither the offender nor the victim knew each other prior to the murder. In 3% of the cases, both people were friends who had seen each other on a regular basis. In 5% of the cases, the offender and victim barely knew each other: the offender knew the victim but the victim did not know the offender. In 1% of the cases, victims had a family relationship. At the time of the murders, 21% of the victims were actively working as prostitutes.

3.2.6 Methodology

3.2.6.1 *Preparing the Data for Analysis*

Sixty-five crime scene variables were selected for the analysis and coded as dichotomous data, where the score of "0" represents absence of the behavior in the crime, and "1" the presence of the behavior in the crime. The data in this study do not represent categorical variables. Coding the data in dichotomous form enabled a particular association matrix of co-occurrence to be produced, thus permitting the SSA program to construct the distance matrix from which geometric mapping is reproduced. Coding the raw data matrix in binary format made the data amenable to a suitable association coefficient. Holsti and Krippendorf argue that dichotomous decision-making in content analysis has the tendency to raise inter-rater reliability from around 60% to above 90%.[74,75]

Three sample raw data matrixes of 96 offenders and 96 offenses formed the association matrix that was analyzed by SSA. The SSA program computes correlations, or in the case of this study, offense behavior of association coefficients of the co-occurrence of behaviors. The SSA then rank–orders these correlations, transforming the original rectangular input data matrix to a triangular distance matrix.

Subjecting variables of a content universe to SSA had two major roles. The first role was exploratory in nature. The exploratory approach is appropriate when the subject matter is relatively new, or where there are no empirical studies arising from the literature. For this research, it is important first to establish that, on an empirical level, there are themes of behaviors in the crime scene actions of serial murderers.

The first SSA analysis was exploratory. SSA was performed on the first murders for each offender's series. The second analysis was confirmatory. In this stage, SSA was employed to confirm the structured elements derived from the exploratory SSA. Two confirmatory SSAs were performed on the middle and last murders for each offender's series.

3.2.7   Smallest Space Analysis (SSA-I)

Smallest Space Analysis (SSA-I) is a non-metric multidimensional scaling procedure most frequently used in facet theory.[75] SSA is appropriate in many psychological studies, such as the present one, as psychological hypotheses are usually about the relative associations between entities rather than their absolute differences. SSA was used to determine the underlying structure in the crime scene actions of serial murderers. The SSA technique examines the structure of the offenders' behaviors, and not the offenders themselves.

The SSA representation of the coefficients matrix is non-metric, meaning that no attempt is made to specify in advance a particular monotonic function that transforms the coefficients into distances. It is only the rank order of the coefficients, not their numerical values, that is preserved by SSA mapping.[76] Other methods of showing relationships between variables of behavior could have been performed on the data in a process of variable-to-variable analysis. For example, cross-tabulation of every variable with every other would have found some co-occurrence, but the results would have not been multivariate and would have been very difficult to interpret. Homogeneity analysis using alternating least squares (HOMALS), factor analysis, or cluster analysis could have been performed on the data. However, SSA has advantages over these techniques, because it imposes little a priori structure on the data. Also, qualitative, dichotomous data are not amenable to examination by methods which assume distribution and mathematically manipulate mean. Rather, a multivariate analysis of the covariance between the variable behaviors is the most interpretable and robust method for data that are produced as qualitative, non-parametric categories in dichotomous form.

The SSA program works by computing iterations, comparing the rank order between the correlation matrix and distance matrix, and adjusting the spatial representation until the minimum of stress is reached within a designated number of iterations. Such a matching of ranks can be shown to give a mathematically more efficient solution as well as being less sensitive to extreme values, and is the reason the procedure is called smallest space analysis.

The analysis provides a stress measurement called the coefficient of alienation, which is used to end the iterations. The coefficient of alienation gives a general indication of the degree to which the variables' inter-correlations are represented in the plot by their corresponding spatial distances. The smaller the coefficient of alienation, the better the fit of the variables in the SSA plot.

An acceptable coefficient of alienation level is 0.2 or below.[77] However, the most important principle of SSA is the interpretability of the structure.

3.2.8 Analysis I — Smallest Space Analysis

3.2.8.1 *Interpretation of SSA Configurations*

SSA configurations are interpreted as regions rather than dimensions.[78–80] Regional interpretation of the SSA space follows naturally from several features of the way the content universe is represented. Regional hypotheses relate to several roles that the variables can play in partitioning the SSA.[78] The SSA configuration was examined to identify regions of the plot in which crime scene behaviors appeared to have coherent interrelationship. The SSA space contains a map of the different variables entered into the analysis as a triangular matrix under the *Principle of Contiguity*.[79] Principle of contiguity means that the closer any two variables are in the SSA plot, the more conceptually related they are, since the program places highly correlated variables together. The plot can be rotated, stretched, translated, and reflected without any effect on the meaning of the solution, because the information is contained in the distances between the variables and not the dimensions.[80] However, this is not the case for metric multidimensional scaling analysis. Therefore, the orientation of the axes in the SSA plot is not meaningful, although as an artifact of the program the axes may correspond to the principal components of the correlation matrix. It is also worth mentioning that SSA regions are not considered clusters. Cluster analysis would not be able to recognize empty spaces in the sampling as the SSA does, because it is a structure-imposing procedure. For example, no indication of empty spaces containing variables which might be conceptually related would be obtained by cluster analysis since the clustering solution is created by iteratively looking at each value in the association or correlation matrix in series, unlike the SSA solution, which looks at them in parallel.

3.2.9 SSA Results for the First Offense Series

Figure 3.2.1 is a plot of the first by second dimension of the three-dimensional solution. The numbers inside the squares correspond to the variable definitions, which are found in Appendix I. The numbers outside of the squares represent frequencies. The SSA of offense behavior produced a coefficient of alienation as 0.26 in 6 iterations. The coefficient of alienation indicates how well the program represents the spatial distance and orientation of the variables to the association matrix. While the coefficient of alienation is high, it is still within the realm of acceptability.[81]

As demonstrated in Figure 3.2.1, the exploratory SSA, using the first offenses from each series, produced variables spread over most of the plot,

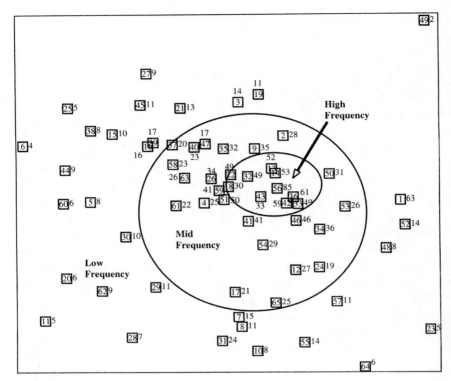

Two-Dimensional Plot
Coefficient of Alienation = 0.268
n = 65 Variables
n = 96 Offenses
n = 96 Offenders
Numbers in squares correspond to variable definitions in Appendix I
Numbers outside of squares are frequency of crime scene actions

Figure 3.2.1 SSA frequency plot of crime scene actions.

with a central core of variables located in the middle, just to the right of the plot. From the central region, the crime scene variables spread out towards the edges of the plot, decreasing in number the further the distance from the central region. Analysis of frequency for the 65 variables across the 96 offenses indicates that this was the result of the presence of a modulating facet for frequency. Briefly, a modulating facet is circular shaped, with bands around a common origin.[78] Levy, in discussing the modular role, points out that a simply ordered facet can play a modular role, namely, have a correspondence with distance from the origin.[78]

3.2.10 Focal Aspects of Serial Murder

In Figure 3.2.1 the highest frequency variables (30 to 85%) are located in the center region, which means that they have co-occurrence with each other and other variables that surround them. However, there is one variable, V1, 63%, plotted in the low frequency band. The location of this variable outside of the center region could be due to using real-world data that is considerably noisy. Variables in the central core are thus items that are shared by the majority of the serial murderers in this study. As such, the variables were not likely to have a discriminating function in describing serial murderers by variations of behavior. The centrality of the highest frequency items is not a function of the coefficient; rather, it simply means that the higher frequency variables have greater co-occurrence of common behaviors in serial murder. The center of the innermost region can be thought of as the center point of the space, and inter-correlations between items in the innermost region will be higher than inter-correlations between items in outer regions.[82] The mid- band of variables in Figure 3.2.1 represents frequencies between 15 to 49%, while variables plotted in the low band represent frequencies between 2 and 20%.

The potential combination of actions in Figure 3.2.1, inherent in the radial order, are derived from the fact that serial murderers have a common focus but with different emphases. This focus and the referents that make it up is given even a clearer meaning by considering those items at the center of the plot for the first offense series. The central core actions shared most with all the others around them are both literally and metaphorically central to the issues being examined, the dominant crime scene behaviors of serial murderers. The following variables or actions are central:

Victim's body hidden
Body moved
Victim found nude
Offender pre-selected a weapon
Personal items stolen from victim
Victim bound by rope
Victim's clothing ripped/torn
Weapon a knife
Anal assault
Vaginal assault

The ten behaviors listed above, which are central to serial murder, give the likely indication that the main focus in serial murder has most to do with controlling the victim (V18, rope), planning the crime (V56, weapon pre-selected), and covering up forensic clues to hinder detection (V13, body hidden). It was expected that if the central focus in serial murder was sex, as suggested in the literature, then variables such as foreign objects, assault of sex organs, and ante-mortem post-mortem sexual activity would be plotted in the central region. However, in this sample of offenders, although sexual

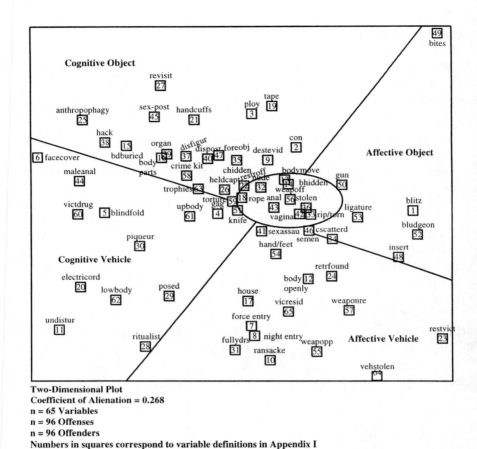

Two-Dimensional Plot
Coefficient of Alienation = 0.268
n = 65 Variables
n = 96 Offenses
n = 96 Offenders
Numbers in squares correspond to variable definitions in Appendix I

Figure 3.2.2 SSA configuration of crime scene behaviors. First murders in the series.

activity was a component in serial murder (V42, vaginal sex; V43, anal sex), it was not the dominant sexual focus that is often propounded in the literature.[45,47,50] The focus of the variables in the central region certainly raises questions about the restricted view of *modus operandi*, implying some signature method of operating.

3.2.11 Regional Themes in Serial Murder

Analysis of the first 96 offenses for 96 serial murderers found that all four of the possible themes were present, as hypothesized, that offense behaviors can be identified in detail of actual discrete events. The two-dimensional solution for the first offense series had a Guttman-Lingoes' coefficient of alienation of 0.26 in 6 iterations, as previously mentioned. Figure 3.2.2 shows the SSA configuration of offense behavior with crime scene themes: Affective-Vehicle (AV),

Affective-Object (AO), Cognitive-Vehicle (CV), and Cognitive-Object (CO) transposed. Variable definitions are listed in Appendix I. The SSA produced a configuration of four structured regions surrounding a central region of highly frequent variables. To repeat, the central region indicates behavior most frequent in serial murders, with the addition of a modulating facet of frequency. The SSA configuration in Figure 3.2.2 is defined as a radex model.[80]

The descriptions assigned to each region express a common origin of the facet element items. The thematic titles are descriptions indicating a general underlying structure of the data. The thematic titles refer to elements that underlie the two facets: behavioral organization and attachment, as hypothesized. It should be emphasized, however, that the thematic approach to classifying the crime scene actions of serial murderers should be seen as behavioral and does not imply personality traits.

3.2.12   Cronbach Alpha Analysis

It is common in research to attempt the measurement of variables for which there is no universally agreed measure. Any variable measurement, but especially data open to different interpretations, such as crime scene actions, must be queried as to its reliability in terms of producing the same results on different occasions. In order to establish, on an empirical level, that the crime scene variables used in this study are structured into meaningful themes with similar psychological meanings, it was necessary to determine that the variables are indeed measuring related phenomena within each theme. Selecting items to form an appropriate scale is therefore a very important step that is both theoretically and technically sound.

An appropriate test for measuring related phenomena is Cronbach's Reliability Alpha Scale.[83] A moderate Alpha scale measure is .60.[83] Variables in each theme were submitted to Cronbach's Alpha Analysis. A total of 55 crime scene actions were analyzed. Variables from the central region were not included in the analysis because the actions occurred most frequently, therefore, they would not be distinctive enough to classify the offenders. All the Alpha scores were acceptable. The Alpha result for each behavioral theme is denoted by the Alpha sign ($\propto$) at the beginning of each thematic section.

3.2.13   Classifying Crime Scene Actions into Themes

3.2.13.1   *Affective-Vehicle Theme ($\propto$ .635)*

Sixteen behaviors in particular seem to indicate that to express his anger and rage, the serial murderer attempts to commit, or at least is not deterred from committing, a completely emotional, unplanned murder where the victim is treated as a vehicle. The following affective-vehicle (AV) thematic variables that co-occurred in this region are:

Weapon hands/feet
Victim's body left openly displayed
Attempt sexual assault
Semen found at crime scene
Victim's clothing scattered
Restraint found at crime scene
Restraint victim's clothing
Crime occurred in a house
Crime at victim's resident
Victim's property ransacked
Forced entry
Entry made during the night
Victim found fully dressed
Weapon found at crime scene
Weapon of opportunity
Victim's vehicle stolen

The variables are located in the low right quadrant of the SSA space. Out of all the themes, the AV theme seems to be the most unstructured. The victim is seen as a "vehicle" on which the offender vents his rage. Interestingly, the AV theme also reveals a subset of serial murderers who target, murder, and leave their victims' bodies in the same location, such as the victim's residence.

For example, in preparation for the crime, the AV offender may stake out a particular house where he will then break and enter to canvass for photos and names of children, and to get a feel for the general layout of the scene. He then will use force (V7) to enter the victim's home — usually during the night (V8).These actions suggest pre-planning; however, the offender's behavior during and after the murder is completely spontaneous and emotional, which is demonstrated by the offender's use of a weapon of opportunity (V55) which is recovered (V57) at the crime scene.

Three variables in the AV theme — attempted sexual assault, (V41), body openly displayed, (V12), and using victim's clothing as a restraint (V23) — are actions that appear to indicate low self-awareness and impersonal attachment to the victim. Often in crimes of this type, the offender's original intent was rape; however during the attack the victim blocks the offender's advances, and he reacts by killing the victim. Due to the emotional component in the AV type killer, the preferred weapon is the offender's hands and feet. Other opportunistic behaviors in the AV theme are scattering the victim's clothing, ransacking the victim's property, and stealing the victim's vehicle. These actions indicate that the crime is expressive with death immediate, and stealing the victim's vehicle, (V64) provides a quick getaway. The AV theme thus accords with Meloy's contention that affective violence results in low mastery and confusion at the crime scene.[84] Possibly exemplifying the affective-vehicle theme is the serial murderer Timothy Spencer, who was executed in Virginia for a series of murders.[85]

3.2.13.2   Affective-Object Theme ($\propto$ .638)

Of the two affective themes, the affective-object (AO) theme presents the more structured crime scene. Variables in the affective-object theme are located in Figure 3.2.2 in the upper right quadrant of the SSA plot. It is notable that there are few variables in this region. Areas in the SSA plot which contain little or no points indicate weak areas in the data or, in fact, missing elements. However, subsequent research on a different sample of serial murderers could be carried out to test for the existence of these missing elements. As it is, six crime scene variables seem to relate to the aspects of the AO theme:

    Blitz attacked
    Weapon — gun
    Ligature
    Bludgeon
    Object found inserted in victim
    Bite marks on victim

These six crime scene variables describe actions which appear to indicate that the offender may have an attachment to his victim as an object. Behaviors that indicate personal attachment to the victim are bite marks and object found inserted. These actions show the offender's callous disinterest in the victim as an actual person. The killer's focus is on degradation of the victim's body; that is, the body has personal symbolic significance. However, the crime remains affective, as some variables indicate that the offender is less than forensically aware; for example, he may leave an object inserted and bite marks on the victim. The emotional component in the AO theme also manifests itself by the victim being blitz attacked (V1).

A rage component in the AO theme is possibly revealed by the victim being bludgeoned to death. Excessive blunt trauma in the face area possibly indicates that the victim knew her attacker.[86,87] The nesting together of their variables bludgeon and blitz on the plot (see Figure 3.2.2) suggests that serial murderers whose method of approach is blitz attack are more likely to kill their victims by bludgeoning them to death.

Two distinct methods of killing the victim are found in the AO theme. The first is the use of a gun (V50) which is an impersonal method of killing, because injury can be accomplished while maintaining a distance from the victim. The second method of death is personal, where the offender has more contact with his victim — for example, ligature strangulation (V53), which requires more involvement and time spent with the victim, and often is a slower method of death.

A personal attachment variable that suggests the victim is used as an object to be exploited is variable (V48), evidence of a foreign object being inserted in the body cavities. Although foreign object is plotted just over the boundary line in the AV theme, it has a higher association (.44) with bludgeon that it does with any of the variables plotted in the AV region. Therefore, it was decided to include the variable in the AO region because it helps define the theme more clearly. Research suggests that inserting objects in the victim is a form of degradation.[87] The act could be considered a form of rage against the victim.

The AO theme seems to reveal a killer whose desire is expressive rage, but one that has a personal focus towards the victim. In this sense, the victim may hold a symbolic importance for the killer. The killer assigns his victims a more active and brutal role in the violent drama. Possibly exemplifying the affective-object theme is the serial murderer David Joseph Carpenter.[88]

3.2.13.3   Cognitive-Vehicle Theme ($\propto .684$)

The clinical literature on serial murder sees its main focus as sadistic sexual components mixed in with impulsive irrational behavior.[50,89,90] However, serial murderers who control their aggression while also committing mutilation and sadistic acts seem to be relatively ignored. Fourteen variables found in the low left quadrant of the SSA space which seem to deal directly with controlled aggression, planning, and torture of the victim seem to represent the cognitive-vehicle (CV) theme. These are:

Blindfolded
Trophies
Victim gagged
Victim torture
Upper body stab wounds
Lower body stab wounds
Ritualistic activity
Piqueurism
Victim's body posed
Victim bound with electrical cord
Male sexual assault
Victim drugged
Victim's face covered
Property at crime scene undisturbed

Although the CV thematic behaviors seem to indicate more personal attachment to the victim than either of the affective themes, the focus is still impersonal. For example, piqueurism (V30) is small jab wounds made to the victim's body. Piqueurism is described as a sadistic act of feeling the ripping and tearing of flesh.[90] The stab wounds are usually found in the lower (V62) and upper (V61) regions of the victim's body. However, since upper stab wounds are plotted near the central region, the victim's chest and facial areas were possibly attacked most often. Stab wounds, in excess of ten or more, are indicated by variable of the victim being tortured to death (V59). The position of lower stab wounds (V62) in the SSA plot indicates that the stabbing of the victim below the waist is more a discriminating behavior. Other research on serial murder found lower stab wounds often occur in the form of mutilation to the victim's sexual organs.[86]

Although the CV theme suggests an offender who pre-plans certain aspects of his crimes, there appear to be some actions which are purely opportunistic. Thus, variables such as the victim being drugged (V60) and property at the crime scene left undisturbed (V11) could be seen as cognitive actions. Conversely, actions such as using an electrical cord (V20) and performing ritualistic (V28) acts on or around the body could be considered opportunistic because the weapon is usually obtained at the crime scene, with ritualistic acts also having a greater possibility of forensic evidence linking the offender to the murder. Several actions in the CV theme also appear to indicate an impersonal attachment to the victim — for example, blindfolding, face covering, and posing the victim's body. Holmes and Holmes, in their interviews with imprisoned serial murderers, suggested that the offenders' impetus to blindfold and cover their victims' faces was because faces screamed with terror.[45] As a result, the offenders sought to distance themselves from their victims.

Another important feature of the CV theme is that more of these offenders murder males. This is indicated by the presence of (V44), male sexual assault. The relative closeness of the variable, male sexual assault, to blindfolding (V5) and victim drugging (V60) accords with Cartel's position that homosexual murderers achieve euphoria through torturing and killing people without experiencing reality disassociation, which accounts for their organization at the crime scene.[91] Serial murderers with behaviors from the CV thematic region can be distinguished from other killers in that the central focus of the attack seems to be to maintain control over the victim. Most interesting, however, is the relationship between gag and torture, which indicates that the CV type of murderer is likely to be associated with controlled aggression and possibly sadistic behavior.

The variable trophy (V63) is also found in the CV region; this action appears to be one way in which the killer reflects psychologically on his or her crimes. The souvenirs may be body parts or small, personal items or clothing of the victim. The souvenirs retained by the offender are usually hidden in a private chamber of horrors along with various devices for torture and murder. For example, Douglas and Burgess suggest that the location may be the offender's basement, attic, or an outside storage building.[92] Possibly exemplifying the cognitive-vehicle theme is the serial murderer Randolph Steven Kraft.[93]

3.2.13.4   Cognitive-Object Theme ($\propto$ .902)

Nineteen variables possibly related to the cognitive-objective (CO) theme are to be found in the upper left quadrant of the SSA. These behaviors are:

> Victim held captive
> Victim's clothing hidden
> Victim bound with tape
> Crime kit
> Restraint pre-selected by offender
> Sex organs assaulted
> Disfigured victim's body
> Evidence of foreign object being inserted
> Dismemberment post mortem
> Body parts scattered
> Victim's body buried
> Evidence destroyed
> Con approach
> Ploy approach
> Handcuffs
> Sex post mortem
> Revisited crime scene
> Body hacked
> Anthropophagy

The variables show a sample of serial murderers who seem to distinctly plan and engage in the most sadistic forms of behavior, while being forensically aware that clues left at the crime scene may link them to the murders. A number of variables relate to the CO offender planning his crime and performing what could be construed as a continuum of sadistic acts. For example, sex post-mortem, the assaulting of sex organs, and anthropophagy, embedded with behaviors such as crime kit and con approach, all indicate that the offender's actions are well thought out.

The cognitive-object theme is characterized by behaviors such as prolonged and bizarre assaults on their victims. The focus of serial murderers found in the CO theme seems to be to possess the victim's body; therefore postmortem sex (V45) is the preferred choice of sexual activity. Balint found a high order of mastery in his description of the qualities of a personal fetish.[94] Here the victim is viewed as a worthless object raised to the dignity of a fetish, a lifeless thing that can be easily taken and possessed. Other evidence of sexual exploration is revealed in the CO theme such as with localized areas of the body in the form of skin tears or inserted objects (V47).

There are a number of other variables that show the offender's focus for continuum of sadism, for example, postmortem sexual activity (V45), assault of sex organs (V40), anthropophagy (V25) (i.e., cannibalism and drinking blood), and evidence of an object being inserted (V47) — all indicating personal attachment to the victim as an object. In this regard, the victim appears to be nothing more to the killer than a symbolic object with which to carry out his sadistic acts. Perhaps there is an implicit mastery of the victim in the form of an object which is fueled through re-enactment due to past traumatic experiences. Katz points out that re-enactment to master negative life experiences is not only to triumph over the object but, like the sacrificial practice it is, to destroy flesh to restore the proper order of being.[95] The proper order of being is the illusion that there is no difference between reality and imitation.[96]

Other evidence suggests that the CO offender has high self-awareness during his crimes. For instance, several variables which indicate the offender is attempting to destroy forensic clues are: destroying evidence at the crime scene, (V9), hacking the body, (V38), burying the body, (V15), and scattering body parts, (V16) — all actions that show forensic awareness.

The CO offender can also be distinguished by his ability to lure victims to their deaths by using his charm, while at the same time he is capable of showing sadistic type behavior. Two variables in particular — con (V2), and ploy (V3) — reflect the killer's ease in luring victims. The finding that more sadistic serial murderers who plan their crimes employ a ruse to trap their victims accords with James' study on 38 serial murderers in which he found that 68% of the killers used some form of con game to get the victim to a location where the killer then believed it was safe to carry out his assault and murder.[97]

Using a plan of action, CO killers may equip themselves with a crime kit (V58) for torturing victims. The victim's body will subsequently exhibit signs of methodical mutilation in the form of ante-mortem and post-mortem cutting, slashing, and stabbing. In these crimes, the victim may also be held captive (V26) for a time prior to the murder. It is also interesting to note that several other variables reflect the high degree of control that the CO offender has over his victims. Two variables in particular are being bound with tape, (V19) and the use of handcuffs, (V21).

Restraints and weapons are preselected and taken from the crime scene. Not leaving a restraint and weapon behind at the scene also suggests the

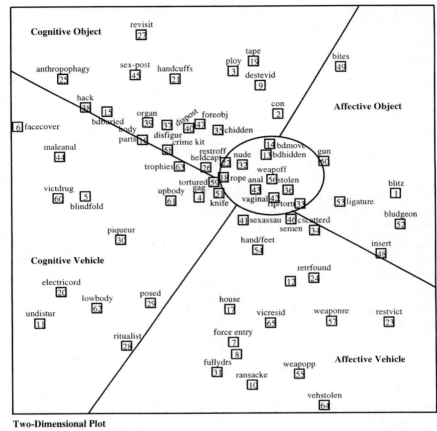

Two-Dimensional Plot
Coefficient of Alienation = 0.265
n = 65 Variables
n = 96 Offenses
n = 96 Offenders
Numbers in squares correspond to variable definitions in Appendix I

Figure 3.2.3 SSA configuration of crime scene behaviors. Middle murders in the series.

offender is forensically aware. In sum, the CO theme reflects a serial murderer who is methodical, calculating, and cunning in the way he carries out his crimes. Possibly exemplifying the cognitive-vehicle theme is the serial murderer Robert Berdella.[98]

3.2.14 Analysis II — Confirmatory SSA Results

The fact that serial murderers commit a series of offenses introduces technical difficulties into developing classifications. One hypothesis explored in the

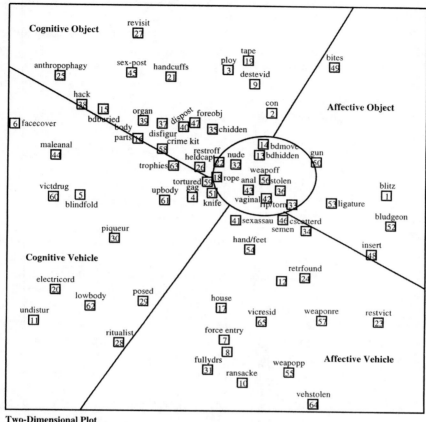

Two-Dimensional Plot
Coefficient of Alienation = 0.268
n = 65 Variables
n = 96 Offenses
n = 96 Offenders
Numbers in squares correspond to variable definitions in Appendix I

Figure 3.2.4 SSA configuration of crime scene behaviors. Last murders in the series.

present study is that the structure of the crime scene behaviors found by SSA for the first offense series is similar for the middle and last offenses. In other words, it may be possible that offenders who change their actions in response to the reactions of the victim are not the same in different offense series. To examine this hypothesis, the offenders' crime scene actions for their middle and last offense were analyzed.

Figures 3.2.3 and 3.2.4 show the SSA plots for the middle and last offenses. For clarity, each point is a variable describing offense behavior. The numbers refer to the variables as listed in Appendix I. The closer any two points are, the more likely the actions they represent will co-occur in offenses in comparison with points that are further apart.

Again, a SSA was carried out on an association matrix of Jaccard coefficients, which are the most appropriate measures of association for this type of binary data. The two-dimensional solution for the middle offense series (Figure 3.2.3) has a Guttman-Lingoes' coefficient of alienation = 0.265 in 22 iterations, while the last offense series (Figure 3.2.4) had the coefficient of alienation = 0.264 in 23 iterations. Looking at the SSA plots, for the middle and last offense series, the configurations turned out to be very similar to the regional structure found for the first offense series, indicating that crime scene behavior, at least in this set of serial murderers, appears to be fairly consistent from one offense to the next.

3.2.15 Assigning Serial Murderers to Themes

The final process in developing an empirical classification model of serial murderers involved taking each of the 96 serial murder cases for the first, middle, and last offense and assigning a unique score that represented the number of crime scene actions present in each theme. So, for example, a theme that has 10 variables possible also has a maximum score of 10. However, in a few cases, where there was a mixture of unequal actions present from each theme, a proportional method was employed to determine whether the case belonged to a theme or not. This process involved taking the number of actions in a particular case and dividing them by the number of actions that were possible. In other words, a case was classified as belonging to one of the 4 themes if the proportional score for that theme was greater than or approximately equal to the score for the other three themes added together. The cognitive-vehicle theme had a total of 14 crime scene actions, while the cognitive-object had a total score of 19 possible actions. The affective-vehicle theme had a total score of 16 possible actions, while the affective-object had a score of 6 actions.

Table 3.2.1 shows the number and percentage of serial murderers who were classified in each theme along with any hybrids, meaning that offenders shared behaviors from different themes. Each serial murderer was classified using the proportional method on 65 variables. In other words, an offender was assigned to a theme if his score in a particular theme over his first, middle, and last offense was greater than his score in the remaining themes. Determining if the themes were mutually exclusive was important for several reasons. First, it allowed a visual inspection of the percentage of offenders assigned to each them, including any hybrids. Second, it provided a way of looking at the consistency of serial murderers by seeing whether offenders in one theme could be classified in the same theme for the middle and last offense. Using the

Table 3.2.1 Frequency of Serial Murderers Assigned to each Behavioral Theme

Theme	N Offenders	% of Offenders in each theme
Affective-Vehicle	16	17
Hybrids AV-AO	10	10
Affective-Object	31	2
Hybrids AO-CV	2	2
Cognitive-Vehicle	6	6
Hybrids CV-CO	1	1
Cognitive-Object	27	28
Hybrids CO-AV	1	1
Hybrids CO-AO	1	1
Hybrids AV-CV	1	1
Total N =	96	99

proportional method, almost all of the serial murder cases (83%) could be classified as pure types, while 15% could be classified as hybrids.

3.2.16 Summary

The sequence of variables in the SSA plot, which make up a serial murderer's crime scene behavior, can now be seen to form a radial order. Equally important is the fact that across the three offense series — first, middle, and last — behavior appears to remain consistent from one offense to the next. The SSA results suggest that is it possible to classify crime scene behavior into four distinct themes describing serial murderers' modes of interaction with their victims, as hypothesized.

The closeness of the activity in the central region, notably actions that showed pre-planning, control over the victim, and destroying evidence, was noted as the central focus for this sample of serial murderers. This finding has considerable investigative weight, because the FBI profilers suggest that serial murderers who mutilate, and perform postmortem sex and cannibalism, are disorganized and careless at their crime scenes, and that little preparation goes into planning their crimes.[47] However, the SSA results clearly point to a different reality. For example, the cognitive-object thematic behaviors that indicated planning, such as using a con approach and destroying forensic evidence, were consistently plotted as neighbors with post-mortem sex, inserting objects, disfiguring the body, and anthropophagy. Similar behaviors were plotted as neighbors in the cognitive-vehicle thematic region. For example, drugging the victim and the use of a blindfold plotted together in all the offense series. These actions suggest pre-planning.

Several important relationships were recognized that are currently not discussed in the serial murder literature. For example, behaviors that formed the affective-vehicle thematic region show that there is a sub-set of serial murderers who primarily targeted, attacked, and murdered their victims indoors. In the affective-vehicle region, we saw behaviors consistently co-occurring, such as forcing entry to the victim's residence, attacking during the night, and leaving the victim fully clothed. These actions appeared in the same region for all three offense series, indicating that there is likely a distinct group of serial murderers who entered their victims' houses to commit murder, who are quite different from those offenders who used a con approach and sadistically tortured their victims.

The results also found a sub-set of serial murderers, mainly those with affective-object thematic behaviors, who show a callous disinterest in their victims as people. The killer's focus was on degradation of the victim's body and its symbolic significance. However, the crime remained affective due to variables, which suggests that the offender was less than forensically aware; for example, he may have left an object inserted or left bite marks on the victim.

The analysis also found a third sub-set of serial murderers, mainly offenders with cognitive-vehicle thematic behaviors. The cognitive-vehicle crime scene seems to reflect an emotional component and an impersonal focus towards the victim. The central issue of the attack for the cognitive-vehicle killer was to maintain control over his victims. Evidence that some victims were tortured and their bodies posed are two examples of control. The final sub-set of serial murderers were classified as cognitive-object. Cognitive-object offenders can be distinguished by their ability to lure victims to their deaths by using charm and, at the same time, exhibiting the most sadistic behavior. The cognitive-object theme reflects serial murderers who are methodical, calculating, and cunning in the way they carry out their crimes. Forensic awareness is a strong attribute of cognitive-object serial murderers.

The finding that the majority of serial murderers classified as belonging to one of the four behavioral themes is due in part to the nature of the SSA structure — that the SSA configuration is produced by groups of consistently co-occurring variables. It is also worth pointing out that the majority of the hybrids were from contiguous regions.

3.2.17   Conclusions and Implications

For any classification system to be really effective, its development must be directly related to the possible utilization of the model by detectives. Awareness of this requirement was central to the research carried out in this study. The results of this study could provide researchers and police with a more heuristic and robust framework for building a computerized linking system. The thematic model presented in this study could also assist profilers in drawing up more accurate offender profiles by using the crime scene behaviors in each theme as a basis for prioritizing offenders.

The techniques used in the research do offer some empirical support for classifying the crime scene behaviors of serial murderers. As Lester has suggested, in order to develop a robust model of serial murder, a large data set must be analyzed.[54] Analyses such as those employed in this study must now look to the future to develop larger and more comprehensive databases and expand the classification types. In doing so, the thematic approach used in this study may give way to concise categorization of many crime scene variables in which observed intensity and scale may be derived that will benefit the law enforcement fight against the serial predator.

3.3   Cluster Analysis of Burglars' Modus Operandi (M/O)*

EDWARD J. GREEN
CARL E. BOOTH
MICHAEL D. BIDERMAN

Excessive case loads are the normal condition for detective divisions in most metropolitan police departments. It is not unusual for a plainclothes officer to be assigned as many as 15 separate cases for follow-up investigation within a one-week period. Every effort is made to assign cases that appear to be related to those already being investigated by the particular police officer, but there is little, apart from intuition on the part of the supervisor, that assists him in the selection of cases for such assignment.

To the degree that a detective is working on a group of related cases, presumably arising from the criminal activities of a single individual or group of individuals, his effectiveness is enhanced. His efforts are not scattered over a series of unrelated incidents, and the concentration of cases provides additional information and leads that can augment his investigatory efforts. Conversely, the random assignment of unrelated cases for follow-up dilutes the effectiveness of investigation and leads all too often to perfunctory efforts of little, if any, value. A low rate of clearance can be the result of a variety of factors, but casual case assignments must rank among the most significant reasons for a poor showing in clearances.

Intuition or experience can go a long way toward effective detective work, as it assists in defining the probable grouping of criminal activities by individuals. Intuition is, fortunately, susceptible to improvement. A hunch is usually based upon real information, although the person having the hunch may be unable to verbalize the basis for his hunch. The hunch is an example of clinical judgment, provided that judgment has validity based upon years of practical experience in the field. To the degree that the judgment is based upon real discriminations, the information that makes possible those discriminations may be clarified.

* Originally published in the *Journal of Police Science and Administration*, 4:382-388, 1976.

3.3.1   Significance of the Technology

House burglaries are perpetrated by persons who have preferred targets and specific Modus Operandi (M/O). A police officer may have little difficulty in recognizing the work of a particular criminal where that person has established a record of operations in his district. The recognition of an individual criminal is based upon certain signatures of M/O. In one city, such a burglar habitually broke through the rear walls of buildings, circumventing burglar alarms. Another group of teenagers developed a method of breaking into residences through windows of homes, taking only loose cash. A drug addict, with an $80-a-day habit who was working the same residential area, only lifted major appliances such as color TVs. He fenced these goods for the money he required for drugs. The characteristics and conditions of the residence burglaries reflected the criminals' behavior with a high degree of reliability.

If these characteristics can systematically be identified, it should be possible to employ techniques of statistical analysis that objectify the bases of the educated guess, hunch, intuition, or whatever else the experienced officer calls his discriminatory abilities. Such a statistical analysis will not provide better information than good judgment, but it can systematically process more information than any single police officer can possibly handle. Cases are reported daily that may never come to the attention of the particular police officer who could readily recognize the M/O. Detectives, lacking complete knowledge of everything that comes into the department, cannot possibly coordinate their efforts in the most efficient manner. It is obviously true that five detectives working on assignments tracking down, for example, five individual burglars who have committed eight break-ins within one week will do better than they will if each is tackling eight random cases where each investigator is crossing the tracks of the others, needlessly duplicating their efforts. Lacking the big picture, each investigator is handicapped by being unable to see the emerging outlines of the characteristics of the criminals' styles.

3.3.2   Description of Innovation

To study the possibility that statistical analysis might assist in identifying such patterns of criminal activity, a series of 38 break-ins were simulated in which differing M/Os were incorporated into the incident reports. The analytic procedures were as follows. First, a measure of similarity of pairs of crimes was defined. This measure was proportional to the number of characteristics that a pair of crimes had in common within seven categories. The categories were location of entry, side of entry, location on block, method of opening, day of week, value of property, and type of material taken. The "type of material" category was divided into eight sub-categories. The measure of similarity was the number of identical characteristics within the first six

Table 3.3.1 Comparison of Two Cases as Analyzed For Similarity

Category	Case 1	Case 2	Similarity
Location of entry	Window	Roof	0
Side of entry	Back	Garage	0
Location on block	Middle	Middle	1
Method of opening	Forced	Broken	0
Day of week	Tuesday	Thursday	0
Value of property	30-50,000	Less than 30,000	0
	Type of material taken		
Small appliance?	No	No	1
Major appliance?	Yes	No	0
Money?	No	No	1
Credit cards?	No	No	0
Checks?	No	Yes	0
Jewelry?	No	Yes	0
Tools?	No	No	1
Gems?	No	Yes	0
	Final measure of similarity 4		

categories and the eight sub-categories of type of material taken. Thus, a pair of crimes could have a similarity value ranging from 0 (no characteristics in common) to 14 (all characteristics in common). For example, consider cases 1 and 2. Table 3.3.1 illustrates how the measure of similarity between these two cases was computed.

Note that this measure of similarity treats the characteristics within the type of material category differently than it does the rest of the categories. For the subcategories within the type of material category, similarity between two cases was increased if a particular type of material was either taken or ignored in both cases; for example, the failure to take small appliances in both cases 1 and 2 in the table. It should also be noted that this measure of similarity gives more weight to the type of material taken than to the rest of the categories. Obviously, many other measures of similarity could be considered. Other possibilities are currently being investigated.

After similarity values between each pair of crimes were obtained, these values were input to a nonmetric multidimensional scaling program.[98] This program was designed to represent the cases by points in a two-dimensional space such that distances between pairs of points corresponded to the similarity between corresponding pairs of cases. Specifically, if a pair of crimes was highly similar, the program positioned the points representing the cases close together. If a pair of crimes was dissimilar, the program positioned the points representing the two cases far apart in the space. In this case, distance between any pair of points varied inversely with the similarity between the corresponding pair of cases.

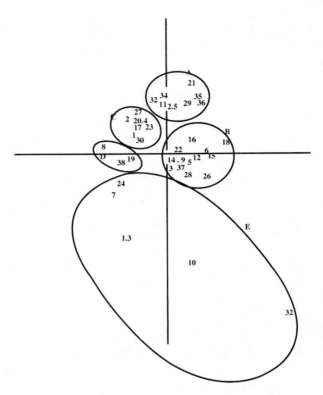

Figure 3.3.1 Two-dimensional representation of 38 simulated crimes. Each number represents a crime. Contours outline subjectively determined clusters and were drawn without prior knowledge of which crimes represented similar M/O's.

The clusters outlined in Figure 3.3.1 were drawn by one of the present authors without prior knowledge of which cases were actually created to cluster together. Other, more objective measures of clustering, based on interpoint distances in a multidimensional space and on the original similarity values themselves, have been investigated.[100]

In the selection of cases for simulation, it was determined in advance that the break-ins should represent five different foci of criminal activity. The M/Os were chosen to simulate the actual patterns of burglars functioning in the city of Chattanooga. One group was constructed where the burglar normally forces entry through a door and takes any small object that can be readily transported, with a preference for tools, guns jewelry, credit cards, and cash. Another group represented an individual with a preference for middle-income housing, who normally force entry through windows, and who had preference for large appliances. A third group represented the M/O described earlier, where entry was effected through a wall in lower-income housing, from which the thief took TV sets. A fourth group had to do with cases involving expensive homes, isolated at the end of a block, from which a variety of materials might be stolen, but which always involved the theft of jewelry. The fifth group again showed a preference for targets that were physically isolated, but where the materials taken were most commonly small appliances, and where entry was most often forced in lower-income homes.

The match achieved by the statistical analysis and the predetermined groupings was very good. The program grouped all the cases of entry through the wall together. Two random cases were also ascribed to this group. Of the seven jewel thefts from high-income residences, three (see Figure 3.3.1) were ascribed to group E, three to group B, and two to group D. The differences in assignment were the result of substantial departures from the pattern of entry through a door, and working the isolated end of the block. Both of these differences might well be significant indicators of M/Os to distinguish among criminals. Consequently, although this classification was fragmented into the three groups by the analysis, the fragmentation could very reasonably be a meaningful separation in practice. Six cases were assigned to a group characterized by window entry of houses in the middle of the block, where entry was forced, major appliances taken, and where there was a preference for middle-income dwellings. Six of the eight cases in group C make up that group. Nine of the cases of group B are made up of the juvenile simulation where the residences were not selected in advance, but were targets of opportunity, where small appliances were the materials taken in most instances, and where the houses were usually isolated at the end of a block. In no case was day of the week a significant discriminator. In short, the analysis achieved what was hoped for. As shown in Table 3.3.2, there was an 80% correspondence between the pre-analysis groups and those derived statistically.

The real test of the technique is, of course, in its application to actual data. Validation depends upon clearances of cases where a determination is made of the actual responsibility for specific burglaries. From this, one can determine the certainty with which one can view the assignment of a case to a particular group as indicative of the working of one individual or group of individuals. Actual cases where clearances have been achieved provides this validation if the analysis is done blind and if the analysis groups crimes together in accordance with cleared data on who was responsible for committing specific crimes. Such an analysis has been completed. Fifteen actual cases were subjected to the analysis described. These cases were cleared and known to have been the work of three different burglars or groups of burglars working in the city of Chattanooga. The clusters derived from computer analysis are shown in Figure 3.3.2. The correspondences between cases for which the three criminal groups were responsible and the statistically derived clusters is presented in Table 3.3.3. The correspondence between actual and analytic groups is 93%.

Table 3.3.2   Correspondence Between Predetermined
Simulated Grouping and Statistically Derived Clusters

					Group				
A		B		C		D		E	
Sim	Stat	Sim	Stat	Sim	Stat	Sim	Stat	Sim	Stat
21	21	5	5	1	1	2	—	3	3
29	29	11	—	4	4	8	8	6	—
31	31	12	12	17	17	19	19	7	7
34	34	14	14	23	23	20	—	9	—
35	35	15	15	27	27	22	—	10	10
36	36	16	16	30	30	38	38	13	13
—	11	18	18	—	2			24	24
—	25	25	—	—	20			32	32
		26	26						
		28	28						
		33	33						
		37	37						
		—	9						
		—	22						

The clusters around which the contours are drawn in Figures 3.3.1 and
3.3.2 are subjectively determined. Groups of crimes do emerge to naive
scrutiny of the data when they are so presented. Obviously, a more objective
means of defining clusters is desirable. Such an objective procedure has been
employed for the 15 actual cases. Figure 3.3.3 shows clusters generated by
PEEP-I, a computer program for nonmetric probability clustering.[101] This
program sequentially partitioned the points until all partitions and sub-
partitions were identified.

In this analysis essentially the same groupings appear as in Figure 3.3.2.
The data upon which this analysis is based are the same as before. The
difference is that the computer program identified the clusters. It is seen that
groups A and B are grouped as before. Group C is, of course, a more loosely
structured group of crimes, one of whose primary characteristics is the very
fact of greater heterogeneity in technique. Case 2 is erroneously assigned to
group C rather than to A as before. In short, the objectified analysis confirms
the subjective clusters.

The phenomenal success of this technique in grouping the crimes of the
three burglars must be noted with some caution, however. We deliberately
chose three criminals with clearly defined M/Os. Moreover, no data were
included from the casual, target-of-opportunity type of burglary whose perpetrator may not soon repeat his crime. Such data would blur the precision
with which this analysis assigns cases. Nevertheless, the basic groupings
would remain. Error would be introduced by the occasional assignment of
random cases to specific groups. This, however, is an error that also occurs
when assignments are based upon human intuition.

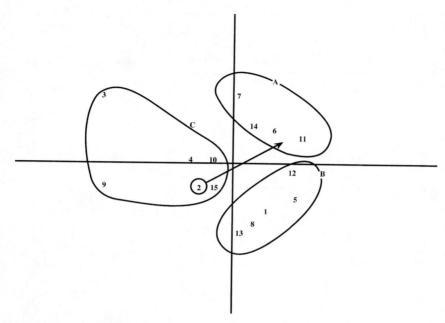

Figure 3.3.2 Two dimensional representation of 15 solved crimes. Each number represents a crime. Contours outline subjectively determined clusters and were drawn without prior knowledge of which crimes were the work of the three separate burglars whose crimes were studied. One case (Case 2) was assigned to an inappropriate group.

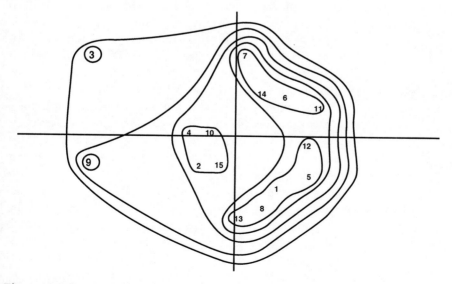

Figure 3.3.3 Two-dimensional representation of 15 solved crimes with contours drawn around computer-identified clusters.

Table 3.3.3   Correspondence Between Actual Criminal Patterns and Statistically Defined Groups

Burglar A		Burglar B		Burglar C	
Actual Cases	Stat Groups	Actual Cases	Stat Groups	Actual Cases	Stat Groups
2	—	1	1	3	3
6	6	5	5	4	4
7	7	8	8	9	9
11	11	12	12	10	10
14	14	13	13	15	15
					2

3.3.3   General Applications

The results of this validation study provide strong encouragement to the belief that this type of data processing can yield benefits of enormous significance in facilitating police operations. Specifically, the analysis described here can be applied to the data of daily incidence reports with the following advantages:

1. An up-to-date running record could be achieved against which new cases could routinely be compared for assignment to investigative teams. A comprehensive assessment of current M/Os could thereby maximize efficient use of the detective division in follow-up investigations.
2. Where current statistics are available, a new incident report could well provide hot lead on the activity of suspects who are already reasonably well identified. The progressive pattern could be determined over time, and anticipation of moves to fence stolen merchandise could lead to more effective surveillance and eventual apprehension.
3. Criminals often work their own neighborhoods, so a geographical separation of sets of burglaries will usually indicate the work of different groups of people. Where crimes are all committed in one general area, other discriminators are needed to identify the work of different parties. Statistical analysis provides the means of making those discriminations.
4. Comprehensive summaries of the M/Os characteristic of particular groups could be built up, against which an evaluation could be made of the probable characteristics of the perpetrator of a new incident. For example, the general profile of thefts by juveniles can be expected to differ from that of the adult addict, or the specialist in the theft of jewels, coins, furs, or silver plate. Once those profiles are determined, a specific case can be compared and probability statement generated to indicate the type of criminal who should be sought. In short, crime statistics could be used to draw the profile of the criminal. The individual's operation is, in general, as characteristic as his fingerprint. The class of criminal can be expected to show similar consistencies.

3.3.4 Note

The authors gratefully acknowledge the cooperation of Sheriff Jerry Pitts and Sergeant William Cox of the Chattanooga Police Department for making available the actual crime statistics used in this report.

References

1. Block, C. R. and Block, R., Street Gang Crime in Chicago, *Natl. Inst. Justice Res. Brief*, Washington, D.C, 1993.

2. Block, C. R. and Christakos, A., Major Trends in Chicago homicide: 1965-1994, *Ill. Crim. Justice Inf. Auth.*, Chicago, 1995.

3. Block, R. L., Homicide in Chicago: a nine-year study (1965-1973), *J. Crim. Law Criminol.*, 66(4): 496-510, 1976.

4. Block, R. L. and Zimring, F., Homicide in Chicago, 1965-1970. *J. Res. Crime Delinquency*, 10: 1-7, 1973.

5. Decker, S. H., Exploring victim-offender relationships in homicide: the role of individual and event characteristics, *Justice Quart.*, 10(4): 585-612, 1993.

6. Decker, S. H., Deviant homicide: a new look at the role of motives and victim-offender relationships, *J. Res. Crime Delinquency*, 33 (4):427-449, 1996.

7. Siegel, L., *Criminology: Theories, Patterns, and Typologies*, 6th ed., West/Wadsworth Publishing Company, Belmont, CA, 1998.

8. Prentky, R., Cohen, M., and Seghorn, T., Development of a rational taxonomy for the classification of rapists: the Massachusetts treatment center system, *Bull. Am. Acad. Psychiatry Law*, 13(1):39-70, 1985.

9. Rosenberg, R., Knight, R. A., Prentky, R. A., and Lee, A., Validating the components of a taxonomic system for rapists: a path analytic approach, *Bull. Am. Acad. Psychiatry Law*, 16 (2): 169-185, 1988.

10. Amir, M., Political terrorism and common criminality, in Ward, R. H. and Smith, H. E., Eds., *International Terrorism: Operational Issues*, Chicago, IL: University of Illinois at Chicago, Chicago, 95-109, 1988.

11. Gelles, R. J., *Violent Home*, Sage Publications, Newbury Park, CA, 1987.

12. Miethe, T. D. and McCorkle, R. C., *Crime Profiles: the Anatomy of Dangerous Persons, Places, and Situations*, Roxbury Press, Los Angeles, 1998.

13. Swanton, B., *Violence and the Public Contact Workers*, Australian Institute of Criminology, Australia, 1989.

14. Whittingham, M.D., Vandalism: the urge to damage and destroy, *Can. J. Criminol.*, 23(1): 69-73, 1981.

15. Rose, H., Black-on-black homicides: overview and recommendations, in Georges-Abeyie, D., Ed., *The Criminal Justice System and Blacks*, Clark Boardman Company, New York, 61-74, 1984.

16. Petersilia, J., Criminal career research: a review of recent evidence, in Morris, N. and Tonry, M., Eds., *Crime and Justice: An Annual Review of Research*, Vol. 2, University of Chicago Press, Chicago, 321-379, 1980.

17. Chambliss, W. J., Types of deviance and the effectiveness of legal sanctions, *Wisc. Law Rev.*, Summer: 703-719, 1967.

18. Parker, R. N. and Smith, M., Deterrence, poverty, and type of homicide, *Am. J. Sociol.*, 85(3): 614-624, 1979.

19. Thomas, C. W. and Williams, J. S., Actors, actions, and deterrence: a reformulation of Chambliss's typology of deterrence, in Riedel, M. and Vales, P. A., Eds., *Treating the Offender: Problems and Issues*, Praeger Publishers, New York, 1977.

20. Clarke, R. V., *Situational Crime Prevention: Successful Case Studies*, Harrow and Heston, New York, 1997.

21. Cornish, D. B. and Clarke, R.V., *The Reasoning Criminal: Rational Choice Perspectives on Offending*, Springer-Verlag, New York, 1986.

22. Polk, K., *When Men Kill: Scenarios of Masculinity Violence*, Cambridge University Press, New York, 1994.

23. Maxfield, M., Circumstances in supplementary homicide reports: variety and validity, *Criminology*, 27(4): 671-695, 1989.

24. Feeney, F., Robbers as decision-makers, in Cornish, D.B. and Clarke, R.V., Eds., *The Reasoning Criminal: Rational Choice Perspectives on Offending*, Springer-Verlag, New York, 53-71, 1986.

25. Gabor, T., Baril, M., Cusson, M., Elie, D., Leblanc, M., and Normandeau, A., *Armed Robbery: Cops, Robbers, and Victims*, Charles C Thomas Publishing, Springfield, Illinois, 1987.

26. MacDonald, J. M., *Armed Robbery: Offenders and Their Victims*, Charles C Thomas Publishing, Springfield, IL, 1975.

27. Felson, R. B., Predatory and dispute-related violence: a social interactionist approach, in Clarke, R. V. and Felson, M., Eds., *Routine Activity and Rational Choice*, Transaction Publishers, New Brunswick, 103-125, 1993.

28. Williams, K. R. and Flewelling, R. F., Family, acquaintance, and stranger violence: alternative procedures for rate calculations, *Criminology*, 25(3): 543-560, 1987.

29. Riedel, M., Nationwide homicide datasets: an evaluation of UCR and NCHS data, in MacKenzie, D. L., Baunach, P. J., and Roberg, R. R., Eds., *Measuring Crime: Large-Scale, Long-Range Efforts*, State University of New York Press, Albany, New York, 1989.

30. Riedel, M., Zahn, M. A., and Mock, L., The Nature and Patterns of American Homicide, National Institute of Justice, *Government Printing Office*, Washington, D.C., 1985.

31. Loftin, C., The validity of robbery-murder classifications in Baltimore, *Violence and Victims*, 1: 191-204, 1986.

32. Loftin, C., Kindley, K., Norris, S. L., and Wiersema, B., An attribute approach to relationships between offenders and victims in homicide, *J. Crim. Law Criminol.*, 78: 259-271, 1987.

33. Fox, J. A., *Uniform Crime Reports [United States]: Supplementary Homicide Reports, 1976-1992*, Computer file, ICPSR version, Northeastern University, College of Criminal Justice [producer], Boston. Ann Arbor, MI: Inter-University Consortium for Political and Social Research [distributor], 1994.

34. Kennedy, L. W. and Sacco, V. F., Crime Counts: A Criminal Event Analysis, Nelson Canada, Scarborough, Ontario, 1996.

35. Miethe, T. D. and Meier, R. F., *Crime and Its Social Context: Toward an Integrated Theory of Offenders, Victims, and Situations*, State University of New York Press, Albany, New York, 1994.

36. Drass, K. A. and Ragin, C. C., QCA: *Qualitative Comparative Analysis*, Center for Urban Affairs and Policy Research, Northwestern University, Evanston, Illinois, 1989.

37. Ragin, C. C., *The Comparative Method: Moving Beyond Qualitative and Quantitative Strategies*, University of California Press, Berkeley, CA, 1987.

38. Ragin, C. C., Introduction to Qualitative Comparative Analysis, in T. Janoski and A. M. Hicks, Eds., *The Comparative Political Economy of the Welfare State*, Cambridge University Press, New York, 1994.

39. Ragin, C. C., Mayer, S. E., and Drass, K. A., Assessing discrimination: a Boolean approach, *Am. Soc. Rev.*, 49:221-34, 1984.

40. Cleveland, W. S., *The Elements of Graphing Data* [Revised Edition], AT & T: Murray Hills, New Jersey, 1994.

41. Turvey, B., Tamlyn, D., and Chisum, J., *Criminal Profiling*, London: Academic Press, 1999.

42. Egger, S., *The Killers among Us: an Examination of Serial Murder and Its Investigation*, New Jersey: Prentice Hall, 1997.

43. Jackson, J. L. and Bekerian, D. A., *Offender Profiling: Theory, Research, and Practice*, West Sussex, England: Wiley, 1997.

44. Godwin, M., *Hunting Serial Predators: a Multivariate Classification Approach to Profiling Violent Behavior*, Boca Raton, FL: CRC Press, 2000.

45. Holmes, R. M. and Holmes, S., *Profiling Violent Crimes: an Investigative Tool*, 2nd ed., CA: Sage, 1996.

46. Hickey, E., *Serial Murderers and Their Victims*, 2nd ed., Belmont, CA: Wadsworth, 1997.

47. Ressler, R., Burgess, A.W., and Douglas, J., *Sexual Homicide: Patterns and Motives*, Lexington, MA: Lexington Books, 1988.

48. Douglas, J. E. and Olshaker, M., *Journey into Darkness*, London: Heinemann, 1997.

49. Michaud, S. G. and Hazelwood, R., *The Evil That Men Do: FBI Profiler Roy Hazelwood's Journey into the Minds of Sexual Predators*, New York: St Martins Press, 1999.

50. Geberth, V. J. and Turco, R. N., Antisocial personality disorder, sexual sadism, malignant, narcissism, and serial murder, *J. Forensic Sci.*, 42: 49-60, 1997.

51. Giannangelo, S. 1996. *The Psychopathology of Serial Murder*, Westport, CT: Praeger.

52. Burgess, A. W., Hartman, C. R., Ressler, R. K., Douglas, J. E., and McCormack, A., Sexual homicide: a motivational model, *J. Interpersonal Violence*, 1:251-272, 1986.

53. Liebert, J., Contributions of psychiatric consultation in the investigation of serial murder, *Int. J. Offender Therap. Comp. Criminol.*, 29:187-200, 1985.

54. Lester, D., *Serial killers: the Insatiable Passion*, Philadelphia, PA: The Charles Press, 1995.

55. Hickey, E., *Serial Murderers and Their Victims*, Pacific Grove, CA: Brooks and Cole, 1991.

56. Groth, A., Burgess. A., and Holmstrom, L., Rape, power, anger, and sexuality, *Am. J. Psychiatry*, 134: 1239-1243, 1977.

57. Keppel, R. and Walter, R., Profiling killers: a revised classification model for understanding sexual murder, *Int. J. Offender Therap. Comp. Criminol.*, 43:417-437, 1999.

58. Dietz, P. E., Hazelwood, R, and Warren, J., The sexually sadistic criminal and his offenses, *Bull. Am. Acad. Psychiatry Law*, 18:163-178, 1990.

59. Meloy, J. R., *Violent attachments*, New Jersey: Aronson, 1997.

60. Sullivan, H. S., *The Interpersonal Theory of Psychiatry*, New York: Norton, 1953.

61. Suttie, H., 1935, Analyzing childhood trauma, in H. Parens, Ed., *The Development of Aggression in Early Childhood*, New York: Aronson, 1979.

62. Klein, M., 1934, On criminality, in M. Klein, Ed., *Love, Guilt, and Reparation and Other Works, 1921-1945*, New York: Free Press, 258-261, 1975.

63. Swann, W. B., Self-verification: bringing social reality into harmony with the self, in J. Suls and A. G. Greenwald, Eds., *Psychological Perspectives on the Self*, Hillsdale, NJ: Lawrence Erlbaum, 2, 1983.

64. Gifford, R. and O'Connor, B., The interpersonal circumplex as a behavior map, *J. Personality and Soc. Psychology*, 52:1019-1026, 1987.

65. Bartholomew, K., Avoidance of intimacy: an attachment perspective, *J. Soc. Personal Relationships*, 7:147-178, 1990.

66. Kagan, J., *The Second Year: the Emergence of Self Awareness*, Cambridge, MA: Harvard University Press, 1989.

67. Miller, R. S., Humiliation and shame: comparison of two affective states as indications of narcissistic stressors, *Bull. Menninger Clin.*, 52: 40-51, 1983.

68. Birtchnell, J., Attachment-detachment, directiveness-receptiveness: a system for classifying interpersonal attitudes and behavior, *Br. J. Med. Psychol.*, 60: 17-27, 1987.

69. Laing, R. D., *The Divided Self*, London: Penguin Books, 1965.

70. Gacono, C. and Meloy, R., A Rorschach investigation of attachment and anxiety in antisocial personality disorder, *J. Nerv. Ment. Dis*, 179,546-552, 1991.

71. Keppel, R. and Weis, J., April. HITS: catching criminals in the Northwest, *FBI Law Enforcement Bull.*, 14-19, 1993.

72. Lingoes, J. C., The multivariate analysis of qualitative data, *Multivar. Behav. Res.*, 3: 61-94, 1973.

73. Canter, D., *Facet Theory: Approaches to Social Research*, New York: Springer-Verlag, 1985.

74. Holsti, O., *Content Analysis for the Social Sciences and Humanities*, Massachusetts: Addison Wesley, 1969.

75. Krippendorf, K., *Content Analysis: an Introduction to its Methodology*, Beverly Hills: Sage, 1980.

76. Shye, S., *Theory Construction and Data Analysis in the Behavioural Sciences*, San Francisco: Jossey Bass, 1978.

77. Donald, I. and Canter, D.,Temporal and trait facets of personnel assessment, *Appl. Psychol. Int. Rev.*, 39: 413-429, 1990.

78. Levy, S., Lawful roles of facets in social theories, in I. Borg, Ed., *Multidimensional Data Representation: When and Why*, Ann Arbor, MI: Mathesis Press, 1981.

79. Foa, U. G., New developments in facet design and analysis, *Psychological Rev.*, 72: 262-274, 1965.

80. Borg, I. and Shye, S., *Facet Theory: Form and Content*, Newbury, CA: Sage, 1995.

81. Brown, J., An introduction to the uses of facet theory, in D. Canter, Ed., *Facet Theory Approaches to Social Research*, New York: Springer-Verlag, 17-57, 1985.

82. Dancer, L. S., Introduction to facet theory and its application, *Appl. Psychol. Int. Rev.*, 39:365-377, 1990.

83. Cronbach, L. J., *Essentials of Psychological Testing*, New York: Harper and Row, 1960.

84. Meloy, J. R., A psychotic sexual psychopath: I just had a violent thought, *J. Pers. Assessment*, 58: 480-493, 1992.

85. Mones, P., *Stalking Justice*, New York: Pocket Books, 1995.

86. Dietz, P. E., Sex offender profiling by the FBI: a preliminary conceptual model, in M. H. Ben-Aron, S. J. Hucker, and C. D. Webster, Eds., *Criminal Criminology: the Assessment and Treatment of Criminal Behavior*, Pittsburgh, PA: American Academy of Psychiatry and Law, 1985.

87. Dietz, P. E., Patterns in human violence, in R. Hales and A. Frances, Eds., *American Psychiatric Association Annual Review*, 6: 465-490, Washington, D.C.: American Psychiatric Press, 1987.

88. Graysmith, R., *The Sleeping Lady: the Trailside Murders above the Golden Gate*, New York: Onyx, 1990.

89. Carlisle, A. L., The divided self: toward an understanding of the dark side of the serial killer, *Am. J. Crim. Justice*, 27:23-36, 1993.

90. De River, J. P., *Crime and the Sexual Psychopath*, Springfield, IL, Charles C Thomas, 1958.

91. Cartel, M. D., *Disguise of Sanity: Serial Mass Murder*, Toluca Lake, CA: Pepperbox Books, 1985.

92. Douglas, J. and Burgess, A., Criminal profiling: a viable investigative tool against violent crime, *FBI Law Enforcement Bull.*, 55: 9-13, 1986.

93. McDougal, D., *Angel of Darkness*, New York: Warner Books, 1993.

94. Balint, M., *The Basic Fault: Therapeutic Aspects of Regression*, London: Tavistock, 1967.

95. Katz, J., *Seductions of Crime*, New York: Basic Books, 1988.

96. Chassequet-Smirgel, J., *Creativity and Perversion*, New York: W.W. Norton, 1985.

97. James, E., *Catching Serial Killers: Learning from Past Serial Murder Investigations*, Lansing, MI: International Forensic Service, 1991.

98. Jackson, T. and Cole, T., *Rites of Burial: the Horrific Account of a Sadistic Serial Killer*, London: Virgin Books, 1992.

99. Johnson, R. M., Pairwise nonmetric multidimensional scaling, *Psychometrika*, 38:11-18, 1973.

100. Johnson, S. C., Hierarchical clustering schemes, *Psychometrika*, 32:241-254, 1967.

101. Lingoes, J. C. and Cooper, T., PEEP-I: a fortran IV (G) program for Guttman-Lingoes nonmetric probability clustering, *Behav. Sci.*, 16:259-261, 1971.

Crime Scene Variables Correspond to SSA Plot

Variable 1
blitz
Blitz Attack   0 = No   1 = Yes
Sudden and immediate use of violence, whether proceeded by a confidence
or ploy approach or not, which incapacitates the victim. Typically, the victim
succumbs to the power and control of the offender.

Variable 2
con
Con Approach   0 = No   1 = Yes
Offender initiated contact with the victim prior to attack by use of a con or
deception. Any verbal contact, questions asked, pseudo introductions or story
told. Any pseudo names or businesses used to gain entry into victims' homes.

Variable 3
ploy
Ploy Approach   0 = No   1 = Yes
Offender initiated contact with the victim prior to the attack by the use of a
ploy or subterfuge. Any role taken, such as faking a broken leg or arm.

Variable 4
gag
Gagging   0 = No   1 = Yes
Use at any time during the attack of any physical article placed in or around
the victim's mouth. This does not include manual gagging. Gag may be used
to prevent noise or associated with sexual role-playing or bondage.

Variable 5
blindfol
Blindfold   0 = No   1 = Yes
Use at any time during the attack of any physical interference with the victim's
ability to see. This included only the use of articles, and not verbal threats
or temporary use of the offender's hands.

Variable 6
facecov
Facecover   0 = No   1 = Yes
Use at any time during the attack of any physical article used to cover the
victim's entire head.

Variable 7
forced
Forced Entry   0 = No   1 = Yes
Entry into the victim's home was by force. Prying open windows and doors,
breaking locks and windows. This does not include physical force upon the
victim.

Variable 8
night
Night Entry   0 = No   1 = Yes
Entry into the victim's home was during the night. Any entry made between
sunset and sunrise.

Variable 9
destevid
Destroyed Evidence   0 = No   1 = Yes
A forensic awareness variable. The offender destroyed or attempted to destroy
physical evidence at the crime scene. The focus of this category is to characterize those offenders who have performed some act which can be interpreted
as interference with the possible forensic examination of the crime scene or
victim. This would not include simply wearing gloves, which is a common
practice among most criminals. This involves activities such as wiping and
washing the victim as well as removing from the scene incriminating articles
or other evidence.

Variable 10
ransacke
Ransacked Property   0 = No   1 = Yes
Condition of the victim's property at the crime scene. Property at a crime
scene whether indoors or outdoors, personal belongings of the victim found
torn apart as if the offender were looking for something specific. The position
or placement of the victim's clothing is not included in these four property
variables. The condition of the victim's clothing would be included.

Variable 11
undistur
Undisturbed (Property)   0 = No   1 = Yes
Victim's property at the crime scene was found in its original form prior to the crime. The property was left undisturbed.

Variable 12
bdopenly
Victim (Body Openly Displayed)   0 = No   1 = Yes
Victim's body when discovered was found openly displayed. The body could be viewed with ease and was not obstructed by any trees or other barriers.

Variable 13
bdhidden
Victim (Body Hidden)   0 = No   1 = Yes
Victim's body when discovered was found hidden. The body could not be viewed with ease, and visibility was obstructed by trees or other barriers. This did not include bodies that were buried.

Variable 14
bodymove
Victim (Body Moved)   0 = No   1 = Yes
Victim's body was moved from the assault or murder site to the disposal site. Moving the body by foot or transport.

Variable 15
bdburied
Victim (Body Buried)   0 = No   1 = Yes
Victim's body was found completely buried in the ground. No part of the body was exposed or could be visually seen. This does not include the body being completely covered up by some article.

Variable 16
bodparts
Body Parts   0 = No   1 = Yes
Victim's body parts were found scattered away from the area where the body was lying. Also, any body part found any distance from the crime scene.

Variable 17
house
Victim (Found in House)   0 = No   1 = Yes
Victims whose bodies were discovered in a house.

Variable 18
bounrope
Victim Bound (Rope)   0 = No   1 = Yes
Victims who were found bound by rope, string, or twine, or who showed evidence of being restrained by same.

Variable 19
bountape
Victim Bound (Tape)   0 = No   1 = Yes
Victims who were found bound by tape or who showed evidence of being restrained by tape. This variable would not include those victims who were gagged with tape.

Variable 20
bouncord
Victim Bound (Cord)   0 = No   1 = Yes
Victims who were found bound by an electrical cord or who showed evidence of being restrained by same.

Variable 21
bouncuff
Victim Bound (Handcuffs)   0 = No   1 = Yes
Victims who were found bound by handcuffs or who showed evidence of being restrained by same.

Variable 22
restroff
Restraint Offender   0 = No   1 = Yes
Offender brought the restraining device(s) to the crime scene.

Variable 23
restvict
Restraint Victim   0 = No   1 = Yes
Victim brought the restraining device(s) to the crime scene. This does not imply that the victim purposely or intentionally carried a restraining device to the crime scene but rather, property owned by the victim was used to restrain or bind them.

Variable 24
restrfound
Restraint Found   0 = No   1 = Yes
Offender left the restraining device at the crime scene.

Variable 25
Cannibal
Cannibalism/Drinking Blood   0 = No   1 = Yes
Offender engaged in cannibalism and/or drinking the victim's blood.

Variable 26
heldcapt
Victim (Held Captive)   0 = No   1 = Yes
Offender held a victim captive for more than eight hours prior to the murder.

Variable 27
revisit
Revisited Crime Scene   0 = No   1 = Yes
Offender revisited the crime scene after the murder. Any trips made back to
the actual murder site if different from the victim's body dump site.

Variable 28
ritualsc
Ritualistic Activity   0 = No   1 = Yes
Any evidence found at the crime scene that suggests the offender performed
ritualistic acts on, with, or near the victim's body. Evidence of candle burning,
stacking of rocks, or dead animals found at the crime scene.

Variable 29
bodposed
Victim Body Posed   0 = No   1 = Yes
Position of the victim's body when found. Intentional posing of the victim's
body for shock value when discovered. This does not include staging the body.

Variable 30
piqueur
Piqueurism   0 = No   1 = Yes
Acts performed on the victim's body with a knife or other sharp instruments
that indicate excessive stabbing, cutting, or ripping of the flesh. These wounds
are usually inflicted near the genital or breast areas.

Variable 31
fullydrs
Victim (Full-dress)   0 = No   1 = Yes
One of four variables that described how the victim was dressed when discovered. This does not include the position of the victim's shoes.

Variable 32
nude
Victim Nude   0 = No   1 = Yes
How the victim was dressed when discovered. Victim completely nude, no clothes were found on the victim's body. This would include whether the victim's shoes were intact or not.

Variable 33
riptorn
Victim Clothes Ripped   0 = No   1 = Yes
How the victim's clothes were removed. Tearing of the victim's clothing.

Variable 34
scatterd
Clothing Scattered   0 = No   1 = Yes
Placement of the victim's clothing (not on the body) found at the crime scene.

Variable 35
hidden
Clothing Hidden   0 = No   1 = Yes
Offender intentionally hides the victim's clothing to avoid detection. Burning of the victim's clothing.

Variable 36
stolen
Personal Items Stolen   0 = No   1 = Yes
The taking of small personal items (other than clothing) from the victim. These items may or may not be valuable, (e.g., photos, driver's license, real or costume jewelry, etc.).

Variable 37
disfigur
Victim's Body Disfigured   0 = No   1 = Yes
Elements of torture or unusual assaults on the victim's body. Removal of body parts, burns, mutilation of body cavities.

Variable 38
hack
Victim's Body Hacked   0 = No   1 = Yes
Dismemberment by hacking or chopping off body parts.

Variable 39
organ
Sex Organs Assaulted   0 = No   1 = Yes
Any evidence suggesting the offender explored the victim's body cavities or
assaulted victim's sexual organs. Any attempts and insertion of fingers or
foreign objects into the victim.

Variable 40
dispost
Dismember Postmortem   0 = No   1 = Yes
Dismemberment by hacking or chopping off body parts post-mortem.

Variable 41
sexassau
Attempted Sexual Assault   0 = No   1 = Yes
Any evidence suggesting the offender attempted to sexually assault the victim.
Any evidence of masturbation on the victim's body.

Variable 42
vaginal
Vaginal Penetration   0 = No   1 = Yes
Intercourse with the victim. This would not include penetration by a foreign
object or fingers.

Variable 43
analsex
Anal Penetration   0 = No   1 = Yes
Anal intercourse with the victim. This would not include any penetration by
a foreign object or fingers.

Variable 44
maleanal
Male Sexual Assault   0 = No   1 = Yes
Anal assault carried out on male victim.

Variable 45
sexpost
Sexual Assault (postmortem)   0 = No   1 = Yes
Necrophilic acts performed on the victim's body.

Variable 46
semen
Semen Evidence   0 = No   1 = Yes
Offender's semen was found on and/or in or around the victim's body.

Variable 47
foreobj
Foreign Object(s)   0 = No   1 = Yes
Foreign object(s) found inside the victim's body.

Variable 48
insert
Foreign Objects Inserted   0 = No   1 = Yes
Evidence that foreign object(s) had been inserted into the victim's body.

Variable 49
bitemark
Bitemarks   0 = No   1 = Yes
Evidence of bite mark(s) on the victim's body. This would include any evidence of chewing on a particular body part.

Variable 50
firearm
Weapon Type (Firearm)   0 = No   1 = Yes
One of five variables that describes the type of weapon that caused the death of the victim. This particular variable would include any type of gun (e.g., shot gun, rifle, or handgun).

Variable 51
knife
Weapon a Knife/Cutting   0 = No   1 = Yes
Any cutting or sharp instrument, such as a knife, sword, or machete.

Variable 52
bludgeon
Bludgeon   0 = No   1 = Yes
Any blunt instrument, such as a club or tire iron.

Variable 53
ligature
Ligature   0 = No   1 = Yes
Any article used to strangle the victim. This would not include the offender's hands, legs, or feet.

Variable 54
hand/feet
Weapon Hands/Feet   0 = No   1 = Yes
Use of the offender's hands, feet, legs, or arms to strangle or beat the victim.

Variable 55
weaponop
Weapon of Opportunity   0 = No   1 = Yes
One of two variables that described where the weapon(s) used in the murders
came from. This particular variable would include any weapon that was
found at the crime scene or brought to the scene by the victim.

Variable 56
weapoff
Weapon Offender   0 = No   1 = Yes
Offender pre-selected a weapon and carried it to the crime scene.

Variable 57
weaponre
Weapon Recovered   0 = No   1 = Yes
The weapon used to commit the murder was found at the crime scene.

Variable 58
crimekit
Crime Kit   0 = No   1 = Yes
Offender possessed a crime-kit for torturing his victims. Electrical devices,
cutters, or pliers, etc. for use in submitting the victim to sadist torture. Items
such as duct tape and rope used to bind the victim.

Variable 59
tortured
Victim Tortured   0 = No   1 = Yes
Offender performed sadistic acts upon the victim's body while victim was
alive. Sadistic acts such as electric shock, cutting, or flagellation. Mental
torture such as forcing victim to write a letter to loved ones prior to death.
Victim suffered 10 or more stab wounds.

Variable 60
victdrug
Victim Drug   0 = No   1 = Yes
Victim was neutralized by chemical soporifics.

Variable 61
upbody
Stabbed/Upper Body   0 = No   1 = Yes
This is one of two variables that described the location of the stab wounds
on the victim's body. Any stabbing or cutting above the waist.

Variable 62
lowbody
Stabbed/Lower Body   0 = No   1 = Yes
Location of the stab wounds on the victim's body. Any stabbing or cutting
wounds below the waist.

Variable 63
trophies
Trophies   0 = No   1 = Yes
Offender retained personal items or body parts of the victim.

Variable 64
vehstole
Vehicle Stolen   0 = No   1 = Yes
Victim's vehicle stolen by the offender.

Variable 65
vicresid
Crime at Victim's Residence   0 = No   1 = Yes
Abduction, death, and body disposal site was the victim's home.

Profiling and Linking Crimes

4

4.1 One Offender – Five Victims: Linking the Offenses of the Serial Killer John Williams, Jr.

MAURICE GODWIN

This study showed the value of using Jaccard's co-efficients as a decision support system in a serial murder investigation. Highlighted was how important the initial selection phase of crime information selected must reflect the degree of variation within one serial murderer's actions, which then can be used to discriminate him from other possible offenders. Another important finding was, regardless of the effect of the representational system chosen to link criminal behavior, the accuracy of the decision maker is inevitably influenced by the appropriateness of the information chosen in the selection phase of the task of discriminating between offenders. Equally important was the finding that the representation of crime information can only be useful provided the information used is a valid measure. The results of this paper support the notion that to correctly link crimes, behavior selection must be valid indices of offender consistency, which can only be achieved through scientific research.

The crime of serial murder poses many difficult problems for law enforcement officials. For example, Egger argues that in stranger-to-stranger murders, lacking forensic evidence or witnesses, criminal investigators are left to deal with a large number of suspects, with only a small probability of including the offender.[1] As a result of the police inability to link, or connect, offenders or offenses, serial murderers are usually caught by "chance or coincidence."[1] In his study on 28 serial murderers, James found that 61% of the cases were solved due to eye witnesses, including victims that lived, rather than any direct investigative effort.[2]

The inability to link a series of crimes is often referred to as linkage blindness.[1] Egger points out that linkage blindness is the "nearly total lack of sharing or coordinating of investigative information and the lack of adequate networking by law enforcement agencies."[1] This applies to the failure of law enforcement agencies to share case information across city, county, and state jurisdictional lines. The author acknowledges that linkage blindness is a major problem, however, there is another form of blindness that occurs when police are faced with a series of unsolved crimes; that is, the inability to link behavioral patterns in offenses committed by a single perpetrator within the same jurisdiction.

The failure to link behavioral patterns is termed by this author as *ampliative blindness*, the failure of police to go beyond the evidence in hand.[3] For example, during an investigation, to arrive at sound investigative decisions, investigators should base their deductive inferences on inductive premises. While it is important for police to share similar case information on unsolved crimes with other police agencies, it is equally important for investigators to recognize similar offenses carried out by a single offender within their own jurisdiction. Without police first recognizing a crime pattern in their own area, there can be no information to share with other law enforcement agencies. Not only does ampliative blindness exist in serial murder investigations, investigators fail to notice the same pattern of behavior from offense to offense in other types of crimes such as rape and arson. The FBI and several states in the U.S.A. have taken some steps, although not truly productive ones, to reduce the effects of linkage blindness and ampliative blindness. The development of computerized data bases to store, manage, and link crimes has played only a minor role in helping link unsolved crimes, as discussed later in this section.

4.1.1   Decision Making in the Linking of Serial Murders

Deciding on the links between offender patterns or crimes is one of the most crucial decisions faced by any investigator. Recognizing similar patterns early can lead to increased resources for the police agency, improve clearance rates, and ultimately save lives. Positive linkage can also help to narrow down the search area for potential suspects. Knowing that one offender is responsible for several murders will allow investigators to make crude estimations of the offender's home base, which then can be used to narrow down the search area.[4] When there is only one offender and one offense location, it is difficult to make similar estimations.

4.1.2   The Use of Modus Operandi to Link Offenses

The traditional use of Modus Operandi (MO), as a basis for linking offenses is premised on the investigator's deductive reasoning that the MO is static and uniquely characteristic to a particular offender. MO is traditionally defined as distinctive actions which link crimes together.[5] As evidenced by this definition, often investigators confuse the offender's MO with his signature. Keppel and Birnes[6] point out:

An MO accounts for the type of crime and property used to commit a crime. The offender's MO includes the victim type, the time and place the crime was committed, the tools or implements used; the way the criminal gained entry or how he approached or subdued his victim, including disguises or uniforms, and ways he represented himself to a victim.

The authors suggests that an offender's MO can and does change over time as he discovers that some things can be done more effectively.[6] Keppel and Birnes also note that the MO of a killer is only those actions which are necessary to commit the murder.[6]

However, using MO to classify or link crime scene behavior is rather unreliable, as it does not take into account the many offense dynamics which can affect an offender's change in behavior due to such influences as changing victim reaction from one offense to another.[7] The offender's MO can change over time as a result of a number of factors, such as experience, which when committing crimes such as rape or murder leads to refinements in conduct to facilitate completion of the crime. These refinements in criminal actions can have a number of causes, for example, the result of being arrested or a result of victim response, causing the offender to change his way of dealing with the victim, including any future victims. The change in behavior could be attributed to factors such as maintaining control over the victim by the use of a weapon or, for example, a rapist progressing to murder in order to avoid identification.

4.1.3   Signature Behaviors

Another way police attempt to deduce what occurred in a series of murders is to record those actions that are unique across the offense series. The unique behaviors that serial murderers repeatedly leave at their crime scenes are referred to by forensic and criminal investigators as the killer's psychological signature.[8] These unique behavior patterns have been explained by the FBI as traits,[9] and they claim that the person variable shows consistency across crimes.[10] However, there lies danger in using the term "trait" as a cause of behavior.[11] To say that an offender left the victim nude after the murder explains nothing. Hilgard points out that traits are inferred from behavior, they cannot then be used to explain behavior.[12]

Ressler and his colleagues argue that signature actions are revealed due to the offender acting out his violent fantasies.[13] According to Ressler and his colleagues, fantasy may be manifested through particular verbal interaction with the victim, or through committing a series of actions on the victim in a particular order.[12] However, an offender's MO, or signature is not present in every murder, due to occurrences such as disturbances during the course of an offense or an unanticipated victim response, or because the body of the victim has decomposed prior to its discovery; therefore the signature aspect has been destroyed.

Signature behavior is defined by Keppel and Birnes[6] as:

> ... types of extraordinary violence similarities. For example, the victim was beaten beyond the point needed to kill her, or the killer seemed preoccupied with the victim's clothing or took some time to pose the victim's body. In leaving his signature, a killer's psychodrama is evolving, although the scene is different, the act contained the same plot, same characters, and same dialogue which came to the same conclusion.

The advantages of recognizing behavioral patterns immediately and linking crimes to a common offender are not straightforward. The difficulties encountered by police investigators when trying to decide whether patterns are similar from offense to offense may also not be as apparent. Forensic clues are rarely available to aid this process, and investigators are frequently required to consider similarities in offense behaviors. This task can be extremely difficult unless an offender has an unique signature. However, determining the underlying structure of offenders' signature behaviors requires extensive empirical analysis beyond any that is currently in use by police forces. Identifying the combinations of behavioral variables and background characteristics which account for an offender's individuality is the most logical way to facilitate an understanding of consistency and the development of offending behavior over time. One example of this empirical process can be seen in Section 3 in the article by this author entitled Death by Detail.

Any crimes that are linked erroneously could cost the police agency, in both financial and time considerations, a considerable amount of money. Providing police investigators with an empirical means of decision support has the potential to facilitate the decision-making process and thereby enhance the efficiency of investigative decision-making concerned with recognition of patterns and subsequently linking of crimes. The ultimate success of any enquiry team may lie with *Investigative Process Management*.[11]

4.1.4 Linking Serial Murders: A Three-Stage Process

4.1.4.1 *Information Management*

The first stage of the three-step process is selection of information. The selection of crime information is vital to the decision-making process when trying to link a series of unsolved murders. Traditionally, decisions of this sort are made deductively on the basis of the experience of a few selected investigators. In contrast to the deductive approach, the *Investigative Process Management* approach is validated through the development of theories based on inductive empirical data relationships. This approach to linking offense behavior minimizes the potential biases of individual experience upon decisions of all the circumstances of any particular case.

Once the boundaries for information selection have been defined, the information has to be represented before decisions can be made. So, the decision as to whether to link offenses can be viewed as a three-stage process. Initially, it requires the selection of information thought to be indicative of consistency. Secondly, once information has been selected, the investigator must structure the material through some representational means. Finally, decisions must be made about the relationships between crimes.

In recent years, information selection and inference derivation which is based upon the experience of the investigator has formed the basis of expert systems for investigative decision-making. Psychological exploration has shown that expert systems work best when the decision environment is stable.[14] The decision-making associated with linking of crimes is a complex process in which consideration must be accorded to the dynamics of the offense behavior. For example, some expert systems rely on production rules, such as IF/THEN statements, although they may have a number of connectives incorporated into the statements, such as, OR. Regardless of the connectives, production rules act to exclude cases that do not satisfy predetermined requirements, such as the example given below.

IF <x number of conditions true> THEN <x number of conclusions can be drawn>

The above approach to linking a series of murders would be appropriate if offenses occurred in a stable environment. However, to assume that behaviors such as those found at a serial murderer's crime scenes will be stable is erroneous, and would result in linked crimes being excluded from further analysis. Therefore, expert systems will not aid in the investigative process using the IF/THEN form of analysis. There are, however, Decision Support Systems (DSSs) which may assist with model building, as opposed to expert systems which simulate models, that could aid law enforcement in serial murder investigations.

4.1.5 The Representation of Crime Information

DSS, defined as a tool to assist with model building, is a way of representing information. This brings us to the second stage of the process, the representation stage. DSSs are used in the representation stage of the process. Having selected the information on which to base the decision to link, the material must be processed in order to structure the similarities and differences between crimes. There are many potential methods of representation that carry with them assumptions about the role of the investigator. These approaches to aid criminal investigations range from the purely graphical to the statistical. The more statistical the DSS chosen, the more processed the information becomes. This results in a more predetermined decision. Conversely, the more graphical the approach, the less processing is carried out on the crime information, and the less predetermined the decision.

There are currently several computerized professional visualization and analysis tools on the market which aid police investigators in making their decisions. One of the most popular is called the *Analyst's Notebook*. This computerized program advertises that it assists investigators by uncovering, interpreting, and displaying complex information in easily-understood chart form. The program claims that it can automatically analyze data sets, navigate through large networks in order to unravel complex relationships, and quickly discover key information and relationships. Another computerized program that is widely used by police forces is called *Watson*, manufactured by Harlequin Group, Inc. Watson is a high-level relational database integration for modeling data and representing information. A similar product used by police forces is SIUSS, a criminal intelligence analysis software program that stores, correlates, and analyzes crime information in order to identify and compare offenders' MOs for serial correlation in chart form. The implications of these three approaches to linking crimes are based on what is referred to as ANACAPA. ANACAPA is purely graphical, rather than assessing the co-occurrence of behaviors in a given series of crimes. Assessing the co-occurrence of behaviors in a crime is purely statistical, as demonstrated in Death by Detail in Section 3.

4.1.6   Defining ANACAPA

ANACAPA is system of information structuring originally developed in American after the assassination of President Kennedy in the 1960s.[15] ANACAPA is named after an island off the West Coast of America that is perpetually shrouded in mist. When the mist rises, all becomes clear. Hence, ANACAPA means "the parting of the mist."

Originally the ANACAPA technique started off as a paper-based system of information analysis. However, since computers have become more powerful and cheaper, programs have been developed to do the same kind of thing. For example, in the paper-based ANACAPA approach, if one has information about a number of people who have met each other, this relationship can be drawn using circles and lines connecting them. The circles would represent the people and the lines some kind of relationship of link. Text was usually written alongside the circles or links to identify the people or describe the relationship, for example, friends or business associates. The link lines can be solid or dotted to indicate the strength or reliability of the information about that link.

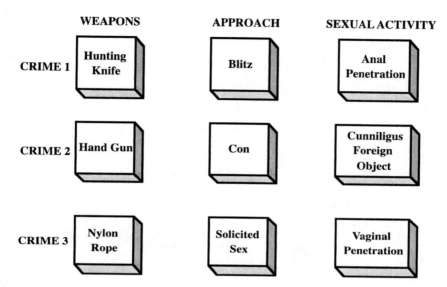

Figure 4.1.1 Part example of the layout and type of information recorded on an ANACAPA chart

In its computer form, ANACAPA is a tabulation process whereby all information considered relevant to an inquiry can be collated in chart form. Figure 4.1.1 demonstrates how crime information is recorded on an ANACAPA chart. From this visual display of relationships between variables, investigators may attempt to define the relationships between information concerning, for example, a series of murders. The technique shown in Figure 4.1.1, and less organized forms of it, is the most frequently used method of structuring crime data in police forces today. Figure 4.1.2 represents the same crime data found in Figure 4.1.1 but coded as an association matrix.

The ANACAPA approach to analyzing and linking crime patterns is thus viewed as a content-oriented approach that records all available information with no attempt to process the information. As a result, the investigator is asked, using all the available information before him or her, to establish links. The limitations of information-processing abilities ensures that this form of information systematization and linking crimes is extremely prone to bias by individual experience during the assimilation and interpretation phase. It is extremely difficult to avoid drawing deductive inferences using past experiences of a similar type of crime with this type of crime information representation. This method of accessing crime information and recognizing behavioral patterns maintains the most reliance on the investigator's personal, subjective judgement. An inductive and systematic approach to linking offenses is discussed below.

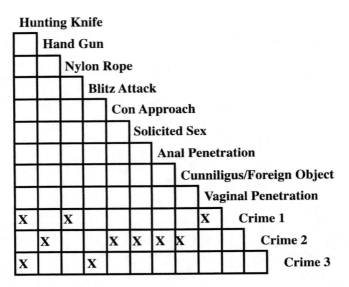

Figure 4.1.2 The crime information from ANACAPA presented as a simplified association matrix

4.1.7   A Case Study of Serial Murder: Linking Crimes

Beginning in 1996 through March 1997, the capital city of Raleigh, North Carolina, located in the eastern part of the state, was faced with a series of unsolved murders of six African-American females. The women were slain inside the Beltline, a major thoroughfare within the city limits. Initially, the Raleigh Police Department assured the public that a serial murderer had not murdered the women.[16] The police stated that beyond the fact that the victims suffered sheer brutality, the cases where not linked in any way.[16] The police views were confirmed later by North Carolina Chief Medical Examiner John Butts, who acknowledged that the circumstances and causes of the deaths were similar, but the crimes lacked a "signature that would point to a serial murderer."[16]

    Throughout 1996, investigators discounted the possibility of a serial murderer; however, by the end of 1996, with the murders still unsolved, police acknowledged that they were looking for one suspect. Later, Raleigh detectives determined that one of the five homicides was not related to the others, and a suspect was arrested and charged on January 17, 1997. On February 4, 1997, Raleigh police arrested John Williams, Jr., 36, an African-American male, a drifter from Augusta, Georgia. He was charged with two of the five murders. The remaining three murders have not yet officially been linked to Williams, and those cases are still open. Williams had a lengthy record of sexual assault, and was trying to rape a woman when he was apprehended by the police. Williams worked at a fast food restaurant and drifted among homeless shelters within the city of Raleigh.

What follows is a general discussion of the five murders which occurred in Raleigh, North Carolina, two of which Williams was arrested, charged, and sentenced to death for committing. DNA tests linked Williams to the two murders. Included are details about each victim and the crime scene evidence. The crime information was obtained from the Medical Examiner's office and published newspaper accounts of the murders. Presented below is the original case analysis and subsequent psychological profile, which was constructed by this author while living in Liverpool, England prior to solving of the murders. The profile presented below formed the backdrop for several newspaper articles about this author.[17]

4.1.8 The Victims

4.1.8.1 Victim One

The body of victim one, a black female, 33, was found the afternoon of January 7, 1996 behind a business in the 1500 block of South Blount Street, Raleigh, North Carolina. She had been strangled and beaten to death by the offender's hands. She had also been sexually assaulted vaginally. The presence of semen was found. The victim was found nude, lying back on a bench, her legs sprawled, and the only article of clothing that remained was her socks. Scratches and abrasions were found on the victim's shoulders, mid back and left buttock. One of the victim's shoes was found under a table, and the other nearby in the snow. The victim was known to work as a prostitute and was a drug user. John Williams, Jr. was charged for victim one's murder.

4.1.8.2 Victim Two

The second victim, a black female, 38, was found at 916 Oakwood Avenue, Raleigh, North Carolina. The victim was found in Oakwood Cemetery by grounds keepers. The victim was found wearing a bra, which was in disarray, and an ankle bracelet. According to the Medical Examiner's report, several upper teeth were missing, which was concluded to be the result of the homicide. There were multiple abrasions and contusions to the face, head, and neck areas. Smaller abrasions and contusions were found on the victim's hands, forearms, lower legs, and back. There were no skull fractures. The presence of blood was found in the victim's mouth. There was no evidence of external genitalia injury, however, semen was found in the anal area. The cause of death was manual or possible ligature strangulation with an article of clothing from the victim, with contributing factor of multiple blunt trauma to the face and head. The victim worked as a prostitute and was a known drug user. No arrests have been made in this case.

4.1.8.3   Victim Three

The third victim, a black female, 30, was found near a homeless camp near railroad tracks under Morgan Street Bridge in Raleigh, North Carolina. The victim was found nude except for a pair of high-top trainer shoes and white socks. Vaginal penetration had taken place, and a condom was found within the vagina. The cause of death was due to acute aortic rupture of the main vessel to the heart. This was caused by blunt chest trauma. Evidence of head and neck trauma was found which was consistent with strangulation. Near the body, police investigators found the possible murder weapon, a brick. There was also a footprint on her head and side. The victim was a known drug user. No arrest has been made in this case.

4.1.8.4   Victim Four

The fourth victim, a black female, 32, was found at the Martin Luther King Boulevard extension project near Dawson Street in Raleigh, North Carolina. She was found at a south side Raleigh construction site. Her body was found lying on its back, partly skeletonized. She had been strangled, and one hand was missing. Her clothing was found scattered nearby. The victim had an extensive record of drug, theft, and prostitution arrests. No arrest has been made in this case.

4.1.8.5   Victim Five

The fifth victim, a black female, 35, was found nude in an empty building being renovated at the intersection of North and West Streets. The victim's body showed signs of trauma. She had been beaten to death. Her clothes were found scattered nearby. There were no forensic reports on whether a sexual assault occurred or not. She had no criminal record, however, she was known to be a drug user. John Williams, Jr. was charged with this victim's murder.

4.1.9   Co-occurrence of Behaviors across a Series of Murders

A review of the case files for the five unsolved Raleigh murders produced a list of variables appropriate for analysis. The nine crime scene actions shown below were chosen for analysis using the Smallest Space Analysis (SSA-I) program. SSA-I is discussed in Section 3; however, a short description is provided here on how SSA can be used to link offenses.

Ligature
Semen found at crime scene
Bludgeon
Restraint victim
Weapon hands/feet
Anal penetration

Vaginal penetration
Clothing scattered
Victims nude

SSA-I is an empirical alternative to purely graphical and deductive methods of establishing links between offenses such as *Analyst's Notebook* and *Watson*. SSA uses the Jaccard's coefficient to measure the association between variables. The results are mapped using the monotone mapping condition.[18] Monotonic relationship states that the greater the similarity between two behavior items, the greater the proximity; that is, the smaller the distance between their geometric image points.[19] In a series of homicides, if a killer performed similar actions in his first two murders, but not in his third and fourth, then it would be expected, under the conditions of a monotonic relationship, that the behaviors from the first two crimes will have higher Jaccard's coefficients. Jaccard's coefficients are represented by 0.00, meaning that two variables do not share any similar behaviors to 1.00, a perfect correlation. The Jaccard coefficient represents the percentage of co-occurrence between two variables; i.e., crime scene behaviors. The use of the Jaccard's coefficient has the luxury of having each incident compared with every other incident.

4.1.10 Preparing the Data for Analysis

Using the crime scene variables gleaned from the unsolved case files, chosen after careful inspection of the offenses, SSA was carried out to test whether particular actions in the Raleigh murders could be linked. To carry out this procedure, 15 serial murder cases were chosen for the analysis, 10 of which came from a larger database, owned by this author, which originally formed the backdrop for Death by Detail in Section 3. The 10 solved serial murder offenses occurred in various regions of the U.S. The additional five serial murder offenses represented the unsolved murders in Raleigh. John Williams, Jr. was convicted for two of the murders. A research assistant from the University of Liverpool combined the crime scene actions from the Raleigh series with serial murder offenses unrelated to the Raleigh crimes. The data matrix was then given to the author for analysis. Prior to the analysis, the author had no knowledge of which offenses or offenders the columns or rows of data belonged to. It was only after the analysis that comparisons and links were made to the actual offenses.

In constructing the data matrix, the columns represented the cases or offenses, while the rows represented the crime scene actions. Presenting the data in this form allowed the SSA program to look at the co-occurrence of how each killer scored across each crime scene action. It should be noted, however, that this process does not classify offenders but rather looks at whether there were similarities (concurrences) between crime scene actions in the same series. This was an important step in the analysis, because it provided an empirical backdrop to test whether the SSA could link the offenses. Using the Investigative Process Management (IPM) approach discussed earlier, the author applied an inductive methodology to link offenses in the five unsolved murders in Raleigh, North Carolina. The results of the analysis are discussed in the next section.

4.1.11 SSA Results of the Raleigh Murders

It is imperative that police investigators recognize early whether a series of murders are linked. With respect to the murders of five black females in Raleigh, the authorities continually denied that the murders were the work of one person. A similar scenario was played out between 1992 and 1994 in Charlotte, North Carolina, where a series of ten murders were not linked to the now convicted Henry Louis Wallace.

Shown in Table 4.1.1 is the Jaccard's coefficient matrix that was derived from the SSA analysis. As previously mentioned, each of the decimal numbers in the matrix are Jaccard's coefficients, representing the percentage of co-occurrence between any two variables. The numbers highlighted by asterisks in the data matrix show the Jaccard's coefficients of co-occurrence between offenses carried out by the same offenders. The empty spaces indicate zero co-occurrence. The numbers that have no asterisks represent the co-occurrence between offenses not related to the same offender. For example, a loading of 0.30 means that 30% of behaviors occur between two offenses. All coefficients with a loading of 0.30 or higher are highlighted by an asterisk. The Jaccard's coefficient does not tell the investigator which behaviors are co-occurring. To determine this, one must revert to the original data matrix for comparison.

Looking at the matrix in Table 4.1.1, both vertically and horizontally, the letters A through D represent 15 offenses. Let us look at the first three offenses, A1, A2, and A3; these murders were carried out by three separate serial murderers, taken from the original data matrix of 288 offenses. The coefficients are rather low for the first three offenses — 0.04, 0.13, and 0.04 — indicating that these offenses had few actions in common. Therefore, it can be concluded that the three offenses are unrelated.

The next series of murders, B1 through B3, were committed by the same serial murderer. Looking at the numbers with asterisks between B1, B2, and B3, we see that the co-occurrence between B3 and B1 has a coefficient of 0.32, indicating that the crimes have similar behaviors. The link between the two remaining offenses, B1 to B2 and B2 to B3, while the coefficients of 0.23 and 0.26, respectively, are less than 0.30, nonetheless approach the 0.30 level. Considering the overall coefficient levels, it can be concluded that the same offender committed these three murders.

Table 4.1.1 Jaccard Co-efficients for 15 Murder Offenses According to Aspects of Crime Scene Behavior

Offenses	A1	A2	A3	B1	B2	B3	C1	C2	C3	C4	D1	D2	D3	D4	D5
Three Separate Killers															
A1															
A2	0.04														
A3	0.13	0.04													
Same Killer															
B1	0.10	0.12	0.26												
B2	0.03	0.20	0.15	0.23											
B3		0.20	0.04	0.32*	0.26										
Same Killer															
C1	0.04	0.30*	0.08	0.35*	0.24	0.50									
C2		0.10	0.07	0.12	0.28	0.25	0.29								
C3	0.03	0.28	0.10	0.22	0.45*	0.25	0.19	0.06							
C4	0.10	0.20	0.10	0.12	0.10	0.14	0.60*	0.32*	0.04						
Raleigh Killer															
D1		0.20	0.00	0.25	0.26	0.47*	0.12	0.12	0.10	0.07					
D2		0.23	0.10	0.22	0.35*	0.30*	0.39*	0.50*	0.10	0.20	0.43*				
D3		0.23	0.10	0.22	0.35*	0.30*	0.39*	0.50*	0.10	0.20	0.43*	1.00*			
D4		0.23	0.10	0.22	0.35*	0.30*	0.39*	0.50*	0.10	0.20	0.43*	1.00*	1.00*		
D5		0.23	0.10	0.22	0.35*	0.30*	0.39*	0.50*	0.10	0.20	0.43*	1.00*	1.00*	1.00*	

N = 6 Serial murderers – N = 15 Offenses – N = 9 Crime scene variables * = Co-efficient above 0.30

In the next offense series, there are four murders carried out by the same serial murderer. These offenses are represented by labels C1 through C4. Following the four rows to the middle of the matrix, we see the numbers with asterisks that represent these four murders. Two offenses show a link, C1 to C4 and C2 to C4, with coefficients of 0.60 and 0.32, respectively. The coefficient of 0.29, between offense C1 and C2, although lower than 0.30, suggests that these offenses are probably linked. The remaining coefficients, 0.04, 0.06, and 0.19 suggest that the behaviors performed in these three murders differ considerably, although they were committed by the same killer.

The final five offenses, D1 through D5, represent the murders of the five black females in Raleigh, North Carolina. John Williams, Jr. was convicted for two of the murders, labeled D4 and D5. Label D4 corresponds to victim one, while label D5 corresponds to victim five. As for the remaining three murders, no individual has been charged with these crimes, although the police suspect Williams. On inspection, the coefficients for the five murders may be linked. For example, beginning with the link between offense D1 and offense D2, the coefficient reached a level of 0.43, indicating that 43% of the crime scene actions that occurred in the first offense also occurred in the second offense. The same co-occurrences were achieved between offense, D1 and offenses D3, D4, and D5; the coefficient between these offenses was 0.43. This finding suggests that the murders were most likely committed by the same individual. However, a remarkable finding was found between the remaining offenses.

It was mentioned above that Williams was convicted of offenses D4 and D5, but that the police could not link the other three murders to Williams. This finding clearly indicates that Williams was probably the same killer in all five murders. To support this hypothesis, let us first examine the coefficients between offenses D4 and D5, the crimes for which Williams was linked through DNA and subsequently convicted. The coefficients are given in the last areas located in the bottom right side of the data matrix in Table 4.1.1. The coefficient of 1.00 indicates a perfect co-occurrence of crime scene actions in these murders. This means that 100% of the crime scene behaviors from offense four were also present in offense five, suggesting that Williams most likely committed the fifth murder. The SSA findings thus support the DNA evidence that Williams did commit these two murders.

Now, let us examine the remaining coefficients for the Raleigh murders that have not been linked to Williams by traditional investigative methods, or by the North Carolina HITS system. Looking at offenses D2 and D3 in relation to the offenses that Williams was convicted of, D4 and D5, we find a remarkable similarly in the crime scene actions. The coefficients between offenses D2, D3, D4, and D5 achieved a perfect score of 1.00, meaning that 100% of the crime scene behaviors in offenses D2 and D3 were also present in offenses D4 and D5. This finding suggests that it can be said with some confidence that Williams was most likely responsible for the three remaining unsolved murders.

The relatively high co-occurrences of crime scene behaviors in the murders of five black females in Raleigh, North Carolina are more than just chance. The present findings clearly show that behaviors from the murders for which Williams was convicted were strikingly similar to crime scene behaviors in the three remaining unsolved murders.

The remaining numbers with no asterisks in Table 4.1.1 are the coefficients between offenses that are not related. The majority of coefficients show no high rate of co-occurrence, which would be expected, since the behaviors in the offenses differ and the crimes were committed by different serial murderers. However, there were a few offenses not associated with the same offender that showed a co-occurrence. The co-occurrences between offense C2 and offenses D2 to D5 was 0.50. Although these crimes are not related, the high coefficients suggests that some crime scene actions performed in offense C2 are similar to actions in offenses D2 to D5. This may appear to be a problem in using SSA to link offenses; however, considering the high coefficients achieved specifically between the Raleigh offences, all other coefficients between offenses can be disregarded as being committed by Williams.

The ANACAPA process, like those methods used in popular computer linking software, are content-oriented, while the use of SSA is process-oriented. ANACAPA charts rely on the decisionmakers' information-processing abilities, while SSA determines the links automatically, therefore, requiring no processing by the decisionmaker, merely the acceptance of a predetermined decision.

4.1.12   Summary

The value of using SSA as a decision support system to link crimes has been demonstrated above. The importance of the initial selection phase of crime information has been shown, where selection must reflect the degree of variation within one serial murderer's actions, which then can be used to discriminate him from other possible offenders. Regardless of the effect of the representational system chosen to link offenses, the accuracy of the decisionmaker is inevitably influenced by the appropriateness of the information chosen in the selection phase of the task of discriminating between offenders. The representation of crime information can only be useful provided the information used in the process is a valid measure. The results herein support the notion that to correctly link crimes, behavior selection must be valid indices of offender consistency achieved only through repeated research.

Two methods of intermediate representation that were outlined illustrated that the actual decisions made by the investigator are determined by the nature of the representational system. In the case of ANACAPA, information processing remains entirely in the control of the investigator or police officer, with the ANACAPA chart merely recording all the available information and displaying it graphically. Recognizing crime patterns using this approach has been successful with aggregated crime data; however, it has proved less productive when considering a series of crimes carried out by one offender.

The use of SSA contrasts with ANACAPA in that it processes all the crime information and provides a predetermined decision, which eliminates biased opinions of the investigator and guess work. The results can then be used in a decision-making process along with any other pertinent evidence. The use of SSA in linking offenses can reduce *ampliative blindness*, the failure of police to go beyond the information in hand and recognize patterns in offending behavior that may be linked to one individual. For example, if Raleigh police investigators had had a system in place that would have recognized similar behavioral patterns in the five murders, the crimes could have been linked earlier, thereby resulting in less money being spent, reduction in man hours, and most important, lives could have been saved.

The linking of serial murder offenses, as evident here, demands considerable resources, not only in the analysis and preparation of the profile document, but in its anticipated usefulness to an investigation. The *Investigative Process Management* approach, as an investigative tool, differs from the FBI and other types of profiling attempts in that the procedures and practices are empirical and are applied to ongoing investigations. The *Investigative Process Management* approach seeks improvement in the investigator's efficiency and provides assistance to ongoing investigations. In this vein, the linking process here can be seen as the systematic examination of unsolved crime constituents and the application of a scientific method to support criminal investigations.

4.2 Nurses Who Kill: Serial Murder in Health Care Institutions*

CAMERON STARK
BRODIE PATERSON
TOM HENDERSON
BRIAN KIDD
MAURICE GODWIN

"You are seriously disturbed. You are cunning and manipulative and you have shown no remorse for the trail of destruction you have left behind you. I accept it is all the result of the severe personality disorder that you have. But you are and remain a very serious danger to others. On the evidence I have heard there is no real prospect that the time will come when you can safely be released."

—Mr. Justice Latham
convicted British murderer Beverly Allitt

Unexplained deaths involving children and health care patients have increased over the past ten years. In the first instance mothers are suspected; the health care patients are often murdered by nurses and health care givers. Yet, very little has been written to improve techniques that could lead to earlier detection of these crimes. This paper suggests that a rapid epidemiological investigation could identify common exposure to one nurse, and therefore prevent further harm to patients.

Many health professionals will regard the deaths at Grantham and Kesteven General Hospital, in which a nurse murdered four children, as an unprecedented event with little risk of repetition. There are, however, case reports from many countries of serial murder of patients by health care staff. Briefly, serial murder is defined as three or more separate murder events separated by a cooling off period.[20] These episodes differed from euthanasia as the patients did not consent to their death and were not usually seriously ill or in great pain.

* First published in *Nursing Times*, Vol. 93, Number 46, pp. 34–37, 1997. With permission.

Cases in which there have been convictions include that of a licensed vocational nurse in Texas, prosecuted for one death and who is likely to have murdered up to nine other infants in a pediatric intensive care unit,[20-22] four nurses in Vienna convicted of forty-one murders or attempted murders of elderly people,[23,24] a nurse responsible for the death of four patients in a New York hospital,[21,25] a nurse convicted for the murder of twelve patients in a Los Angeles intensive care unit,[21,22] a nursing sister in Wuppertal, West Germany who was responsible for at least five murders in an intensive care unit,[26] and a nurse in the former East Germany who murdered four patients on a surgical ward.[26] Other murders include a nurse in Florida who plead guilty to five murders at a nursing home,[21] a nurse convicted of one murder in a Georgia intensive care unit and who may have killed five others and attempted to murder a further three patients,[27] and a nurse's assistant who admitted to twenty-nine counts of aggravated murder, in a series of deaths from 1970 to 1987 and extending to three separate hospitals.[21] There are other reported cases in which epidemiological evidence suggests that a particular individual was associated with a series of deaths, but in which the outcome is not reported, or in which the accused individual was acquitted or not brought to trial.[28-30] These incidents continued, and in 1995, a trial in the Netherlands was continued for further psychiatric assessment of a nursing assistant who admitted to killing nine patients in a nursing home between 1992 and 1995.[31]

These murders were place-specific, and most were committed by women. Hickey describes women who commit serial murders as "the quiet killers."[27] Female serial murderers tend to use non-violent methods (e.g., poison), to be place-specific, and to confine their activities to vulnerable groups, in contrast to male perpetrators of serial murder who are usually violent and may mutilate their victims in ways which often allow crimes to be linked to the same individual. In Hickey's series of thirty-four female serial murderers in the United States, six were nurses.[27] They were, on average, slightly older than male serial murderers and had often killed for several years before being identified. Nursing homes and hospitals were the commonest locations for place-specific female murderers. Although reported episodes suggest an over-representation of nurses and nursing assistants, there is no reason to believe that other professions will be free of such individuals, and the true number of murders — the "dark figure of crime" — remains unknown.[31] It is not possible to conclude whether nurses are more or less likely to kill than any other professional or occupational group.

Methods used by convicted murderers included injection of benzo-diazepine, drowning by pouring water into the airways,[24] suffocation with a plastic bag or a pillow,[20] poisoning by arsenic, digoxin,[20,26] cyanide,[20] and injection of insulin, succinylcholine, potassium chloride, or lignocaine.[31] In suspected cases, likely methods included administration of digoxin, pancuronium bromide, potassium chloride, and insulin.[27,29,30,33,34]

Cases have not been distributed evenly across all patient groups. Most proven or suspected cases have occurred among older people, children, or patients in intensive care units. In the reported series, risk has been associated with receiving intravenous fluids,[30] with being in a bed out of sight of a nursing station, and with evenings or nights.[34,35] In some cases, victims have experienced repeated cardiopulmonary arrests, but only at one particular time of day, reflecting the shifts worked by the murderer.[22]

Early epidemiological investigations used examination of time trends in cardiopulmonary arrests and case control studies of suspicious and non-suspicious cases.[30] This work demonstrated that crude mortality rates alone could fail to identify a problem, while monitoring of critical incidents such as cardiopulmonary arrests could identify the threat earlier. Two later studies examined staff schedules and identified strong associations between the relative risk of death and the duty times of particular staff members.[23,29] In one case, the nurse identified had moved to another job, and was convicted of murdering a child in her new job.[23] The other case, at a children's hospital in Toronto, resulted in a long-lasting controversy. A nurse was arrested and charged with four murders before the epidemiological evidence was available. The case against the nurse was dropped. Buehler and his colleagues found that the presence of another nurse was statistically associated with the deaths, although no further charges were brought.[29] A Canadian researcher has argued that these deaths were part of a wider medication problem affecting many hospitals, and that allegations of murder were incorrect.[36]

This criticism reflects a frequent comment on epidemiological investigations of unexplained deaths, that "statisticians ... play at Sherlock Holmes."[24] Yorker has argued that media attention may result in a hospital having to explain an increased death rate, and that nurses are an easy target for investigation. As one lawyer suggested, "being accused of murder may be an emerging occupational hazard for nurses." In one case in Las Vegas, however, a nurse found herself accused of the murder of patients in an intensive care unit and was the subject of intense media speculation before charges were withdrawn. It was later established that there had been no unexplained deaths and no evidence of murder. Rather, the case was based on gossip and unfounded suspicions.[37] An epidemiological investigation may have ended the case before it began.

There are many possible causes of unexpected adverse events in health care settings. Recent epidemiological investigations have attempted to preempt criticism by using rigorous methods. In an examination of deaths in a nursing home in Florida, Sacks et al. compared the incidence of deaths across all homes in the same chain to help exclude a widespread problem before conducting a case control study. In a separate incident in an intensive care unit, Sacks and his colleagues conducted the most satisfactory examination to date, using a cohort study with a nested case control study combined with independent blind expert assessment of the deaths examined in the case control study.[30] Using logistic modeling to take other risk factors into account, they found that risk of death on the unit was most strongly associated with primary care by one nurse (adjusted odds ration 47.5). The judge in the case commented that statistical evidence alone was insufficient to convict someone of murder. The nurse was acquitted.

The importance of these murders and suspected murders lies in the possibility for prevention. Series of murders with a low murder rate would be difficult to detect, but most reported episodes, perhaps predictably, have involved a rapid increase in the number of critical incidents and murders. The shortest reported case occurred in a surgical intensive care unit in Georgia.[35] A nurse supervisor identified an increase in the number of cardiac arrests in a three-week period. A rapid epidemiological investigation identified common exposure to one nurse, who was removed from duty and subsequently convicted of aggravated assault. Rapid recognition of increases in adverse incidents and appropriate investigation may, therefore, prevent further harm to patients.

Pre-employment screening, as recommended by the Allitt inquiry,[38] cannot eliminate the possibility of recurrence.[39] While some perpetrators show a similar psychological pattern, reports of others show no such features.[22,27] Our review of previous cases indicates that there is no consistent psychological profile of these murderers. The features identified in some murderers, such as the repeated hospital attendance and probable fabrication of illness seen in at least two cases, may be of some help.[26] The number of other staff who display such behaviors must be far higher than the very small number of murderers, and so the positive predictive value of these behaviors when used as a screening test is likely to be small.

Other characteristics of these cases may be of more value. In most cases, the initial episodes involve an increase in unexpected cardiac or respiratory arrests. The number of these critical incidents will vary over time in any case, but epidemiological techniques can help to identify an increase which is greater than that which would be expected by chance. Routine monitoring of critical incidents is practiced in many units. Most cases will prove to have been caused by chance, or by other factors such as alterations in case mix or medication errors.[41] The Georgia case cited above is an example of the speed with which an episode can be identified and investigated if staff respond to an unexplained increase in critical incidents or unexpected deaths. Public Health departments are one source of advice on the application of appropriate epidemiological techniques.

Previous cases suggest that some clinical areas are more vulnerable than others, such as wards with children, older people, or intensive care units.[40] Some reports suggest that wards with low staffing or inadequate supervision may be associated with such episodes.[25,42–44] It is unclear whether occupational stress was related to these incidents or, as may be more likely, decreased supervision and increased stress on other staff delayed recognition of the events. Several episodes occurred in well run units with adequate staffing, however, so no unit is immune.

Several case reports describe staff concerns which were not initially taken seriously by supervisors, possibly because they believed the allegations to be improbable.[20,40] Similarly, such disbelief may result in an inordinate delay in involving the police.[20] Some episodes have ended with no clear resolution because of the lack of physical evidence. It is essential to involve police forces when there is a serious suspicion of murder. These events are very rare, but have enormous potential for harm. The best defense from them is likely to be awareness of the possibility, a willingness to listen and act on staff concerns, and knowledge of the methods used to investigate suspected episodes.

4.3 Weaknesses in Computerized Linking Data Bases

MAURICE GODWIN

Several projects have been undertaken to develop computerized classification systems based on the offender's actions in the crime.[44] These include the use of computer technology to coordinate large databases to link offenders' crime scene antecedents across different jurisdictions. A small number of police agencies in the U.K. have developed their own computerized database for linking violent criminals, such as HOLMES. In the U.S.A., the FBI has a linking system called the Violent Criminal Apprehension Program (VICAP).[45] VICAP is a computer database which depends on local and state police agencies to complete a check list of 186 questions about solved and unsolved crimes in their jurisdictions.[45] The computer system is designed to flag similarities that might otherwise go unnoticed, for example, in unsolved murders. Other state linking systems are HALT in New York state and HVITS in North Carolina. While these technological advancements have provided law enforcement officials with more efficient ways of storing and managing data, there are inherent problems.

One of the main problems of these computerized database classification systems is that there are no empirical operational definitions for the questions asked on the questionnaires. No attempts have been made to see if the right questions are asked or if too many of the same question are asked. Research by Guttman pointed out that grand theories about relationships are rather useless from a scientific point of view if they do not include an a priori definition system for observations.[47] In light of these weaknesses, there has been no consideration given to explore the validity of questionnaires such as VICAP using techniques evolving out of the literature on psychometric theory. Psychometrics has a long tradition for providing an empirical way to test the reliability and validity of questionnaires.[47]

The starting point for developing a robust database linking system for inquiries into the nature of criminal action is the fact that the questions asked on forms such as VICAP do make distinctions between offenders. The application of psychological tests such as psychometrics to VICAP questions would be used to measure individual differences between offenders, and between the actions of the same offender on different occasions. Information that originates from VICAP questions is supposed to provide investigators with clues to what behaviors the instrument really measures. It appears that the VICAP questionnaire and similar crime linking questionnaires fail to measure the differences between offenders. Even recent attempts to improve the reliability of the VICAP questionnaire have not made any significant improvements, because no attempt has been made to empirically validate the questions on the questionnaire. A brief review of some VICAP questions and the difficulties they pose is discussed below.

4.3.1   Reliability of Linking Data Base Questions

VICAP questions require investigators to answer with subjective opinions, i.e., hunches, and these personal biases could lead to extravagant claims regarding what a particular question truly says about an offender's behavior. One question that requires the investigator to draw suppositions is VICAP question 99, which refers to the offender's method of initial contact with his victim. The possible responses to this question are 1) immediately and physically overpowered the victim; 2) hit victim with hand, fist, or clubbing weapon; 3) choked; 4) stabbed; 5) shot; or 6) other direct assault.

The first response, physically overpowered his victim, is rather vague because this type of information is not likely to be known until after the offender has been arrested. Information concerning whether the offender physically overpowered a victim is usually gleaned from offenders' self-reports, which tend to be biased. It is not exactly clear what part of the offender's behavior is being measured in responses 2 through 6. The FBI suggests that a variety of triggering factors can activate the offender's violence, and that many triggering factors center around some aspect of control and dominance.[45] Hence, is the initial method of contact with the victim or the degree of power the offender used to gain control over the victim being measured by this question?

Response one, immediately and physically overpowered the victim, seems to measure the behavior rather than functioning as one of the six responses. So, in essence, question 99 addresses two totally different emphases. One is the method of initial contact with the victim, and the other is the degree of power used to gain control of the victim. Therefore, it seems more reasonable to view responses 2 through 6 as a set of actions that reflect how the offender physically overpowered his victim. The responses to question 99 are not mutually exclusive. There is no clear indication of what behavior is being measured. There is no theory used to support the relationships between the possible range of responses or the individual differences between offenders who use various methods of contact and power to subdue their victims.

Determining which response to check on question 99 is determined solely by deductive hunches made by an investigator.

The next VICAP question that we will look at shows how additional reliability problems are encountered when investigators interpret the same questions differently. For example, question number 145 on the VICAP form addresses whether the binding of the victim was excessive, much more than necessary to control the victim's movements. The response to this question is either yes or no.

VICAP question 145 is clearly vague, and no indication is given of what behaviors the question is attempting to measure. The degree of excessiveness can vary from one investigator to another, resulting in different responses to the same question. Therefore, any future interpretation of the answers to this question as part of an investigation could be misleading. The reliability problem in criminal database questions, as demonstrated by question 145, exist because there are no empirical operational definitions for the questions asked on the forms. Similar problems also exist with individuals who use deductive profiling to draw conclusions about a crime scene.

4.3.2 Validity of VICAP Questions

The validity of the questions asked on questionnaires such as VICAP is supposed to provide a direct check on how well this function is fulfilled. The determination of validity usually requires independent, external criteria of whatever the questions are designed to measure. However, there have been no attempts to determine the validity of the questions asked on VICAP or similar questionnaires in linking the behaviors associated with unsolved crimes. For example, VICAP question number 137 asks about evidence of how the offender disposed of the victim's body. The possible responses to VICAP question 137 are 1) openly displayed or otherwise placed to insure discovery; 2) concealed, hidden, or otherwise placed to insure discovery; or 3) the body was disposed with an apparent lack of concern as to whether or not is was discovered.

Referring to response one for question 137, body openly displayed, several hypotheses can be proposed, none of which can be answered. To what extent was the body openly displayed? What behavior is being measured by this question? The question offers a number of possibilities that are propounded in the FBI literature. One possibility seems to originate from the belief that when offenders openly discard their victims, somehow this "contributes to the offender's overall fantasy."[45] Although this may be one of many possibilities, no evidence is given to support this theory as it relates to the VICAP question. It is highly unlikely that choosing response one will tell an investigator anything about the behavior of an offender.

The second response for question 137 is concealed or hid the victim's body. Again, this action raises a number of hypotheses, none of which can be supported by the range of responses to the question. One hypothesis seems to suggest that concealing or hiding the victim's body "expresses the killers' relationship with or feelings towards another person by keeping the body close to them."[45] Another hypothesis is that concealing or hiding the body fuels the killer's fantasy,[45] which is also given as possible hypothesis for openly displaying the body. VICAP question 137 tells us nothing about offenders who conceal or hide victims' bodies.

The response to question 137 that requires the investigator to draw broad assumptions about the offender's post-offense behavior is response three, an apparent lack of concern as to whether or not the body was discovered. It is doubtful that any investigator would have knowledge about whether the offender was concerned about discovery of the body. Information of this nature can only be gleaned from offenders' self-reports, and that information is questionable. The face validity of question 137 is misleading. Face validity refers not to what the question measures, but to what it appears superficially to measure. The method of body disposal on the VICAP form, openly displayed, concealed or hidden, or an apparent lack of concern as to whether the body was discovered, does not advance our knowledge of criminals who perform these actions.

The lack of face validity can be found in another VICAP question. VICAP question number 166 addresses whether there is evidence that the offender disfigured the victim's body in order to delay or hinder identification. The range of responses to this question is yes or no. Like the other VICAP questions discussed earlier, question 166 requires different investigators to draw broad and unsubstantiated conclusions about the offender's intent prior to the offender being identified. For example, the question clearly suggests that the offender disfigures victims' bodies in order to hinder identification. Disfiguring to hide the victim's identity may be one of many hypotheses that can be discerned from this type action. However, there are other possibilities. One is the offender disfigures the body to retain certain parts as souvenirs, for reflection about the murder.[45] If both of these hypotheses are possibilities, then which behavior is VICAP question 166 supposed to be measuring?

4.3.3 Utility of the VICAP System

Essentially, most of the criminal database linking systems are built on assumptions propounded in the serial murder literature.[45] In one study of the relationship between organized and disorganized crime scenes, background characteristics were measured using analysis of variance procedures.[49] The problem with generating serial murder classifications using results from this type of test is the fact that the explained variance is sensitive to the particular distribution that exists within a given sample, so the variable relationships are not usually stable across samples. The differences between the offenders and variations that occur within offenders across a set of related crime scene actions are hidden when comparisons between group averages are made. Therefore, significant relationships between offense actions and offenders are less likely to be revealed through group comparisons. The problem is further compounded when the data is skewed to sexually sadistic offenders only, i.e., organized and disorganized typology.

The offender and offense data entered in current crime linking database systems have not been empirically tested, and seem to originate from *post hoc* reasoning by a few investigators without any attempt to validate the assumptions. The previous discussion of the VICAP questions demonstrates the ambiguities in interpreting what the questions truly measure. For instance, the relationships between crime variables in VICAP are produced by a few key individuals using work experience and intuition as a foundation. What is derived from this deductive profiling process is that the investigator's assumptions about what historical events might be connected to the behavior under study will determine what variables are studied. Consequently, no framework has been empirically established for identifying the crucial or salient signature behaviors for linking cases and, as a result, database systems such as VICAP have been qualified failures.

4.3.4 Conclusions

Two important reasons highlighted why the computerized linking databases are unreliable. One is that flat databases are unlikely to pick up on one-to-one variable comparisons or variations between offenders and offenses. The problem is exacerbated when comparisons between group averages are made. The second reason has to do with how questions are designed and what behaviors are measured. Questions on VICAP and other similar offense-linking forms seem to originate from *post hoc* reasoning by a few investigators about the motivations of criminals based on work experience and gut feelings. Consequently, there is no empirical research on the validity of such questions or the data that is collected from the questionnaires.

Many of the questions are vague and provide no direct measurement on offense behaviors or offender background characteristics. The questions require investigators to draw speculative opinions about what each question implies, resulting in different responses to the same question. For example, VICAP staff determines if "similar pattern characteristics exist among the individual cases in the VICAP system."[45] This is rather an informal approach in determining whether crime scene behaviors have a relationship. In light of these questionnaire weaknesses, no consideration has been given to improve the reliability and validity of the questionnaires using tests construction procedures, i.e., psychometrics theory. Through psychometrics and factor analytic techniques, linking databases such as VICAP questions can be more systematically identified and defined. Each question could then be selected to represent the best available measure of the behavior under review or factors identified by factor analysis.

References

1. Egger, S., *The Killers Among Us: an Examination of Serial Murder and its Investigation*, New Jersey: Prentice Hall, 1997.

2. James, E., *Catching Serial Killers: Learning from Past Serial Murder Investigations*, Lansing, MI: International Forensic Service, 1991.

3. Pierce, C. S., *Philosophy of Logic*, England: Oxford Press, 1950.

4. Godwin, M. and Canter, D., Encounter and death: the spatial behavior of U.S. serial killers, *Policing Int. J. Police Manage. Strategies*, 20, 24-38, 1997.

5. Douglas, J. E. and Munn, C., Violent crime scene analysis: Modus Operandi, signature, and staging, *FBI Law Enforcement Bull.*, February, 1-10, 1992.

6. Keppel, R. and Birnes, W., *Signature Killers*, New York: Pocket Books, 1997.

7. Godwin, M., *Inner Themes-Outer Behaviors: A Multivariate Facet Model of U.S. Serial Murderers' Crime Scene Actions*, unpublished doctorate dissertation, University of Liverpool, England, 1998.

8. Grubin, D., Offender profiling, *J. Forensic Psychiatry*, 6, 259-263, 1995.

9. Allport, G. W., *Personality: a Psychological Interpretation*, New York: Henry Holt, 1937.

10. Douglas, J. E., Ressler, R. R., Burgess, A. W., and Hartman, C.R., Criminal profiling from crime scene analysis, *Behav. Sci. Law*, 41, 401-421, 1986.

11. Godwin, M., *Hunting Serial Predators: a Multivariate Classification Approach to Profiling Violent Behavior*, Boca Raton, FL, CRC Press, 2000.

12. Hilgard, E. R., *Divided Consciousness: Multiple Controls in Human Thought and Action*, New York: Wiley, 1977.

13. Ressler, R. K., Burgess, A. W., and Douglas, J. E., *Sexual Homicide: Patterns and Motives,* Toronto: Lexington Books, 1988.

14. Tversky, A. and Kahneman, D., Judgment under uncertainty: heuristics and biases, *Science*, 185, 1124-1131, 1974.

15. Gordon, P., *Technical Support*, i2 Limited, Cambridge, England, 1998.

16. Jarvis, C. and Swindell, S., *News and Observer*, Raleigh, North Carolina, January 11, 1997.

17. Jarvis, C., *News and Observer*, Raleigh, North Carolina, January 10, 1997.

18. Shye, S., Elizur, D., and Hoffman, M., *Introduction to Facet Theory: Content Design and Intrinsics in the Behavioral Research*, Applied Social Research Methods Series, CA: Sage, 1994.

19. Shye, S., *Theory Construction and Data Analysis in the Behavioral Sciences*, San Francisco: Jossey Bass, 1978.

20. Ressler, R. K., Douglas J. E., Burgess, A. W., and Burgess, A. G., *Crime Classification Manual*, London: Simon & Schuster, 1993.

21. Yorker, B. C., Nurses accused of murder, *Am. J. Nursing*, 10, 1327-1332, 1988.

22. Istre, G. R., Gustafson, T. L., Baron, R. C., Martin, D. L., and Orlowski, J. P., A mysterious cluster of deaths and cardiopulmonary arrests in a pediatric intensive care unit, *N. Engl. J. Med.*, 313: 205-211, 1985.

23. Martin, D., Nurses who murder, *Nursing Stand.*, 46:19-20, 1989.

24. Missliwetz, J., Die mordserie im krankenhaus Wien-Lainz, *Arch. Kriminol.*, 194:1-7, 1994.

25. Repper, J., Munchausen syndrome by proxy in health care workers, *J. Advanced Nursing*, 21: 299-304, 1995.

26. Durwald, W., Totungsdelikte in krankenhasuern, *Versicherungmedizin*, 45: 3-6, 1993.

27. Hickey, E. W., *Serial murderers and their victims*, Pacific Grove, CA: Brooks/Cole, 1991.

28. Buehler, J. W., Smith, L. F., Wallace, E. M., Heath, C. W., Kusiak, R., and Herndon, J. L., Unexplained deaths in a children's hospital: an epidemiologic assessment, *N. Engl. J. Med.*, 313: 211-216, 1985.

29. Stross, J. K., Shasby, D. M., and Harlan, W. R., An epidemic of mysterious cardiopulmonary arrests, *N. Engl. J. Med.*, 295: 1107-1110, 1976.

30. Sacks, J. J., Herndon, J. L., Lieb, S. H., Sorhage, F. E, McCaig, L. F., and Withum, D. G., A cluster of unexplained deaths in a nursing home in Florida, *Am. J. Public Health*, 78: 806-808, 1988.

31. Sheldon, T. D., Deliverance, *Nursing Times*, 91:51, 1995.

32. Creighton, H., Nurses and murder charges, *Nursing Manage.*, 19:16-20, 1988.

33. Kroll, P., Silk, K., Chamerlain, K., and Ging, R., Denying the incredible: unexplained deaths in a Veterans Administration hospital, *Am. J. Psychiatry*, 12:1376-1380, 1977.

34. Sacks, J. J., Stroup, D. F., Will, M. L., Harris, E. L., and Israe, E., A nurse-associated epidemic of cardiac arrests in an intensive care unit, *JAMA*, 259:689-695, 1988.

35. Franks, A., Sacks, J. J., Smith, J. D., and Sikes, R. K., A cluster of unexplained cardiac arrests in a surgical intensive care unit, *Crit. Care Med.*, 1075-1076, 1987.

36. Hamilton, G., The nurses are innocent, *Canadian Nurse*, 89: 27-32, 1993.

37. Kalisch, P. A., Kalisch, B. J., and Livesay, E., The angel of death: the anatomy of a major 1980s news story about nursing, *Nursing Forum*, 19: 212-241, 1980.

38. Clothier, C., MacDonald, C. A., and Shaw, D. A., *The Allitt Inquiry: Independent Inquiry Relating to Deaths and Injuries on the Children's Ward at Grantham and Kesteven General Hospital during the Period February to April 1991*, London: HMSO, 1994.

39. Bowles, N., Methods of nurse selection: a review, *Nursing Standard*, 9:25-29, 1995.

40. Stark, C. and Sloan, D., Audit critical incidents in patients at risk, *BMJ*, 308:477, 1994.

41. Hiedkamp, B., Angels of Death: The Lianz Hospital Murders, in Birch, H., Ed., *Moving Targets: Women, Murder and Representation*, London: Virago, 1993.

42. Rogers, R., Qualified in caring? *Nursing Standard*, 8:21-22, 1993.

43. Naish, J., The Allitt case: getting close to the facts? *Nursing Standard*, 7:20-22, 1993.

44. Keppel, R. and Weis, J., HITS: catching criminals in the Northwest, *FBI Law Enforcement Bull.*, (April), 14-19, 1993.

45. Ressler, R., Burgess, A. W., and Douglas, J., *Sexual Homicide: Patterns and Motives*, Lexington, MA: Lexington Books, 1988.

46. Guttman, L., What is not what in theory construction, in I. Borg, Ed., *Multidimensional Data Representations: When and Why*, Ann Arbor: Mathesis, 1979.

47. Bijou, S. W., Psychometric similarities between habitual criminals and psychotics, *Del. State Med. J.*, May, 4, 1939.

48. Ressler, R., Burgess, A. W., and Douglas, J., Sexual killers and their victims: identifying patterns through crime scene analysis, *J. Interpersonal Violence*, 1, 288-308, 1986.

Cyber-Crimes
5

5.1 Hackers, Phreakers, and Pirates: The Semantics of the Computer Underground

GORDON R. MEYER

The advancement of the computer age has introduced many new terms into our everyday vocabulary. One of these words, "hacker," has to do with computer related deviance and crime. We are all familiar with the stories of teenage whiz-kids breaking into various computers and generally causing havoc in corporate computerized America, but it is my contention that the term "hacker" is one of the most misunderstood, misapplied, and inconsistently used words of the computer age. Considering all the confusing techno-terms that computing has brought us, that's a pretty bold statement to make, so allow me to illustrate. Popular culture defines hackers as those who, through use of exceptional computer skills, are able to break into the computers owned by banks and government agencies. They snoop through information that does not belong to them, they steal expensive software, and they transfer funds from bank account to bank account.

Criminologists have described hackers in less glorified terms. Donn Parker calls them "electronic trespassers"[1,2] and August Bequai[1-3] describes them as "electronic vandals." Both of them, while they acknowledge that the activity of hackers is generally illegal, shy away from the label of "computer criminal." They draw a clear distinction between the joyriding hacker and the trusted white collar employee who turns bad. Thus, we are seemingly left with a definition that has two extremes. The modern day bank robber at one end, the trespassing teenager at the other. Either activity (and any which falls in between) could be classified as "hacking." Hardly what one would consider to be a precise and insightful conceptualization.

A large part of the ambiguity of the term hacker can be traced to the origin and uses of the word over the past (roughly) twenty years. The term first came into use in the early 1960s when it was applied to a group of pioneering computer afficionados at M.I.T.[4] Back then, and on through most of the 1970s, a hacker was someone obsessed with understanding and mastering computer systems. The designers of the Apple computer, Jobs and Wozniack, are hackers in this sense of the word.

In the early 1980s, fueled by the release of the movie *War Games* and the much publicized arrest of a "hacker gang" known as the 414s, hackers became known as young whiz-kids capable of breaking into corporate and government computer systems.[3] Unfortunately, the news media and the social scientific community has made little effort to move beyond this definition. The problem of drafting a more precise definition of hackers is compounded not only by the little information that is known about their daily activities, but by the fact that what is known does not always fall under existing criminal labels. That is to say, there is no legal definition of what it means to be a hacker, nor are all their activities in violation of criminal law. This results in applications of the term that change on a case-by-case basis depending on the charges that have been filed, not on any clear understanding of what it is that they actually do.

This problem, and the lack of any clear understanding of what it means to be a hacker, result in the label being overused and applied to too many forms of electronic intrusion. Parker and Bequai, two leaders in the scientific study of computer crime, use the term hacker in slightly different ways. Parker recognizes that hacking does not include the entire range of activity associated with the electronic trespassers, however, he prefers it to the term "phreaking," which he rejects as being too obscure and dated.

Bequai, on the other hand, has not rejected the term phreaking, and often applies it to acts that Parker would call system hacking. Bequai further confuses the issue by describing a hacker as someone who uses illicit telephone credit cards to access a system that illegally distributes commercial software.[1,2] We'll come back to this description later, and we'll see that it has little to do with hacking per se, but is illustrative of other types of underground computer activity.

This chapter is drawn from ethnographic research on the computer underground. Much of the information here has been gathered in interviews, conducted both on-line and in person, with people actively involved in hacking activities. Hacking, phreaking, and piracy are presented and defined as they are used by those who embrace these roles. Reference for this chapter is the computer underground — not the laws that have been written to control it. The typification and conclusions presented here should be regarded as somewhat tentative. This chapter reflects my research work-in-progress, and the author fully expects to re-order these terms around a sociological framework. The raw classifications are a necessary first step in making sociological sense of the computer underground community.

Our first discussion will focus on the area of hacking and hackers. In the vernacular of the computer underground, hacking can refer to two activities:

1) the attempt to gain access to a computer system; or 2) the more general goal of exploring and learning to operate a computer system. In the first connotation, hacking encompasses the tools and tricks used to obtain valid user accounts on computer systems that would otherwise be unavailable to the hacker. One can think of the word hack as being closely related to the repetitive nature of the break-in attempts. Also, once a successful entry is made, the illicit accounts are sometimes shared with associates and described as being "freshly hacked." This is the stereotypical media image of the hacker — a computer-wise teenager, hunched over his computer keyboard, endlessly searching for an un-used account or a weak link in the security system. While this image is not entirely accurate, it does fairly represent this aspect of the term hacking.

The second dimension of hacking has to do with the activity that occurs once access has been secured — once a password has been "hacked out." Since the system is being used without permission, the hacker does not, generally speaking, have access to the usual operating manuals and other resources that are available to legitimate users of the system. Therefore, the intruder must experiment with command structures and explore files in order to understand and effectively use the system. This is sometimes called hacking around, or simply hacking a system. As opposed to the first aspect of hacking, activity here is not solely to gain access (although one might be looking for ways to obtain even more powerful access levels), but rather to learn more about the general operation of a computer type. Contrary to the media image, most hackers will not go about deliberately destroying data or damaging the system. To do so would go against their goal of blending in with the average user so as not to attract undue attention to their presence and cause the account to be deleted. After spending what may be a substantial amount of time getting the account, the hacker places a high priority on not being discovered using it.

Despite the obvious relationship between the two types of hacking, the label of 'hacker' is generally reserved for those engaged in the second type of hacking. In other words, a hacker is someone who has the knowledge, ability, and desire to fully explore a computer system. The mere act of gaining entry — of guessing a password — is not enough to warrant the hacker moniker. There must be a desire to master, explore, and use the system after access has been achieved. This distinction seems logical in light of the fact that not everyone is skilled at hacking out passwords, and not all intruders retain interest in a system once the challenge of gaining entry has been surmounted. In the computer underground community, passwords and accounts are often traded and made available for general use. Thus, gaining entry can almost be viewed as the easy part, so those who actually use and explore the systems hold the position of higher prestige.

The second activity that we will discuss is phone phreaking. Usually called just "phreaking," it came into general practice after the adventures of John Draper, aka Capt. Crunch, were publicized in a 1971.[3] Phreaking is a way to circumvent the billing mechanisms of the telephone company. It allows one to call anywhere in the world, quite literally without cost. In many cases it also prevents, or at least inhibits, the possibility of calls being traced to their source, thereby helping the offender to avoid being caught.

For most members of the computer underground, phreaking is simply a tool that allows them to call long distance without amassing enormous phone bills. The number of people who consider themselves to be phreakers as opposed to hackers is proportionately small. However, those who do consider themselves to be phreakers are into it for exploring the telephone system. Most people, although they use the phone system every day, know little about phreaking. The phreakers, on the other hand, want to learn all they can. This desire to master the system is best summarized by an active phreak:[7]

> The phone system is the most interesting, fascinating thing that I know of. There is so much to know. Even phreaks have their own areas of knowledge. There is so much to know that one phreak could know something fairly important and the next phreak not. The next phreak might know ten things that the first phreak doesn't though. It all depends upon where and how they get their info. I myself would like to work for the telco, doing something interesting, like programming a switch. Something that isn't slave labor bull. Something that you enjoy, but have to take risks in order to participate unless you are lucky enough to work for the telco. To have access to telco things, manuals, etc. would be great.

Most members of the underground do not approach the telephone system with such passion. They are simply interested in exploiting its weaknesses in order to pursue other interests. In the above case, phreaking is more of a means than a pursuit unto itself. Another respondent, one who identifies himself as a hacker, explains:[7]

> I know very little about phones....I just hack. See, I can't exactly call these numbers direct. A lot of people are in the same boat. In my case, phreaking is a tool, an often used one, but nonetheless a tool.

In the world of the computer underground, the ability to "phreak a call" is taken for granted. With the break-up of the Bell system came the advent of the telephone credit card. These cards opened the door to wide-scale phreaking. Today no special knowledge or equipment is required to phreak a call. Only a touch-tone phone and a valid credit card number, known as c0dez, are needed to call any location in the world. Just as the more skilled and motivated participants may be called hackers, those with the desire to master the phone system are called phreakers. Utilizing the tools of the phreak is not limited to those who are known as phreakers, but use alone is not enough to earn the distinction.

Finally, we come to software "tele-piracy." Tele-piracy is the illegal distribution of copyrighted software. Tele-piracy does not refer to disk-copying and trading that occurs among colleagues (which is equally illegal), but rather the activity that centers around computer bulletin board systems that specialize in such traffic. Access to these systems is obtained by contributing, via a telephone modem, a copy of a commercial program. This self-incriminating act allows the user to copy, or download, between three to six programs that others have contributed. Thus, for the expense of only a phone call, one can quickly amass great amounts of valuable software. Of course, in many cases even the cost of the phone call is avoided by phreaking. Note that unlike the two-dimensional activities of hacking and phreaking, there is not a more prestigious or motivated side to being a tele-pirate. In this case, committing the act earns the title.

Tele-piracy is computer deviancy for the masses. Unlike even the basic hacking and phreaking, it requires almost no skill to perform. Anyone who possess a modem-equipped computer and some copyrighted software has the needed components to enter the world of tele-piracy. Because tele-piracy is unskilled underground activity, the role of a pirate inspires no admiration or prestige among those in the computer underground. A possible exception are those tele-pirates who have to the programming ability necessary to remove the copy protection from commercial software.

While the hackers and phreakers of the computer world probably don't disapprove of piracy, and undoubtedly individually participate in it to some extent, they are less active (at least visibly so) on the bulletin board services that cater exclusively to tele-piracy. They tend to avoid these boards because most tele-pirates lack phreak/hack skills, and thus are known for over-abusing the telephone network in pursuit of the latest computer game program. One hacker theorizes that the tele-pirates are responsible for most of the telephone credit card fraud, and pointed out:[7]

> The media claims that it is solely hackers who are responsible for losses pertaining to large telecommunication companies and long distance services. This is not the case. We (hackers) are but a small portion of these losses. The rest are caused by pirates and thieves who sell these codes to people on the street.

Another hacker explains that the process of exchanging large commercial programs via modems frequently takes many hours to complete, and it is these calls, not the ones placed by telecommunications enthusiasts (a popular euphemism for phreakers and hackers) that the telephone company is upset about. But regardless of whether it is the lack of phreak/hack skills, the reputation for abusing the network, or some other reason, there does seem to be some division between the worlds of phreakers/hackers and the tele-pirates.

Having outlined the three roles found in the computer underground, we can see that the earlier definition of a hacker as someone who uses a stolen credit card to download the latest game does not reflect the definitions found in the computer underground. Obviously, this description is of a tele-pirate phreaking a call, not the actions of a hacker or phreaker.

Some caveats are in order here. It is not my intent to give the impression that individuals are either hackers or phreakers or tele-pirates exclusively. The categories are not always mutually exclusive. Certainly, many individuals are capable of acting in more than one of these roles. So, in light of this role multiplicity, how can sociologists, reporters, and investigators adopt accurate definitions of the activities found in specific cases? The answer lies in focusing on the goals that have been discussed. A hacker's goal is not just to break into the system, but to learn about how it operates. The phreaker's goal is not just to place long distance calls for free, but to discover what the phone company won't explain about its network, and the tele-pirates goal is to obtain a copy of the latest software for his computer. So, even if a particular individual is knowledgeable about the telephone system, when he phreaks a call to download a game he is acting as a tele-pirate.

To a certain extent, this is merely an argument of semantics. Regardless of whether a hacker is mislabeled as a tele-pirate, unauthorized access and illegal copying of commercial software will continue. However, if we are to accurately understand this new development of the computer age, we must identify and recognize the three types of activity that face us. Grouping all three together under one label is inaccurate; it ignores the functional relationships and differences between them.

Admittedly, there are some who will disagree with the distinctions drawn between the groups presented here. In conducting this research, it became obvious that individuals who are actually engaged in the activities cannot agree where the boundaries lie. The categories and roles, as indicated earlier, are not mutually exclusive. The phreak/hack worlds in particular are very much intertwined. However, just as we shouldn't group all underground activity under the generic term hacking, we shouldn't insist that our definitions be artificially stringent to the point of ignoring the reality of the actions they represent. The typologies presented here are broad, and need to be refined. However, they are a step forward in the accurate representation, specification, and identification of activities in the computer underground.

5.2 A Sociology of Hackers*

TIM JORDAN
PAUL TAYLOR

The growth of a world-wide computer network and its increasing use both for the construction of online communities and for the reconstruction of existing societies means that unauthorized computer intrusion, or hacking, has wide significance. The 1996 report of a computer raid on Citibank that netted around $10 million indicates the potential seriousness of computer intrusion. Other, perhaps more whimsical, examples are the attacks on the CIA world-wide web site, in which its title was changed from Central Intelligence Agency to Central Stupidity Agency, or the attack on the British Labour Party's web-site, in which titles like 'Road to the Manifesto' were changed to 'Road to Nowhere'. These hacks indicate the vulnerability of increasingly important computer networks and the anarchistic, or perhaps destructive, world-view of computer intruders. It is correct to talk of a world-view because computer intrusions come not from random, obsessed individuals but from a community that offers networks and support, such as the long running magazines *Phrack* and *2600*. At present there is no detailed sociological investigation of this community, despite a growing number of racy accounts of hacker adventures. To delineate a sociology of hackers, an introduction is needed to the nature of computer-mediated communication and of the act of computer intrusion, the hack. Following this, the hacking community will be explored in three sections: first, a profile of the number of hackers and hacks; second, an outline of its culture through the discussion of six different aspects of the hacking community; and third, an exploration of the community's construction of a boundary, albeit fluid, between itself and its other, the computer security industry. Finally, a conclusion that briefly considers the significance of our analysis will be offered.

In the early 1970s, technologies that allowed people to use decentered, distributed networks of computers to communicate globally were developed.[8] By the early 1990s, a new means of organizing and accessing information contained on computer networks was developed that utilized multi-media "point and click" methods, the World-Wide Web. The Web made using

* First published in *The Sociological Review*, 46:4, 1998. With permission.

computer networks intuitive, and underpinned their entry into mass use. The size of this global community of computer communicators is difficult to measure; however, in January 1998 there were at least 40 million.[8] Computer communication has also become key to many industries, not just through the Internet but also through private networks, such as those that underpin automated teller services. The financial industry is the clearest example of this, as John Perry Barlow points out, "cyberspace is where your money is." Taken together, all the different computer networks that currently exist control and tie together vital institutions of modern societies including telecommunications, finance, globally distributed production, and the media. Analysis of the community who attempt to illicitly use these networks can begin with a definition of the "hack."[10,11]

Means of gaining unauthorized access to computer networks include guessing, randomly generating, or stealing a password. For example, in the Prestel hack, which resulted in the Duke of Edinburgh's mailbox becoming vulnerable, the hacker simply guessed an all too obvious password (222222 1234).[12] Alternatively, some computers and software programs have known flaws that can be exploited. One of the most complex of these is "IP spoofing" in which a computer connected to the Internet can be tricked about the identity of another computer during the process of receiving data from that computer. Perhaps most important of all is the ability to "social engineer." This can be as simple as talking people into giving out their passwords by impersonating someone, stealing garbage in the hope of gaining illicit information (trashing), or looking over someone's shoulder as they use their password (shoulder surfing). However, what makes an intrusion a hack or an intruder a hacker is not the fact of gaining illegitimate access to computers by any of these means, but a set of principles about the nature of such intrusions. Turkle identifies three tenets that define a good hack: 1) simplicity — the act has to be simple but impressive; 2) mastery — however simple it is, the act must derive from a sophisticated technical expertise; and 3) illicit — the act must be against some legal, institutional or even just perceived rules.[13] Dutch hacker Ralph used the example of stealing free telephone time to explain the hack:

> It depends on how you do it, the thing is that you've got your guys that think up these things, they consider the technological elements of a phone-booth, and the they think, 'hey wait a minute, if I do this, this could work', so as an experiment, they cut the wire and it works, now *they're hackers*. Okay, so it's been published, so Joe Bloggs reads this and says, 'hey, great, I have to phone my folks up in Australia', so he goes out, cuts the wire, makes phone calls. He's a stupid ignoramus, yeah?

Ralph, hacker, interview

A second example would be the Citibank hack. In this hack, the expertise to gain unauthorized control of a bank was developed by a group of Russian hackers who were uninterested in taking financial advantage. The hacker ethic to these intruders was one of exploration and not robbery. However, drunk and depressed, one of the hackers sold the secret for $100 and two bottles of vodka, allowing organized criminals to gain the expertise to steal ten million dollars. Here, the difference between hacking and criminality lay in the communally held ethic that glorified being able to hack Citibank but stigmatized using that knowledge to steal. A hack is an event that has an original moment and, though it can be copied, it loses its status as a hack the more it is copied. Further, the good hack is the object in itself that hackers desire, not the result of the hack.[12]

The key to understanding computer intrusion in a world increasingly reliant on computer-mediated communication lies in understanding a community whose aim is the hack. This community makes complex computer intrusion possible and a never-ending threat, through the limitless search for a good hack. This community stands forever intentionally poised at the forefront of computer communications and on the wrong side of what hackers see as dominant social and cultural norms.

5.2.1   Computer Underground: Demographics

Analyzing any intentionally illicit community poses difficulties for the researcher. The global and anonymous nature of computer-mediated communication exacerbates such problems because generating a research population from the computer underground necessitates self-selection by subjects, and it will be difficult to check the credentials of each subject. Further methodological difficulties involved in examining a self-styled outlaw community that exists in cyberspace are indicated by the Prestel hacker:[12]

> There used to be a hacking community in the U.K., the hackers I used to deal with 8 or 9 years ago were all based in North London where I used to live and there were 12 of us around the table at the local Chinese restaurant of a Friday night...within about 20 minutes of me and my colleague Steve Gold being arrested: end of hacking community. An awful lot of phone calls went around, a lot of discs got buried in the garden, and a lot of people became ex-hackers and there's really no-one who'll talk now.

Schifreen, hacker, interview

Demographic data is particularly difficult to collect from an underground community. However, some statistics are available. Following presentation of these, an in-depth exploration of the hacking community on the basis of qualitative research will be presented. After investigating the U.S. police force's crackdown on the computer underground in the early 1990s, Sterling estimated there were 5,000 active hackers with only around 100 in the elite who would be "skilled enough to penetrate sophisticated systems."[14] For the same time period, Clough and Mungo estimated there were 2,000 of "the really dedicated, experienced, probably obsessed computer freaks" and possibly 10,000 others aspiring to this status.[15] Though no more than an indication, the best, indeed only, estimates for the size of the hacking community or computer underground are given by these figures.

Another means of measuring the size of the computer underground is by its effects. Though this cannot indicate the actual number of hackers, as one hacker can be responsible for extensive illicit adventures, measuring the extent of hacking allows one indication of the underground's level of activity. Three surveys are available that generate evidence from the hacked rather than hackers: the 1990 U.K. Audit Commission's survey, the 1993 survey conducted as part of this research project, and the 1996 WarRoom Research, information systems security survey.[8,16] Results from all three sources will be presented, focusing on the amount of hacking.

The 1990 U.K. Audit Commission surveyed 1500 academic, commercial, and public service organizations in the United Kingdom. This survey found that 5% of academic, 14% of commercial, and 11.5% of public service organizations had suffered computer intrusion.[9] A survey was conducted as part of this research project (hereafter referred to as the Taylor survey) and received 200 responses, of which 64.5% had experienced a hack, 18.5% a virus only, and 17% no detected illicit activity.[12] The 1996 WarRoom survey received 236 responses from commercial U.S. firms (Fortune 1,000 companies) of which 58% reported attempts by outsiders to gain computer access in the 12 months prior to July 1996, 29.8% did not know, and 12.2% reported no such attempts. The types of intrusions can be categorized as 38.3% malicious, 46.5% unidentifiable as malicious or benign, and 15% benign.[8,12]

The level of hacking activity reported in these surveys varies greatly between the Audit Commission on the one hand and the Taylor and War-Room surveys on the other. A number of possibilities explain this. The lower level of hacking comes from a survey of U.K. organizations, while Taylor was over half from the U.S. and a third U.K., and WarRoom was solely U.S. This might suggest a higher level of hacking into U.S. organizations, though this says nothing about the national source of a hack. Next, the Audit Commission survey has a much larger sample population and consequently should be more reliable. However, the WarRoom and Taylor surveys stressed the confidentiality of respondents. This is a key issue, as organizations show a consistently high level of caution in reporting hacks. The WarRoom survey found that 37% of organizations would only report computer intrusion if required by law, 22% would report only if "everyone else did," 30% would only report if they could do so anonymously, and only 7% would report anytime intrusion was detected.[16] From this perspective, the Audit Commission survey may have under-reported hacking because it did not place sufficient emphasis on the confidentiality of responses. Also, the Taylor and WarRoom surveys were conducted later than the Audit Commission and NCC surveys, and may reflect either rising levels or rising awareness of hacking. Unfortunately, there is no way of deciding which of these factors explains the differences in reported levels of hacking.

The available statistics suggest that the computer underground may not be very large, particularly in the number of elite hackers, but may be having a significant effect on a range of organizations. If the Taylor and WarRoom surveys are accurate, nearly two-thirds of organizations are suffering hacks. To grasp the nature of hackers requires turning to the qualitative fieldwork conducted in this project.

5.2.2 Internal Factors: Technology, Secrecy, Anonymity, Membership Fluidity, Male Dominance, and Motivations

> To find 'hacker culture' you have to take a very wide view of the cyberspace terrain and watch the interactions among physically diversified people who have in common a mania for machines and software. What you will find will be a gossamer framework of culture.
>
> Marotta, hacker, interview[12]

The imagined community that hackers create and maintain can be outlined through the following elements: technology, secrecy, anonymity, membership fluidity, male dominance, and motivations. Community is here understood as the collective identity that members of a social group construct or, in a related way, as the collective imagination of a social group. Both a collective identity and imagination allow individuals to recognize in each other membership of the same community. The computer underground, or at least the hacking part of it, can be in this way understood as a community that offers certain forms of identity through which membership and social norms are negotiated. Even though some of these forms are externally imposed, the nature of internet technology; for example, the way these forms are understood, allows individuals to recognize in each other a common commitment to an ethic, community, or way of life. This theorization draws on Anderson's concept of the imagined community and on social movement theories that see movements as dispersed networks of individuals, groups, and organizations that combine through a collectively articulated identity. Anderson names the power of an imagined identity to bind people, who may never meet each other, together in allegiance to a common cause. Social movement theories grasp the way movements rely on divergent networks that are not hierarchically or bureaucratically unified but are negotiated between actors through an identity that is the subject of much of the negotiation.[12] These perspectives allow us to grasp a hacking community that can use computer-mediated communication to exist world-wide and in which individuals often never physically meet.

5.2.3 Technology

The hacking community is characterized by an easy, if not all-consuming, relationship with technology, particularly with computer and communications technology. As one professor pointed out:[12]

> We are confronted with ... a generation that has lived with computers virtually from the cradle, and therefore have no trace of fear, not even a trace of reverence.

Professor Herschberg, academic, interview

Hackers share a certain appreciation of, or attitude to technology in the assumption that technology can be turned to new and unexpected uses. This attitude need not be confined to computer-mediated communication. Dutch hacker Dell claimed to have explored the subterranean tunnels and elevator shafts of Amsterdam, including government fallout shelters (Dell, hacker, interview), while Utrecht hacker Ralph argued that hacking "pertains to any field of technology. Like, if you haven't got a kettle to boil water with and you use your coffee machine to boil water with, then that in my mind is a hack, because you are using technology in a way that it's not supposed to be used."[12] It is the belief that technology can be bent to new, unanticipated purposes that underpins hackers' collective imagination.

5.2.4 Secrecy

Hackers demonstrate an ambivalent relationship to secrecy. A hack demands secrecy, because hacking is illicit, but the need to share information and gain recognition demands publicity. Sharing information is key in the development of hackers, though it makes keeping illicit acts hidden from law enforcement difficult. Hackers often hack in groups, both in the sense of physically being in the same room while hacking and of hacking separately but being in a group that physically meets, that frequents bulletin boards, on-line places to talk and exchange information. It is a rare story of a hacker's education that does not include being trained by more experienced hackers or drawing on the collective wisdom of the hacking community through on-line information. Gaining recognition is also important to hackers. A member of the Zoetermeer hacking group noted, "hacking can be rewarding in itself, because it can give you a real kick sometimes. But it can give you a lot more satisfaction and recognition if you share your experiences with others. ... Without this group I would never have spent so much time behind the terminals digging into the operating system."[12] A good hack is a bigger thrill when shared, and can contribute to a hacker gaining status and access to more communal expertise. For example, access to certain bulletin boards is only given to those proven worthy.

A tension between the need to keep illicit acts away from the eyes of police and other authority figures but available to peers or even the general public defines hackers' relationship to secrecy. No hack exemplifies this more than a World-Wide Web hack, where the object is to alter an internationally accessible form of public communication but not be caught. In the case of the Labour Party hack, the hacker managed to be quoted on the front page of U.K. national newspapers by ringing up the newspapers to tell them to look at the hack before it was removed, but also kept his/her identity secret. A further example is that many hackers take trophies in the form of copied documents or pieces of software, because a trophy proves to the hacking community that the hacker "was there." The problem is that a trophy is one of the few solid bases for prosecuting hackers. Ambivalence toward secrecy is also the source of the often-noted fact that hackers are odd criminals, seeking publicity. As Gail Thackeray, one-time police nemesis of hackers, noted, "what other group of criminals ... publishes newsletters and hold conventions?"[14]

5.2.5   Anonymity

The third component of the hacking community is anonymity. As with technology, what is distinctive is not so much online anonymity, as this is a widely remarked aspect of computer-mediated communication, but the particular understanding of anonymity that hackers take up. Anonymity is closely related to secrecy but is also distinct. Secrecy relates to the secrecy of the hack, whereas anonymity relates to the secrecy of a hacker's offline identity. Netta Gilboa notes one complex version of this interplay of named and hidden identity on an on-line chat channel for hackers.

Gilboa pointed that hackers can log into the hack channel using software that allows them to come in from several sites and be on as many separate connections, appearing to be different people.[17] One of these identities might then message you privately as a friend while another is being cruel to you in public.[17] Gilboa experienced the construction of a number of public identities all intended to mask the real identity of a hacker.[17]

A second example of this interplay of anonymity and publicity is the names, or "handles" that hackers give themselves and their groups. These are some of the handles encountered in this research: Hack-Tic (group), Zoetermeer (group), Altenkirch (German), Eric Bloodaxe, Faustus, Maelstrom, Mercury, Mofo. Sterling notes a long list of group names such as Kaos Inc., Knights of Shadow, Master Hackers, MAD!, Legion of Doom, Farmers of Doom, the Phirm, Inner Circle I, and Inner Circle II. Hackers use names to sign their hacks (sometimes even leaving messages for the hacked computer's usual users), to meet on-line, and to bolster their self-image as masters of the hack, all the while keeping their offline identity secret.[12]

5.2.6 Membership Fluidity

The fourth quality of the hacking community is the speed at which membership changes. Hacking shares the characteristics ascribed to many social movements of being an informal network rather than a formally constituted organization and, as such, its boundaries are highly permeable.[12] There are no formal ceremonies to pass or ruling bodies to satisfy to become a hacker. The informal and networked nature of the hacking community, combined with its illicit and sometimes obsessional nature, means that a high turnover of hackers occurs.[15] Hackers form groups within the loose overall structure of the hacking community, and these may aspire to be formally organized, however the pressures of law enforcement mean that any successful hacking group is likely to attract sustained attention at some point.[19]

> People come and go often, and if you lay off for a few months and then come back, almost everyone is new. There are always those who have been around for years ... I would consider the hacking community a very informal one. It is pretty much anarchy as far as rule-making goes. ... The community was structured only within the framework of different hacking groups. Legion of Doom would be one example of this. A group creates its own rules and usually doesn't have a leader ... The groups I've been in have voted on accepting new members, kicking people out, etc.

Eric Bloodaxe, hacker, member of Legion of Doom, interview[12]

Gilboa claims that the future of hacking will be a split between life-long hackers, often unable to quit because of police records and suspicion, and 90% of hackers who will move on when they get a job they care about or a girlfriend who sucks up their time.[17] A more prosaic, but equally potent, reason the hacking community's membership is fluid is given by hacker Mike: "If you stop, if you don't do it for one week, then things change, the network always changes. It changes very quickly and you have to keep up and you have to learn all the tricks by heart, the default passwords, the bugs you need,"[12] The sheer speed at which computer communications technology changes requires a powerful commitment from hackers.

5.2.7   Male Dominance

The fifth component of hacking culture is male dominance and an associated misogyny. Research for this project and literature on hackers fails to uncover any significant evidence of female hackers.[12] Gilboa states: "I have met more than a thousand male hackers in person, but less than a dozen of them women."[17] This imbalance is disproportionate even in the field of computer-mediated communication.[19] A number of factors explain the paucity of women generally in the computer sciences: childhood socialization, where boys are taught to relate to technology more easily than girls; education in computers occurs in a masculine environment; and a gender bias towards men in the language used in computer science.[12,13,19] With these factors producing a general bias towards males in relation to computers, the drive towards the good hack exacerbates this as it involves a macho, competitive attitude.[20] Hackers construct a more intensely masculine version of the already existing male bias in the computer sciences.

> When Adam delved and Eve span...who was then the gentleman? Well, we see that Adam delves into the workings of computers and networks and meanwhile Eve spins, what? programmes? Again, my wife programmes and she has the skills of a hacker. She has had to crack security in order to do her job. But she does it as her job, not for the abstract thrill of discovering the unknown. Eve spins. Females who compute would rather spend their time building a good system than breaking into someone else's system.
>
> **Mercury, hacker, interview**[12]

Whether Mercury's understanding of differences between men and women is accurate or not, the fact that he, and many other hackers, take such attitudes means the hacking community will almost certainly feel hostile to women. Added to these assumptions of, at best, separate spheres of male and female expertise in computing is the problem that anonymity often fuels sexual harassment. "The fact that many networks allow a user to hide his real name...seems to cause many males to drop all semblance of civilization. Sexual harassment by email is not uncommon" (Freiss, hacker, interview.)[12]

In Gilboa, a woman recounts an epic tale of harassment that included hackers using her on-line magazine as a tutorial example of how to charge phone calls to someone else, taking over her magazine entirely and launching a fake version, being called a prostitute, child molester, and drug dealer, having her phone calls listened to, her phone re-routed or made to sound constantly engaged, and having her e-mail read.[17] One answer to Gilboa's puzzlement at her treatment lies in the collective identity hackers share and construct that is in part misogynist.

5.2.8   Motivations

Hackers often discuss their motivations for hacking.[12] They are aware of, and often glory in, the fact that the life of a dedicated hacker seems alien to those outside the hacking community. One result of this is that hackers discuss their motivations. These are sometimes couched as self-justifications, sometimes as explanations, and sometimes as agonized struggles with personal obsessions and failures. However, whatever the content of such discussions, it is the fact of an ongoing discourse around the motivation to hack that builds the hacking community. These discussions are one more way that hackers can recognize in each other a common identity that provides a collective basis for their community. A number of recurring elements to these discussions can be identified.

First, hackers often confess to an addiction to computers and/or to computer networks, a feeling that they are compelled to hack. Second, curiosity as to what can be found on the worldwide network is also a frequent topic of discussion. Third, hackers often claim their offline life is boring compared to the thrill of illicit searches in online life. Fourth, the ability to gain power over computer systems, such as NASA, Citibank, or the CIA web site, is an attraction. Fifth, peer recognition from other hackers or friends is a reward and goal for many hackers, signifying acceptance into the community and offering places in a hierarchy of more advanced hackers. Finally, hackers often discuss the service to future computer users or to society they are offering because they identify security loopholes in computer networks. Hackers articulate their collective identity, and construct a sense of community, by discussing this array of motivations:[12]

> I just do it because it makes me feel good, as in better than anything else that I've ever experienced … the adrenaline rush I get when I'm trying to evade authority, the thrill I get from having written a program that does something that was supposed to be impossible to do, and the ability to have social relations with other hackers are all very addictive…For a long time, I was extremely shy around others, and I am able to let my thoughts run free when I am alone with my computer and a modem hooked up to it. I consider myself addicted to hacking…I will have no moral or ethical qualms about system hacking until accounts are available to the general public for free…Peer recognition was very important, when you were recognized you had access to more.
>
> **Maelstrom, hacker, interview**

Maelstrom explores almost the whole range of motivations including curiosity, the thrill of the illicit, boredom, peer recognition, and the social need for free or cheap access. By developing his own interpretation out of the theme of motivation, he can simultaneously define his own drives and develop a sense of community. It is this double movement, in which individual motivations express the nature of a community, that makes the discussions of motivations important for hackers. Finally, the motivations offered by perhaps the most notorious of all hackers, Kevin Mitnick, provide another common articulation of reasons for hacking:[12]

> You get a better understanding of cyberspace, the computer systems, the operating systems, how the computer systems interact with one another, that basically was my motivation behind my hacking activity in the past. It was just from the gain of knowledge and the thrill of adventure, nothing that was well and truly sinister as trying to get any type of monetary gain or anything.

Mitnick, hacker, interview

5.2.9   Internal Factors: Conclusion

These six factors all function largely between hackers, allowing them a common language and a number of resources through which they can recognize each other as hackers and through which newcomers can become hackers. These are resources internal to the hacking community, not because they do not affect or include non-hackers, but because their significance is largely for other hackers. Put another way, these are the resources hackers use to discuss their status as hackers with other hackers, they are collectively negotiated within the boundaries of the hacker community. This raises the issue of how an external boundary is constructed and maintained. How do hackers recognize a distinction between inside and outside? How do hackers adjust, reinvent, and maintain such a distinction? This is the subject of the third and final section of this definition of the hacker community.

5.2.10   External Factors: The Boundary between Computer Underground and the Computer Security Industry

Hackers negotiate a boundary around their community by relating to other social groups. For example, hackers have an often spectacular relationship with the media. Undoubtedly the most important relationship with another community or group is their intimate and antagonistic bond to the computer security industry (CSI). This relationship is constitutive of the hacking community in a way that no other is. Put another way, there is no other social group whose existence is necessary to the existence of the hacking community. Here is a sample of views of hackers from members of CSI:[12]

Hackers are like kids putting a 10 pence piece on a railway line to see if the train can bend it, not realizing that they risk derailing the whole train.

Mike Jones, security awareness division, Department of Trade and Industry, U.K., interview

Electronic vandalism

Warman, London Business School, interview

Somewhere near vermin

Zmudsinski, system engineer/manager, U.S., interview

Naturally, hackers often voice a similar appreciation of members of CSI. For example, while admitting psychotic tendencies exist in the hacking community, Mofo notes:[12]

My experience has shown me that the actions of "those in charge" of computer systems and networks have similar "power trips" which need to be fulfilled. Whether this psychotic need is developed or entrenched before one's association with computers is irrelevant.

Mofo, hacker, interview

However, the boundary between these two communities is not as clear as such attitudes might suggest. This can be seen in relation to membership of the communities and the actions members take.

Hackers often suggest the dream that their skills should be used by CSI to explore security faults, thereby giving hackers jobs and legitimacy to pursue the hack by making them members of CSI. The example of a leading member of one of the most famous hacker groups, the Legion of Doom, is instructive. Eric Bloodaxe, aka Chris Goggans, became a leading member of the hacking community before helping to set up a computer security firm, Comsec, and later became senior network security engineer for WheelGroup, a network security company.[18] On the CSI side, there have been fierce debates over whether hackers might be useful because they identify security problems.[21] Most striking, a number of CSI agencies conduct hacking attacks to test security. IBM employs a group of hackers who can be hired to attack computer systems, and the U.K. government has asked intelligence agents to hack its secure e-mail system for government ministers. In the IBM case, an attempt at differentiating the hired hackers from criminal hackers is made by hiring only hackers without criminal records (a practice akin to turning criminals who have not been caught into police). Both sides try to assure themselves of radical differences because they undertake similar actions. For example, Bernie Cosell was a U.S. commercial computer systems manager and one of the most vehement anti-hackers encountered in this study, yet he admitted he hacked:[12]

> ...once or twice over the years. I recall one incident where I was working over the weekend and the master source hierarchy was left read-protected, and I really needed to look at it to finish what I was doing, and this on a system where I was not a privileged user, so I "broke into" the system enough to give myself enough privileges to be able to override the file protections and get done what I needed...at which point I put it all back and told the systems administrator about the security hole.

Cosell, U.S. systems manager, interview

More famous is the catalogue of hacks Clifford Stoll had to perpetrate in his pursuit of a hacker, which included borrowing other people's computers without permission and monitoring other peoples' electronic communications without permission.[22] Such examples mean that differences between the two communities cannot be expressed through differences in what they do but must focus on the meaning of actions. Delineating these meanings is done chiefly through ethical debates about the nature of hacking, conducted through analogies drawn between cyberspace and non-virtual, or real, space.

CSI professionals often draw analogies between computer intrusion and a range of widely understood crimes. These analogies draw on the claim that a computer is something like a bank, car, or house that can be "gotten into." Using this analogy makes it easy to understand the danger of hackers. People who break into banks, schools, or houses usually do so for nefarious purposes. The ethical differences between hackers and the CSI become clearly drawn. The problem with such analogies is that, on further reflection, hackers seem strange burglars. How often does a burglar leave behind an exact copy of the video recorder they have stolen? But this unreal situation is a more accurate description of theft in cyberspace because taking in cyberspace, overwhelmingly means copying. Further, hacker culture leads hackers to publicize their break-ins, sometimes even stressing the utility of their break-ins for identifying system weaknesses. What bank robbers ring up a bank to complain of lax security? The simple analogy of theft breaks down when it is examined, and must be complicated to begin to make sense of what hackers do:[23]

There is a great difference between trespassing on my property and breaking into my computer. A better analogy might be finding a trespasser in your high-rise office building at 3 am and learning that his back-pack contained some tools, some wire, a timer and a couple of detonation caps. He could claim that he wasn't planting a bomb, but how can you be sure?

Cosell, U.S. systems manager, interview

Cosell's analogy continues to draw on real world, or physically based images of buildings being entered, but tries to come closer to the reality of how hackers operate. However, the ethical component of the analogy has been weakened, because the damage hackers cause implies, where is the bomb? Cosell cannot claim there will definitely be a bomb, only that it is possible. If all possible illegal actions were prohibited, many things would become illegal, such as driving because it is possible to speed and then hurt someone in an accident. The analogy of breaking and entering is strong on implied dangers but weak on the certainty of danger. The analogies that CSI professionals use continue to change if they try to be accurate. My analogy is walking into an office building, asking a secretary which way it is to the records room, and making some Xerox copies of the records. Far different than breaking and entering someone's home.[12] Clearly there is some ethical content here, some notion of theft of information, but it is ethically far muddier than the analogy burglary offers. At this point, the analogy breaks down entirely because the ethical content can be reversed to one that supports hackers as whistle-blowers of secret abuses everyone should know about.

The concept of privacy is very important to a hacker. This is because hackers know how fragile privacy is in today's world. In 1984, hackers were instrumental in showing the world how TRW kept credit files on millions of Americans. Most people had not even heard of a credit file until this happened. More recently, hackers found that MCIs "Friends and Family" program allowed anybody to call an 800 number and find out the numbers of everyone in a customer's "calling circle." As a bonus, one could also find out how these numbers were related to the customer. In both the TRW and MCI cases, hackers were ironically accused of being the ones to invade privacy. What they really did was help to educate the American consumer.[24]

The central analogy of CSI has now lost its ethical content. Goldstein reverses the good and bad to argue that the correct principled action is to broadcast hidden information. If there is some greater social good to be served by broadcasting secrets, then perhaps hackers are no longer robbers and burglars, but socially responsible whistle blowers. In the face of such complexities, CSI professionals sometimes abandon the analogy of breaking and entering altogether; "it is no more a valid justification to attack systems because they are vulnerable than it is valid to beat up babies because they can't defend themselves."[12] Here many people's instinctive reaction would be to side with the babies, but a moment's thought reveals that in substance Cohen's analogy changes little. A computer system is not human, and if information in it is needed by wider society, perhaps it should be attacked.

The twists and turns of these analogies show that CSI professionals use them not so much to clearly define hacking and its problems, but to establish clear ethical differences between themselves and hackers. The analogies of baby-bashing and robbery all to try establish hacking as unethical. The key point is that while these analogies work in an ethical and community building sense, they do not work in clearly grasping the nature of hacking, because analogies between real and virtual space cannot be made as simply as CSI professionals would like to assume.[12]

> Physical (and biological) analogies are often misleading as the appeal to an understanding from an area in which different laws hold....Many users (and even "experts") think of a password as a "key" despite the fact that you can easily guess the password, while it is difficult to do the equivalent for a key.

Brunnstein, academic, Hamburg University, interview

The process of boundary formation between the hacking and CSI communities occurs in the creation of analogies by CSI professionals to establish ethical differences between the communities and their reinterpretation by hackers. However, this does not exclude hackers from making their own analogies.[12]

> Computer security is like a chess game, and all these people that say breaking into my computer systems is like breaking into my house: bull-shit, because securing your house is a very simple thing, you just put locks on the doors and bars on the windows and then only brute force can get into your house, like smashing a window. But a computer has a hundred thousand intricate ways to get in, and it's a chess game with the people that secure a computer.

Gongrijp, Dutch hacker, interview

Other hackers offer similar analogies that stress hacking is an intellectual pursuit. "I was bored if I didn't do anything ... I mean why do people do crosswords? It's the same thing with hackers." (J.C. Van Winkel, hacker, interview) Gongrijp and van Winkel also form boundaries through ethical analogy. Of course, it is an odd game of chess or crossword that results in the winner receiving thousands of people's credit records or access to their letters. Hackers' view that a game of chess has no result but a winner and a loser at a game of chess, whereas hacking often results in access to privileged information, means their analogies are both inaccurate and present hacking as a harmless, intellectual pursuit. It is on the basis of such analogies and discussions that the famed hacker ethic is often invoked by hackers. Rather than hackers learning the tenets of the hacker ethic, as seminally defined by Steven Levy, they negotiate a common understanding of the meaning of hacking, of which the hacker ethic provides a ready articulation.[26] Many see the hacker ethic as a foundation of the hacker community, whereas we see the hacker ethic as the result of the complex construction of a collective identity.

The social process here is the use of analogies to physical space by CSI and hackers to establish a clear distinction between the two groups. In these processes the construction of boundaries between communities that are based on different ethical interpretations of computer intrusion, can be seen in a situation where other boundaries, such as typical actions or membership, are highly fluid.

5.2.11   Conclusion

The nature of the hacking community needs to be explored in order to grasp the social basis that produces hacking as a facet of computer networks. The figures given previously and the rise of the World-Wide Web hack, offering both spectacular publicity and anonymity, point to the endemic nature of hackers now that world-wide computer networks are an inescapable reality. Hackers show that living in a networked world means living in a risky world. The community found by this research articulates itself in two key directions. First, there are a number of components that are the subject of ongoing discussion and negotiation by hackers with other hackers. In defining and redefining their attitudes to technology, secrecy, anonymity, membership change, male dominance, and personal motivations, hackers create an imagined community. Second, hackers define the boundaries of their community primarily in relation to the Computer Security Industry. These boundaries stress an ethical interpretation of hacking because it can be difficult to distinguish clearly the activities or membership of the two communities. Such ethics emerge most clearly through analogies used by members of each community to explain hacking.

Hackers are often pathologized as obsessed, isolated young men. The alien nature of online life allows people to believe that hackers communicate more easily with machines than humans, despite hackers constant use of computers to communicate with other humans. Fear of the power of computers over our own lives underpins this terror. The very anonymity that makes their community difficult to study makes hackers an easy target for pathologizing. For example, Gilboa's experience of harassment outlined earlier led her to pathologize hackers, suggesting work must be done exploring the characteristics of hackers she identified — such as lack of fathers or parental figures, severe depression, and admittance to mental institutions.

Similar interpretations of hackers are offered from within their community. As one hacker pointed out, "All the hackers I know in France have (or have had) serious problems with their parents."[12] Our research strongly suggests that psychological interpretations of hackers that individualize hackers as mentally unstable are severely limited because they miss the social basis of hacking. Gilboa's experience is no less unpleasant but all the more understandable when the male dominance of the hacking community is grasped.

The fear many have of the power of computers over their lives easily translates into the demonization of those who manipulate computers outside of society's legitimate institutions. Journalist Jon Littman once asked hacker Kevin Mitnick if he thought he was being demonized, because new and different fears had arisen with society becoming increasingly dependent on computers and communications.[26] Mitnick replied, "Yeah ... that's why they're instilling fear of the unknown. That's why they're scared of me. Not because of what I've done, but because I have the capability to wreak havoc."[26] The pathological interpretation of hackers is attractive because it is based on the fear of computers controlling our lives. What else could someone be but mad, if he is willing to play for fun on computer systems that control air traffic, dams, or emergency phones? The interpretation of hackers as members of an outlaw community that negotiates its collective identity through a range of clearly recognizable resources does not submit to the fear of computers. It gains a clearer view of hackers, who have become the nightmare of information societies despite very few documented cases of upheaval caused by hackers. Hacking cannot be clearly grasped unless fears are put aside to try and understand the community of hackers, the digital underground. From within this community, hackers begin to lose their pathological features in favor of collective principles, allegiances, and identities.

References

1. Bequai, A., *Computer Crime*, New York: Lexington Books, 1978.
2. Bequai, A., *Techno Crimes*, New York: Lexington Books, 1987.
3. Landreth, B., *Out of the Inner Circle*, Bellvue, WA: Microsoft Press, 1985.
4. Levy, S., *Hackers*, New York: Dell Books, 1984.
5. Parker, D. B., *Crime by Computer*, New York: Charles Scribner and Sons, 1976.
6. Parker, D. B., *Fighting Computer Crime*, New York: Charles Scribner and Sons, 1983.
7. Meyer, G. R., private ethnographic research files.
8. It is of course impossible to provide an adequate history of computer networking here and would distract from the main purpose of present arguments. A summary and full references for such a history can be found in Jordan, 1998a.

9. See Jordan, 1998a for a full discussion of methodologies for counting Internet users.

10. Hackers do indeed hold conferences, such as HoHoCon, SummerCon, PumpCon and DefCon (Rosteck, 1994), see Littman, 1996: 41-44 for a description of such a conference.

11. Anonymity also enables some of the darker fears that emerge about hackers. Finding fearsomely named gangs of hackers running amok in supposedly secure systems can give rise to exaggerated fears, which hackers are often happy to live up to, at least rhetorically, Barlow, 1990.

12. Taylor, P., *Hackers*, London: Routledge, 1999.

13. Turkle, S., *The Second Self: Computers and the Human Spirit*, London: Granada, 1984.

14. Sterling, B., *The Hacker Crackdown: Law and Disorder on the Electronic Frontier*, London: Viking, 1992.

15. Clough, B. and Mungo, P., *Approaching Zero: Data Crime and the Computer Underworld*, London: Faber & Faber, 1992.

16. WarRoom, 1996 information systems security survey, *WarRoom Research, LLC*, available at *http://www.infowar.com*, 1996.

17. Gilboa, N., Elites, lamers, narcs and whores: exploring the computer underground, in Cherny, L. and Weise, E. R., *Wired Women: Gender and New Realities in Cyberspace*, Seattle: Seal Press, 1996.

18. Quittner, J. and Slattalla, M., *Masters of Deception: The Gang that Ruled Cyberspace*, London: Vintage, 1995.

19. Spertus, E., *Why are There so Few Female Computer Scientists?* unpublished paper, MIT, 1991.

20. Keller, L. S., Machismo and the hacker mentality: Some personal observations and speculations, *paper presented to WiC (Women in Computing) Conference*, 57-60, 1990.

21. Denning, D. E., Concerning hackers who break into computer systems, *paper presented at the National Computer Security Conference*, Washington, DC, 1-4, October, 1990.

22. Stoll, C., *The Cuckoo's Egg: Tracking a Spy Through the Maze of Computer Espionage*, New York: Doubleday, 1989.

23. Cosell, B., Is hacking the same as breaking and entering? *Comput. Underground Dig.*, 3, file 2, 1991.

24. Goldstein, E., Response to telecom digest's views, *Comput. Underground Dig.*, 1, July, 1990.

25. Levy, S., *Hackers: Heroes of the Computer Revolution*, New York: Bantam Doubleday, 1984.

26. Littman, J., *The Fugitive Game: Online with Kevin Mitnick, the Inside Story of the Great Cyberchase*, Boston: Little, Brown & Co., 1996.

Psycho-Geographical Profiling

6

6.1 The Serial Rapist's Spatial Pattern of Victim Selection

JONATHAN D. ALSTON

The victim selection pattern of serial rapists in British Columbia is examined against several models derived from Environmental Criminology. Information about offender activity nodes and routine pathways was compared with information about the location of the initial contact scenes of the offenses. Data for a population of thirty British Columbia, Canada series were selected from case files held by the Royal Canadian Mounted Police (RCMP) at "E" division headquarters in Vancouver, Canada.

The research supports the importance of the serial rapist's awareness space in shaping victim selection patterns. The initial contact scenes were consistently found to be close to the activity nodes and especially the routine pathways of this serial rapist population. The research suggests that the target selection process used by serial rapists is not random and may be predictable.

In Canada in 1992, the latest year for which crime statistics are available, there were 33,017 reported incidents of sexual assault, 937 reported incidents of sexual assault with a weapon, and 398 reported incidents of aggravated sexual assault. In total, about 125 reported incidents of sexual assault (all three levels combined) occurred per 100,000 persons in Canada for 1992. Traditionally, British Columbia has a higher rate of crime than the national average and is usually the highest of all provinces in rates of violent crime. In 1992, there were about 173 reported incidents of sexual assault (all three levels combined) per 100,000 persons in B.C.[1] Although many sexual assaults are committed by serial rapists, very little academic research has been conducted on this behavior. Here we examine the victim selection pattern of serial rapists in B.C. against several models derived from Environmental Criminology.[2,3]

The theory suggests that most individuals, including serial rapists, spend most of their daily life engaged in non-criminal activities such as work, school, recreation, and activities with family and friends. The immediate area surrounding these particular locations form what are called activity nodes.

Presumably, the most central node will be the offender's residence, while other activity nodes such as work, school, a boyfriend or girlfriend's residence, or a shopping center will branch out from the central node and determine an offender's routine pathways. Moving to and from these nodes creates the area called the awareness space. Environmental Criminology suggests that offenders will choose targets within their own awareness spaces. Exploration of unknown areas will not be part of the target selection process. It should be noted that locations such as tourist sites, landmarks, rivers, mountains, well-known buildings, and highways may become a part of the person's awareness space without actually being a part of their routine activity space. It will be argued later in this chapter that including highways near the offender's primary activity node as a portion of the awareness space is a legitimate procedure.

The suppositions made by environmental criminology are distinctive, as the theory, in essence, is suggesting that the need to feel secure or familiar within an area is more important to the offender than the need to minimize chances of recognition or detection, especially if the crime does not unfold according to the offender's expectations (e.g., the victim escapes, a bystander interrupts the crime, or a witness views the crime taking place). Detection and recognition are, of course, much more likely if an offender is known and associated with an area. Admittedly, this is a simplified description of the much more comprehensive theory.

Here we attempt to answer whether a test of domocentric and nodally influenced behavior can identify spatial patterns of target selection within a set of serial rapists. Furthermore, we attempt to determine whether incorporating the offender's routine pathways into the analysis strengthens the statistical results and improves the identification of spatial patterns in serial rape.

The data set used contains information about the location of the offender's residence and other activity nodes such as work locations, friends' residences, and other locations frequented at the time the offense occurred, and the location of the initial contact scene between the victim(s) and offender(s). This information makes it possible to extrapolate a vital portion of the offender's awareness space. Measuring the distance between the activity node and the initial contact scene for many offenders and offenses will allow the researcher to state whether serial rapists do fit into an identifiable model in their selection of targets.

6.1.1   Perspectives on Rape and Serial Rape

The National Center for the Analysis of Violent Crime (NCAVC), under the auspices of the Behavioral Science Services Unit of the FBI, has conducted numerous law enforcement-based studies of serial crime, including serial rape.

Researchers from the NCAVC monitored interviews with 41 incarcerated serial rapists responsible for 837 rapes and over 400 attempted rapes. The number of rapes committed by those in the sample ranged from 10 to 59. The researchers studied only serial rapists who had committed 10 or more rapes. The first of this NCAVC literature was the Hazelwood and Burgess study, which provided background for the future articles.[4]

Hazelwood, Reboussin, and Warren focused on the relationship of force to victim resistance, on the pleasure experienced by the rapist, and on how these variables change over time.[5] Hazelwood and colleagues examined the demographics and characteristics of the serial rapist sample. In a separate study, Hazelwood and Warren examined specific aspects of the behavior of these rapists during and following the commission of their sexual assaults.[6]

In addition to their work on serial rape, the NCAVC and affiliated researchers have published valuable information on serial sexual murderers. As will be explained later, sexually related homicides are included in the tabulation of serial rapes. Of this research, Burgess and Hartman,[7] FBI,[8] Hazelwood, Dietz, and Warren,[5] Ressler, Burgess, and Douglas,[9] Ressler, Burgess, Douglas, Hartman, and D'Agostino,[10] and Ressler, Burgess, Hartman, Douglas, and McCormack[11] offer insight into this crime and this type of criminal.

Ressler, Burgess, and Douglas, researchers affiliated with the NCAVC, focused on the psycho-dynamics of a single serial rapist/murderer.[12] This offender committed 12 known offenses over a 4 year period. All 12 offenses occurred within the offender's awareness space. The offender noted the times that police patrols frequented his home area by monitoring them from his high rise apartment. Most of the victims were taken by knifepoint from the elevator at the offender's apartment complex. Prentky et al. also examine serial sexual homicide.[14] Money also based his research on a single incarcerated serial rapist.[15] He argues that the causes of the psychiatric disorders of serial rape and lust murder are linked to a pathological condition or brain disease.

Groth is often cited as a definitive work in the analysis of the motivation of rapists.[15] Groth identifies three types of rapists: the *anger* rapist, the *power* rapist, and the *sadistic* rapist. He states that the sadistic rapist is sensationalized and overrepresented in the media as the typical rapist. Groth suggests that any of the three types of rapists may become a serial rapist, although the sadistic rapist is the most likely to repeat his offense behavior.[15]

Maume argues that inequality produces lifestyles that are associated with the opportunity for offenders and victims to come into contact with each other, and this relationship would be established using rape rates.[16] Some measures used by Maume are suspect as measures of opportunity. James LeBeau has published several works on serial rape.[17] His research on serial rape is based on a sample of rapes in a five year period (1971 to 1975) in San Diego, California. During this period there were 612 reported rapes that met LeBeau's standard for research. LeBeau examined the intraracial versus interracial characteristics of reported rape offenses.[17] LeBeau also examined the capacity of the serial offender to skew descriptions, measurements, and generalizations about the offense of rape.[18] He discovered a clear indication that geographic locations and the ecological distribution of offenses vary radically from one year to the next. In this study, LeBeau examined whether this crime followed the distance-decay effect proposed by Burgess in 1925.[19] He found support for this supposition and noted that serial offenders continue their series in the same relative area. LeBeau concluded that any numerical, geographical, and ecological descriptions concerning rape are short-lived or require revision after accounting for the effects of the serial offender, which tend to skew findings,[19] a conclusion supported by Groth et al.,[20] Hamparian et al.,[21] and Wolfgang et al.[22] The effect of serial rape on aggregate rape rates is also suggested by Lisak and Roth, who reported that of the 15 rapists in their sample, 6 were serial offenders.[23] These serial rapists skewed many of the findings of their research.

LeBeau found significant differences between the geographic nature of serial and single rapists.[24] At large (i.e., unapprehended) serial offenders traveled the shortest distance with the victims, whereas single offense rapists traveled a relatively long distance with the victims. More relevant was the finding that serial offenders, though they may travel long distances to the crime scenes, will often restrict their attacks within a small diameter. LeBeau cautions that this finding occurred only for chronic serial offenders (serial offenders who commit five or more offenses before apprehension).[24]

In another study, using Manhattan metric, LeBeau focused on the distance traveled by the rapist from his residence to the initial contact scene, the place where he first encountered the victim.[25] The mean journey length for serial offenders was 1.77 miles, and for single offense rapists 3.5 miles. LeBeau also used *centrography* to examine similar spatial trends.[26]

LeBeau examined the activity of four chronic serial rapists in the San Diego sample. He discussed common patterns of date, hour of the day, relationship with the victim, *modus operandi*, type of crime scene, and travel distance.[27] Although the sub-sample was too small to apply the findings to the larger serial rapist population, these are intriguing patterns.

Canter and Larkin's research is one of the more valuable works on serial rape.[28] Canter and Larkin examined the spatial activity of 45 British male serial rapists who had been convicted of at least two rapes of women they had not known before the offense (i.e., they were stranger rapists).[28] The researchers tested two spatial activity hypotheses called the *marauder* hypothesis and the *commuter* hypothesis. Canter and Larkin found strong statistical support for the *marauder* hypothesis but not for the *commuter* hypothesis. They found that by using the two most widely separated crime scenes as diameter points of a circle, it was likely that all offenses in a particular series would be encompassed by the circle and, more importantly, that the residence of the offender would also be found within the circular area (i.e, the marauder hypothesis).[28] Canter and Larkin did note that there were some individuals who exemplified the *commuter* offender schema. They suggest that more experienced serial rapists are more likely to become *commuters.*

Canter and Larkin also found strong support for the range hypothesis, which states that the distance serial rapists travel to offend should correlate positively with the distances between offenses. The average minimum distance the rapists traveled from their base was 1.53 miles.[28] The sample of serial rapists traveled a minimum of 0.61 miles from their residence or base of activity. This "minimum safe distance" is supposedly a buffer zone where an offender will likely not select victims for fear of recognition, a notion first suggested by Brantingham and Brantingham.[2]

6.1.2 Journey to Crime Research

Journey to crime research is based on the theoretical assumptions of environmental based analysis. Few studies have explicitly examined the journey to crime of serial rapists. Exceptions to this are LeBeau,[26,27] Canter and Larkin,[28] and Topalin.[29] Topalin examined rape and serial rape in London in the 1980s and found that the serial rapist group traveled a mean distance of 2.81 miles from node to target contact scene.[29] Some 20% of the offenses Topalin studied occurred in or close to the offender's residence.[29]

Journey to crime research on rape in general is valuable background to this chapter. Amir examined rape in Philadelphia for 1958 to 1960 and found that 72% of his sample of rapists attacked their victims within 5 city blocks of the rapist's home area.[30] Rand also examined rape in Philadelphia for 1968 to 1975 and reported that 53% of rapes occurred within the home census tract of the offender.[31] Pyle examined rape in Akron, Ohio in 1972 and reported a 1.34 mile mean distance from offender residence to crime site.[32] Some decades ago, Erlanson examined the journey of rapists in Chicago and found that 87% of rapes occurred within the offender's home neighborhood (defined as the police precinct).[33] An earlier study by White in Indianapolis, Indiana, found that rapists traveled a mean distance of 1.52 miles.[34] Gabor and Gottheil also examined rapists and found 1.43 miles as the mean distance traveled from residence to crime site by their sample of offenders from Ottawa, Ontario.[35] Finally, a study by Rhodes and Conly in Washington, D.C., for 1974 found a 1.15 mile mean and a 0.73 mile median journey to crime for their sample of rapists.[36]

This research supports the idea that rapists and serial rapists will remain close to their area of familiarity and that this phenomenon is consistent for different locations, different cultures, and even different periods of time. This chapter builds on journey to crime literature. Distances from the offender's awareness space to the initial contact scene will be noted and analyzed. The next section explains the research design and includes definitions of the terms and variables used in this research.

6.1.3   Research Design

6.1.3.1   Definition of Terms

The following terms will be used throughout the chapter. An explanation of how the particular term was defined is also provided. The explanations given here have been abridged somewhat from an earlier work.[37]

6.1.4   Serial Sexual Assault (Stranger to Stranger)

In this analysis, only stranger-stranger serial sexual assaults were examined. A stranger to stranger rape or sexual assault is defined as a sexual assault that occurs between one or more offenders and one or more victims when the offender(s) and victim(s) had no personal relationship prior to the day the offense was committed.

6.1.5   Serial Rapist

A serial rapist is any individual who has committed two or more serious sex offenses. Applicable sex offenses are:

1. Sexual assault or attempted sexual assault as defined by the Criminal Code of Canada (CCC) in s. 271-273
2. A sexually related homicide as defined by the CCC in s. 231 (5) (b) (c) (d) (6)
3. Sexual interference with an individual under the age of 14 as defined by the CCC in s. 151
4. Sexual exploitation of an individual under the age of 14 as defined in the CCC in s. 153
5. Criminal anal intercourse as defined in the CCC in s. 159.

It may seem questionable to categorize a serial offender who murders his victims as a serial rapist, even if the crimes were sexually related. It is argued that differentiating behavior according to the outcome of a crime is not a valid basis, in academic research, for studying the behaviors separately (e.g., the exact amount of violence may be fatal in one rape while it may wound but not kill the victim in a different rape).

6.1.6   Series

A series is comprised of two or more sex offenses committed by:

Class I: A <u>single</u> offender acting alone.

Class II: <u>Two or more</u> offenders acting together, where <u>all</u> offenders are common to <u>all</u> cases.

Class III: <u>One</u> offender acting alone or two or more offenders acting together, where at least one offender is common to <u>all</u> cases.

Class IV: <u>Two or more</u> offenders acting together, where <u>each</u> offender participated in <u>at least</u> two cases.

Class V: Two or more offenders who have committed one or more cases alone, and where all offenders have <u>only one</u> case in common.

There is no minimum or maximum time interval that must occur between offenses in order for an incident to be included in a series. Furthermore, events such as incarceration, that interrupt a series do not preclude offenses taking place after or before the said event from being included in a series. The data set population is comprised of 29 separate series that contributed to the total 102 stranger-stranger sexual assaults. To be precise, this paper examines series, <u>not</u> individual serial rapists.

6.1.7   Activity Node

An activity node is a locus of familiarity for the offender.[2,3] For most of the series only a single activity node, the offender's residence at the time of the offense, is known. In some cases, more extensive information about the offender's routine activities is available, and in such cases the measured journey to crime distance is taken from the initial contact scene to the nearest activity node. To avoid tautology, a researcher must be discriminatory in the nodes used in analysis and only utilize sites that would, on theoretical grounds, be primary to the offender in anchoring his spatial pattern of target selection.

6.1.8   Initial Contact Scene

If the serial rapist uses a blitz or surprise attack in the offense, the initial contact scene is the exact location where the offender first comes into personal contact with the victim. If the offender uses a "con" or uses a mutual acquaintance to gain access to the victim, the initial contact scene is the exact location where the offender comes into contact with the victim immediately prior to the commission of the act.

6.1.9   Distance

Distances in this study will be measured from the initial contact scene to the particular activity node using both curvimeter measures and "as the crow flies" distances. Each distance was remeasured at least once to ensure an accurate reading. The initial contact scenes and offender nodes were obtained from a database held by a ViCLAS unit at "E" Division RCMP headquarters in Vancouver, B.C. These points were then plotted on individual road maps. In total, there were 102 offenses contained in 29 series.

"As the crow flies" measurements were simply taken with a straight-edged ruler, measuring the distance from initial contact scene to closest node and multiplying this distance by the scale of the map. Curvimeter measurements are more subjective than straight line distances, as the measurements are the *perceived distance* that the offender traveled. In some cases, the actual route taken by the offender was noted in the case file. In the former cases, a probable route from the node to initial contact scene was plotted on the roadmap and measured using the curvimeter. Routes were plotted along the obvious traffic thoroughfares which, in most cases, had a B.C. highway designation.

It is possible that the offender may take a different route as a short cut. In such cases, the curvimeter distance measure would be a more conservative measurement of distance. It is not as likely, though still probable, that a serial rapist could take a route that is further than the perceived distance measurement. It is argued, on the basis of the geography of movement literature, that any discrepancy between actual distance traveled and the imputed distance will be insignificant in the cognitive notion of distance in the offender's mind.[38] Distances were also measured from the routine pathways of the offender to the initial contact scene. Routine pathway is defined in the next paragraph. These distances were measured using curvimeter distance measures. There were 102 measured distances representing the total number of offenses.

6.1.10   Nearest Node or Routine Pathway

Another vital portion of an individual's awareness space are the pathways between activity nodes. An analysis of the serial rapist's spatial pattern of target selection should also take into account the area along pathways. The area of high probability for target selection along a routine pathway would probably be much narrower than the area of high probability for target selection around an essential node.

In order to explore the effect of including the routine pathway portion of the offender's awareness space, analysis will be conducted on the distance to the nearest node of activity <u>or</u> the nearest routine pathway of the offender. *Routine pathway* is defined as a roadway that can be extrapolated as the probable route between two known activity nodes, and also as the major commuter routes (routes that have a highway designation) near the offender's activity nodes. If information from the RCMP case file mentions other routes commonly used by the offender, they will also be included as valid portions of the awareness space.

Using major commuter routes with a highway designation is an appropriate and conservative measure. Highways, like any major geographical feature such as a river, mountain, or landmark cannot pass unnoticed by an offender who drives to and from an initial contact scene (only two series included offenses in which a vehicle was not used to travel to or away from the initial contact scene). Therefore, they can be utilized as a pathway that the offender is aware of and probably uses fairly often. The 102 offenses occurred in 10 population centers throughout British Columbia. Only routes near the offender's primary node will be used in the analysis.

6.1.10.1   Research Design

The Kolmogorov-Smirnov test for goodness of fit was used in this analysis.[39,40] This is a test of the density of data points in relation to a given site or node. Hodder and Orton state that in the Kolmogorov-Smirnov test, the greatest cumulative distance (Dmax) is compared with a critical value that depends on the number of sites.[41] The test uses the basic principles of distance decay analysis, but in a more efficient manner.

In the present work, and as mentioned earlier, there were 29 series which contributed 102 distance measurements. These distances range from a minimum distance of 0 km (i.e., the initial contact scene was at, or very near, a primary activity node) to a distance of over 100 km. It should be noted that only a small proportion of the measurements were any great length from the offender's known awareness space and are therefore treated as outliers.

Using the Kolmogorov-Smirnov process, zones were created using constant distance increments. Although the exact distances could be used, this option was discarded in favor of the more conservative distance increment zones. A number of tests were conducted using different maximum distances as the final zone. Table 6.1.1 notes the final zone that was used for each test and the size of the incremental constant.

Conducting such a battery of tests by different maximum ranges is an important procedure. It is probable that the cumulative frequency of the data may be significantly different from a standardized distribution using a larger final zone such as 25 or 50 km than a distribution that uses a smaller final zone such as 2.5 or 5 km. This is intuitively logical, as journey to crime distances are much more likely to be normally or uniformly distributed within a 5 km range than a 50 km range. This is primarily due to the amount of time spent within the different ranges. Significance levels will be lower in

Table 6.1.1   Maximum Distance From Node of Activity for Each Kolmogorov-Smirnov Test for Goodness of Fit by Incremental Constant

Maximum Distance	Increment Constant
50 km	1 km
25 km	1 km
15 km	0.5 km
10 km	0.5 km
7.5 km	0.5 km
5 km	0.25 km
2.5 km	0.15 km

these smaller final distance increment categories, and if the Kolmogorov-Smirnov tests reveal that serial rapists choose targets in a non-uniform or non-normal pattern within smaller ranges, it would suggest that the node or site is strongly influencing target selection.

However, one important point should be noted. In the smaller maximum distance tests such as the test that uses 2.5 km as the final zone, the test may begin to be influenced by the buffer zone of the offender.[2,3,42] This may alter the power of the nodal influence within the range and lead to a result in the statistical test which shows a decreased level of significance.

These tests will also be conducted for the distances measured to the nearest node of activity <u>or</u> routine pathway of the offender. When including the routine pathways of the offender, only a few distances were found beyond 3.5 km of the offender's awareness space. Two tests were conducted on these data using 2.5 and 3.5 km as the final zonal and using a 0.15 km incremental constant.

Two auxiliary Kolmogorov-Smirnov tests will be conducted to explore the robustness of the previous results. These tests will exclude different series to see whether there is any change in the levels of significance that could be attributed to the presence of these series. This is an important step. It will allow the researcher to argue that various idiosyncrasies in the data have not affected the results and conclusions.

The first of these auxiliary tests will exclude a single series that was responsible for 25 offenses. This series is of such magnitude that the presence of the series may skew the results. The second auxiliary test will answer concerns about the possibility that *commuter* serial rapists may affect the results of such a study. As described in Canter and Larkin, the *commuter* serial rapist is one who attacks his victims far away from any area in which he is well known.[28] His criminal range does not overlap his home range. It is possible that if this type of offender exists in inordinate numbers, the results of the study will be skewed. If excluding such offenders strengthens the levels of significance greatly, then it is probable that an analysis of the serial rapist's spatial pattern of target selection must control by type of rapist — *marauders* or *commuters*. To explore this, a battery of tests was conducted, excluding those series that did not have at least one offense within 2.5 or 5 km of a primary activity node. Offenders who select all their targets beyond this range are defined here to be commuters.

6.1.11   The Population of Serial Rapists

A brief word about the information used in this study is important. Material on the series of offenses committed by the different offenders was obtained from the records of a specialized crime analysis unit of the RCMP. Most of the series have occurred since the 1991 inception of this unit. Only two series, included for their notoriety, occurred completely before 1991. This crime analysis unit has a great number of records on sex crimes and sexually related crimes that occur in British Columbia. The 29 series used in this paper are the entire number of series in this database which fit the criterion of a stranger-stranger serial sexual assaulter defined earlier. Therefore, the set of series should be referred to as a population and <u>not</u> as a sample. It is likely that there are series that fit this criterion of which the RCMP is not aware or about which they do not have sufficient data. As the ViCLAS unit has no specific policy regarding the type of series they collect information about, it is argued that the series used in this paper are not significantly different from any other series that occurred in British Columbia during this time.

6.1.12   Results of Research

The first set of tests was run on straight line, or "as the crow flies" distance measures. Separate tests were run with an ever-decreasing final distance increment. Proportions representing the fraction of data points that were within the final distance increment will be noted below the reported significance values. Two tests were conducted for each final distance increment category using normal and uniform distributions as standards for comparison. It should be remembered that a successful test merely indicates that the distribution of data points is neither normal nor uniform. The significance values for the first test are as follows:

Table 6.1.2   Significance Values Using Straight Line Distance Measures From the Nearest Node of Activity

	Final Distance Increment and Length of Incremental Constant						
	50 km (1 km)	25 km (1 km)	15 km (.5 km)	10 km (.5 km)	7.5km (.5 km)	5 km (.25 km)	2.5km (.15 km)
Normal Distribution	.0000	.0000	.0006	.0010	.0013	.0033	.0495
Uniform Distribution	.0000	.0000	.0000	.0000	.0000	.0000	.0000
Proportion of Data	0.98	0.95	0.88	0.87	0.84	0.76	0.58

Two Kolmogorov-Smirnov tests, the 50 and the 25 km final distance increment test, included a comparison of the data to a Poisson distribution. The significance values for both tests were less than .0001.

The second set of tests was run on distances using curvimeter measurements of the imputed route taken by the offender to the initial contact scene. As in the first set of tests, separate tests were run with an ever-decreasing final distance increment. The *P* values for each of the separate tests are as follows:

Table 6.1.3   Significance Values Using Curvimeter Measured Perceived Distances From the Nearest Node of Activity

	Final Distance Increment and Length of Incremental Constant						
	50 km (1 km)	25 km (1 km)	15 km (.5 km)	10 km (.5 km)	7.5km (.5 km)	5 km (.25 km)	2.5km (.15 km)
Normal Distribution	.0000	.0000	.0001	.0001	.0001	.0051	.2431
Uniform Distribution	.0000	.0000	.0000	.0000	.0000	.0000	.0000
Proportion of Data	.97	.92	.87	.84	.80	.72	.54

The significance values in this battery of tests appear to be only slightly different from the previous aggregate tests. As above, two Kolmogorov-Smirnov tests, the 50 and the 25 km final distance increment test, included a comparison of the data to a Poisson distribution. The significance values for both tests were less than .0001.

The next battery of tests was run on distances using curvimeter measurements of the imputed route from the nearest node of activity or routine pathway of the offender. Only a small number of offenses occurred at any great length from the putative awareness space when the routine pathways of the offender were included as probable portions of the awareness space. Thus, only two tests were run on these data using 2.5 and 3.5 km as the final distance increments. The *P* values for each of the two tests are as follows:

Table 6.1.4   Significance Values Using Curvimeter Measured Perceived Distances From the Nearest Node of Activity or Routine Pathway of the Offender

Final Distance Increment and Length of Incremental Constant		
	3.5 km (.15 km)	2.5 km (.15 km)
Normal Distribution	.0000	.0000
Uniform Distribution	.0000	.0000
Proportion of Data	.97	.94

The high proportion of offenses that occur near a routine pathway strongly suggest that almost all offenders are most comfortable near their own awareness spaces.

As mentioned earlier, two auxiliary Kolmogorov-Smirnov tests were conducted that were designed to investigate the robustness of the previous results. The first of these auxiliary tests excluded a 25 offense series. It is possible that the large number of offenses in the series could have skewed the results reported above. Subsequent tests that excluded this series made little difference. As above, the only test that was greater than a .05 level of significance was the 2.5 km final distance increment test compared to a normal distribution. However, this was found for <u>both</u> straight line and curvimeter measured distances. Excluding this 25 offense series has no apparent affect on the significance of these results.

The second auxiliary test was concerned with the possibility that commuter serial rapists may affect the results of such a study. If this type of offender exists in inordinate numbers, they will skew any results. A battery of tests was conducted for all series excluding those series that do not have at least one offense within 2.5 or 5 km of a primary activity node. Offenders who select all their targets beyond this range are said to be commuters. As in the first battery of tests, the only test that was greater than a .05 level of significance was the 2.5 km final distance increment test compared to a normal distribution using curvimeter distance measures. Controlling by series type, such as by excluding commuters, apparently has little effect.

6.1.13 Discussion

The first set of aggregate tests shows that serial rapists exhibit a clear spatial pattern of target selection. All 16 Kolmogorov-Smirnov tests using straight line distance measures to the nearest node were significant at the .05 significance level or better. All tests compared to a uniform distribution were significant to at least the .0001 level. The distribution of target selection data points is not statistically comparable to either a normal or uniform distribution, and did not conform to a Poisson distribution in the tests on that distribution. The node of activity is clearly affecting the choice of victims. The proportion of data used in each test is an important consideration. Even at the smallest final distance increment test of 2.5 km, the bulk of the data was used in the test. Confidence in tests of such data would be in jeopardy if only a small portion of the data were used in the analysis.

This pattern was also identified in the tests using curvimeter measures. Fifteen of these 16 Kolmogorov-Smirnov tests were beyond a .01 level of significance. The only test that did not exhibit this pattern was the test with a final distance increment of 2.5 km using 150 m increments and compared to a normal distribution. An explanation for this is difficult in that the same test compared to a uniform distribution was significant beyond the .0001 level of significance. It is possible that the buffer zone of the offenders affected the results for this 2.5 km test. If the serial rapist was affected by such a phenomenon, the distribution at this 2.5 km level would certainly not be uniform, but may appear to be normally distributed in that there would be few victims within three or four of the first 150 m increments but would increase to a peak in the next few increments (at 2.5 km there were seventeen 150 m increments). The effect of a buffer zone on larger distance tests would be weak, and the zone would probably only influence results in the smaller increment tests.

The strength of these findings is especially evident in the significance of the tests in the smaller final zone tests (7.5, 5, and 2.5 km). It could be argued that an offender will, logically, not choose victims uniformly or even normally within a 50 km span. An offender who chooses victims in a non-uniform or non-normal pattern within 7.5, 5, or even 2.5 km of a node of activity is clearly affected by the presence of a powerful variable.

Using the routine pathway as part of the awareness space created significance levels beyond the .0001 level. Even more intriguing is that 97% of the rapes occurred within 3.5 km of this portion of the probable awareness space, and 94% of the incidents occurred within 2.5 km. The proportion of offenses that occurred close to the nodes was also very high. Fifty-eight and 54% of the incidents occurred within 2.5 km of a primary activity node of the offender, using straight line measures and curvimeter-perceived distance measures, respectively.

The routine pathway proportions are impressive. It is possible that this is due largely to the fact that automobiles played an important part in all but two of the series used in this study. Most often, serial rapists used automobiles to travel to, and to flee from, the initial contact scene. In a number of series the automobile was used by the offender as part of his *modus operandi.* Offenders who victimize hitchhikers or prostitutes, for example, usually need to have a vehicle to gain access to this victim type. The propensity for the use of automobiles may create a cognitive state in the offender's search pattern whereby the routine pathways become a more salient portion of the awareness space in searching for potential victims than the nodes these pathways connect. It must be reiterated that most of the routine pathways used in this analysis were not expressly described as such in the case files. They were extrapolated or assumed portions of the awareness space. Therefore, any conclusions using the results from the routine pathway, as described in the study, must take into account this characteristic of the data.

The second battery of tests excluded a 25 offense series. Strong evidence was found showing that the pattern described above exists with or without the presence of this series. The first set of tests using the straight line distance measures clearly showed this. Fifteen of the 16 Kolmogorov-Smirnov tests were significant beyond the .05 level. All of the tests comparing the frequencies to a uniform distribution were significant beyond a .0001 level of significance.

This shows, of course, that the distribution of data in most of the tests was neither uniform nor normal. Like the first aggregate tests, the large proportion of data that was analyzed even for the 2.5 km test (56%) adds strength to the findings of this research.

The second set of tests, using the curvimeter distance measures, added further support to this conclusion. Again, 15 of the 16 Kolmogorov-Smirnov tests were significant beyond the .05 level, and all tests comparing the frequencies to a uniform distribution were significant beyond a .001 level of significance. Not surprisingly, the final set of tests that incorporated the use of the routine pathways of the offender were significant beyond the .0001 level of significance.

This series has a negligible effect on these data. This is an important finding as, more than almost any other series, this series exhibited a distinct node-centered pattern. Even an "eyeball" examination of the initial contact scenes in relation to the different primary activity nodes and routine pathways of the offender show that the offender was obviously predisposed towards his awareness space. It was felt that the series might effect the findings such that the results would appear to be stronger than they actually were.

The third battery of tests excluded series that did not have at least one offense within 2.5 km of an activity node for one set of tests and 5 km for a second set of tests. It was thought that removing these apparent commuter series would strengthen the results of the Kolmogorov-Smirnov test. These tests demonstrate that the same pattern found in the two previous batteries of tests reappears with or without the presence of these commuter series. The four tests using the straight line distance measures clearly showed this. All four of the tests were significant beyond the .05 level of significance, and the tests comparing these frequencies to a uniform distribution were beyond the .0001 level of significance. A large proportion of data was analyzed in each test, 80% for the 5 km test and 71% for the 2.5 km test. These percentages are only representative of the series included in these two batteries of tests, not the entire data set or population.

The curvimeter-measured distance tests were, for the most part, significant. Three of the four Kolmogorov-Smirnov tests were significant beyond the .01 level. Both tests on the uniform distribution were significant beyond the .0001 level. The 5 km test included 77% of the applicable data, and the 2.5 km test included 69% of the applicable data. As in the previous tests on curvimeter distances, the 2.5 km final distance increment test was not significantly different from a normal distribution. When routine pathways are considered as part of the awareness space, all four Kolmogorov-Smirnov tests were significant beyond the .0001 level. There seems to be little or no difference between the results of this battery of tests and previous tests. Removing the commuter series has no real effect.

In all, 84 Kolmogorov-Smirnov tests were performed on these data. Eighty of these tests were significant beyond the .05 level and many of those beyond even a .0001 level of significance. The only test that failed to show a consistent pattern of non-uniformity and non-normality with regard to the distribution of distances was the 2.5 km final distance increment test. As previously mentioned, a number of factors may be responsible for the anomalous results of the 2.5 km test. Serial rapists exhibit a distinct pattern that seems to be centered on and strongly affected by the awareness space of the offender. A distance decay pattern is distinctly displayed by this type of serial offender.

It should be mentioned that similar levels of significance would be found if the actual distribution was clustered at any point along the distance axis. The research hypothesis suggests that this clustering occurs in the smallest distance increments. An examination of the actual frequency distributions by distance increment shows that the clustering does indeed occur towards the smaller final distance increments. This phenomenon was evident for all of the data distributions except for the 2.5 km final distance increment distribution which was discussed earlier.

6.1.14   Other Important Results

A second test, called Criminal Geographic Targeting (CGT), developed by Rossmo, was used to examine some of the longer series.[42] This test is based on the assumptions of Environmental Criminology. It predicts, on the basis of the location of crime scenes, the most likely area where the offender resides. The results of these tests were impressive. Most impressive was the result of a CGT test on an 81-incident series that had to be excluded from the Kolmogorov-Smirnov tests because of its inordinate length. Upon entering the initial contact scenes for all 81 offenses, the CGT test predicted the exact location of the offender's residence. Alston (1994) discusses CGT and the results of these various tests.

More general information concerning the serial rapist's journey to crime were also gathered. The mean distance traveled by this population of serial rapists using straight line distance measures to the nearest activity node was 3.47 km. The median distance using straight line distance measures to the nearest activity node was 1.02 km. The standard deviation was 6.82 km.

The mean distance traveled by this population of serial rapists using curvimeter distance measures to the nearest activity node was 4.17 km. The median distance using curvimeter distance measures to the nearest activity node was 1.27 km. The standard deviation was 8.02 km. The mean distance traveled by this population of serial rapists using curvimeter distance measures to the nearest node or routine pathway was 2.98 km. The median distance using curvimeter distance measures to the nearest activity node or routine pathway was 0.62 km. The standard deviation was 5.59 km.

These figures support the general findings of other journey to crime literature regarding rape and serial rape. This type of offender seems to be greatly affected by their home area or, more specifically, their awareness space.

6.1.15 Conclusion

Serial sexual assault is a criminal behavior that has not received much academic attention. This work attempted to answer questions or hypotheses regarding the geographic patterns that the serial rapist exhibits in the selection of his victims. The Kolmogorov-Smirnov tests suggested that the research distributions were non-normal and non-uniform and that the spatial selection of targets is clustered around the serial rapists awareness spaces. One test, on a smaller portion of the data, suggested the possibility that there may be a buffer zone immediately surrounding activity nodes where the serial rapist will not select targets. A number of other tests were conducted to examine the robustness of these results. Likely routine pathways were included in one battery of tests; in another set of tests, a large volume series was excluded to see if its inclusion in the original tests had any skewing effect on the findings; and in another test, serial rapists who always attacked some distance from the activity node were excluded to see if they had a skewing effect on the original tests. These subsequent tests support the overall validity of the findings in the first battery of Kolmogorov-Smirnov tests.

This suggests that the awareness space is a powerful variable that must be considered when examining criminal behaviors such as serial rape. An offender searches for targets along familiar routes between and near established primary activity nodes. This conclusion is supported by a great deal of research concerning this and other criminal behaviors. A large amount of research, some of which was reviewed earlier, such as Amir,[30] Canter and Larkin,[28] Erlanson,[33] Gabor and Gottheil,[35] LeBeau,[26] Pyle,[32] Rand,[31] Rhodes and Conly,[36] Topalin,[29] and White[34] all examined rape or serial rape and reached the same conclusion, that the awareness space, or principal portions of it, seems to affect spatial selection patterns. In turn, these findings are generally consistent with journey to crime research on other criminal behaviors such as Rengert and Wasilchick's,[43] and Cromwell, Olson and Avary's[44] examination of burglary, and Feeney's[45] analysis of robbery. The findings set forth here are generally consistent with this research in Environmental Criminology and related fields.

This is one of the first studies to examine how cognitive elements (i.e., using routine pathways, primary activity nodes other than the residence of the offender, and probable travel routes) affect the microspatial behavior of the serial rapist. It is also quite unique in that it is potentially applicable to law enforcement practice. Although something of a pioneer study in this field, it is hoped that, in collaboration with future research, major advancements in the efficiency of investigative and linkage analysis units will be noted. The work was produced with the cooperation and invaluable input of law enforcement personnel. They were able to suggest what research would be most beneficial to their own work and suggested potential pitfalls in the research. This led to research that has greater utility and applicability.

Future studies should control for the specific geographical range occupied by the preferred victims of given offenders. This is not to suggest that all, or even most, serial rapists choose victims who occupy a specific range, but such offenders do exist in enough numbers to warrant the careful consideration of this contingency. Future studies also should control for the *modi operandi* employed by different serial rapists, as some *modi operandi* are affected more strongly by the awareness space of the offenders than others. Future studies should control for violence-escalating serial rapists. Only a few offenders actually demonstrated a marked increase in either fantasy-driven or incidental violence, yet this factor may introduce a sizable amount of error into research findings. The researcher should be attentive to environmental factors that may be responsible for the shift in the escalation of violence used in the series. Finally, future studies must control for the geographic type of series within a sample of data such as the proportion of marauders and commuters in a data set.

6.1.16   Notes

To place this in perspective, the 1992 homicide rate was 2.7 per 100,000 persons. The robbery rate was 121 per 100,000 persons. The rate for all three levels of non-sexual assault (CCC s. 266 - 268) combined was 791 per 100,000 persons.

The term "serial sexual assaulter" is technically more accurate for such offenders in Canada. Rape legislation in the United States and sexual assault legislation in Canada, as defined in sections 271-273 of the *Criminal Code of Canada*, are largely consistent, although there are important differences. Few researchers differentiate between the terms, and in this paper they are used synonymously.

A serial rapist can belong to more than one series, but a case cannot exist in more than one series.

A tool used in geography to measure curved distances on maps. It is usually shaped like a writing utensil with a small wheel on the tip that, when rolled along the map surface, measures the distance in centimeters or inches. This distance, when multiplied by the scale of the map, determines the precise distance between the given points.

The Kolmogorov-Smirnov statistic states that the sample distribution function or: $F_n(x) = j/n$, for $X_{(j)} <$ or $= x < X_{(j+1)}$, $j = 0, ..., n$, (with $X_{(o)} = -\infty$ and $X_{(n+1)} = \infty$) will significantly differ from the stated population distribution. The numerical difference of $|F_n(x) - F(x)|$ is the value of comparison.

The Canter and Larkin (1993) definition of a commuter was found to be problematic.

The definition of a commuter used in these Kolmogorov-Smirnov tests differs from Canter and Larkin's (1993) definition.

6.2 Victim Target Networks as Solvability Factors in Serial Murder[*]

MAURICE GODWIN

The situational context in which the serial killer targets his victims is critical to understanding the hunting patterns of a predator. However, police and researchers eschew victim target networks (VTN). Rather, their attention is overwhelmingly concerned with the offender's characteristics. As an alternative to traditional police investigations, this study suggests that by directing attention to victim target networks, inferences about the decision-making process underlying the selection of crime locations, victims, and locating offenders' home bases can be made. A decision-making model that the serial predator uses to scope out potential victim target networks is presented, and it is demonstrated how proactive policing in victim target areas can deter the killer. The study also posits that by directing investigative attention to victim social networks, police can first identify a set of prospective victims targeted by a serial killer. The study closes with suggestions about the applicability of law enforcement use of victims' targeting networks and how victim social networks can be used to link serial murder victims.

It has been established that there is a relationship between solving homicides and having information about a number of important locations. A recent study of the factors that contributed to solving serial murder investigations found that time and distance proved significant, suggesting that the more information on "the location of the original contact between the victim and the killer, where the assault occurred, the murder site, and the body recovery site, the more likely a murder case will be solved." Yet despite the importance of these locations and the great cost of extended police investigations, they are rarely researched. A few anecdotal illustrations are recorded by retired Agents from the FBI Behavioral Science Unit in their memoirs.[47,48] They acknowledge that determining where victims are targeted and dumped is an

[*] First published in *Social Behavior and Personality: An International Journal*, Vol. 26, No. 1, 1998.

important factor in solving serial murders, but these have not been related to empirical studies testing hypotheses about the distances serial killers travel to carry out various crime related activities. Consequently, an understanding of the processes that shape serial killers' spatial behavior has not been developed.

There is one notable exception, the work of Rossmo.[49] Calling his approach criminal geographical targeting (CGT), Rossmo has combined concepts from environmental criminology with a mathematical model based on a distance decay function, derived from the locations in which killers leave their victims' bodies, to indicate the area in which a serial killer may be living. The reasons for the proposed decay are not exactly clear but are usually presented in relation to the least-effort principle. This postulates that when multiple destinations of equal desirability are available, all else being equal, the closest one will be chosen.[50] Another principle that is incorporated into Rossmo's geographical profiling technique, that has been put forward as a basis for determining crime locations, is that there will be a tendency for offenders to avoid committing crimes close to where they live, often referred to as a buffer zone.[51,52] The proposed reason for this is to avoid leaving incriminating evidence near to where they live. However, the evidence for this is sparse. Davies and Dale find no evidence for it in their limited study of single rapists.[53] Although Rossmo has not published any studies demonstrating the validity of his distance decay algorithms or how they compare with other approaches, he has provided illustrations of the utility of his technique.[51]

A variety of distance-related processes have been propounded in the literature on the importance of crime locations in serial murder. These geographical processes are mainly derived with an environmental criminology bias (notably Brantingham and Brantingham[51]) that could be seen to be logically in conflict. One is a tendency to minimize effort close to home, which would predict that crimes are in a closely circumscribed area. A second is the tendency to keep a minimum distance away from home. These two processes combined would lead to the prediction of an optimum distance from home to all of a particular type of offense. However, the general finding is one of an aggregate decay of the frequency of crimes as their distances increase from home. These processes are derived from two considerations. The first are instrumental crimes often with a tangible material benefit, such as theft or robbery. Crimes of this nature usually require some degree of planning. The second are crimes of opportunity that rarely involve preplanning. So, although these processes have relevance to violent crimes, such as serial murder, there are questions about how important emotional issues are ignored by such rational models.

Two further complexities raise questions about the relevance of these rational processes to geographically profile serial killers. The first is that there is typically more than one location involved in their activities. However, besides the location of the site where the victim's body is dumped, there is usually at least one other important site, the point at which the victim is first encountered or targeted. Rossmo's geographical profiling model takes into account mainly victims' body disposal sites when predicting the home base of a serial killer.

Other researchers argue that victims' body dump locations are more reliable than sites in which victims are targeted, however, they provide no data supporting their opinions.[55] Canter and Hodge point out that abduction sites are usually not known to a police investigation; therefore, body dump sites provide investigators an immediate and more accurate description of the killer's foraging grounds. The theory put forth in the Canter and Hodge study seems to originate from animal foraging theories, and from the popular belief and research by Reppetto[56] that criminals have routine activities and a limited awareness space. It is reasonable to assume that criminals learn about space through their daily routine activities; however, there is the question whether serial killers are active agents in the environment rather than simple reactors to physical and social elements within this environment. Rengert and Wasilchick[57] demonstrated that crime trips of suburban burglars are more likely to be skewed in the direction of nodal centers such as workplaces and city center districts. In a later study, Rengert concurred with his earlier findings that locations of crime sites are most likely to be skewed.[58]

In a similar vein, research[58] by this author suggests a directional bias in serial killers' trips to target and dispose of their victims rather than a circular pattern as proposed by Canter and Larkin.[59] This directional bias could be due to the offender's routine activities and general knowledge of the area. However, there is also the possibility that it results from pre-planning, as is the case in many serial murders. Rengert and Bost demonstrated that robbers living in housing projects exhibited behavior designed to avoid recognition by traveling a distance from home to commit their crimes.[60]

Through daily travel, the home environment becomes a unique place of familiar and predictable activities, people, and physical elements, a focal point of one's experiential space.[61] Thus, through habitual, focused, and satisfying involvement in a residential locale, the tangible home area becomes an enduring symbol of self, of the continuity of one's experiences, and of that which is significant and valued by the inhabitant. The landscape around the home may thus be hypothesized to provide serial killers with those enduring symbolic experiences and a relatively conformable environment in which to hunt for their prey. Conversely, since the victim's body carries the most evidential clues, it could be expected that serial killers will distance their crimes from their domiciles. In a recent study of 54 U.S. serial killers, Godwin and Canter found that the mean distance from the offenders' home bases to the victims' abduction sites was 1.46 miles, and 5.0 miles for the body dump locations.[62] The study also found that serial killers progressively traveled closer to their homes as they targeted more victims.

6.2.1 Victim Targeting Networks (VTN)

The victimological approach to serial murder begins with the assumption that serial killers carry geographical templates in their mind. They have a certain kind of place in mind where experience has taught them that suitable victims can be found. Each subsequent trip to these crime locations forms something of an analogy with previous successes, modified by experience and perhaps intelligence gained from previous murders. The killer's perception will be shaped by both actual characteristics and those inferred from factors such as where a victim spends time, and with whom.

Routine activities enable the killer to make contact with targeted victims and to shape expectation for interaction. The situational context within which network interactions occur is critical to understanding the hunting patterns of a predator. For example, if the killer targets victims in a location at which contact is likely to be witnessed, the chance of detection will increase. An analysis of the ecology of possible victim-offender contact settings can help to narrow the focus of an investigation to promising areas for locating witnesses, including surviving victims, and the general home base area where the killer lives.

6.2.2 Decision-making Process in Target Network Areas

Figure 6.2.1 shows the decision-making process that a serial killer may use while hunting for a suitable target area and victim. His immediate question is, are there available victims to grab where the risk is low for being noticed? After the offender has made this decision, he scans the potential target area for easy and accessible victims. Similar decision-making processes have been found in burglars. For example, Rengert and Wasilchick analyzed decision-making processes of suburban burglars, and they found that most burglars spent hours driving around different communities during the day to determine ideal targets and times for their criminal activities.[57]

Once the offender has made his decision to target a specific location, he then uses the argument by contradiction decision-making process to determine the level of risk involved in the attack. For example, he may ask, are there surveillance cues to contradict that someone will witness me make the abduction? This is a major concern for the serial killer. For example, James' study on 28 U.S. serial killers found that 61% of the cases were solved due to eye witnesses compared to a direct result of police investigative work.[63] The killer may also look for the presence of police in the area. If the killer

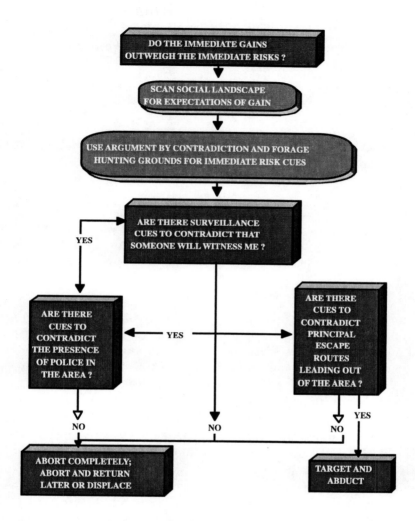

Figure 6.2.1 The serial killer's decision-making process in victim targeting network areas.

has no cues to contradict that the abduction may be witnessed and that he will be noticed by the police, he is likely to abort the crime completely and return later, or displace to another location. In the event, however, the killer has cues to contradict that the abduction will not be witnessed and that he will not be seen by police, he then scans the area for principal escape routes. If there are easy escape routes, then the killer will most likely target and

Table 6.2.1   Victim Social Networks — Areas of Highest Risk for Victimization From Serial Killers

• Urban Subcultures (heterosexual and homosexual bars, night clubs, and red light areas)
• Isolated Landscapes (parking lots, jogging paths, and rest areas)
• Areas with high concentration of elderly and poor individuals
• Skid Row (derelict areas of a city)
• University Campuses

abduct his victim. If there are no easy escape routes, he will likely abort his plan of attack or displace to another area.

The decision-making process demonstrated in Figure 6.2.1 shows that police presence in potential victim target network areas can affect the killer's decision to attack. However, as is often the case in a serial murder investigation, determining how to link victims can be difficult. One way to accomplish this is for police to know the high risk areas and the environmental networks that tie potential victims together. This is done by looking at victim social networks.

6.2.3   Victim Social Networks

Victim social networks provide the serial killer with opportunities to prey on transient persons; for example, lost or runaway children, mental patients, and prostitutes. Victim social networks are also important for determining where the killer resides and works. Table 6.2.1 lists the geographical areas in the U.S. with the highest risks for victimization from serial killers. These landscape layouts provide the serial killer with easy access and escape routes to avoid detection. For example, from the five high risk victim targeting areas, the university campus appears to be a safe place. However, university campuses, at least in the U.S., have certain landscape features which make them ideal for hunting and abducting victims. Isolated parking lots provide ample opportunities for serial killers to abduct victims. Increasing lighting on university campuses has improved safety, however, the serial killer is still willing to take his chances in open areas. Theodore Bundy, a contemporary serial killer, provides a classic example of an offender who targeted many of his victims on college campuses.[64]

Victim social networks also relate to the incidence and location of street-walking. Different landscape features are used by prostitutes to manipulate the environment for their own purposes, and potential victims of crime often seek out these types of locations for their solicitations.[65] Symanski[66] pointed out that streetwalkers tend to stand near bus and taxi stops, and research on victims of serial killers has confirmed that these two social networks are important features in the selection of victims.[67] The serial killer Bobby Joe Long provides a classic example of an offender who targeted prostitutes in red light districts in Tampa, Florida.[68]

Another feature that sets the five victim social networks apart from less valuable areas is locations where individuals have little or no bond to the neighborhood. These include transient people who lack a strong network of friends, acquaintances, and family ties. Egger refers to these victims as "the less-dead" victims.[69] He points out that these are society's throwaways due to the irritant symbols they represent.[69] Because of society's lack of regard for these victims, it is not unusual for a person not to be seen for days or weeks in these types of areas. Therefore, police are likely to regard their disappearance as trivial. Police investigators should make contact with the victim's family members including any significant others who may have information regarding recent change in lifestyle or personality. This information can provide police with victim availability and susceptibility.[70]

6.2.4   Summary and Conclusions

With every act that leaves behind evidence associated with each crime in the series, the killer provides information that can indicate with increasing accuracy the location of his home base. It is posited that the location of the initial offender-victim contact may be of more direct assistance in helping to delimit the area in which the offender resides than the sites where victims' bodies are discovered. Clearly, though, the body dump sites are more likely to be objectively established by the police than the initial victim target areas. However, by using the decision-making process in Figure 6.2.1, police investigators can initiate proactive policing strategies in victim targeting areas in order to detect possible suspects and possible future victims who may be targets of a serial killer. Or, if the suspect displaces, this would usually indicate to investigators that their proactive policing in the victim target network areas is having an affect.

The application of VTN strategies can have direct implications for systems such as criminal geographical targeting,[54] leading to the hypothesis that this procedure might be more efficient if it commenced with abduction sites followed by body dump locations.[62] However, investigators should view body dump sites with caution for predicting the home area of a serial killer. The systematic changing of locations and distances relative to the home base may be a deliberate ploy to distract police attention from the killer's home base. This study certainly supports the view that investigative efforts should go into interviewing people within the neighborhood from which victims go missing in order to pinpoint precisely the address or location where the victim may have last been seen. The victim's last seen site can be developed from any number of sources: 1) eyewitness accounts; 2) visual sightings; 3) telephone conversations; 4) official documents such as traffic citations, police field reports, jail booking logs, long distance calls, toll records, and credit card receipts.

6.3 Encounter and Death: The Spatial Behavior of U.S. Serial Killers*

MAURICE GODWIN
DAVID CANTER

A small but growing research literature indicates that offense locations have a systematic relationship to where the offender resides. In the case of individuals who carry out a number of killings over a period of time, mainly of strangers, this relationship between residence and offense sites may be of significance in helping to clarify the psychological mechanisms underlying this most heinous of crimes.

Two central aspects of the geography of serial killers' behavior provide a useful index of the psychological processes involved. First is the fact that usually the point at which the victim is first encountered (PFE) is different from the location at which their body is eventually dumped or buried (BD). It is hypothesized that if the serial killer is evolving his criminal behavior from his normal daily activities, the PFE is likely to be closer to his home than the BD. However, if his activities are specially and carefully planned with very specific targeting, the PFE would be hypothesized to be further, or at least a similar distance from home to the BD.

The second important consideration is the progression of the offenses over time. One hypothesis is that the offender becomes ever more committed to his crimes as distinct activities, and this is likely to be reflected in their distance from home increasing over the series of murders. A more challenging hypothesis is that over time the offender incorporates the killings into his daily life and therefore the later offenses may be committed nearer home than the earlier ones. These three issues, a) the psycho-geographical impact of the home location, b) the differences in distance from home of PFE and BD and, c) the change in distance from home of both the PFE and the BD will be

* First published in *Policing: An International Journal of Police Strategy and Management*, Vol. 20, No. 1, 1997, pp. 24-38.

examined through the study of 54 U.S. serial killers. The present study will have a number of practical consequences for police investigations, and if replicated with other data sets could form the basis of a powerful investigative decision support tool.

For the years 1986-90, the average number of murders reported in the U.S.A. annually, according to the Uniform Crime Reports, was over 20,000. Of these 20,000 murders, an average of about 5,000 are classified as unsolved each year.[71] Furthermore, so-called stranger murders account for an average of 15% of all murders reported in the U.S. each year.[71] It is suspected that many of these stranger-related murders are committed by episodic, sequential murderers, often referred to as "serial killers."[72] In addition to the significant loss of life, which may be attributed to a few individuals who commit a number of murders, there are indications that since the 1970s there has been a distinct increase in serial killings, even after taking better reporting methods into account.[73-75]

As Jenkins has emphasized, the increasing impact of serial killers is likely to be a product of both the actions of individuals and the ability of law enforcement and other agencies to respond to those actions.[76] He states that "no amount of aggressive or destructive behavior can result in a career of murder lasting months or years unless a number of other factors are present that create a victim population, and a weak or confused law-enforcement response."[76] As a consequence, a fuller understanding of serial killing has academic merit and will facilitate more effective law enforcement.

Serial killers present a particularly challenging problem for investigators because they generally murder strangers.[77] Once their activities are established, they are likely to become more skillful, and as Holmes and DeBurger[78] and Holmes and Holmes[79] stress, it is consequently important to have early identification of such killers to afford control by police. Skogan and Antunes have asserted that "the availability and reliability of information about incidents and offenders plays a key role in determining the ability of the police to solve crimes and apprehend offenders."[80]

It has been established that there is a relationship between solving homicides and having information about a number of important locations. A recent study of the factors that contributed to solving serial murder investigations found that time and distance proved significant, suggesting that the more information on "the location of the original contact between the victim and the killer, where the assault occurred, the murder site, and the body recovery site the more likely a murder case will be solved."[81] Yet despite the importance of these locations and the great cost of extended police investigations, the detailed consideration why they may be important is rarely researched. A few anecdotal illustrations are recorded by retired agents from the FBI Behavioral Science Unit when they write their memoirs,[82,83] acknowledging that the distance the offender travels is an important factor in solving serial murder investigations, however, these have not been related to empirical studies testing hypotheses about the distances serial killers travel to carry various crime related activities. Consequently, an understanding of the processes that shape serial killers' journeys to crime has not been developed.

One notable exception has been the work of Rossmo.[84–86] Calling his approach criminal geographical targeting (CGT), Rossmo has combined concepts from environmental criminology with a mathematical model based on a distance decay function, derived from the locations in which killers leave their victims' bodies, to indicate the area in which a serial killer may be living. Although Rossmo has not published any studies demonstrating the validity of his algorithms or how they compare with other approaches, he has provided illustrations of the utility of his technique.

The psychological principles on which Rossmo's work is based are not articulated in detail, but appear to derive from Brantingham and Brantingham, who suggest that victims are "probably spatially biased toward the offender's home base," illustrated by a study in Washington, D.C. that found that offenders in general victimize areas they know best, concentrating on targets within their immediate environments and surrounding areas.[88] This bias is the proposed cause of a decay function such that the further an offender is from home, the less likely he is to commit an offense.

The reasons for the proposed decay are not exactly clear but are usually presented in relation to the least-effort principle. This postulates that when multiple destinations of equal desirability are available, all else being equal, the closest one will be chosen.[89] However, it is usually modified by two further considerations. One is supported most readily by Pettiway's (1982) results, which found that specialist selectivity is reflected in the effort an offender puts into planning a crime. This leads to more selective and more carefully planned crimes committed further away from home. This has been supported by comparisons across different types of crime, where it has been shown that the apparently more impulsive crimes of rape are committed nearer to home than robbery (Pyle, 1974) and that armed robbers travel further on average than those who are not armed (Capone and Nicholas, 1975, 1976) and tend to net larger sums of money. However, such considerations have not been included in Rossmo's computerized predictions of serial killers' residential locations.

Another principle, incorporated into Rossmo's algorithm and put forward as a basis for crime locations, is that there will be a tendency for offenders to avoid committing crimes close to where they live, often referred to as a "buffer zone" (Brantingham and Brantingham, 1981, 1984). The proposed reason for this is to avoid leaving incriminating evidence near where they live. However, the evidence for this is sparse. Davies and Dale (1995), for example, find no evidence for it in their limited study of single rapists. Furthermore, the actual distances proposed as buffer zones are often larger than would be consistent with leaving local clues.

A variety of distance-related processes have thus been outlined by those with an environmental criminology bias (notably Brantingham and Brantingham, 1981) which could be seen logically to be in conflict. One is a tendency to minimize effort close to home, which would predict that crimes are in a closely circumscribed area. A second is the tendency to keep a minimum distance away from home. These two processes combined would lead to the prediction of an optimum distance from home to all of a particular type of offense. However, the general finding is one of an aggregate decay of the frequency of crimes as their distances increase from home. These processes are derived from a consideration of instrumental crimes often with a tangible material benefit, such as theft or robbery. So, although they doubtless have relevance to violent offenses, there are questions about how important emotional issues are ignored by such rational models.

Two further complexities raise questions about the relevance of these rational processes to serial killers. First, there is typically more than one location involved in their activities. Besides the location of the site where the victim's body is dumped (BD), there is also usually at least one other important site, the point at which the victim is first encountered (PFE). All three of the processes indicated above, least effort, buffer zone, and decay function, would predict the BD and PFE to be close together. Second, none of the three processes would lead to any predictions in the changes over time of the distance of the crimes from home.

A different emphasis from these essentially economic, rational processes would lead to predictions of differences between BD and PFE site distances from home as well as differences over time. This is an emphasis drawn from the role of the crimes in the unfolding life "narrative" of the offender (Canter, 1994). Briefly, within this framework, the crimes are seen as a product of the lifestyle of the offender, but also by virtue of the experience of the crimes, the offender changes his view of himself and the ways he commits his crimes. This leads to the proposal that the home, being an important focus for life activities, acts as a structuring device for the development of the criminal activity. Within any particular crime there will be some activities, notably those to do with the leaving of evidence, that may be guided by buffering processes and the optimization of locations away from home to maximize value for effort, but overall it would be predicted that as the crimes proceed, they will be incorporated more fully into the domestic ambit.

The theoretical analysis of people's bonds with the tangible surroundings of the home environs is found in several disciplines (Buttimer, 1980; Copper, 1974; Fried, 1963). Through daily travel, the home environment becomes a unique place of familiar, known, and predictable activities, people and physical elements, a focal point of one's experiential space (Feldman, 1988). Thus, through habitual, focused, and satisfying involvement in a residential locale, the tangible home area becomes an enduring symbol of self, the continuity of one's experiences, and that which is significant and valued by the inhabitant. The landscape around the home base may thus be hypothesized to provide serial killers with those enduring symbolic experiences. If their crimes, as hypothesized, do indeed develop as an elaboration of their daily activities, rather than as some distinct work-life activity, then it would be predicted that the home would be geographically as well as symbolically central to their criminal activities.

A study of serial rapists (Canter and Gregory, 1994) does show that the home can be used as a basis for defining the area in which crimes were committed; they showed that very few offenders "commuted" like workers into areas to commit their crimes, but that in 86% of the cases the home was within a circle defined by the two crimes furthest from each other. A number of other studies have also shown that criminals are apparently reluctant to travel very far from their home base to commit their crimes (Baldwin and Bottoms, 1976; Rhodes and Conly, 1981). However, none of these studies have dealt with serial killers and considered both the BD and the PFE as well as considering the possibility in changes in distances traveled over time.

The present study, therefore, set out to explore three sets of hypotheses of serial killers' journey to crime:

H1: The home operates as a focus for the activities of serial killers in apprehending their victims and leaving their bodies. The focus is hypothesized as being the most likely center of gravity of their actions.

H2: There will be differences in the distances traveled to apprehend victims and to leave their bodies. It is proposed that the dumping of the body carries most evidential implications and therefore is likely to be at a further distance as well as being more likely to be shaped by buffering processes.

H3: The distances serial killers travel to dump the victims' bodies are likely to change systematically over time, while the victims' points of fatal encounter locations are not. The counter-intuitive possibility that this change relates to an increasing incorporation of all his killing activities into his domestic area will also be tested.

6.3.1 Data sample

The study involved 54 male U.S. serial murderers. All the cases were solved. Each offender was convicted of at least ten murders, committed on different dates and in different locations. Most of the killers were suspects in additional murders; however, those cases were not included in the study because the offenders were never charged with the additional crimes. Only the first ten murder victims were considered in the present study, so in total the details on 54 serial killers and 540 victims were used.

The data were collected from various police departments throughout the U.S. including, but not limited to, intelligence sources such as the Homicide Information Tracking System (HITS), Violent Crime Apprehension Program (VICAP), and Homicide Assessment and Lead Tracking System (HALT). Additional data on specific cases were obtained from court transcripts by accessing Lexus and Westlaw, the on-line law databases. The material used to generate the data matrix was derived from police eyewitness accounts, including visual sightings and telephone conversations, police field reports, detective reports, and medical examiners' reports. Independent corroboration was used when necessary. Considerable effort was taken to locate and record the physical addresses of the offenders' home bases, the victims' points of fatal encounter (PFE), and the victims' body dump sites (BD). Throughout the study, home base is defined as the location where the offender was living during the time he were committing the crimes. In most instances the data included one offender and one home base. Point of fatal encounter is defined as the initial contact site or last seen location of the victim. Body dump location is defined as the final resting place where the victim's body was discovered. Additional care was used to determine and record the killings in sequence as they were committed.

In 92% of the cases, neither the offender nor the victim knew each other prior to the encounter. In 3% of the cases, both people were friends who had seen each other on a regular basis. In just 1% of the cases, victims had a family relationship. In 4% of the cases, the offender and victim barely knew each other, seeing each other perhaps once in a year; this included one-way acquaintance, where the offender knew the victim but the victim did not know the offender. At the times of the murders, 28% of the victims were actively working as prostitutes.

6.3.2   Mapping the Crimes

The physical address of each serial killer's home base along with the address of each victim's abduction and body disposal site was mapped using Map Expert. This is a commercially available mapping program which features state boundaries, major lakes and oceans, and the interstate highway network. The map projection displays information about the terrain and topography of the area being viewed. In addition, the map program provides viewing down to street levels for all parts of the U.S., including cities.

Direct point-to-point Euclidean (i.e., as the crow flies) distance measurements were performed on the geographical locations. The distances were recorded in miles. For each offender the distances from the offender's home to every one of his PFE and BD sites were calculated, as well as the distances between every PFE and BD. The distance matrix so created was the basis for all subsequent analysis.

6.3.3   Results

6.3.3.1   Smallest Space Analysis and the Home as a Focus of Serial Murder

In order to explore the role of the home in the geographical locations of both BD and PFE sites, it is necessary to consider the relationship that every location has to every other. This can be posed as the question, what is the best approximation to a two-dimensional representation of the average distance between every location? If one location, say the home, was on average typically a long distance from most of the PFE sites, then such a representation ought to place the home in a region that is at some distance from the PFE sites. But in order for such a geometric representation of the average spatial distances to be valid, it must take into account the distance that every location has from every other location. In doing so, such a representation can also represent the relative average distances between the PFE and BD sites.

In effect, a geometric representation of the distances between all the locations across the whole sample allows the testing of a multivariate model of offender geography. That model contains the following facets:

- The nature of the location, with the elements home, PFE, and BD — with the hypothesis that there will be some order in the distances such that typically the distance from home to PFE will be less than the distance from home to BD. If the home has a significance for both the PFE and the BD, then if there is the order hypothesized, the home will be central.
- The temporal sequence of the offenses. Some difference between earlier and later offenses in the distances and directions traveled is hypothesized.

An appropriate statistical procedure for testing this model is smallest space analysis (SSA), which is a multi-dimensional scaling technique that finds the best fit within a specified dimensionality between, on one hand, a matrix of associations, in this case the mean distances between all locations across the 54 offenders, and on the other, a geometric representation of those associations as distances in a Cartesian space (i.e., the axes have no external reference).

6.3.4   Smallest Space Analysis

Smallest space analysis was developed by Guttman (1968) and computerized by Lingoes (Bloombaum, 1970). The program deals with the off-diagonal elements of a square, symmetric matrix of association coefficients (Lingoes, 1973). The advantage of SSA over other algorithms lies in its robustness and rational step-size (Lingoes, 1973). This is mainly because the algorithm only attempts to find the best fit between the ranks of the association coefficients and the ranks of the distances in the geometric space. Such a matching of ranks can be shown to give a mathematically more efficient solution as well as being less sensitive to extreme values, and is the reason the procedure is called "smallest" space analysis. It also leads to the procedure being recognized as non-metric. It is also appropriate in many psychological studies, such as the present one, as psychological hypotheses are usually about the relative associations between entities rather than their absolute differences. The hypotheses here are not precise enough to say how much bigger or smaller the relative distances are in comparison with each other, merely that there are consistent differences in rank. The resulting geometric representation is thus often more amenable to direct interpretation in relation to a set of hypotheses than would be procedures using metric algorithms or specific externally defined axes.

A triangular association matrix was generated for the SSA analysis using the mean interpoint distances that serial killers traveled between all their home bases, victims' points of fatal encounter, and body dump sites. The mean interpoint distances were calculated for each killer by taking the Euclidean distance between each crime site and every other and dividing by the number of locations recorded. The result for a two-dimensional SSA is shown in Figure 6.3.1.

6.3.5   The Home as Focus

The goodness of fit between the empirical coefficients and the resulting representation is measured by a Guttman and Lingoes (GL) coefficient of alienation (Shye, 1985). The smaller the coefficient of alienation, the better the fit (Brown, 1985; Shye, 1985). A generally acceptable coefficient of alienation is 0.24. The SSA plot in Figure 6.3.1 has a (GL) coefficient of alienation of 0.30, which is a little high, indicating that the original matrix of average distances may require more than two dimensions to represent all their nuances. The distance metric used to generate the SSA in Figure 6.3.1 is based on "Manhattan" distances. This provided the interpretable plot in two dimensions. A similar result using Euclidian distances was found in three dimensions. For simplicity and clarity, the city block solution is presented here. However, as Shye and Borg (1995) have clearly argued, measures of goodness of fit can only be taken as broad indications, and the actual interpretability of the solution carries considerable scientific weight.

Each point in the SSA plot represents an average location, so the relative distances across the plot represent the relative distances the killers traveled on average from their home bases to abduct victims and dispose of their

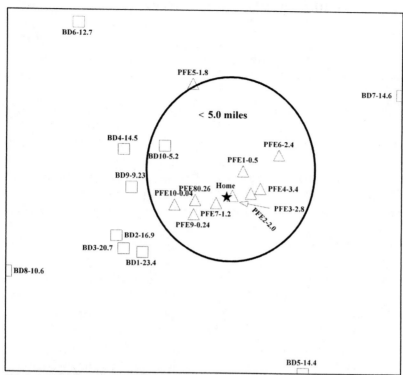

BD - Victims' Body Dump Sites
PFE - Victims' Points of Fatal Encounters
Variables represent mean distances - Figures are in miles
G-L Coefficient of Alienation = 0.302
N=54 Serial killers

Figure 6.3.1 Two-dimensional SSA plot mean distances offenders traveled from their home bases to victims' points of fatal encounter and body dump locations.

bodies. The serial killers' home base is represented by the star. So, for example, Figure 6.3.1 shows that the distance from home to the first point of encounter (PFE1) was considerably less than the distance between the seventh and eighth body dump sites (BD7 to BD8).

The interpretation of Figure 6.3.1 is assisted by recognizing that the home is located by the computer within a region that is surrounded by the PFE sites, which are in turn surrounded by the BD sites. This thus clearly demonstrates that the home plays the role of the geographical focus for these offenses. The relative geometry is such that the best solution the SSA algorithm can find does place the home in a position such that all the distances between each of the locations, in effect, surround the home. This accords well with the studies cited earlier that argue for a central significance to the offender in the location of his home.

6.3.6 PFE Victim and BD Locations

Nine of the PFE sites are located on the SSA closer to the home than any of the BD sites. This indicates that the offenders, on average, tended to make initial contact with their victims closer to home than the locations in which they eventually place the bodies. The fifth PFE, while still within the same general region as indicated on the SSA plot, is nonetheless further from the home than a number of the BD sites. This is worthy of note but may be an artifact of this particular data set and the two-dimensional solution.

The finding that the PFEs are relatively closer to the home than the BD sites is of considerable interest because it indicates that an emphasis towards lifestyle considerations rather than rational modeling may be valid for these types of offenses. It suggests that if a buffering process is present, it is more obviously apparent for the BD sites than for the initial encounter with the victim.

6.3.7 Temporal Sequences

The SSA does indicate that the first six PFEs are closer to each other and a little separate from the remaining four. This indicates that the offender has a tendency to move to a slightly different area on the other side of the home after the first abductions. A similar but more complex process is revealed for the BD sites. The first three are located on average quite close to each other, interestingly on the opposite side of the home from the initial points of encounter. Subsequent dump sites are spread out on differing axes, such that BD5 is across the plot from BD4, BD6 is across the plot again, with BD7 and BD8 at opposite ends of an axis that is orthogonal to the BD5-BD6 axis. This certainly supports the idea of offenders who are attempting to spread the locations of their dump sites and thus, presumably, reduce the risk of detection.

As mentioned, the SSA results are based on non-metric algorithms that find the best fit; in this case, a two-dimensional solution. There are thus approximations in these results that, although valuable in supporting the general model, do not allow more precise testing of the various related hypotheses. A further set of parametric statistical analyses were therefore carried out.

6.3.8 Distances to PFE and BD Sites over the Ten Offenses

Figure 6.3.2 shows the mean distances serial killers traveled from their home bases to victims' abduction and body dump locations. This provides another way of considering the results already found from the SSA. This graph cannot indicate the central significance of the home, but because it uses conventional interval metrics, it does show clearly how much further serial killers traveled to dispose of their victims' bodies on average than to abduct them. The overall home-to-BD mean is 14.3 miles (SD = 5.0). The overall mean distance serial killers traveled from their home bases to abduct their victims is 1.46 miles (SD = 1.25).

Table 6.3.1 *T*-tests Mean Distances Serial Killers Traveled From Home Bases to Victims' Points of Fatal Enounter and Body Dump Locations

Offense	Home to PFE χ (SD)	Home to BD χ (SD)	t-value
1	0.55 (1.9)	23.4 (64.7)	2.24**
2	2.03 (3.9)	16.9 (25.9)	3.04*
3	2.86 (3.8)	20.7 (40.8)	2.64**
4	3.40 (4.0)	14.5 (19.1)	3.61*
5	1.87 (3.6)	14.4 (21.4)	3.91*
6	2.24 (2.1)	12.7 (26.9)	3.02*
7	1.20 (3.0)	14.6 (21.2)	2.09**
8	0.26 (2.2)	10.6 (21.0)	4.36*
9	0.24 (1.6)	9.23 (8.0)	1.27
10	0.04 (1.7)	5.28 (7.7)	0.33

t-test at 95% CI

df = 53

T *Significance at $p < 0.01$

T **Significance at $p < 0.05$

Each offense equals 54 crime sites

The differences in the average distances for each PFE and each BD in the sequence is statistically significant for the first eight offenses as summarized in Table 6.3.1. This provides further strong support for the conclusions derived from the SSA, but shows that these differences are of a considerable size. In this sample at least, it can be claimed with some confidence that the point at which the offender makes contact with the victim and abducts her is typically close to his home, but he then will travel some distance, often choosing different directions for each offense, to get rid of the body.

6.3.9 Changes over Time

Table 6.3.1 does show that the differences between the travel distances for PFE and BD are not significantly different for the last two offenses in this series of ten. The basis for this can be seen in Figure 6.3.2. The PFE distances do not appear to change consistently over time, whereas the BD distances decrease from first to tenth. Statistical tests show the scale of these apparent trends.

6.3.10 Changes in Distance to PFE

Table 6.3.2 summarizes the one-way analysis of variance that examined the distances traveled to the PFE for each of the ten offenses, across all 54 offenders. This shows that none of the distances are statistically different from each other. Further analysis was performed using one-way repeated measures ANOVA (Scheffe test) on the group differences between the victims' points

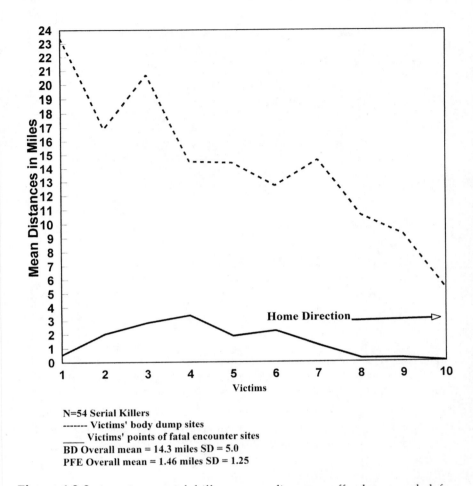

N=54 Serial Killers
------- Victims' body dump sites
_____ Victims' points of fatal encounter sites
BD Overall mean = 14.3 miles SD = 5.0
PFE Overall mean = 1.46 miles SD = 1.25

Figure 6.3.2 American serial killers mean distances offenders traveled from their home bases to victims' point of fatal encounter and body dump locations.

of fatal encounter sites. The difference within the groups (victims) is not significant over time (F[10,530] = 0.222 p > 0.05). The mean distance serial killers traveled from their home bases to abduct the first victims in the series was 0.5 miles. The mean distance serial killers traveled from their home bases to abduct their tenth victims was 0.2 miles. Thus, a remarkably consistent closeness to home in the distances the offenders traveled to make contact with their victims is revealed.

6.3.11 Changes in Distance to the Body Dump Locations

The mean for all the first body dump locations was 24.5 miles and the mean for all the tenth body dump ten locations was 0.4 miles from the offender's

Table 6.3.2 One-way Analysis of Variance of Distances That Serial Killers Traveled From Their Home Bases to Victims' Points of Fatal Encounter Sites

Source	Sum of Squares	DF	Mean Square	F-Ratio	F-Probability
Mean (Between)	127.47	9	14.16	1.775	0.07
Linear Term	8.29	1	8.29	1.039	0.31
Deviation	119.17	8	14.89	1.867	0.06
Linear Error (Within)	672,533.1	530	1,268.93		
Total	676,961.0	531			

Notes: Tukey's HSD significant at $p < 0.05$

Levene's (homogeneity of variance) $F (10,530) = p < 0.01$ two-tailed

N= 540 PFE distances

Table 6.3.3 One-way Analysis of Variance of Distances That Serial Killers Traveled From Their Home Bases to Victims' Body Dump Sites

Source	Sum of Squares	DF	Mean Square	F-Ratio	F-Probability
Mean (Between)	28,190.5	9	3,132.2	4.09	0.0000*
Linear Term	6.6	1	6.6	0.08	0.9258
Deviation	28,183.8	8	3,522.9	4.61	0.0000*
Linear Error (Within)	404,965.54	530	764.08		
Total	433,156.06	531			

Notes: *Tukey's HSD Significant at $p < 0.001$

Levene's (homogeneity of variance) $F (10,530) = p < 0.01$ two-tailed

N = 540 BD distances

home. The one-way ANOVA results are given in Table 6.3.3. Tukey's HSD post hoc test was run on the body dump distances. Tukey's HSD test is a more conservative test of significance. It would be expected that if a significance is found using the Tukey's HSD for the BD sites, then the actual significance could be expected to be greater. The linear polynomial function was chosen. The polynomial linear function allows the data to be partitioned using sum of squares polynomial trend components. Each victim, then, was a treatment. The ANOVA results on the BD means are given in Table 6.3.3. To test the within group differences between the victims' body dump sites, a one-way repeated measures ANOVA (Scheffe test) was run on the BD mean distances. The differences within the groups (victims) over time is significant ($F[10,540] = 54.60$ p < 0.001). The relationship between distances serial killers traveled from their home bases to dispose of victims changes over time ($F = 4.09$, p < 0.0001). As the number of victims increased, the distances from home decreased in a broadly linear way, as illustrated in Figure 6.3.1.

6.3.12 Conclusions

6.3.12.1 Home, Abduction, and Dumping

The results of the present study indicate that as the number of murders increases, killers generally cover a narrower area in which to leave the bodies of their victims, until the ninth and tenth offenses, where the offender may be disposing of bodies quite close to his home. This pattern contrasts markedly with the locations at which the initial contact is made with the victim. All ten of the murders in the sequences studied here tended to be close to the home base of the offender, typically less than a couple of miles from his residence. Such findings are in accord with a perspective that sees serial killings growing out of the daily activities and contact patterns of the offender. Rather than seeing the offender as balancing some economic effort against perceived gain, as may be relevant to crimes that are directly financially motivated, these results indicate the offenses evolving out of day-to-day dealings with others. A recognition of potential victims in the area around his home to which the offender normally has access is hypothesized as the first stage in this process.

Once a victim has been abducted and killed, then an attempt is made to distance the body from known haunts of the offender. Subsequent victims are found in similar ways — see the marauding model proposed for serial rapists.[89] The removal and placing of the bodies, however, involves a more conscious process, in which the evidential implications are likely to be considered by the killer. The sites at which the bodies are left are thus more likely to be dispersed away from the home. The finding, possibly counter-intuitive, for the present set of serial killers, that the sites at which they dump the bodies get closer to their homes as the series progresses, is most intriguing. It accords with the proposal that their offenses become increasingly integrated with their daily lives, and that some sort of growing confidence, or growing determination to reduce the risk of transporting the bodies, leads to the dump sites and the encounter sites being closer together. Clearly, future research is required to explore more closely this important process.

6.3.12.2 Psycho-Geographical Profiling in Relation to Ongoing Police Investigations

With every act that leaves behind evidence associated with each crime in the series, the killer provides information that can indicate with increasing accuracy the location of his home base. The results reported indicate, however, that the location of initial contact with the victims may be of more direct assistance in helping to delimit the area in which the offender resides than the sites at which victims' bodies are discovered. Clearly, though, the BDs are more likely to be established objectively by the police than the PFEs. In this case, the indications are that the later BDs may be of more assistance, being closer to the home than the earlier BDs. Such a finding has direct implications for systems such as criminal geographical targeting,[84] leading to the hypothesis that this procedure might be more efficient if it commenced with the most recent offenses, adding earlier BD offenses subsequently.

The results also indicate, as shown clearly in the SSA, that when considering any number of body dump locations that have been determined to be linked, the police should view these sites with caution for predicting the home area of a serial killer. The systematic changing of locations and distances relative to the home base may be a deliberate ploy to distract police attention from the killer's home base.

This raises another interesting point. What if police do not know exactly what number of victims were murdered in the series or their sequence? In a serial murder case, where any number of victims may have previously been linked through other forms of forensic analysis (e.g., DNA or fingerprints), then the body dump sites found furthest apart may be hypothesized to be the first victims in the series. Those clustered together, near any number of abduction sites, are more likely recent murders. The latter areas should be the sites at which investigators focus their proactive policing efforts.

These results certainly support the view that investigative efforts should go into interviewing people within the neighborhood from which victims go missing in order to pinpoint precisely the address or location where the victim may have been last seen. The victim's last seen site can be developed from any number of sources: eyewitness accounts, visual sightings, telephone conversations, official documents such as traffic citations, police field reports, jail booking logs, long distance calls, toll records, and credit card receipts. As Ford has elaborated, it is imperative for investigating officers to follow up on where the predator met his prey.[90]

Note: The distances represented in Figure 6.3.1 are slightly different from the distances reported in the text. The numbers reported in the text are correct. This error was discovered after the article was originally published. The slight inconsistencies are due to the nature of the graphic program used, and in no way affect the result of the study.

6.4   Geographical Profiling[*]

MAURICE GODWIN

Over the last two decades, numerous research studies using the theory of
mental maps and home range have been applied to study criminals' spatial
behavior. These studies reflect the importance of the journeys criminals habitually take around the areas close to their homes. The research also points out
that such journeys provide criminals with information around which they
are likely to plan their next crime. Locations frequently passed by the criminal
while traveling home, such as bars, shops, and restaurants are therefore proposed as defining the criminal's range and thus tuning his or her perceptions
as to which areas are likely to be safe, both geographically and psychologically.

The concept of home range is based upon the notion that there is a geographical area around our homes in which we travel and use more regularly
than areas a greater distance from our homes. This area would typically
include shopping areas, homes of friends and relatives, and social activity
areas. Trowbridge in 1913 suggested that home range can be thought of as a
kind of cognitive or mental map; that is, images strongly related to residential
location.[91] Cognitive maps are representations of what is possible and where,
built up through our daily activities and social transactions. As such, the
mental maps we draw of an area change over time, reflect how much time
we spend in an area and the variability of our purposes for being there.

Each of these spatial approaches has a defining role to the specific aspect
of geographical behavior investigated; for example, the location of the
offender's home base, the location where the crime occurred, and the
relationship between offender's home base and occurrence locations. However, it is the latter area which has the most significance to the emerging field
of geographical profiling. The identification of an offender's home base and
the distances that the offender travels from home to commit his or her crime
has value to police investigators who are investigating a series of crimes; for
example, serial murder, rape, or arson.

[*] First published in *Encyclopedia of Forensic Science*, Siegel, J., Saukko, P., and Knupfer, G.,
Eds., London: Academic Press, 2000.

6.4.1   The Ecological Approach

Approaches to the study of geographical movements of criminals originated from what has become known as "the ecological tradition," which developed in America between 1900 and the early 1970s. The ecological tradition is closely linked to a particular theoretical concept originally developed at the Chicago School of Sociology. Research in the Chicago School of Sociology in 1929, 1931, and 1969 exemplified the ecological principles. Using the ecological principles in 1942, Shaw and McKay confirmed the geographical coincidence of a number of social problems with high rates of delinquency and criminality.[92] They found that crime rates in American cities tended to be highest in the wealthier areas that were juxtaposed to poorer areas where there were identifiable concentrations of criminal residences. Shaw and McKay demonstrated the persistence of areas with a high rate of criminality over time and through changes in the ethnic makeup of these cities.[92] Their research findings had a major impact on police procedures, and consequently have become accepted as facts. Shaw and McKay's studies have influenced all subsequent sociological theory dealing with the geography of crime and delinquency.

However, the confusion in Shaw and McKay's ecological principles is they assumed that the characteristics of an area that had a high proportion of criminal residents also identified and described the social characteristics of individuals who were likely to commit crimes. The attempt to use general data as an explanation for individual behavior has been termed "the ecological fallacy" by criminologists critical of the Chicago School of Sociology. As Brantingham and Brantingham pointed out in 1981, the problem comes when ecological data on the location of criminal residences is expected to answer questions about criminal motivations. The weakness of the ecological approach is that its findings are based on patterns of association between crime and its potential causes at an aggregate level, and does not consider individualistic offending data. However, the ecological studies of the Chicago School of Sociology did draw attention to the potential of studying the spatial distribution of various urban, social, and criminal indices.

6.4.2   Environmental Criminology

Deriving out of the ecological tradition, Brantingham and Brantingham in the late 1970's termed the phrase "environmental criminology."[93] Environmental criminology is concerned with criminal mobility and the relationship between offenders' home bases and their target areas. Environmental criminology attempts to predict the geographical area that an offender will victimize, based not on demographic features but on the individual's own mental image of the area. The Brantinghams proposed a theoretical spatial model for

Table 6.4.1 Major Elements of the Brantingham's Hypothesized Spatial Model

1	Individuals exist who are motivated to commit specific offenses
2	The environment emits many signals about its physical, spatial, cultural, legal, and psychological characteristics
3	The commission of an offense is the result of a multistaged decision process which seeks out and identifies a target or victim positioned in time and space
4	As experimental knowledge grows, an individual learns which individual cues, clusters of cues, and sequences of cues are associated with good victims or targets. These can be considered a template which is used in victim selection
5	An individual who is motivated to commit an offense uses cues from the environment to locate and identify targets
6	This template becomes relatively fixed and influences future behavior

looking at journeys to crime as they occur in urban space.[94] The Brantinghams' model uses concepts of opportunity and offender motivation together with the concepts of mobility and perception to predict the next likely target area and the offender's residence. In Table 6.4.1, six major components are listed that make up the Brantinghams' hypothesized spatial model.[93]

One element not shown in Table 6.4.1 is the spatial pattern of hunting and target selection. However, in an attempt to fill this void, the Brantinghams expanded their model using theoretical cases. The simplest case scenario and subsequently the foundation for current geographical profiling systems is the basic search area for an individual offender. An example of the hypothesized search area can be seen in Figure 6.4.1. The initial conditions in this figure are single offender, uniform distribution of potential targets, and the offender based in a single home location.[93]

The Brantinghams refer to the phenomenon of "distance decay" in describing the location of an offender's crimes. Briefly, distance decay refers to the reduction of activity or interaction as distance from the home increases. In the hypothesized case shown in Figure 6.4.1, the expected range would be circular, and most offenses would occur close to home, with the likelihood of an offense taking place in a particular location decreasing with distance from home.

The Brantinghams suggest that offenders will have more cognizant mental maps about potential crime opportunities close to their home bases. They also proposed that offenders are more likely to be noticed and identified close to their home bases by other individuals who live in the same vicinity. Consequently, the Brantinghams argue that there would be a "confront zone" directly around the offender's home base where little criminal activity would occur, which is referred to as a "buffer zone."[93] Phillips suggested that it takes effort, time, and money to overcome distance; these things are what have been termed the "friction" of distance.[95]

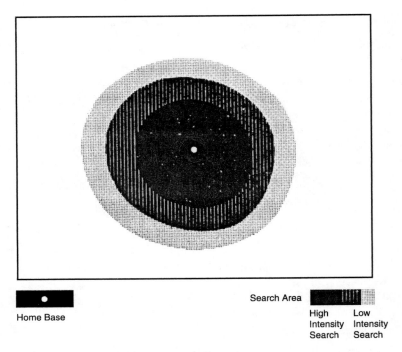

Home Base

Search Area

High Intensity Search

Low Intensity Search

Figure 6.4.1 Brantingham's hypothetical offense area for a single offender. From Brantingham, P. L. and Brantingham, P. J. (1981), *Environmental Criminology*, Sage: London. With permission.

In later research, the Brantinghams refined their hypothesized spatial model and proposed a complex search area for offenders. An example of this hypothesized model is shown in Figure 6.4.2. The initial conditions allow for the fact that criminals, like non-criminals, are not tied to just geographical locations near their home base. Rather, offenders, like non-offenders, go to work, shop, and relax, and the pathways between these activities combine to form what the Brantinghams' termed the individual's awareness space. Arguably, the Brantinghams hypothesized spatial theories suggest that given equally distributed opportunities, offenders will tend to offend within a minimum and maximum range of distance from the offender's home, independent of direction and other physical or psychological constraints. Research that tends to echo this hypothesized spatial model was carried out by Pyle.[96] Pyle found that in Cleveland, Ohio, property offenders tended to travel further from home than personal offenders did. Conversely, a study by Pettiway found that black robbers and not burglars traveled longer distances to their crime sites.[97] However, there are exceptions to these findings. A study by Turner did not find any significant differences based on offense type and the distances between the offenders' residences and crime locations for 1960 Philadelphia data.[98] Also, a

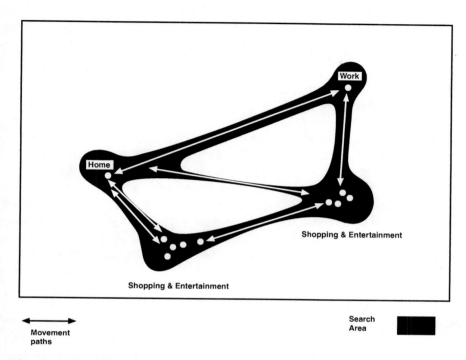

Figure 6.4.2 Brantinghams' hypothetical offense area for an individual offender, taking into account his or her action space. From Brantingham, P. L. and Brantingham, P. J. (1981), *Environmental Criminology*, Sage: London. With permission.

study by Bullock as far back as 1955 showed that 40% of all Houston homicides, including domestic homicide, between the years 1945 and 1949, occurred within one city block of the offenders' residences.[99]

6.4.3 Computerized Geographical Profiling

Following on from the work of Brantingham and Brantingham, Dr. Kim Rossmo, calling his technique criminal geographical targeting (CGT), has combined concepts from environmental criminology with a mathematical model, based on a distance decay function, derived from the locations in which killers leave their victims' bodies, to indicate the area in which an offender may be living.[100,101] As discussed previously, the psychological principles on which Rossmo's work is based are not articulated in any detail but appear to derive from the postulate propounded by Brantingham and Brantingham, who suggest that victims are probably spatially biased toward the offender's home base. This theory was illustrated in a study by the Brantinghams in 1981 in Washington, D.C., where they that found offenders generally victimize areas they know best, concentrating on targets within their immediate environments and surrounding areas. This spatial bias is the proposed cause of a decay function such that the further an offender is from home, the less likely he is to commit an offense.

The reasons for the decay proposed in Rossmo's criminal geographical targeting model are not exactly clear, but appear to be based on the least-effort principle. As defined by Zipf, least-effort principle postulates that when multiple destinations of equal desirability are available, all else being equal, the closest one will be chosen.[102] However, the notion that criminals choose targets in their confront zones is usually modified by two further considerations. One is most readily supported by Pettiway's 1982 study, which found that specialist selectivity is reflected in the effort an offender puts into planning a crime. This choice would lead to more selective and more carefully planned crimes being committed further away from home. This theory has been supported by comparisons across different types of crime. For example, in a series of studies by Capone and Nichols, it was found that the apparently more impulsive crime of rape is committed nearer to home than robbery, and that armed robbers travel further on average than those who are not armed, and tend to net larger sums of money.[103,104]

Dr. Kim Rossmo incorporates another principle into his geographical profiling system that has been put forward as a basis for crime locations, that there will be a tendency for serial killers to avoid committing crimes close to where they live, which was referred to earlier as a buffer zone. The proposed reason for this so-called confront zone is so criminals will avoid leaving incriminating evidence near where they live. However, the evidence for this is sparse. For example, Godwin and Canter's[105] study of 54 American serial killers found that offenders, on average, tended to make initial contact with their victims closer to home than the locations in which they eventually placed the bodies, which could suggest that a buffer zone is highly probable for body disposal sites, however, not for the abduction sites. Davis and Dale found no evidence for a buffer zone in their limited study of single rapists.[106] Furthermore, the drawback to relying on the distance decay theory is that the actual distances proposed as buffer zones are often larger than would be consistent with leaving local clues.

A variety of geographical profiling processes have thus been outlined by those with an ecological and environmental criminology bias that could be seen to be logically in conflict.[93,103] One process is a tendency to minimize effort close to home, which would predict that crimes are in a closely circumscribed area. A second is the tendency to keep a minimum distance away from home. These two processes combined would lead to the prediction of an optimum distance from home to all of a particular type of offense. However, the general finding is one of an aggregate decay of the frequency of crimes as their distances increase from home. These processes are derived from a consideration of instrumental crimes often with a tangible material benefit, such as theft or robbery. So, although they doubtless have relevance to geographical profiling, there are questions about how important emotional issues are ignored by such rational models.

Two further complexities raise questions about the relevance of these rational processes to the geographical profiling of criminals. Godwin points out that there is typically more than one location involved in serial killers' activities.[107] Besides the location of the site where the victim's body is dumped, there is also usually at least one other important site, the point at which the victim is first encountered. For example, in a series of murders, all three processes indicated above — least effort, buffer zone, and decay function — would likely predict that the abduction and body dump sites would be close together. However, research on 54 serial killers by this author found that the locations where victims go missing were on average 1.5 miles from the offenders' home bases, compared to 5 miles for the body dump locations.[105] Furthermore, none of the three processes would lead to any predictions in the changes of distance of the crimes from home over time.

6.4.4 Environmental Psychology

Following on from the environmental criminological theories proposed by Brantingham and Brantingham is the emerging field of environmental psychology. Environmental psychologists see the journey to crime as an expression of a complex interaction between the offender, his or her background characteristics, predispositions, knowledge and perceptions, and the location and type of target, in terms of perceived risks, rewards, opportunities, and attractions. For example, in 1989, environmental psychologist Professor David Canter hypothesized that the actual nature of the location selected may be indicative of the purpose and experiences of the offender.[108] Canter pointed out that there may be patterns of space use typical of different criminals, relating to where they are living at the time of their crimes.

Using an environmental psychology approach, David Canter and his colleague proposed research into the relationship that may exist between the criminal range and the location of the home base of serial sexual offenders.[109,110] The proposed model of individual sexual offenders' spatial activity was based upon 45 British male sexual assaulters who had committed at least two assaults on strangers. The study hypothesized two general models to characterize the relationship between the home base and criminal area of offenders. The first assumption that was suggested regarded the geometry of a criminal's domain; that it would be an area defined by a circle around the offender's home, which Canter and his colleague defined as the *commuter hypothesis*. According to this theory, the area around the home and the area in which the crimes are committed are represented as circles. An example of the *commuter hypothesis* is shown in Figure 6.4.3.[109]

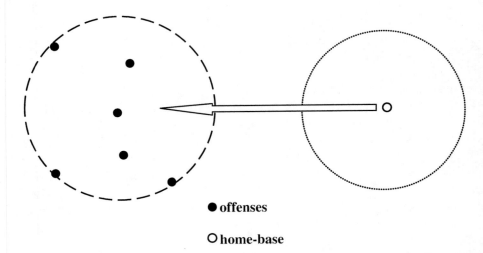

Figure 6.4.3 Commuter hypothesis. Adapted from Canter and Gregory (1994), identifying the residential location of rapists, *JFSS*, 34(3): 169-175.

In describing the commuter process, Canter suggests that an offender travels from his or her home base into an area to offend.[109] Central to this hypothesis is that there will be no clear relationship between the size or location of the criminal's domain and its distance from an offender's home. As such, the *commuter hypothesis* model proposes little or no overlap between these two areas, suggesting that the offender moves an appreciable distance to a district outside his home range to offend.

The second model proposed by Canter and his colleague is based upon the *marauder hypothesis*.[109] An example of this hypothesized model is shown in Figure 6.4.4. This theory argues that the offender's home base acts as a focal point for his or her crimes; it is suggested that the offender moves out and returns to his or her home base each time he commits a crime. Arguably, this hypothesis would predict that, on average, the further the distance between crimes, the further the offender must be traveling from home to offend. However, research on 54 serial murderers found that the marauding process may be viable for victims' body dump locations but not for their abduction sites.[105]

Canter found that 91% of the sample of offenders had all their crimes located within the circular region, which was termed as the *circle hypothesis*.[109,110] It was also found that 87% of the offenders had a base within the *circle hypothesis* prediction area. These results provided strong support for the general *marauder hypothesis* as most applicable to this set of offenders; that is, that the majority of the sample had operated from a home base from which they traveled to commit their crimes.

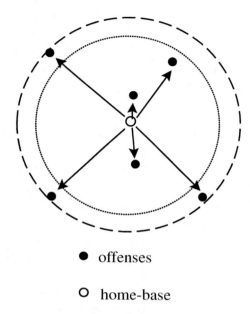

● offenses

○ home-base

Figure 6.4.4 Marauder hypothesis. Adapted from Canter and Gregory (1994), identifying the residential location of rapists, *JFSS*, 34(3): 169-175.

6.4.5 Home Range and Directional Travel of Criminals

There is a complexity about environmental criminology, Rossmo's geograph-ical profiling model, and the *circle hypothesis* processes to consider; that is, the hypothesized spatial models fail to take into account directional bias. Research by Rengert and Wasilchick demonstrated that crime trips of sub-urban burglars are more likely to be skewed in the direction of nodal centers, such as workplaces and city central districts, and crime trips were more likely to be wedge-shaped.[111] Considering the plethora of research literature on the sectoral mental maps (directionality) of intra-urban travel patterns and migration of people, the consideration of directionality in geographical pro-filing has been moot. In 1969, Adams argued that intra-urban migration takes place in accordance with sectoral and directional biases in the urban spatial cognition.[112] Adams' findings suggested that intra-urban migration patterns are sectorally biased towards the center business districts in that they are wedge-shaped.[112]

The theoretical analysis of people's bonds with the tangible surroundings of the home environs is found in several disciplines; for example, migration and shopping behavior studies. As Feldman pointed out, the home environment becomes a unique place of familiar, known, and predictable activities, people, and physical elements; a focal point of one's experiential space.[113] Thus, through habitual, focused, and satisfying involvement in a residential locale, the tangible home area becomes an enduring symbol of self, of the continuity of one's experiences, and of that which is significant and valued by the inhabitant. The landscape around the home base may thus be hypothesized to provide criminals with those enduring symbolic experiences. If their crimes, as hypothesized, do indeed develop as an elaboration of their daily activities rather than as some distinct work-life activity, then it would be predicted that the home would be geographically as well as symbolically central to their criminal activities.

6.4.6   Geographical Profiling the Angles between Crimes Using Predator©*

Predator is a geographical profiling system developed from research carried out by this author. The basic platform for the program is written in Visual Basic for Windows 98. The Predator system employs two location-allocation theories. Firstly, it employs a method that looks at the location of central facilities and the allocation of flows to them. Such a method projects, theoretically, the probable trips of the offender to the center. Secondly, Predator employs an analysis of a dispersing offender and reverses the directional assumption of the location-allocation model, while also keeping the assumptions of a monotonous plain and of optimization. Rather than assuming that the victim travels to the offender's home base, it assumes that the offender travels outward from his or her home, so the allocation of flows is "from" rather than "to" the center. This process allows the criminal's spatial movements to be modeled from all directions, whether they are moving in or out.

Mapping the crime data involves recording each killer's crime locations and home base and their respective latitude and longitude geographical coordinate. Once this task is completed, the geographical coordinates of latitude and longitude are converted into the Universal Transverse Mercator (UTM) Grid System. Converting the latitude and longitude coordinates into the UTM coordinate system allows the data to be entered into the Predator geographical profiling system. Each distance is entered separately into the Predator system. The program then creates a scale of the actual crime area in miles or kilometers. For each event, the Northing and Easting UTM coordinate serves to express the unique, absolute location of each crime event. Equally important, the UTM coordinate system is impartial, and the values of locations are independently verifiable. The geographical program then plots each of the crime locations on the computer screen. Each case is analyzed separately.

To demonstrate how offense angles can be calculated, Figure 6.4.5 shows cognitive maps of four American serial killers that were calculated by the Predator system. The degree of the angles are reported next to each offenders'

* Registered Trademark of Grover Maurice Godwin, 2000.

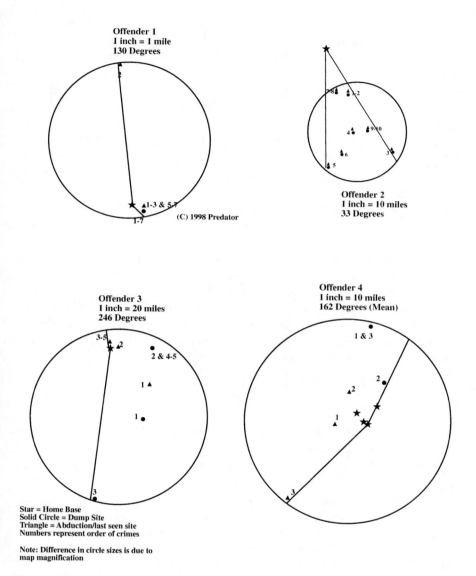

Figure 6.4.5 Cognitive maps of killers' movements between home bases, victims' abduction, and body dump sites.

map. The data were collected, as part of this author's doctorate dissertation, from the Homicide Investigating Tracking System (HITS) in Seattle, Washington. Where there was more than one home base, the mean of the angles between the crimes is reported. The finding that serial killers' spatial behavior has a tendency to be wedge-shaped has several implications for geographical profiling and predicting the likely home base area of a serial killer. In the study of British sex offenders discussed earlier, the home base was found 71% of the time between the two furthest crime sites, as Canter's circle hypothesis suggests. However, there is still a rather substantially large search area for the police to investigate. If police were to rely on the wedge-shaped theory as a function in geographical profiling, the search area including the offender's home base would be considerably smaller. It is therefore argued that the wedge-shaped theory has heuristic value when developing geographical profiles of serial killers. Reboussin, Warren, and Hazelwood carried out a limited study on serial rape and found that crime patterns had a distinct sense of directionality that could be described as a windshield wiper pattern.[114]

In another study on directional bias, Mercer suggests that the sectoral mental map may not be anchored on downtown, based on regular daily activities, but may instead focus upon recreation areas beyond the city which are visited weekly.[115] To be sure, there is ample basis for the argument that criminals' spatial patterns depend on limited mental maps or mental images of the city and areas surrounding their homes. When they carry out their crimes, the locational choices are affected by reliable knowledge of the city or area which forms wedge-shaped images that are in focus for places close to home or other parts of the home sector, and blurry or blank for distant places, such as the other side of town. This study certainly supports the view that investigative efforts would be greatly enhanced if geographical profiles took into consideration the directionality of crime locations.

6.4.7   Conclusions

Theories and concepts associated with the geographical behavior of criminals with particular focus on four principle approaches, ecological school, environmental criminology, environmental psychology, and the wedge theory have been discussed. Research into geographical profiling originated from the ecological approach and was concerned with the identification of crime areas in relation to offender demographics rather than the location of specific criminal events.

The environmental criminology approach provided a new perspective on the relationship between an offender's home base area and the location of his or her offenses. Hence, it moved away from looking at the causes of crime, and emphasized the importance of where victims are targeted and where crimes occur. Although the foundations on which environment criminology is built are entirely theoretical, it does suggest that criminals have patterns in their spatial behavior that could have implications for predicting future target areas. In a different vein, geographical profiling from the environmental psychological approach deals directly with the prediction of the likely behavior of the serial offender, as demonstrated in research on rape by Canter and his colleague. Environmental psychology holds more promise than previously non-psychological based geographical profiling methods.

Evidence has been presented suggesting that criminals have limited spatial knowledge, and that these patterns appear to be wedge-shaped. Such findings are in accord with a perspective that sees journeys to crime growing out of the daily activities and contact patterns of the offender. When serial killers make environmental choices involving locational considerations, their mental maps are used as preferences as to which areas to forage for potential victims and dispose of their bodies. The fact that serial killers' spatial behavior is sectorally biased suggests that police investigators are not dealing with economic killers, with his or her perfect knowledge, but rather real individuals with imperfect knowledge and a predilection for satisfying behavior. Such a finding has direct implications for systems such as Rossmo's criminal geographical targeting system, leading to the hypothesis that his procedure might be more efficient if it considered the directionality of crimes.

Admittedly, the interpretations of this paper are *ex post facto*, and one has to speculate whether there are additional features of the criminal's spatial behavior that can be predicative. Further research is needed to find out what additional psychological and environmental factors influence the geographical behavior of criminals.

6.5 A Psycho-Geographical Profile of a Series of Unsolved Murders in Raleigh, North Carolina

MAURICE GODWIN

The application of geographic predication was best stated by Harries: "Prediction, depending on the level of its reliability, may be the most valuable end product of any social science investigation."[116] Even some success in predication is often worthwhile, since it creates an awareness of tendencies within a system without necessarily specifying either the parameters of those tendencies or underlying causes.

Psycho-geographical profiling is concerned with the spatial analysis and psychological behavioral patterns of criminals. The technique employs a variety of methods, including distance to crime research, demographical analysis, environmental psychology, landscape analysis, geographical information systems, point pattern analysis, crime site residual analysis, and psychological criminal profiling. This process has both quantitative and qualitative (landscape analysis) dimensions to its application. Moreover, psycho-geographical profiling seems to be a particularly effective method for police investigators attempting to solve complex serial crimes. The technique examines the spatial data connected to a series of crime sites and, more specifically, victims' body dump sites and abduction/last seen sites.

While several sciences specialize in such matters as crime scene analysis, none can analyze the site and situation of the entire crime better than geography in conjunction with environmental psychology. Qualities of places and the relationships among places are stock in trade for developing geographical profiles. While the quantitative methods, at least at first aim at general patterns of crimes in the aggregate, the qualitative method used here aims at reconnecting the known facets of the crimes to the actual landscape. In this vein, psycho-geographical profiling attempts to reconstruct the courses of travel of the killer and the victim from before the crime until well after it. Every reasonable effort is made to lay down a complete trail for each person involved in the crime.

Psycho-geographical profiling does not "solve" cases. Rather, the method provides an additional avenue of scientific investigation that, with the many other forensic specialities, may provide some help for the investigation. The actual search for the perpetrator remains completely in the hands of the police. Psycho-geographical profiling techniques could provide an additional perspective that may assist police during serial murder investigations in which bodies of victims are scattered over a large geographical area. Psycho-geographical profiling also has the possibility to indicate that a sequence of murders belong in one series, even when the police deny such an interpretation. Such was the case when this author developed a psycho-geographical profile in 1997 on a series of unsolved murders in Raleigh, North Carolina, for which John William, Jr. was later charged and convicted. Following is the psycho-geographical profile developed in the unsolved murders in Raleigh, North Carolina. From all accounts, the geographical profile presented here predicted the killer's home base more accurately than any previous attempts to geographically profile a murder or rape case.

6.5.1   Predator Geographical Profiling System

The geographical profiling system that was used at the time of the Raleigh crimes was only in the early stages of development. The program has since been upgraded, and is now called Predator. A brief explanation of Predator was given previously. Predator uses the actual discrete crime locations along with several distance-decay functions to geographically profile the crime series. Predator does not use the rather aggregated "mean interpoint distance" that is used in some other geographical profiling systems. Predator uses the more reliable UTM coordinates for plotting crime locations. Predator does not assume a buffer zone but does, make allowances for buffer zones, especially when analyzing the victims' abduction sites. This is contrary to current popular geographical profiling systems, which do not make allowances for buffer zones.

Most geographical profiling systems used to predict the likely home area of an unknown offender employ presumptuous mean interpoint distances between crime locations that the creators assume represent a "monotonous plain," which is a theoretical surface only analogously related to the actual surface of the earth. Their monotonous plain lacks rivers, cliffs, streets, shopping centers, and so forth.

Predator employs two location-allocation theories. First, it employs a method that looks at the location of central facilities and the allocation of flows to them. Such a method projects, theoretically, the probable trips of the offender to the center. Second, Predator employs an analysis of a dispersing offender, and reverses the directional assumption of the location-allocation model while also keeping the assumptions of a monotonous plain and optimization. Rather than assuming that victims travel to the offender's home-base, it assumes that the offender travels outward from his home, so

Function Calculate Slope (x1 As Variant, y1 As Variant, x2 As Variant, y2 As Variant)
As Variant

This function calculates the slope between two points using the Arctangent function (Atn). Atn is passed the ratio of the two sides of the right-angled triangle and returns the angle of the hypotenuse in radians. Special cases like 90 degrees and 270 degrees are identified and handled individually.

If the two x values are the same then the angle is 90 or 270 degrees. If not then it is safe to divide by (x2-x1).

If Not (x1 = x2) Then

    Calulate the angle in radians by passing the tangent (dy/dx) to the Atn function

    angle = Atn((y2 - y1) / (x2 - x1))

If the second point is higher than the first

If y2 >= y1 Then

    and the second point is to the left of the first

    If x2 <= x1 Then

        then the line is in the second quadrant and the required angle is therefore pi radians (180 degas) minus the angle from Atn

        CalculateSlope = pi - Abs(angle)

    Else the second point is to the right and the line is in the first quadrant, in which case the angle returned by Atn is the one needed

    Else

        CalculateSlope = angle

    End If

Else, the second point is below the first and the line is in the third or fourth quadrant

Else

    If the second point is to the left then the line is in the third quadrant, so the angle required is the angle from Atn, plus pi.

    If x2 <= x1 Then

        CalculateSlope = angle + pi

Else the line is in the fourth quadrant and the angle required is 2 pi minus the angle from Atn

    Else

        CalculateSlope = (2 * pi) - Abs(angle)

    End If

    End If

Else x1 = x2 so the angle is 90 or 270. If the second point is higher then it's 90 or (pi/2).

ElseIf y2 > y1 Then

    CalculateSlope = pi / 2

Or if the second point is below the first, it's 270 degrees or (3 pi/2)

Else

    CalculateSlope = (3 * pi) / 2

End If

End Function

Figure 6.5.1 Function for calculating the slope between two points using the arctangent function (Atn).

the allocation of flows is "from" rather than "to" the center. This process allows the criminal's spatial movements to be modeled from all directions, whether they are moving in or out.

One advantage that Predator has over other popular geographical pro-filing systems is that it does not assume that the crime area is circular, but rather looks at the locations from all angular positions. Ongoing research by this author shows that the directionality of crime locations of serial U.S. killers is wedged-shaped, as demonstrated earlier in this chapter. Although not used in the Raleigh analysis because the function had not been incor-porated in the program at that time, the Predator program now has a function that calculates the angle of crimes by calculating the two sides of two points using the Arctangent function (Atn), as shown below. Neither Rossmo's system nor the Dragnet geographical profiling system consider the angle of crimes.

6.5.2   Geographical Analysis of the Crime Locations Using Predator

Figure 6.5.2 depicts a map showing the locations where the victims' bodies were found in Raleigh, North Carolina. The body of victim one, a black female, 33, was found the afternoon of January 7, 1996 behind a business in the 1500 block of South Blount Street, Raleigh. The second victim, a black female, 38, was found at 916 Oakwood Avenue. The third victim, a black female, 30, was found near a homeless camp near railroad tracks under Morgan Street Bridge in Raleigh. The fourth victim, a black female, 32, was found at the Martin Luther King Boulevard extension project near Dawson Street. The fifth victim, a black female, 35, was found nude in an empty building being renovated at the intersection of North and West Streets.

The street addresses of each victim's body dump site were entered into the geographical profiling system for analysis. To determine a monotonous plan to represent the radius of the crime locations for the computer analysis, Universal Transverse Mercator (UTM) coordinates were used. These UTM numbers are given in meters north of an arbitrary beginning point, as well as east of another such point. For each event, then, a Northing and an Easting figure was obtained. The meters were converted to miles. These coordinates serve to express the unique, absolute location of each crime event. The crime locations encompassed a 2.2 mile radius.

Figure 6.5.3 shows the probability plot produced by the geographical pro-filing system. Each of the black center dots represents the original crime loca-tions. Although on visual inspection of the plot there are slight differences, these do not affect the results of the study. The program incorporates three distance-decay functions. Considering the relevant small radius of 2.2 miles, a

Function Calculate Slope (x1 As Variant, y1 As Variant, x2 As Variant, y2 As Variant)
As Variant

This function calculates the slope between two points using the Arctangent function (Atn). Atn is passed the ratio of the two sides of the right-angled triangle and returns the angle of the hypotenuse in radians. Special cases like 90 degrees and 270 degrees are identified and handled individually.

If the two x values are the same then the angle is 90 or 270 degrees. If not then it is safe to divide by (x2-x1).

If Not (x1 = x2) Then

Calulate the angle in radians by passing the tangent (dy/dx) to the Atn function

angle = Atn((y2 - y1) / (x2 - x1))

If the second point is higher than the first

If y2 >= y1 Then

and the second point is to the left of the first

If x2 <= x1 Then

then the line is in the second quadrant and the required angle is therefore pi radians (180 degrs) minus the angle from Atn

CalculateSlope = pi - Abs(angle)

Else the second point is to the right and the line is in the first quadrant, in which case the angle returned by Atn is the one needed

Else

CalculateSlope = angle

End If

Else, the second point is below the first and the line is in the third or fourth quadrant

Else

If the second point is to the left then the line is in the third quadrant, so the angle required is the angle from Atn, plus pi.

If x2 <= x1 Then

CalculateSlope = angle + pi

Else the line is in the fourth quadrant and the angle required is 2 pi minus the angle from Atn

Else

CalculateSlope = (2 * pi) - Abs(angle)

End If

End If

Else x1 = x2 so the angle is 90 or 270. If the second point is higher then it's 90 or (pi/2).

ElseIf y2 > y1 Then

CalculateSlope = pi / 2

Or if the second point is below the first, it's 270 degrees or (3 pi/2)

Else

CalculateSlope = (3 * pi) / 2

End If

End Function

Figure 6.5.1 Function for calculating the slope between two points using the arctangent function (Atn).

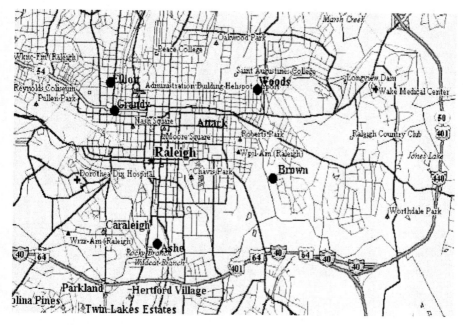

Figure 6.5.2 John Williams serial murder case victims' body dump locations.

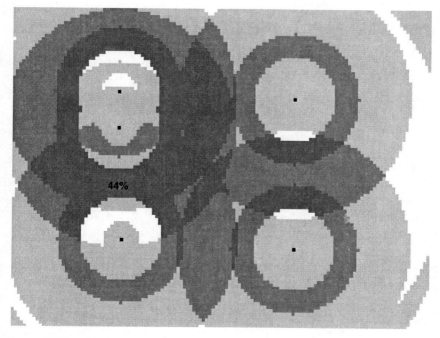

Figure 6.5.3 Probability geographical plot, John Williams, Jr. serial murder case.

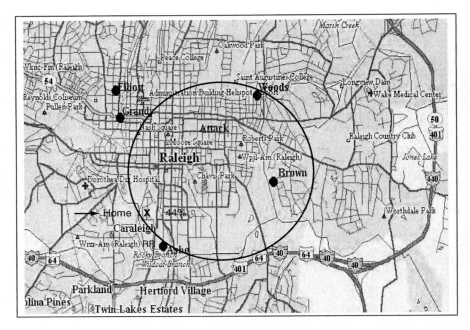

Figure 6.5.4 Psycho-Geographical profile John Williams serial murder case.
→ = Williams home base
44% Represents the predicted location

distance-decay function was chosen that is programmed to simulate short radiuses. The medium gray and lightest regions represented geographical areas with low probabilities, which suggested that the offender's home base was unlikely to be located in those areas. The darkest region represented the higher probability of the offender living in those areas. The probability at any given point in Figure 6.5.3 can be determined by clicking on the right side of the mouse.

Looking at Figure 6.5.3, we see the probability 44%. This exact location represented the highest probable area of where the offender lived. The plot in Figure 6.5.3 was superimposed over the map of Raleigh shown in Figure 6.5.2 using a GIS system. Figure 6.5.4 shows the probability plot superimposed over the Raleigh map, and the offender's predicted home base is marked as "x" (the exact spot of the 44%), while the circle in Figure 6.5.4 represents all the darkest region from the probability plot in Figure 6.5.3. Briefly, in the darkest region there was no other location found to have a matching or higher probability than 44%. This is why this particular location was chosen as the predicted home base.

The location marked with an "x" in Figure 6.5.4 indicates the predicated home base of the killer using the geographical profiling system. The location marked as "HB" in Figure 6.5.4 indicates where Williams actually lived while committing his crimes. Remarkably, although where Williams was living was located just outside of the circle, it was roughly one block from the predicted home base area. An interesting finding in Figure 6.5.4 is the area marked with a square, which is located in the upper middle of the circle. This location shows the region where the police discovered Williams attacking another victim and subsequently arrested him.

The Williams serial murder case also provided a wealth of information on the importance of examining victims' abduction sites. Williams abducted most of his victims along railroad tracks, which can be seen in the lower left side of the circle in Figure 6.5.4 near the body of Patricia Ashe. Starting with the Patricia Ashe body discovery site, the railroad tracks run northwest near where Williams was actually living. Due to the limited capabilities of the geographical profiling system at that time, the victims' abduction sites were not included in the analysis. However, it is now apparent that analysis of the victims' abduction sites along the railroad tracks could have made the geographical profile more accurate than one block.

References

1. Canadian Centre for Justice Statistics, *Canadian Crime Statistics*, Ottawa: Statistics Canada, 1994.

2. Brantingham, P. J. and Brantingham, P. L., Mobility, notoriety, and crime: a study in crime patterns of urban nodal points, *Journal of Environmental Systems*, 11: 89-99,1981.

3. Brantingham, P. J. and Brantingham, P. L., *Patterns in Crime*, New York: Macmillan, 1984.

4. Hazelwood, R. and Burgess, A. W., An introduction to the serial rapist, *FBI Law Enforcement Bulletin*, 56:16-24, 1987.

5. Hazelwood, R., Reboussin, R., and Warren, J., Serial rape: correlates of increased aggression and the relationship of offender pleasure to victim resistance, *Journal of Interpersonal Violence*, 7:65-78, 1989.

6. Hazelwood, R. and Warren, J., The criminal behaviour of the serial rapist, *FBI Law Enforcement Bulletin*, 59:11-16, 1990.

7. Burgess, A. W. and Hartman, C. R., Sexual homicide: a motivational model, *Journal of Interpersonal Violence*, 1:251-272, 1986.

8. Federal Bureau of Investigation, Classifying sexual homicide crime scenes: inter-rater reliability, *FBI Law Enforcement Bulletin*, 54:12-17, 1985.

9. Ressler, R. K., Burgess, A. W., and Douglas, J. E., *Sexual Homicide: Patterns and Motives*, Lexington, MA: Lexington Books, 1988.

10. Ressler, R. K., Burgess, A. W., Douglas, J. E., Hartman, C. R., and D'Agostino, R. B., Sexual killers and their victims, *Journal of Interpersonal Violence*, 1:288-308, 1986.

11. Ressler, R. K., Burgess, A. W., Hartman, C. R., Douglas, J. E., and McCormack, A., Murderers who rape and mutilate, *Journal of Interpersonal Violence*, 1:273-287, 1986.

12. Ressler, R. K., Douglas, J. E., and Burgess, A. W., Rape and rape murder: one offender and twelve victims, *American Journal of Psychiatry*, 140:36-40, 1983.

13. Prentky, R. A., Burgess, A. W., Rokous, F., Lee, A., Hartman, C., Ressler, R., and Douglas, J., The presumptive role of fantasy in serial sexual homicide, *American Journal of Psychiatry*, 146:887-891, 1989.

14. Money, J., Forensic sexology: paraphilic serial rape, *American Journal of Psychotherapy*, 44: 26-36, 1990.

15. Groth, A. N., *Men Who Rape: The Psychology of the Offender*, New York: Plenum Press, 1979.

16. Maume, D. J., Inequality and metropolitan rape rates: a routine activities approach, *Justice Quarterly*, 6:513-528, 1989.

17. LeBeau, J. I., Rape and racial patterns, *Journal of Offender Counselling, Services and Rehabilitation*, 9:123-148, 1984.

18. LeBeau, J. I., Some problems with measuring and describing rape presented by the serial offender, *Justice Quarterly*, 2:385-398, 1985.

19. Burgess, E. W., The Growth of the City, in Park, R. E., Burgess, E. W., and McKenzie, R. D., Eds., *The City*, Chicago: University of Chicago Press, pp. 47-62, 1925.

20. Groth, A. N., Longo, R. and McFadin, B., Undetected recidivism among rapists and child molesters, *Crime and Delinquency*, 28:450-458, 1982.

21. Hamparian, D. M., Schuster, R., Dinitz, S., and Corad, J. P., *The Violent Few: A Study of Dangerous Juvenile Offenders*, Boston: Lexington, 1978.

22. Wolfgang, M. E., Figlio, R. M., and Sellin T., *Delinquency in a Birth Cohort*, Chicago: University of Chicago Press, 1972.

23. Lisak, D. and Roth, S., Motivations and psychodynamics of self-reported, non-incarcerated rapists, *American Journal of Orthopsychiatry*, 60: 268-279, 1990.

24. LeBeau, J. I., Patterns of stranger and serial rape offending: factors distinguishing apprehended and at-large offenders, *The Journal of Criminal Law and Criminology*, 78: 309-326, 1987.

25. LeBeau, J. I., The journey to rape: geographic distance and the rapist's method of approaching the victim, *Police Science and Administration*, 15:129-136, 1987.

26. LeBeau, J. I., The methods and measures of centrography and the spatial dynamics of rape, *Journal of Quantitative Criminology*, 3, 125-141, 1987.

27. LeBeau, J. I., Four case studies illustrating the spatial-temporal analysis of serial rapists, *Police Studies*, 15:124-145, 1992.

28. Canter, D. and Larkin, P., The environmental range of serial rapists, *Journal of Environmental Psychology*, 13:63-6, 1993.

29. Topalin, J., *The Journey to Rape*, Reading, U.K.: unpublished master's thesis, University of Surrey, 1992.

30. Amir, M., *Patterns in Forcible Rape*, Chicago: University of Chicago Press, 1971.

31. Rand, A., Mobility triangles, in Figlio, R. M., Hakim, S., and Rengert, G. F., Eds., *Metropolitan Crime Patterns*, Monsey, NY: Willow Tree Press, pp. 117-126, 1986.

32. Pyle, G. F., *The Spatial Dynamics of Crime*, Research Paper No. 159, Chicago: Department of Geography, University of Chicago, 1974.

33. Erlanson, O. A.,The scene of sex offences, *Journal of Criminal Law and Criminology*, 31:339-342, 1946.

34. White, R. C., The relation of felonies to environmental factors in Indianapolis, *Social Forces*, 10, 498-509, 1932.

35. Gabor, T. and Gottheil, E., Offender characteristics and spatial mobility: An empirical study and some policy implications, *Canadian Journal of Criminology*, 26:267-281, 1984.

36. Rhodes, W. M. M. and Conly, C., Crime and mobility: an empirical study, in P. J. Brantingham and P. L. Brantingham, Eds., *Environmental Criminology*, California: Sage, 1991.

37. Alston, J. D., *The Serial Rapist's Spatial Pattern of Target Selection*, Burnaby, Canada: unpublished master's thesis, Simon Fraser University, 1994.

38. Lowe, J. C. and Moryadas, S., *The Geography of Movement*, Boston: Houghton Mifflin, 1975.

39. Lindgren, B. W., *Statistical Theory*, New York: Macmillan, 1960.

40. Massey, F. J., The Kolmogorov-Smirnov test for goodness of fit, *Journal of the American Statistical Association*, 46:68-78, 1951.

41. Hodder, I. and Orton, C., *Spatial Analysis in Archaeology*, Cambridge: Cambridge University Press, 1989.

42. Rossmo, D. K., *Geographical Profiling*, Boca Raton, FL: CRC Press, 2000.

43. Rengert, G. and Wasilchick, J., *Suburban Burglary: A Time and a Place for Everything*, Springfield, IL: Charles C Thomas, 1985.

44. Cromwell, P. F., Olson, J. N., and Avary, D. W., *Breaking and Entering: An Ethnographic Analysis of Burglary*, Newbury Park, CA: Sage, 1991.

45. Feeney, F., Robbers as decision makers, in Cornish, D. and Clarke, R., Eds., *The Reasoning Criminal*, New York: Springer-Verlag, pp. 53-77, 1986.

46. Keppel, R. and Weis, J., Time and distance as solvability factors in murder cases, *Journal of Forensic Science*, 39, 386-401, 1994.

47. Ressler, R. K. and Shachtman, T., *Whoever Fights Monsters*, London: Simon & Schuster, 1992.

48. Douglas, J. and Olshaker, M., *Mindhunter*, London: Heinemann, 1996.

49. Rossmo, D. K., Multivariate spatial profiles as a tool in crime investigation, presentation, *Workshop on Crime Analysis through Computer Mapping*, Chicago, IL, August, 1993.

50. Zipf, G., *The Principle of Least Effort*, Reading, MA: Addison Wesley, 1950.

51. Brantingham, P. J. and Brantingham, P. L., Mobility, notoriety, and crime: A study in crime patterns of urban nodal points, *Journal of Environmental Systems*, 11: 89-99,1981.

52. Brantingham, P. J. and Brantingham, P. L., *Patterns in Crime*, New York: Macmillan, 1984.

53. Davies, A. and Dale, A., Locating the stranger rapist, *London Home Office Police Department*, Special Interest Series, Home Office: London, Paper 3, 1995.

54. Rossmo, D. K., *Geographical Profiling*, Boca Raton, FL: CRC Press, 2000.

55. Canter, D. and Hodge, S., *Predatory behavior in serial killers*, unpublished research paper, University of Liverpool Investigative Psychology Research Unit, 1997.

56. Reppetto, T. A., *Residential crime*, Cambridge, MA: Ballinger Publishing, 1974.

57. Rengert, G. and Wasilchick, J., *Suburban Burglary: A Time and a Place for Everything*, Springfield, IL: Charles C. Thomas, 1985.

58. Godwin, M., Geographical Profiling, in Siegel, J., Saukko, P., and Knupfer, G., Eds., *Encyclopedia of Forensic Science*, London: Academic Press, 2000.

59. Canter, D. and Larkin, P.,The environmental range of serial rapists, *Journal of Environmental Psychology*, 13:63-6, 1993.

60. Rengert, G. and Bost, R., *The spillover of crime from housing project*, paper presented to Academy of Criminal Justice Sciences, St. Louis, 1987.

61. Feldman, R. M., *Psychological bonds with types of settlements: looking back to the future*, IAPS 10 Proceedings, 2:335-342, Delft: Delft University Press, 1988.

62. Godwin, M. and Canter, D., Encounter and death: the spatial behavior of U.S. serial killers, *Policing: An International Journal of Police Strategies and Management*, 20:28-38, 1997.

63. James, E., *Catching serial killers: Learning from past serial murder investigations*, Lansing, MI: International Forensic Services, Inc., 1991.

64. Keppel, R. and Birnes, W., *Riverman: Ted Bundy and I hunt for the Green River killer*, NY: Pocket Books, 1995.

65. Ricci, J., Streetwalkers, *Environment and Behavior*, 24:300-308, 1992.

66. Symanski, K., The incidence and location of streetwalkers, *Environment and Behavior*, 11:91-100, 1981.

67. Douglas, J. E., Ressler, R. R., Burgess, A. W., and Hartman, C. R., Criminal profiling from crime scene analysis, *Behavioral Sciences and the Law*, 41:401-421, 1986.

68. Schechter, H. and Everitt, D., *The A to Z encyclopedia of serial killers*, NY: Pocket Books, 1996.

69. Egger, S., *The killers among us: An examination of serial murder and its investigation*, NJ: Prentice Hall, 1997.

70. Holmes, R. and Holmes, S., *Profiling violent crimes: an investigative tool*, 2nd ed., Newbury Park, CA: Sage, 1996.

71. U.S. Department of Justice, *Serial/mass murder*, (National Institute of Justice topical search TS 011664) Government Printing Office, Washington, D.C., 1991.

72. Hickey, E., *Serial murderers and their victims*, Pacific Grove, CA: Brooks and Cole, 1991.

73. Canter, D., Missen, C., and Hodge, S., A case for special agents? *Policing Today*, 2:23-7, 1996.

74. Newsweek, *Murder: A Week in the Death of America*, August, pp. 23-49, 1994.

75. Stote, R. and Standing, L., Serial and multiple homicide: is there an epidemic? *Social Behavior and Personality*, 23: 313-18, 1995.

76. Jenkins, P., Chance or choice? The selection of serial murder victims, in Wilson, A. V., Ed., *Homicide: The Victim/Offender Connection*, Cincinnati, OH: Anderson Publishing Company, 1993.

77. Rogers, R., Delores, C., and Anderson, D., Serial murder investigations and geographic information systems, presentation, Annual Meeting, *Academy of Criminal Justice Sciences*, Nashville, TN, 1991.

78. Holmes, R. and DeBurger, J., *Serial Murder*, Newbury Park, CA: Sage, 1988.

79. Holmes, R. and Holmes, S., *Profiling Violent Crimes: An Investigative Tool*, 2nd ed., Sage, Newbury Park, CA., 1996.

80. Skogan, W. G. and Antunes, G. F., Information, apprehension, and deterrence: exploring the limits of police productivity, *Journal of Criminal Justice*, 7:219-34, 1979.

81. Keppel, R. and Weis, J., Time and distance as solvability factors in murder cases, *Journal of Forensic Science*, 39, 386-401, 1994.

82. Ressler, R. K. and Shachtman, T., *Whoever Fights Monsters*, London: Simon & Schuster, 1992.

83. Douglas, J. and Olshaker, M., *Mindhunter*, London: Heinemann, 1996.

84. Rossmo, D. K., Multivariate spatial profiles as a tool in crime investigation, presentation, August, *Workshop on Crime Analysis through Computer Mapping*, Chicago, IL, 1993.

85. Rossmo, D. K., Place, space, and police investigations: hunting serial violent criminals, in Eck, J.E. and Weisburd, D., Eds., *Crime and Place*, Monsey, N.Y.: Criminal Justice Press, 1995.

86. Rossmo, D. K., Geography, profiling, and predatory criminals, in Holmes, R. and Holmes, S., *Profiling Violent Crimes: An Investigative Tool*, 2nd ed., Newbury Park, CA: Sage, 1996.

87. Brantingham, P. J. and Brantingham, P. L., Mobility, notoriety, and crime: a study in crime patterns of urban nodal points, *Journal of Environmental Systems*, 11:89-99, 1981.

88. Zipf, G., *The Principle of Least Effort*, Reading, MA: Addison Wesley, 1950.

89. Canter, D. and Larkin, P., The environmental range of serial rapists, *Journal of Environmental Psychology*, 13:63-6, 1993.

90. Ford, D., Investigating serial murder: the case of Indiana's gay murders, in Egger, S., Ed., *Serial Murder: An Elusive Phenomenon*, New York, N.Y.: Praeger, 1991.

91. Trowbridge, C., On fundamental methods of orientation and imaginary maps, *Science*, 38:990, 1913.

92. Shaw, C. R. and McKay, H. D., *Juvenile Delinquency and Urban Areas*, Chicago: University of Chicago Press, 1942.

93. Brantingham, P. L. and Brantingham, P. J., *Environmental Criminology*, London: Sage, 1981.

94. Brantingham, P. J., A thoeretical model of crime site selection, in M. Krohn and R. L. Akers, Eds., *Crime, Law, and Sanction*, Beverly Hills, CA: Sage, 1978.

95. Phillips, P., Characteristics and typology of the journal to crime, in Georges-Abeyie, D. E. and Harris, K. D., Eds., *Crime: A Spatial Perspective*, New York: Columbia University Press, 1980.

96. Pyle, G. F., The spatial dynamics of crime, *Chicago: University of Chicago, Department of Geography*, Research Paper No. 159, 1974.

97. Pettiway, L. E., Mobility of robbery and burglary offenders: ghetto and non-ghetto spaces, *Journal of Urban Affairs Quarterly*, 18: 255-269, 1982.

98. Turner, S., Delinquency and distance, in M. E. Wolfgang and T. Sellin, Eds., *Delinquency: Selected Studies*, New York: John Wiley, 1969.

99. Bullock, H. A., Urban homicide in theory and fact, *Journal of Criminal Law, Criminology and Police Science*, 45: 565-575, 1955.

100. Rossmo, D. K., Multivariate spatial profiles as a tool in crime investigation, *Workshop on Crime Analysis through Computer Mapping*, Chicago, IL, 1993.

101. Rossmo, D. K., Place, space, and police investigation: hunting serial violent criminals, *Crime Prevention Studies*, 4: Crime and Place, 1995.

102. Zipf, G., *The principle of least effort*, Reading, MA: Addison Wesley, 1950.

103. Capone, D. L. and Nicholas, W. Jr., Crime and distance: an analysis of offender behaviour in space, *Proceedings of the Association of American Geographers*, 45-49, 1975.

104. Capone, D. L. and Nicholas, W. Jr., Urban structure and criminal mobility, *American Behaviour Scientist*, 20: 199-213, 1976.

105. Godwin, M. and Canter, D., Encounter and death: the spatial behavior of U.S. serial killers, *Policing: An International Journal of Police Management and Strategies*, 20: 24-38, 1997.

106. Davies, A. and Dale, A., *Locating the Stranger Rapist*, Police Research Group Special Interest Series: Paper 3, 1995.

107. Godwin, M., Victim target networks as solvability factors in serial murder, *Social Behaviour and Personality: An International Journal*, 26, 75-84, 1998.

108. Canter, D., Offender Profiles, *The Psychologist*, 2:12-16, 1989.

109. Canter, D. and Larkin, P.,The Environmental range of serial rapists, *J. Environmental Psychology*, 13: 63-69, 1993.

110. Canter, D. and Gregory, A., Identifying the residential location of rapists, *JFSS*, 34: 169-175, 1994.

111. Rengert, G. F. and Wasilchick, J., *Suburban Burglary*, Springfield, IL: Charles C. Thomas, 1985.

112. Adams, J., *Directional bias in intra-urban migration*, Economic Geography, 45, 302-323, 1969.

113. Feldman, R. M., *Psychological bonds with types of settlements: looking back to the future*, IAPS 10 Proceedings 2:335-342, Delft: Delft University Press, 1988.

114. Reboussin, R., Warren, J., and Hazelwood, R., *Mapless mapping in analyzing the spatial distribution of serial rapes*, conference proceedings Workshop on Crime Analysis through Computer Mapping, Illinois Criminal Justice Information Authority, 1993.

115. Mercer, D., Discretionary travel behavior and the urban mental map, *Australian Geographical Studies* 9: 133-143, 1971.

116. Harries, K. D., *The geography of American crime and justice*, New York: McGraw-Hill, 1974.

Ethics in Profiling

7

7.1 The Role of Ethics in Criminal Profiling

LYNN BARKLEY BURNETT

Set forth hereunder are recommendations for the ethical conduct of behavioral profiling. No longer are profilers solely affiliated with law enforcement; rather their services may be retained by a wide variety of clients, including criminal defense counsels, members of the civil bar representing plaintiff or defendant, insurance companies, and the news media. Furthermore, as with the explosion aboard the USS Iowa, the murder of Jon-Benet Ramsey, and the crash of Egypt Air 990, profilers may be asked to offer an opinion as to whether a specific person fits the profile of someone who would engage in a particular criminal act, in addition to their traditional role of drafting a profile of an unknown subject. Thus, these recommendations are broadly written, a reflection of the multiple settings in which profilers may practice.

Integrity is one of several paths, it distinguishes itself from the others because it is the right path, and the only one upon which you will never get lost.

M.H. McKee

A recent headline in *The New York Times* proclaimed "America Flunks Civics."[1] Since civic virtue is served — or disserved — to the degree that decisions are made in a manner that makes central their moral significance,[2] such a headline has, unfortunately, the ring of truth. Indeed, in the period of history that saw actions by the highest elected official in the United States which were called "reprehensible" and "egregious" by members of his own political party, many of America's social institutions, in addition to the presidency, have also sustained damage. Evidence of such harm is all too easy to identify:

- Of biomedical researchers in the United States who were accused of scientific fraud and subjected to formal investigation, one-half were found to have committed misconduct.[3] Government-funded scientists who conducted research on behalf of the U.S. Public Health Service were guilty of falsification, fabrication, and plagiarism, according to

the report *Scientific Misconduct Investigations 1993-1997*, released by
the U.S. Office of Research Integrity.

• A report by the American Medical Association indicated that examples
abound of false and/or misleading testimony given by physicians in
legal proceedings, including the misquoting of standard journals and
texts, and deliberate omission of important facts and knowledge as it
pertained to the expert opinion that was offered.[4]

• A corruption of our legal system that "stain[s] our judicial system and
mock[s] the ideal of justice under law" is how The Supreme Court of
Appeals of West Virginia characterized the actions of State Trooper Fred
Zain.[5] The opinion of the court cited multiple findings of fact that Zain,
assigned to the Serology Section of the State Police Laboratory, had a
long history of falsifying evidence in criminal prosecutions, including
trials for murder. These acts of misconduct included overstating the
strength of results; overstating the frequency of genetic matches on
individual pieces of evidence; reporting the testing of multiple items,
when in fact only a single item had been tested; reporting inconclusive
results as conclusive; grouping results to create the erroneous impression that genetic markers had been obtained from all samples tested;
failing to report conflicting results; implying a match with a suspect,
when testing supported only a match with the victim; and reporting
scientifically impossible or improbable results. The opinion of the
Court also noted that these irregularities were "the result of systematic
practice rather than an occasional inadvertent error."[5]

Through each of these examples of unprofessional misconduct runs a
common thread — the absence of a moral foundation that guided the actions
of the professionals cited. Derived from the Latin *mores*, the word "moral"
means character.[6] Yet another term for character is the Greek word *ethos*,
from whence comes "ethics." Ethics deals with values, with good and bad,
and with right and wrong.[7] The failure to address ethics fosters the potential
for negative consequences, many of immense significance, as reflected above.

In this chapter, whose primary purpose is to educate criminal justice and
behavioral science professionals as to the state-of-the-art of criminal profiling, it is vital to recall "It may well be that the most significant quality in
educated persons is the informed judgment that enables them to make
informed moral choices.[8]" Thus, this chapter on ethics.

7.1.1 The Chapter in Context

Set forth hereunder are recommendations for the ethical conduct of behavioral profiling. No longer are profilers solely affiliated with law enforcement;
rather their services may be retained by a wide variety of clients including

criminal defense counsel, members of the civil bar representing plaintiff or defendant, insurance companies, and the news media. Furthermore, as with the explosion aboard the USS Iowa, the murder of Jon-Benet Ramsey, and the crash of EgyptAir 990, profilers may be asked to offer an opinion as to whether a specific person fits the profile of someone who would engage in a particular criminal act, in addition to their traditional role of drafting a profile of an unknown subject. Thus, these recommendations are broadly written as a reflection of the multiple settings in which profilers may practice.

The recommendations are based, in part, on statements concerning professional ethics published by several organizations. Many of these societies have a forensic orientation, and each is well-recognized for its standards of conduct. Reviewed were the codes of ethics of the American Medical Association,[9] the American Psychiatric Association,[10] the American Psychological Association,[11] the American Academy of Psychiatry and the Law,[12] the American Statistical Association,[13] and the American Academy of Forensic Sciences.[14]

7.1.2 Ethical Guidelines

7.1.2.1 *Integrity*

"If you don't have integrity, *nothing else* matters." Those words of former U.S. Senator Alan Simpson reflect the primacy of integrity, and set the framework for these guidelines on ethics. The profiler has an individual obligation to professional integrity, as well as a more general responsibility to promote integrity in the science and practice of profiling.[11]

The key element of integrity is truth-telling. One should deal honestly with clients, colleagues, and others.[9] When describing or reporting services, fees, findings, opinions, research, or teaching, the profiler should make no statements that are false, misleading, or deceptive.[11] The profiler's qualifications should be presented accurately and precisely,[12] without misrepresentation of education, training, experience or area of expertise.[14] Furthermore, expertise should be claimed only in areas of actual knowledge, skills, training and experience.[12]

When making professional judgments or when engaging in scholarly or professional endeavors, reliance should be placed on scientifically and professionally derived knowledge.[11] Assessments and evaluative statements, as well as reports, should be based on information that is sufficient to provide appropriate substantiation for the opinion. The profiler should refrain from providing any misrepresentation of the information (facts) upon which an expert opinion or conclusion is based.[12]

The profiler functions as an expert within the legal system. Thus, although s/he may be retained by one side in a criminal or civil matter, the profiler should adhere to the principle of honesty, and strive for objectivity in the evaluations performed and expert opinions rendered.[12] Contingency fees challenge honesty and objectivity, and should neither be requested nor accepted. Retainer fees are appropriate, as are fees for professional services rendered. When a report is generated; if the profiler speaks publicly, in an appropriate form and forum; or when testimony is offered; the identity of the ultimate financial sponsor of the evaluation performed should be disclosed, when such is not obvious.[13] A diligent effort should be made to avoid conflict of interest or the appearance thereof. Should any conflict exist, it should be disclosed, and a good faith effort should be made to resolve same.

Forensic opinions, forensic reports, and forensic testimony should be based on all of the relevant data that is available to the profiler,[12] with the sources and assessed adequacy of the data reported.[13] An exception to revealing the source of information would be a situation wherein doing so would place in jeopardy the life of an informant.

Statements should be made truthfully, honestly, and candidly.[11] Consistent with applicable legal procedures, the bases for testimony and conclusions should be fairly described. To avoid misleading testimony, any limitations on data or conclusions should be acknowledged; for example "including those due to the limits of scientific or professional knowledge, as well as those specific to a particular case."[15] Honesty, efforts to obtain objectivity, and the soundness of professional opinion are communicated when the profiler distinguishes verified versus unverified information, as well as between "facts," "inferences," "impressions," or "opinions."[12]

When the profiler's opinion is based on an idiosyncratic theory or interpretation of the literature, the expert must make clear the minority status of those views.[15] The failure to do so, deliberately or by neglect, would be misleading as to the *prima facie* weight that should be ascribed to the expert's opinion, and would be violative of the obligation of truthfulness.

7.1.3 Preventing the Misuse of Profiling

A corollary to integrity is preventing the inappropriate use of one's professional work. The scientific and professional judgments and actions of the profiler have great potential to affect the lives of others; one must therefore be alert to — and guard against — personal, financial, social, organizational, or political factors that might lead to misuse of his or her influence.[11]

The profiler should recognize limits to the certainty with which judgments or predictions can be made about individuals, and indicate any reservations about the accuracy or limitations of interpretations.[11] The profiler should not participate in activities in which it appears likely that his or her skills or opinions will be misused by others.[11] Furthermore, one should not become a participant in a case investigation unless there is a reasonable expectation that valid results may be achieved,[13] and confidence that the profiler's name will not be associated with a case or resulting publications without explicit consent.

Upon learning of the misuse or misrepresentation of one's work, the profiler should take reasonable steps to correct or minimize the misuse or misrepresentation.[13] In a like manner, any errors discovered after release of a publication should be promptly and publicly corrected.[13]

7.1.3.1 Competence

The profiler should strive to maintain high standards of competence.[11] The profiling professional should initially seek to develop a valid and reliable body of scientific knowledge concerning human behavior. In order to then maintain knowledge of relevant scientific and professional information, including developments within the discipline, profilers should be mindful that theirs must be a lifetime of learning.[10,11] As a professional, the individual profiler is responsible for his or her own continuing education.[10] Effort directed toward the advancement of scientific knowledge is also a desirable characteristic in a behavioral science professional.[9]

The profiler should recognize the boundaries of his or her own particular competencies and limitations of expertise, and provide only services for which s/he is qualified by education, training, or experience.[11] The profiler should obtain consultation and use the talent of other scientific, professional, technical, and administrative resources when indicated.[11] When engaged in services in areas in which recognized professional standards do not yet exist, careful judgment should be exercised and appropriate precautions should be taken to protect the welfare of those with whom the profiler may work.

7.1.4 Professionalism

The profiler has a social obligation to contribute to human welfare by the application of specialized knowledge in a professional, competent, and ethical manner. Professional activities should be conducted with responsible attention to: the social value of the work, and the consequences flowing from how well or poorly it is performed; the science of profiling, including the evolution of understanding, and acknowledgment that just as an established body of scientific knowledge exists, so do unresolved issues that deserve frank discussion; and finally, avoidance of any tendency to slant findings toward predetermined outcomes.[13]

The profiler is also a citizen. Good professional citizenship encourages: acceptance of responsibility for one's behavior;[11] fulfilling all commitments; collegiality and civility with other professionals, including respect for and acknowledgment of the intellectual property of others;[13] support for sound profiling science, especially when it is unfairly criticized; support for improved public understanding and respect for profiling; exposure of the dishonest or incompetent use of profiling; and service to one's profession, including participation in formal or informal ethics review panels.

7.1.5   Consent

When conducting an interview, there is a need to make clear for which side the profiler is working, and the limits on confidentiality of any such interview.[15] Furthermore, any person charged with a crime should not be contacted prior to access to, or the availability of, legal counsel;[10,12] nor without permission of the attorney, once the defendant has obtained representation.

7.1.6   Confidentiality

The profiler should not release confidential information pertaining to an ongoing criminal investigation. In the same fashion, the profiler should not disclose the trial strategy of one side when meeting with opposing counsel. When contacted by an attorney who may desire to retain the profiler, clarification should be made as to whether or not an initial screening conversation, prior to a formal agreement, will interdict consultation with the opposing side should the profiler not wish to accept the consultation.[12]

In rare instances, to protect an individual or the community, it may be necessary to disclose confidential information obtained from interviews.[10] Such unusual circumstances notwithstanding, private information [9] obtained during an investigation should not, within the constraints of the law, be released if the data did not contribute to the profiler's assessment. Privileged information of the employer or client should be guarded as well.[13]

7.1.7   Profiling and Society

Scientific tools and methods should only be employed for the social good of society.[13] The professionalism encouraged by these ethical guidelines is predicated on their use in socially responsible pursuits, in morally responsible societies, by responsible governments and employers. Valid findings are best achieved from competent work in a moral environment.[13] Employers, attorneys, clients, policy makers, journalists, and the public should be urged to expect that profiling will be conducted in an ethical fashion; in like manner, they have a responsibility to provide a moral environment that fosters the practice of professional ethics. It should be recognized that the opinion of a profiler cannot be guaranteed to conform to the expectations or desires of those who commissioned a study, and that any measures taken to insure a particular outcome, such as pressure on the profiling practitioner to deviate from ethical guidelines, markedly lessens the validity of the analysis and is likely to damage the professional credibility of the practitioner.

7.1.8   Preventing and Responding to Misconduct

In questionable situations, the profiler should seek the counsel of colleagues in order to prevent or avoid unethical behavior.[11] The profiler should also be concerned about the ethical compliance of his or her colleagues in their scientific and professional conduct, and may deem it necessary to obtain consultation to discuss concerns about possible ethical problems on the part of other professionals. The profiler should not condone, or appear to condone, careless, incompetent, or unethical practices, neither in his or her working environment nor elsewhere. All types of professional misconduct should be deplored, including plagiarism, professional dishonesty — by commission or omission, and unjustified detraction from the reputations of fellow professionals. One who regularly practices outside his or her area of professional competence should be considered unethical.[10] Thus, the profiler should ensure that those with whom s/he deals is a recognized member of his/her own profession, and is capable of carrying out any task(s) required. Whenever the profiler has significant doubts about the training, skill or ethical qualifications of other individuals, s/he should refrain from consulting, collaborating, or associating with them.[13] While the profiler should strive to expose those who are deficient in character or competence, or who engage in fraud or deception,[9] it should be kept in mind that differences of opinion and honest error do not constitute misconduct; they warrant discussion, not accusation.[13]

7.1.9 Conclusion

Consideration of these guidelines may assist the profiling practitioner in preventing misconduct, or the appearance thereof, in arriving at an ethical course of action when the appropriate decision is not obvious, and in communicating ethical decisions.[13] Of far greater importance than these guidelines, however, is a personal commitment on the part of the professional profiler to a lifelong effort to act ethically, and to encourage similar ethical behavior on the part of his or her colleagues.[11]

7.2 Ethics and Forensic Psychology

ANDREW DAY
PAUL WHETHAM

Our interest in ethical issues stems from our work as clinical psychologists with offenders in institutional settings. In the course of this work we encountered numerous situations where we saw potential conflicts of interest between our work with an individual client and our work as part of a correctional organization. At the same time, we had difficulty in locating resources to help us resolve ethical dilemmas as they arose. In this chapter, we hope to outline some of the areas of ethical practice that may affect the forensic psychologist and the psychologist who is called upon to do some forensic work. As a starting point to this work, we try to remember that our clients are already disadvantaged before any psychological assessment or treatment begins. That is, they are often in a vulnerable emotional state and lack adequate information about the treatment process, their legal situation, their rights, and the accountability mechanisms that govern our behavior. As practitioners we believe that we have a responsibility to improve all aspects of our practice so that our clients are not further disadvantaged and so that they can have confidence in the professional service they are receiving.

When the term "unethical behavior" is used we often think of gross violations of established standards. The truth is, however, that most ethical violations are subtle and can occur inadvertently. There are times when we are unaware that our behavior may adversely effect our clients. For example, a psychologist in a struggling private practice may extend the number of sessions with clients and justify his actions on theoretical, and not financial, grounds. In prisons we have encountered situations where prisoners are denied transfers on the grounds that they are currently consulting with a psychologist. Conversely, there may also be times in which we have intentionally violated these standards. In a national survey of American psychologists, the majority (57%) of respondents had intentionally violated the law or a similar formal standard because they believed not to do so would have injured the client or violated some deeper value. Further, one in ten participants reported having sex with a client using the same rationale.[16]

Ethical dilemmas are a particularly common feature of forensic work. Thomas-Peter and Howells describe a series of typical ethical challenges in just one week's work as a forensic psychologist in a mental health setting.[17] Forensic settings differ from other settings in which psychologists work in several respects. Perhaps the most significant difference relates to the adversarial nature of legal activity and the pressures on the psychologist to act as an advocate. Forensic clients are often unwilling participants in assessment and treatment, and are rightly concerned about the services they will receive, how information will be stored, and whether any reports and records will be shared. There may also be differences in how organizations manage issues such as consent and confidentiality, and how psychologists believe they should respond to clients. The forensic context thus dictates that ethical issues have to be particularly carefully considered by the forensic practitioner. In addition, the work of the forensic practitioner is likely to undergo a high level of public and judicial scrutiny.[17]

One of the greatest sources of confusion in forensic psychology is the apparent lack of consensus about the role of the forensic psychologist. Around the world there are now multiple models of training ranging from clinical psychology with forensic specialisms through to law-psychology.[18] Tomkins and Ogloff distinguished between law/psychology training and forensic psychology training. They argue that the former addresses the interface between law and psychology, whereas the latter "is a branch of clinical psychology which addresses criminal and civil clinical issues." This division is reflected in the development of graduate programs in law and psychology with two distinct streams.[19] These programs offer both a law and psychology stream offering training in research and applied policy skills, and a clinical-forensic stream preparing clinical psychologists with the skills required to provide clinical services in forensic areas.[19] At present there does not appear to be any generally accepted and well codified training model in forensic psychology.[20] However, there is "a developing consensus that the future of forensic psychology depends upon its ability to apply the scientist-practitioner model to psychological questions."[21]

One of the important ethical debates in forensic psychology concerns the role that the psychologist adopts when working with clients, whether therapeutic or evaluative. Most commentators now argue for a clear separation of the evaluative role from the therapeutic role.[22,23] Greenberg and Shuman argue that forensic evaluators, that is, those who prepare court reports, differ from those who work therapeutically in ten important ways.[24] Most importantly, evaluators work for the lawyer rather than the client, and confidentiality is between the lawyer and psychologist rather than the client and psychologist. Secondly, the tasks of the relationship differ — whereas therapists may be supportive, accepting, and empathic, the evaluator is required to be neutral, detached, and objective. Treatment techniques and diagnoses are for psycho-legal purposes rather than for the purpose of therapy. Self-report information from clients is more likely to be scrutinized and corroborated from other sources. In short, while a therapeutic role aims to develop a helping relationship that is rarely adversarial, the role of the forensic evaluator is to provide critical, unbiased opinion for the court.

A common area of confusion for practitioners with little experience of the courts is the distinction between "expert" witness and witness of fact. When a psychologist testifies factually about the nature of a contact with a client, s/he is adopting a different role than acting as an expert witness who provides opinions based on professional knowledge skill and techniques. In practice, it is suggested that treating practitioners should refrain from offering legal opinion (restricting themselves in legal settings to acting solely as witnesses of fact), and that practitioners who undertake evaluative roles for the courts should not subsequently make themselves available for therapeutic work.

For forensic practitioners to act ethically, they have to take a clear position which role they are adopting. For forensic evaluators, the client will be the court, for clinical-forensic practitioners, we see a major responsibility towards the client, within the limits set out later in this chapter. This distinction helps to clarify the nature of client-practitioner relationships and overcomes any criticisms of partisanship that may undermine professionalism.

In this chapter, we are particularly interested in ethical issues as they apply to those working in clinical-forensic roles within prisons or juvenile justice settings. Within this role, most professionals recognize that their primary accountability is to the person they are working with. We agree substantially with the view of Brandon who argues that "an important task for professionals is to help consumers (sic) gain more power and control, both over their lives, and over the running of the services."[25] Brandon raises the idea of practical citizenship involving consultation, information systems, and devolution of decision making.

These ideas, although credible in clinical mental health settings, have different connotations when applied to correctional settings. Ideas of giving offenders more responsibility for their lives, and being active participants in treatment have been seen as anathema by some (though not all) prison managers. The literature on prison management styles tends to emphasize models that see prisoners as passive recipients of services. For example, Dilulio outlines three managerial approaches in prisons that varied as to the degree of rigidity and control imposed on administrations.[26] The "control" model refers to a high degree of administrative control with an emphasis on formalized procedures.[26] At the other extreme, the "responsibility" model minimizes official control mechanisms and devolves more decision making to prisoners.[26] In between, Dilulio describes a "consensual" model that incorporates features of both other models.[26] Dilulio argues that many prisons tend to adopt control models of management, where prison staff tend to avoid rather than initiate contact with prisoners, who feel powerless and depersonalized.[26] This may be a feature of many institutional environments. Barrowclough and Fleming argue that institutional environments are strongly associated with the development of passivity and dependence, factors which are likely to result in difficulties in collaborative decision-making processes.[27]

A notable exception to this would be the small number of prison therapeutic communities, which have been shown to have positive effects on recidivism, particularly for drug using offenders.[28] Such communities work to establish a less institutional atmosphere and encourage participation in decision making.

Other initiatives include the introduction of unit management approaches designed to encourage responsibility and self-determination, where prisoner management is targeted to meet the individual needs of prisoners.[29] Case management similarly implies an individualistic approach to treatment, which contrasts with a focus on the application of universal laws enshrined in control models of management. It is the individual rather than organizational approach which is generally enshrined in law and professional codes of conduct.

Despite these exceptions, our experiences of prisons and juvenile justice settings in the Australia and the U.K., lead us to believe that organizations generally operate on hierarchical control models of management. Organizationally, we have encountered expectations that *all* information will be shared, with only restricted assurances of confidentiality and little emphasis on issues of consent. Working within such settings as a professional psychologist creates dilemmas of accountability — how can we manage the competing demands of accountability to the client, the profession, and the organization?

Laws and ethical codes are the two major mechanisms of professional accountability and have been developed to protect the individual client. Both of these offer the psychologist guidelines for ethical behavior. While they both use a different formulation of standards, there may be considerable overlap. It is often the case that the behavior of a psychologist may be unethical, yet not form the basis for a criminal charge.

Remley defines laws as the minimum standards society will tolerate. These standards are enforced by government.[30] By contrast, ethical codes are used to regulate, educate, and inspire practitioners, often represent the maximum or ideal standards set by the profession, and are enforced by professional associations, national association boards, and government boards that regulate professions. There are instances in which legal opinion may not coincide with a profession's ethical code.[31]

Most professional associations have ethics committees. Their main function is to educate their members about ethical codes and protect the public from unethical practice. Committee meetings are held regularly to process formal complaints lodged by clients against their members. When a complaint is made, the committee typically launches an investigation and deliberates on the case. A decision is reached over time which could include the complaint being dismissed, specific charges within the complaint may be dismissed, or ethical standards are found to be violated and sanctions imposed. Sanctions vary and include reprimand, suspension, or expulsion. Members also have the right of appeal.

While ethical codes are necessary for ensuring accountability, they have numerous shortcomings. Corey and his colleagues identified a number of problems which we can encounter in our efforts to be ethically responsible practitioners.[32] For example, some issues cannot be dealt with solely by relying on ethical codes; some codes are vague, lacking clarity and precision, making enforcement difficult. Codes are designed more for professions than the public; ethical codes tend to be reactive rather than proactive.

It has been argued that ethical codes are often inadequate in forensic mental health cases.[33] The bottom line is that ethical codes are static guidelines and cannot guarantee ethical behavior. Simply learning ethical codes will not prepare psychologists for ethical practice. Both the legal and ethical codes delineate some extreme areas of unacceptable behavior and uphold areas of desirable behavior. However, they cannot replace the active and often painstaking struggle that each of us must go through in arriving at ethical outcomes, mainly because each client's situation is unique and calls for a different response. As Ellis points out, what professional codes cannot give is precisely what many people would like them to give — moral guidance.[34]

7.2.1   Common Areas of Concern

When we consider which areas of practice psychologists might require guidance for, three general areas have been identified by Swenson.[35] These areas pose the highest risks of malpractice lawsuits for counselors. These are:

- violations of clients' personal rights (typically related to sex, privacy, or wrongful commitment)
- failure to protect others from clients (alleged in failure to warn, failure to commit, and wrongful release cases)
- incompetent treatment of clients (often alleged in suicide cases)

When we refer to codes of conduct from professional psychology societies and associations, we find that these areas are typically covered under general headings of confidentiality, duty to warn, consent, and competency.

7.2.2   Confidentiality

Most codes endorse the principle of confidentiality in psychologist-client relationships unless "there is an overriding legal or social obligation to do so."[36]
As a general principle, confidentiality should not be broken without the client's
consent "except in those unusual circumstances in which not to do so would
result in clear danger to the person or to others."[36] Confidentiality is a central
right of the client. When clients seek professional confidential help, that is
what they expect. The problem is, however, a promise of total confidentiality
by the psychologist is unrealistic, particularly in forensic settings. Authors such
as Ahia and Martin, and Herlihy and Corey have identified circumstances
when it is permissible (or required) to breach confidentiality:[37,38]

- when a client poses a danger to self or others
- when a client discloses an intention to commit a crime
- when the psychologist suspects abuse or neglect of a child, an elderly
  person, a resident of an institution, or a disabled adult
- when a court orders a psychologist to make records available.

Confidential information must be divulged under certain legal conditions; for example, if a client discloses s/he has committed a criminal offense,
or if the client is deemed to be a "clear danger" to either him/herself or others.
While these examples are relatively straightforward, there are many occasions
where the decision to keep or break confidentiality becomes a cloudy issue
for the practitioner. For instance, it is a necessary ethical and legal requirement to break confidentiality when it becomes clear that clients might do
serious harm to themselves or others. However, are all verbal threats by a
client to be immediately put into a report and sent to the appropriate authorities? What if the threat is not verbal but the psychologist has a strong hunch
that the client could be homicidal or suicidal? Ethical codes offer little specific
guidance by way of decision making in these situations (for example, what
constitutes a clear danger, or an over-riding social obligation).[33]

We have an ethical and legal responsibility to inform our clients at the
beginning of any professional relationship about the limits of confidentiality.
If we do not mention these limits, clients may reasonably assume that their
disclosures are strictly confidential. This is reflected in a study assessing the
public's general knowledge and beliefs about confidentiality in counseling.
The majority believed that everything discussed in counselling would be
strictly confidential (69%), and with no exceptions (74%). Interestingly, the
vast majority (96%) wanted more information about confidentiality.[39] The
words of Geldard are appropriate here: "When a client comes to you for
confidential help, you have an implied contract with her to give her that,
unless you tell her something otherwise."[40]

7.2.3   Duty to Warn

If a psychologist determines that a client poses a serious danger of violence to others, s/he is obliged to exercise reasonable care to protect the would-be victims. Costa and Altekruse argue that the duty to warn and to protect presents a major challenge to practitioners.[41] Generally, the duty to warn and to protect is indicated when these three conditions are present: a) a special relationship exists between client and therapist; b) a reasonable prediction of harmful conduct (based on a history of violent behavior) is made; and c) a potential victim can be identified. Monahan (1993) describes some guidelines for risk containment in duty to warn and protect cases.

Hess and Weiner give an example of the ethical conflict that may occur regarding confidentiality and duty to warn in the area of correctional sex offender group treatment.[42] While offenders are encouraged to disclose their information relevant to their offenses in detail as a part of their treatment, there is a risk of the psychologist violating the offender's privacy by reporting progress regarding parole decisions, and reporting high risk behavior. In such cases, it is paramount to discuss the limits of confidentiality prior to commencing treatment. As Hess and Weiner argue, "psychologists who ask for personal revelations without regard to such limits to confidentiality, or without regard to their inability to control the use of information by other group members, and who do not inform the member accordingly, are practicing unethically."[42]

7.2.4   Suicidal Clients

Just as we have an obligation to warn and protect others from dangerous clients, we also have a similar obligation to fulfill with clients who are a danger to themselves. Certainly not every mention of a suicidal thought or feeling justifies extraordinary measures such as hospitalization. Again, the key issue is knowing the signposts and using professional judgment to determine whether these are serious enough to report the condition. Rosenberg describes a model of assessing the suicidal client which includes the initial interview, assessment of depression and suicidal ideation, and identification of relevant risk factors and interventions.

7.2.5   Consent

The issue of consent is sometimes an area that highlights conflicts between professional ethics and the demands of an organization. This is sometimes the case for psychologists who work in institutional settings as part of a treatment team, and who as individuals have little power to affect organizational policy. Ethically, where conflicts with organizations exist, psychologists have a responsibility to take reasonable steps to resolve the conflict, including the ethics code requirement.

7.2.6   Competence

Forensic psychology is a specialized area. Psychological reports often play an important role in determining what happens to a client in the criminal and civil justice systems, whether through trial, sentencing, compensation, or release plans from prison. As a minimum, psychologists doing forensic work should have a reasonable degree of knowledge of the judicial system. Competence refers to practicing within one's own area of expertise and training. However, much of the work of the forensic psychologist relates to specific populations (e.g., sexual offenders, violent offenders, drug and alcohol related crime, child custody work) about which they should be informed. For example, it is difficult to make recommendations for sentencing for a sexual offender without being aware of the literature on the risk of re-offending.

7.2.7   Ethical Decision Making

In response to the ethical and moral issues that we are confronted with in our practice, we can draw on a variety of levels of moral wisdom or knowledge. Kitchener proposed four discrete levels of moral reasoning — personal intuition, ethical guidelines developed by professional organizations, ethical principles, and general theories of moral action.[43] When neither personal intuition nor ethical guidelines can provide a solution to our ethical or moral issue, we need to refer to more abstract principles or theories. These underpin and inform both our personal and professional codes.

The following five ethical principles form the basis of our ethical practice:[43]

- Autonomy refers to the fundamental western value, freedom of choice and action.
- Non-maleficence means that above all else we are to do no harm to clients, intentionally or unintentionally. We must avoid actions that seek to meet our own needs at the expense of clients.
- Beneficence refers to promoting human welfare.
- Justice means providing equal treatment to all people regardless of gender, age, race, disability, socio-economic status, religion, or sexual orientation.
- Fidelity refers to loyalty, reliability, and action in good faith.

General theories of moral philosophy can be called upon to resolve complex ethical problems. Mill's utilitarianism approach, for example, asks us to consider an ethical decision in light of the cost and benefits for every participant involved (e.g., the client, the client's family, other associated people, and the psychologist). Mill defined ethical behavior as that which brought about "the greatest good for the greatest number." Alternatively, Kant proposed that ethical decisions should be universal. In other words, if it is considered right to breach an ethical code in one case, it must be right to do so in all similar cases in the future.

7.2.8   Decision-Making Models

When faced with a situation where concerns are raised about the most appropriate course of ethical action, it is useful to refer to decision making models. While these usually follow a problem solving format, decision trees are valuable in that they highlight areas to consider, encourage reflection and consultation, and offer a logical pathway through decision making. Corey and his colleagues proposed a very practical model that is helpful in dealing with ethical dilemmas.[33] This model has eight stages, starting with a problem recognition stage, followed by consultation with relevant laws, professional codes and colleagues, before outlining a problem-solving method. It is important to note that the model should not be thought of as a straight linear or cognitive way of reaching a resolution on ethical matters. It allows for complex decision making involving feelings, values, and personal intuition. However, its aim is to provide useful steps that stimulate reflection and encourage discussion with your clients and colleagues, in the hope that it will help one to find the best solution.

7.2.8.1   Identify the Problem

In consultation with your client, gain as much information as you can in relation to the issue. Remember the first step is to recognize that a problem or dilemma exists, and identify its specific nature. Ethical issues are complex and defy simple solutions, so you will be challenged by the ambiguity.

7.2.8.2   Identify Potential Issues Involved

Having gathered all the necessary information, clarified critical issues, and discarded irrelevant ones, evaluate the rights, responsibilities, and welfare of everyone affected by the situation. Consider the five moral principles and apply them to the situation. It may help to prioritize these principles and think through ways in which they can support a resolution to the dilemma.

7.2.8.3   Review the Relevant Ethics Codes

Ask yourself whether the principles or standards of your professional organization offer a possible solution. Consider if these relevant codes are consistent with your own values and ethics. If you disagree with a particular part of the code, do you have a rationale to support your stance? You can also call the organization to clarify and seek guidance on any specific aspect of the code.

7.2.8.4　Know the Applicable Laws and Regulations

It is essential to keep up to date on relevant laws that apply to ethical dilemmas. This is especially critical in matters such as reporting abuse, confidentiality, record keeping, assessment, and grounds for malpractice. Also, be informed of the current rules and regulations of your workplace.

7.2.8.5　Obtain Consultation

At this point, it is generally helpful to consult with colleagues to obtain other perspectives on the problem. Do not limit yourself by consulting with those whom you know share a similar view to your own, as this is an important opportunity to test out your reasoning with people who differ. If there is a legal concern, seek legal advice. It is wise to document the nature of your consultation, including the suggestions of those you have consulted.

7.2.8.6　Consider Probable and Possible Courses of Action

Creatively brainstorm different courses of action, even unorthodox ones that may be useful. Remember, one alternative is that no course of action is required. As you think about the many possibilities for action, discuss these options with your client as well as with other professionals.

7.2.8.7　Enumerate the Consequences of Various Decisions

Consider the implications of each course of action for the client, for others who are related to the client, and for you as the counselor. Again, a discussion with your client about the consequences for him or her is most important. Use the five fundamental moral principles as a framework for evaluating the consequences of a given course of action.

7.2.8.8　Decide on What Appears to Be the Best Course of Action

To make the best possible decision, consider the information you have received from various sources. After you have made your decision, choose your course of action, then evaluate the outcomes and see if any further action is required. You may realize later that another action might have been more beneficial. However, this hindsight does not invalidate the decision you made based on the information you had at the time. To obtain the most accurate picture, involve your client in the process.

7.2.9　Malpractice Lawsuits

Finally, it is worth commenting on ways of preventing ethical problems from arising. While the above model offers guidance as to how to respond when faced with an ethical dilemma, it may also be possible to reduce the risks of ethical problems arising. Obviously, the greater awareness we have of ethical issues, the more likely we are to anticipate difficulties and be aware of appropriate courses of action. A four-step process to reduce unethical behavior and potential litigation has been highlighted by Calfee.[44] Calfee's risk management model includes:

- identify potential risk areas
- evaluate whether the risk area is serious enough to merit further attention
- employ preventative and risk control strategies at work
- review treatments periodically to ascertain their effectiveness

Clarifying expectations with clients about the assessment/treatment process is another simple safeguard against the risk of malpractice. Further, it is also good clinical practice, as well as educative and empowering for the client, to give out information at the outset of any professional relationship.

However, if you are faced with a malpractice law suit, some recommendations by Bennett and his colleagues are worth mentioning.[45] First, Bennett and his colleagues suggested to treat the lawsuit seriously, even if it represents a client's attempt to punish or control you. Do not attempt to resolve the matter with the client directly, because anything you do might be used against you in the litigation. Become familiar with your liability policy, including the limits of coverage and the procedures the company will use. If a client threatens to sue you or if you receive a subpoena notifying you of a lawsuit, contact your insurance company immediately. Never destroy or alter files or reports pertinent to the client's case. Promptly retain an attorney. In consultation with your attorney, prepare summaries of any pertinent events about the case that you can use. Do not discuss the case with anyone other than your attorney. Avoid making self-incriminating statements to the client or to his or her attorney.

Determine the nature of support available to you from professional associations to which you belong. Do not continue a professional relationship with a client who is bringing a suit against you.

7.2.10 Summary

To summarize, working within forensic settings raises many ethical issues for those engaged in counseling or clinical services. The philosophy and management of the organization are likely to be inconsistent with the professional models that we bring with us to the workplace. We see ethical codes as important and worthwhile in providing general guidance about what is reasonable and acceptable practice.

Codes identify areas such as confidentiality, informed consent, and competency that help alert the practitioner about when an ethical issue might arise. However, they offer little specific advice about how to resolve ethical dilemmas. In some ways, it would be unreasonable to expect them to. The problem is not that the codes are poorly written or ill-thought through, but that ethical behavior cannot be legislated for. For many decisions in clinical practice, psychologists rely upon their own sense of morality and duty to act in the interests of the client, where possible. In this chapter, we have described an ethical decision-making model which we believe is useful in resolving ethical dilemma. First, it requires that the psychologist identify precisely what the issue is, before advising reference to laws and codes. Then it suggests a consultation and problem solving process which allows scope for applying our own moral principles and identifying our own blind spots and weaknesses. Ultimately, we need to be clear and comfortable about how we work, and take responsibility for our decisions. We see this framework as a starting point for practicing ethical forensic psychology.

7.3 The Unexplored Ethics of Criminal Psychological Profiling

RICHARD N. KOCSIS
STEPHEN COLEMAN

Criminal psychological profiling is the investigative technique of analyzing crime behaviors for the construction of a descriptive template of the probable offender. The technique attracts enormous interest from its various portrayals in the media. However, the infamy of profiling has allowed the proliferation of the technique despite a surprising lack of examination of its actual utility and accuracy. Of equal significance has been the absolute absence of guidelines in the application of this technique in criminal investigations. This paper highlights ethical problems associated with the development and application of the technique, especially in regard to misuses of the technique, and the scientific basis of the technique.

Like any police investigative technique, criminal psychological profiling has advantages and disadvantages. It may be a legitimate tool for police to use in the same way that it is legitimate for police to use coercive force, deception, and surveillance. However, like these other techniques, it is not morally unproblematic, and it may be misused. Coercive force can lapse into brutality, deception into entrapment, surveillance into harassment. Criminal psychological profiling has its own special ethical problems, and if misused it can cause harm to individual members of society, and to society as a whole.

7.3.1 What is Criminal Psychological Profiling?

- A forensic technique which seeks to provide investigative agencies with specific information which will help focus attention on individuals with personality traits that parallel traits of other perpetrators who have committed similar other offenses.[46]
- The process of identifying personality traits, behavioral tendencies, and demographic variables of an offender based on characteristics of the crime.[47]

The primary purpose of criminal psychological profiling is to provide a descriptive template of the probable offender or offenders which will assist in solving the crime by focusing investigative resources in a particular direction. This is done by analyzing behavioral features of a crime, and from these compiling typical offender characteristics observed in similar previous crimes. Indeed, profiling can be viewed as a form of retro-classification. Other uses of criminal psychological profile information include search warrant and offender interview suggestions.

Some sexual murderers have been noted to exhibit a behavior known as souvenir collection, where items from the scene of the crime or from the victim are retained for sentimental value. Such material is frequently discarded in the common forms of homicide, and consequently such blatantly incriminating evidence has been overlooked in past police investigations of sexual murders. Profilers experienced in identifying such behavior patterns may alert police to the possibility of souvenir collection behavior, thus allowing such evidence to be discovered and brought before the court.

A criminal psychological profile will commonly predict such things as the offenders race, age, employment, religion, marital status, and education, and may also include psychological and behavioral characteristics likely to be displayed by the offender.

7.3.2   Misuses of the Criminal Psychological Profile

There are several ways in which a criminal psychological profile can be misused. Examining these misuses of the criminal psychological profile serves as a reminder that the limitations and proper uses of a technique must be fully understood if the technique is not to cause unintended harm. All of these misuses raise important ethical issues, since they will all cause harm to either an individual or the police service involved, and thus will cause harm to society in general. As far as criminal psychological profiling goes, the harm that may be caused is especially important, because up to this time it has not generally been recognized.

So what are the ways a criminal psychological profile can be misused? First, it can be assumed that a person is guilty because he fits the profile. This is an invalid assumption. Just because a person's fingerprints are found at the scene of a crime, this does not make them the offender; after all, the victim's fingerprints are also likely to be found at the crime scene. In the same way, just because a person fits the composed profile of the probable offender, this does not make him guilty of a crime. Many people may fit the profile, but they cannot all have committed the crime. Other evidence is required to establish a case against a guilty party.

Although not receiving the same level of publicity as profiling successes, examples of such mis-identifications abound. Richard Jewell, the private security guard who discovered a bomb during the 1996 Atlanta Olympics, was targeted for extensive investigation due to his congruence with a criminal psychological profile of the suspected bomber.[48,49] The profile of Jewell as the primary suspect of the investigation became public knowledge, and as a result of media persecution he was forced into seclusion for over 10 months. However, despite extensive and highly sophisticated forensic investigation, it was impossible to identify any physical evidence that could support any charges against Jewell.

Another example was in April 1989, when profiling techniques were employed in the investigation of an explosion aboard the U.S.S. Iowa.[50] The Iowa battleship's main gun turret exploded, killing several naval officers including seaman Clayton Hartwig. The profiling analysis of this explosion identified Hartwig as a saboteur who purposely caused the explosion, resulting in his own death and the murder of his colleagues. However, after extensive judicial appeals by Hartwig's family, indisputable forensic evidence was discovered that proved the explosion was purely accidental in origin, and that Clayton Hartwig was simply a hapless victim of mechanical failure along with the other individuals killed in this incident. Both of these cases clearly illustrate the harm that can be caused by the misuse of profiling by targeting innocent individuals for investigation without any corroborating evidence.[50]

Another way that a profile may be misused is assuming that a person is innocent because he does not fit the profile. The profile contains characteristics likely to apply to the offender, but not certain to apply to the offender. No one should ever be ruled out of suspicion simply because they do not fit the given profile.

Profiling is a limited technique and can only provide probable characteristics of an offender. This highlights yet another way in which a profile may be misused. There is a tendency for investigators to focus on particular aspects of the profile, rather than the profile as a whole. This may lead to suspects being ignored even though they fit most aspects of the profile, if they do not fit one or two particular characteristics.

An example to highlight both of these shortcomings was the investigation into the 1989 Mosman "Granny Killer" on Sydney's north shore.[51] In this murder case, a criminal psychological profile was created that was accurate in most aspects except for two pivotal features of age and race. The profile directed police investigations to the pursuit of an adolescent and possibly African American offender. For a period of time, the focus of the investigation was upon possible adolescent offenders to the exclusion of other possibilities. After exhausting this avenue, a tangential investigation of petty sexual assaults in the same area accidentally identified "Granny Killer" John Glover, who was a 57 year old pie salesman of rigid Anglo Saxon heritage.

A profile can also be misused if the profiler gives evidence in court. As previously mentioned, a person cannot be assumed guilty simply because he fits the profile. If a suspect is brought before the court, it would be wrong for a profiler to suggest in evidence that a particular person is likely to be the guilty party simply because they fit the profile well.

An example of this situation is the case of T. Cullen Davis.[52] On the night of August 2, 1976, a gunman dressed in black entered the mansion owned by Davis and shot four people, killing the new boyfriend of Davis' ex-wife and the boyfriend's daughter, and seriously wounding Davis' ex-wife and another person.[52] Davis quickly became the prime suspect. He was charged with the killings, but was acquitted. In a later civil case, a retired FBI profiler, who had created a criminal psychological profile of the offender, compared this profile with two psychological evaluations of Davis that were made in the months following the killings. This profiler testified under oath that the evaluations "fit the psychological profile to a 'T.'"[52] As we have already pointed out, that just because a person fits the profile, this does not mean that he is the guilty party. In any event, no criminal psychological profile will be of sufficient detail to allow one to make the assertions that were made in this case.

Another problem for criminal psychological profiling may arise when someone fits a profile well and there is also some circumstantial evidence against that person. In their zeal to bring the presumed offender to justice, investigators may well misuse other police powers, particularly if the profiler, inexperienced in law, is heavily involved in the investigation. An example of such a circumstance occurred in the Rachel Nickell investigations in the United Kingdom.[53] Here, having exhausted all other avenues, the police investigators undertook a covert operation to gather evidence on a suspect who matched the criminal psychological profile. A highly extensive and elaborate ruse operation began in which an attractive female undercover officer initiated an eight month long liaison with the suspect, Colin Stagg.

This constable, acting under the advice of the psychologist who drew up the profile of Rachel Nickell's killer, attempted to elicit a confession from Stagg by sharing violent sexual fantasies with him, "confessing" to the sexual murder of a baby, and even telling him that she wanted a man like the killer of Rachel Nickell.[53] The operation failed to elicit a confession of the murder from Stagg, but after reading the masses of letters and transcribed conversations obtained through the operation, the profiling psychologist concluded that Stagg possessed knowledge only available to the killer. This led police to arrest Stagg and charge him with the murder. Upon review of the case, the presiding judge ruled that the vast majority of circumstantial evidence brought against Stagg was inadmissible in court, and that the conduct of the police operation was a "blatant attempt to incriminate a suspect by positive and deceptive conduct of the grossest kind."

Another potential danger of the misuse of the criminal psychological profile may arise if too much weight is placed on profiling information. An inaccurate profile may mean that a suspect is not apprehended as quickly as he might be. A particular person (who happens to be guilty) may be high on the police suspect list for a particular crime, but is not investigated because he does not fit the inaccurate profile that has been developed. This could, of course, mean serious harm to the community, which might have been avoided had a profiler not been consulted.

All of the above problems show the need for all involved in the use of profiles, the profilers themselves and the investigators who consult them, to be aware of the limitations of the technique. Failure to consider carefully whether criminal psychological profiling is appropriate and justified can cause great harm to individuals and to the community as a whole. The technique needs to be fully understood, and only used appropriately and in an ethical manner.

It is this point that gives rise to the most serious problem with the technique of profiling, for while the technique is widely used in many countries, its scientific basis is still practically nonexistent. If a technique has a poor basis in science, it would appear at the very least to be irresponsible, and more likely unethical, to continue to use the technique until it has been properly scientifically verified. Without this verification, one risks inadvertently causing harm to individuals and to society. The technique may be unreliable, biased, or even fundamentally flawed.

7.3.3 Scientific Basis for Profiling

Most people's knowledge of criminal psychological profiling comes from a couple of movies, a few television series, and maybe a popular press book or two. The frightening part is that, apart from a handful of academic articles, this is almost all the literature available to the average profiler as well.

The usual basis for any form of scientific discipline is a body of work published in peer-reviewed journals. New ideas and techniques are continually being published and undergo rigorous testing and assessment by peers. In the area of criminal psychological profiling, such work is in its infancy. There is no peer-reviewed journal dedicated to any form of profiling, few profilers undertake any original quantitative research, and most of the little research that is done can seldom be described as independent. For example, a recent issue of the *Journal of Contemporary Criminal Justice* (an academic, peer-reviewed journal) was entirely dedicated to the topic of criminal psychological profiling; however, it did not contain a single article reporting the results of an original quantitative study.[54] There is also no criteria as to qualifications or experience necessary to become a profiler, and generally it is simply assumed that those who call themselves profilers are better at determining the characteristics of a particular criminal than any other member of society would be.

At this point in time, the public perceptions produced by the fame of profiling grossly exceed the real scientific capabilities of the discipline.

7.3.4 What Sort of Scientific Basis is There?

When offender profiling was investigated in the U.K. by a subcommittee of the Association of Chief Police Officers, the committee created a guideline policy for use by U.K. police services. This policy was based on a number of key principles, which were described as "Articles of Faith" and "Articles of Purpose." The first of the articles of faith was that offender profiling be considered essentially viable, even though it must be understood that it has not yet been properly scientifically validated.[55] This is a somewhat frightening concept. An investigative technique is being accepted as viable, as a matter of faith, even though it is acknowledged that it has not yet been scientifically validated. The second article of faith hints at one of the main reasons the technique has not yet been scientifically validated, that offender profiling should be "owned" by the police service.[55]

By insisting on ownership of the technique of profiling, the police service is effectively locking highly qualified researchers out of the process, thus perpetuating the problem of scientifically verifying the technique. This "ownership" idea, with its associated ideas of secrecy and "need to know" is a particular problem for the technique of criminal psychological profiling. It is a clearly understood principle of military operations that the "need to know" principle has to be carefully examined in any operation, otherwise one stands a good chance of excluding from the operation those who possess information vital to its success. It must be recognized that very few police personnel have the requisite expertise and qualifications to conduct the type of empirical research that is needed for profiling to attain the necessary scientific verification. By excluding expert researchers such as behavioral scientists, police are eliminating the precise qualifications that are specifically needed for profiling's scientific development.

The common rationale for this exclusion of the scientific community has been that normal scientific methods such as the publication of articles in publicly available peer-reviewed journals would inadvertently educate potential offenders on how to evade apprehension.[56]

We must recognize the irrationality of this claim, given the low level of readership of most scientific journals in any discipline, even among skilled academics. This, coupled with the fact that the majority of serial sexual offenders seldom hold any standard of tertiary education,[57] makes it extremely unlikely that these types of people would troll university libraries to obtain these materials. Furthermore, we must realistically consider what their useful level of comprehension of such highly technical literature would be.

While it is conceivable that this could be a consequence of allowing normal scientific research in this area, the risks must be balanced against the gains. There are numerous potential gains for the integration of scientific rigor into profiling. The most obvious is attainment of scientific credibility. Stemming directly from this is the issue of reliability of the technique. That is, how accurate are the predictions of profiling? This is an obvious question, yet the answer to this fundamental question seems to be so elusive.

Currently, claims of profiling accuracy are limited and not well substantiated. The most commonly quoted statistic in this area is the claim of the U.S. FBI Behavioral Science Unit, which claims 80% accuracy in predictions.[58,59] However, documentation which conclusively demonstrates how this figure was obtained is not available in the public domain. This circumstance obviously detracts from the claim's credibility. Beyond this statistic, no other material appears to be available citing what degree of accuracy profiling has actually achieved.

What has been undertaken as a poor substitute for this obvious question of accuracy are studies gaging the degree of satisfaction police investigators derive from consulting with a profiler, irrespective of what actual benefits the profile may contribute to the investigation of a crime. For example, a study on offender profiling conducted by the English Metropolitan Police entitled *Coals to Newcastle* completely skirted the issue of how accurate profiles were once the offender was apprehended.[60] Instead, the study extensively discussed the amount of personal satisfaction investigating officers obtained from profile information irrespective of its actual utility or accuracy in their investigation.

While there appear to be no available empirical studies on the exact accuracy ratio of profiling predictions, there have been some studies that have examined whether profilers can out-perform other individuals in making accurate predictions. The first study of this kind was undertaken by Pinizzotto and Finkel,[61] and the second by Kocsis and colleagues, which can be found in Section 2 of this book.

In the Pinizzotto and Finkel study, a solved homicide and a solved rape case were submitted to a group of profilers, detectives, psychologists, and university students. The results of this study demonstrated that profilers outperformed the other groups in the rape case but not the homicide. However, a critical point of this finding was that the profilers produced more extensive reports. By providing more extensive reports, which included more predictions, profilers were skewing the results of the study somewhat, since providing more verifiable predictions increased the profilers probability of making accurate predictions. The percentage of confirmable predictions that were accurate was similar for all groups.

Going beyond the results of the study, we must critically consider the various methodological issues in this study. A key point is the statistical power of the samples utilized. Most significant is the extremely small sample size, six participants in each group. Consequently, the statistical power of the conclusions drawn from this study must be extremely limited. Beyond methodology, and focusing on the purpose of the study, we must consider the circumstances under which the study was undertaken. Principally it was not undertaken by an independent body, but rather by individuals with a vested interest in the result. The problems of a scientific technique being "verified" by those with a significant career investment in the result can be illustrated by reference to another scientific development, that of voiceprint identification.

In the early 1970s, a scientist by the name of Lawrence Kersta wrote and published several articles about a technique he called "voiceprint identification," which utilized a sound spectrograph that had been specially adapted to identify individuals by their speech. When Kersta first published these results, he did not make public the exact technique that he had used, and no one was in a position to challenge his claims.

Then, as now, the usual standard for a technique to be accepted in court as scientific evidence is that the technique has achieved general acceptance in that particular field of scientific endeavour, as described in Frye v. United States.[62] When voiceprint identification was first presented to a court of law, the court held that the technique had not, at that time, attained the necessary degree of scientific acceptance and reliability to be admissible in court. Two years later, after Kersta had published more articles that confirmed his earlier results and had also trained several other "experts" to use the technique, voiceprint identification was accepted in the Minnesota high court as scientific evidence.[63]

The rationale for this decision was that additional testing and research had now been done, and the technique appeared to be "extremely reliable." The Massachusetts Supreme Judicial Court also accepted voiceprint identification as scientific evidence, since the principle appeared to be generally accepted by those who would be expected to be familiar with its use.[64] Apparently this court failed to realize that the only people who could be expected to be familiar with the use of voiceprint identification were those who had been personally trained by Kersta. However, five years later, the California Supreme Court rejected voiceprint identification, and ruled that:[63]

> It had not been shown that the test had received general acceptance in the scientific community, but only among that limited group of individuals, most of whom were connected with a law enforcement agency, whose professional careers depended entirely upon acceptance of the reliability of the technique.

The Michigan Supreme Court concurred with this decision, stating that:[63]

> General scientific recognition may not be established without the testimony
> of disinterested and impartial experts, disinterested scientists whose liveli-
> hood was not intimately connected with the new technique.

These two rulings clearly point out the problem of a technique being
"verified" by those who stand to gain from general acceptance of that technique. If the technique of criminal psychological profiling is to achieve general scientific acceptance, then it must be properly scientifically verified by
disinterested and impartial experts. This will not and can not happen while
the technique is "owned" by the police service.

The research undertaken by Kocsis and colleagues in Section 2 is of
particular interest because the primary researchers (being full time university
academics with no financial stake in the success of profiling) can claim to be
disinterested and impartial experts. Briefly, this study involved groups of
profilers, detectives, psychologists, science students, and psychics.

In the study, a solved homicide was presented which requested a profile
of the offender, based on a multiple choice questionnaire. Using this procedure, the results of this study were not prone to any subjective claim of
accuracy. The overall result showed that profilers did outperform all other
non-profiler groups. However, of more interest were the comparisons
between the group of profilers, the group of psychologists, etc. In these
results, although profilers demonstrated a trend of the highest accuracy, the
next most accurate group were psychologists, followed by university students,
then police detectives, and finally psychics. Although this result offers tentative support for the validity of the process of profiling, it does not support
a commonly reported requisite of profiler expertise, that experience as a
police officer is a quintessential element for profiling. The study gave a
contrary result, that possibly the most important factor in profiling expertise
is knowledge of the discipline of psychology, or just some form of tertiary
education. This certainly suggests that the current trend of only employing
detectives as profilers should be resisted.

Another incidental and surprising finding from the study was the participation rate of self-professed professional profilers. Despite all assurances of
confidentiality, and the offer of payment of a consultation fee, out of a subject
invitation pool of over sixty profilers, only five suitable profilers chose to
participate in the study. This raises a critical issue of the professional credibility
of such individuals, who will not consent to any independent scrutiny.

Another key point of the study is its various methodological strengths.
Foremost among these were the quantitatively sufficient sample sizes, to make
empirically valid conclusions between the groups (with the limitation of the

profiler group). Furthermore, as already highlighted, the use of an objective questionnaire in a quasi-experimental condition allows true insight into the various skills which are purported to occur in the profiling process.

The result of the study strongly highlights the problematic and counter-productive circumstance in which profiling is currently found. With police ownership of the technique and the data, the expansion of profiling into some tertiary context, perhaps with a focus in the discipline of psychology, cannot occur. The Kocsis study suggested that it is knowledge, not experience, that allows one to make accurate predictions about an offender. Police ownership of profiling and the need to know principle have been applied to exclude those with this knowledge. The common practice of only allowing police to access data that relates to profiling has meant that professional researchers, with the skills and expertise to improve the technique, have been excluded from the discipline, to the detriment of the discipline specifically, and serious crime investigation as a whole.

More problematically, this ownership means that the technique is unable to be properly verified, and if it were to be verified somehow, it would be unlikely to improve. Once again, this leads to a host of ethical problems. Is it ethical to continue to use an unverified technique? And to continue to use that technique for so long without verification? What if the technique turns out to be flawed in some way, or consistently biased against certain groups? Then what harm might the technique have already caused?

Now that we have discussed the problems with the development of profiling, we need to consider the limitations of the technique in its actual application. A surprising flaw which constantly re-emerges in various contexts of profiling is the substantial generalization of the technique beyond the areas for which it was originally developed. One of the few empirical studies in profiling was in proposition of the FBI's organized/disorganized behavior dichotomy.[57,64] Here, a select sample of U.S. sexual murderers was studied. The result of the analysis was the proposition that future sexual homicide crimes could be interpreted and profiled based on the level of behavioral sophistication demonstrated at the crime scene. The measure of sophistication allowed the categorization of the offense behavior into either an organized, methodical pattern, or a disorganized, haphazard pattern.

This study was undertaken virtually two decades ago and has only recently received a replication study attesting to its validity. In this study undertaken by Kocsis, Irwin, and Hayes, support could be found for the general concept of interpreting crime by its general level of sophistication.[65] However, the valid application of this principle via a simple dichotomous categorization could not be supported. In cavalier ignorance to the untested validity of this principle, profilers for the past two decades have utilized this dichotomy for profiling predictions, and continue to do so today, even after the Kocsis study. Furthermore, the FBI's one concept, taken from a small sample of a select subgroup of offenders, has been generalized to all manner of crimes beyond those which it was originally hypothesized upon. For example, today we see applications of the organized/disorganized dichotomy in cases of burglary,[67] yet there are few similarities between a crime of criminal enterprise and the sexual murders upon which the dichotomy was originally based. Another example of this gross generalization of profiling is its application between nations in which it was not originally developed.

Profiling as a technique is highly dependent on the demographics of the country, and even the domestic localities, where a crime occurs. A key example of this was the previously mentioned "Granny Killer" investigation. A profile was developed based on research undertaken within North America.[51] In accordance with this, the profile predicted demographic features which were highly implausible in the Australian context.

Other studies have shown that while some features of crime are similar between countries, environmental and demographic factors may in some cases make it inappropriate to transfer techniques and procedures directly between countries. For example, the application of geographical profiling techniques in the Australian context have shown that while viable, they require substantial adaptation to operate within the varying demographic and geographic features of the Australian nation.[67] Profilers must take such features into account when transferring techniques between countries, and should not use techniques in other countries and regions until their validity in those areas has been demonstrated. To simply assume that profiling techniques will directly transfer between countries would be unprofessional and unethical in the extreme.

7.3.5 Ethical Uses of Criminal Psychological Profiles

Criminal psychological profiling appears promising as an investigative tool in certain types of crimes. However, as with any investigative or scientific technique, all those involved in using the technique need to be aware of its capabilities and limitations. In this respect, criminal psychological profiling can be compared to fingerprinting. All police and other investigators need to have some basic knowledge of fingerprinting. Those who continually investigate crimes in which fingerprints are an important piece of evidence need to have a better understanding of how the technique is used, and its limitations. Those who actually take fingerprints need an even better understanding, and those who analyze them need to be experts in the technique, understanding how it can and cannot be used, and all its limitations. In a similar vein, all those investigating crime should have a rudimentary understanding of criminal psychological profiling. Those who investigate crimes in which these profiling techniques are likely to be used need to have a better understanding of the technique, especially in regard to its limitations. Those who actually create criminal psychological profiles need to be experts, with a full understanding of how the techniques work, their foibles, and especially their limitations.

Unfortunately, it would appear that many people are calling themselves profilers without being experts of any sort. The studies of Pinizzotto and Finkel, and Kocsis et al. do not agree on what the most important qualifications for profiling are, but they both suggest that profilers are holders of specialized knowledge. This would suggest that those who seek to be recognized as profilers need to have some extensive knowledge of human criminal behavior and expertise in the application of profiling techniques.

Given the potential harm to others, as evidenced by the cases we have mentioned (the Jewell, Hartwig, and Davis cases), to claim expertise in the area of profiling due to some qualification obtained in a short course would be extremely dangerous and of highly dubious morality. Such courses may educate someone about the process of profiling, but will not make them an expert profiler, in the same way that a short course on fingerprinting would not make someone a fingerprint expert.

Criminal psychological profiling clearly has its limitations. Its validity has not been proven in analyzing many types of crime, and it would be unprofessional and unethical to attempt to use these techniques to profile offenders in crimes for which the technique has not been validated. Many of the problems that we have discussed arise from the use of these technique for analyzing crimes that have absolutely no connection with the types of crimes the techniques were developed from. For example, the Richard Jewell and Iowa cases involved bombings, for which profiling techniques certainly have not been empirically validated.

Some uses of the technique will be clearly unethical, for example, the investigative suggestions that were made in the Rachel Nickell case. If something would be unethical without the involvement of a profiler, adding the profiler will not change the ethics of the situation. So when is it ethical and appropriate to use criminal psychological profiling in an investigation? When all other conventional avenues of inquiry have been exhausted, criminal psychological profiling may be used to augment the inquiries. It should not be the primary coordinating element of the investigation, but should rather be used as a management tool for the effective allocation of investigative resources. It should only be used for crimes for which its use has been validated, and where these validation studies have made recognition of the individual geographic and demographic factors of the region in which the crime has been committed. Clearly profiling's most beneficial role, and most ethical use, is in the domain of the limited scientific research that has been undertaken — the area of aberrant violent sexual crime, which is not easily solved by conventional police methods.

Any technique used by law enforcement agencies has the potential to be both beneficial and harmful. A technique may be harmful if it is misused, if it is used inappropriately, or if the limitations of the technique are not fully understood. Criminal psychological profiling has clearly caused harm in all three of these ways, and will continue to cause harm until it is fully investigated, improved and refined, and clear guidelines are laid out for its use.

References

1. Wolfe A., America flunks civics, *The New York Times*, December 25, 1998.

2. Pratte, R., *The civic imperative: examining the need for civic education*, Teachers College Press, New York, 16, 1988.

3. Pownall, M., Falsifying data is main problem in U.S. research fraud review, *Western Journal of Medicine*, 170:377, 1999.

4. Expert witness testimony, Report of the Board of Trustees 5-A-98, *American Medical Association*, http://www.ama-assn.org/meetings/public/annual98/reports/bot/bot05.htm, 1998.

5. In the Matter of an Investigation of the West Virginia State Police Crime Laboratory, Serology Division, *The Supreme Court of Appeals of West Virginia*, 190 W. Va 321, 438 S.E.2d 501 (1993), http://www.state.wv.us/wvsca/DOCS/FALL93/21973.htm, 1993.

6. Fletcher, J. C., Miller, F. G., Spencer, E. M., Clinical ethics: history, content, and resources, *Introduction to Clinical Ethics*, Fletcher, J. C., Hite, C. A., Lombardo, P. A., Marshall, M. F., Eds., University Publishing Group, Inc., Frederick, Maryland, 6, 1995.

7. Singer, P., *Introduction: A Companion to Ethics*, Blackwell Publishers Ltd., Oxford, v, 1993.

8. Rosovsky, H., *The University: An Owner's Manual*, Norton, New York, 107, 1990.

9. Principles of Medical Ethics, *American Medical Association*, http://www.ama-assn.org/ethic/pome.htm, 1996.

10. The principles of medical ethics with annotations especially applicable to psychiatry, *American Psychiatric Association*, http://www.psych.org/apa_members/ethics_index.html, 1998.

11. Ethical principles of psychologists and code of conduct, *American Psychological Association*, http://www.apa.org/ethics/code.html, 1992.

12. Ethical guidelines for the practice of forensic psychiatry, *American Academy of Psychiatry and the Law*, http://www.cc.emory.edu/AAPL/ethics.htm, 1995.

13. Ethical guidelines for statistical practice, *American Statistical Association*, http://www.amstat.org/profession/ethicalstatistics.html, 1999.

14. Code of ethics and conduct, *American Academy of Forensic Sciences*, http://www.aafs.org/AAFSBylaws.htm, 1998.

15. Forensic psychiatrists need unique ethics rules, *Psychiatric News*, http://www.appi.org/pnews/nov15/forensic.html, 1996.

16. Pope, K. S. and Bajt, T. R.,When laws and values conflict: a dilemma for psychologists, *American Psychologist*, 43:828, 1988.

17. Thomas-Peter, B. and Howells, K., Professional and ethical challenges of forensic clinical psychology, *Psychiatry, Psychology and Law*, 3:63-70, 1996.

18. Tomkins, A. J. and Ogloff, J. R., Training and career options in psychology and law, *Behavioral Sciences and the Law*, 8: 205-216, 1990.

19. Ogloff, J. R. P., Graduate training in law and psychology at Simon Fraser University, *Professional Psychology: Research and Practice*, 30(1), 99-103, 1999.

20. Freeman, L. M. and Roesch, R., Psycholegal education: training for forum and function, in D. K. Kagehiro and W. S. Laufer, Eds., *Handbook of Psychology and Law*, pp. 567-576. New York: Springer-Verlag, 1992.

21. Bersoff, D. N., *Ethical Conflicts in Psychology*, American Psychological Association, Washington D.C., 1997.

22. Hess, A. K. and Weiner, I. B., Eds., *The Handbook of Forensic Psychology 2nd Ed.*, New York: John Wiley & Sons, 1999.

23. Strasburger, L. H., Gutheil, T. G., and Brodsky, A., On wearing two hats: role conflict in serving as both psychotherapist and expert witness, *American Journal of Psychiatry*, 15, 448-456, 1997.

24. Greenberg, S. A. and Shuman, D. W., Irreconcilable conflict between therapeutic and forensic roles, *Professional Psychology: Research and Practice*, 28(1), 50-57, 1997.

25. Brandon, D., User power, in Barker, P. J. and Baldwin, S., Eds., *Ethical Issues in Mental Health*, pp. 3-12 London: Stanley Thornes, 1997.

26. Dilulio, J. J., *Governing Prisons*, New York: Free Press, 1987.

27. Barrowclough, C. and Fleming, I., Ethical issues in working with older people, in Barker, P. J. and Baldwin, S., Eds., *Ethical Issues in Mental Health*, pp. 68-81 London: Stanley Thornes, 1997.

28. Cullen, E., Jones, L., and Woodward, R., *Therapeutic Communities for Offenders*, Chichester: Wiley, 1997.

29. Harmsworth, P., (1993) Managing Violent Offenders in the Correctional Setting: A Coordinated Approach, in Gerull, S.A. and Lucas, W., Eds., *Serious Violent Offenders: Sentencing, Psychiatry and Law Reform*, Canberra: Australian Institute of Criminology, ACT, 1993.

30. Remley, T. P., Consultation contracts, *Journal of Counseling and Development*, 72: 157-158, 1993.

31. Greenberg, S. A. and Shuman, D. W., Irreconcilable conflict between therapeutic and forensic roles, *Professional Psychology: Research and Practice*, 28(1), 50-57, 1997.

32. Corey, G., Corey, M. S., and Callanan S., *Issues and ethics in the helping professions*, 5th ed., California: Brooks and Cole, 1998.

33. Thomas-Peter, B. and Howells, K., Professional and ethical challenges of forensic clinical psychology, *Psychiatry, Psychology and Law,* 3, 63-70, 1996.

34. Ellis, T., The nature of morality, in Barker, P.J. and Baldwin, S., Eds., *Ethical Issues in Mental Health,* London: Stanley Thornes, 13-26, 1997.

35. Swenson, L. C., *Psychology and Law for the Helping Professions,* Pacific Grove, CA: Brooks and Cole, 1997.

36. APS, *Code of ethics,* Melbourne: Australian Psychological Society, 1986.

37. Ahia, C. E. and Martin, D., *The Danger-to-Self-or-Others Exception to Confidentiality,* Alexandria, VA: American Counseling Association, 1993.

38. Herlihy, B. and Corey, G., *Boundary Issues in Counseling: Multiple Roles and Responsibilities,* Alexandria, VA: American Counseling Association, 1997.

39. Miller, D. J. and Thelen, M. H., Knowledge and beliefs about confidentiality in psychotherapy, *Professional Psychology: Research and Practice,* 17:15-19, 1986.

40. Geldard, D., *Basic Personal Counseling: A Training Manual for Counselors,* 3rd ed., Sydney: Prentice-Hall, 1998.

41. Costa, L. and Altekruse, M., Duty to warn guidelines for mental health counselors, *Journal of Counseling and Development,* 72(4), 346-350, 1994.

42. Hess, A. K. and Weiner, I. B., Eds., *The Handbook of Forensic Psychology,* 2nd ed., New York: John Wiley & Sons, 1999.

43. Kitchener, K. S., There is no more to ethics than principles, *The Counseling Psychologist,* 24: 92-97, 1996.

44. Calfee, B. E., Lawsuit prevention techniques, in *The Hatherleigh Guide to Ethics in Therapy,* New York: Hatherleigh Press, 1997.

45. Bennet, B. E., Bryant, B. K., VandenBos, G. R., and Greenwood, A., *Professional Liability and Risk Management,* Washington, DC: American Psychological Association, 1990.

46. Geberth, V. J., *Practical Homicide Investigation,* 3rd ed., New York: Elsevier, 1996.

47. Bartol, C. R. and Bartol, A. M., *Psychology and Law,* Pacific Grove, CA: Brooks and Cole, 1994.

48. CNN, *Olympic Bomb Chronology,* 10/26/96.

49. CNN, *Richard Jewell Faces Cloudy Future,* 7/7/97.

50. Jeffers, H. P., *Profiles in Evil,* London: Warner, 1992.

51. Simpson, L. and Harvey, S., *The Killer Next Door,* Sydney: Random House, 1994.

52. *The Dallas Morning News,* Ex-FBI agent testifies Davis fits mental profile of slayer, 1987, June 6.

53. Crace, J., Inside the criminal mind, *The New Statesman and Society,* (1995, 17 December), pp. 29-30.

54. Holmes, R. M., Ed., Psychological Profiling, (Special Issue), *Journal of Contemporary Criminal Justice,* 15, 1999.

55. Copson, G. and Marshall, N., Mind over matter, *Police Review*, 16-17, June, 1999.

56. Stevens, J., Profiling criminals, *Police Review*, 22-23, August, 1996.

57. Ressler, R., Burgess, A., and Douglas, J., *Sexual Homicide: Patterns and Motives*, Washington: Lexington, 1988.

58. Ressler, R. and Shachtman, T., *Whoever Fights Monsters*, London: Simon & Schuster, 1992.

59. Pinizzotto, A. J., Forensic psychology: criminal personality profiling, *Journal of Police Science and Administration*, 12: 32-40, 1984.

60. Copson, G., *Coals to Newcastle, Part 1*, British Home Office Police Dept: Internal Report, 1990.

61. Pinizzotto, A. J. and Finkel, N. J., Criminal personality profiling: an outcome and process study, *Law and Human Behavior*, 14:215-233, 1984.

62. Frye v. United States, 293 Fed. 1013, 1923.

63. Thomas, O., *Applied Epistemology: How Courts Should Define Scientific Knowledge*, paper presented at Australian Association of Philosophy conference, Melbourne Australia, July, 1999.

64. Hazelwood, R. R. and Douglas, J. E., The lust murderer, *FBI Law Enforcement Bulletin*, 49:18-22, 1980.

65. Kocsis, R. N., Irwin, H. J., and Hayes, A. F., Organized and disorganized criminal behavior syndromes in arsonists: a validation study of a psychological profiling concept, *Psychiatry, Psychology and Law*, 5:117-131, 1998.

66. Douglas, J. and Olshaker, M., *Mindhunter*, New York: Scribner, 1995.

67. Kocsis, R. N. and Irwin, H. J., An analysis of spatial patterns in serial rape, arson, and burglary: the utility of the circle theory of environmental range for psychological profiling, *Psychiatry, Psychology and Law*, 4, 195-206, 1997.

Index

A

Acid
  grassland, 6
  resistant microfossils, 15, 23
  study of, 15
ACL, see Adjective Check List
Activity nodes, 231
  offenders, 231
  primary, 247
Adair, Thomas W., xvii
Adjective Check List (ACL), 85
Aerial photography, 4
Aerial thermal imagery, 5
Affective violence, 140
Aggregated crime data, 192
Aggregation techniques, 54
Aggression, Megargee's algebra of, 71
Aggressive revenge drive theory, 64
Algae, 15
Allitt, Beverly, 193
Alston, Jonathan D., xvii
American Academy of Forensic Sciences, 305
American Academy of Psychiatry, 305
American Medical Association, 304
American Psychiatric Association, 305
American Psychological Association, 305
American serial killers, 284
American Statistical Association, 305
Ampliative blindness, 178, 192
ANACAPA, 182, 191
Analysis tools, 182, see also specific types of
        analysis
Analyst's Notebook, 182
Anger rapist, 74, 233
Angiosperms, 15

Animal
  foraging theories, 253
  microfossils, 15
ANOVA, 88, 112, 269, 271
Anthropology, 1
Anthropophagy, 145
Applied psychology/criminology, xi
Aqueous safranine, 25
Arapahoe County, Colorado, 35
Archaeological conservators, 10
Archaeological excavation, 9
Arctangent function, 291, 292
Armed Forces Institute of Pathology, 33
Arsenic digoxin, 194
Arson, 275
Articles of Faith, 328
Asocial serial murderer, 64
As the crow flies distances, 238
Atlanta Olympics, 325
Augers, 8
Australia
  state police service, 84
  university, 84
Awareness spaces, 242

B

Ballistics, 3
Behavioral profiling, ethical conduct of, 303
Behavioral Science Unit, FBI (BSU), 61, 80,
        126, 232, 251, 260, 329
Behavior dichotomy,
        organized/disorganized, 332,
        333
Benzo-diazepine, injection of, 194